THE ULTIMATE EU TEST BOOK
Assistant (AST) Edition 2012

Also from John Harper Publishing

The Ultimate EU Test Book now exists in separate ADMINISTRATOR and ASSISTANT editions

The companion edition to this book is *The Ultimate EU Test Book – Administrator (AD) Edition 2012* ISBN 978-0-9564508-9-0

To keep up to date with developments on EPSO exams and any updates on *The Ultimate EU Test Book*, visit ***www.eu-testbook.com***, from which you can also link to the *Ultimate EU Test Book* Facebook page to gather information from and make contact with others taking the exams.

Information on useful further resources can be found from page 387.

For the latest details of our guides to the institutions of the European Union, visit ***www.europesparliament.com***

THE ULTIMATE EU TEST BOOK

ASSISTANT (AST) EDITION 2012

András Baneth

JOHN HARPER PUBLISHING

Published by John Harper Publishing
27 Palace Gates Road
London N22 7BW, United Kingdom.

www.johnharperpublishing.co.uk

The Ultimate EU Test Book
First edition, November 2005
Second edition, May 2007
Third edition, March 2008
Fourth edition, April 2009
Fifth edition, March 2010
1st Assistant edition, November 2010
1st Administrator edition, February 2011
2nd Assistant edition, October 2011
2nd Administrator edition, October 2011

ISBN 978-0-9564508-8-3

Typeset in 9 & 10/11pt Palatino

Printed and Bound in Malta at the Gutenberg Press.

TABLE OF CONTENTS

About the Authors vi
Foreword vii

Introduction. The EU Personnel Selection and Recruitment Process for Assistants 1

PART I: PRE-SELECTION – PSYCHOMETRIC TESTS

1. Verbal, Numerical and Abstract Reasoning Tests in EPSO Assistant Exams 27
2. Succeeding in Verbal Reasoning Tests 33
3. Verbal Reasoning Test
   – Questions 47
   – Answers 90
4. Succeeding in Numerical Reasoning Tests 109
5. Numerical Reasoning Test
   – Questions. 125
   – Answers 155
6. Succeeding in Abstract Reasoning Tests 169
7. Abstract Reasoning Test
   – Questions 179
   – Answers 212
8. Succeeding in Situational Judgement Tests 223

PART II: PRE-SELECTION – PROFESSIONAL SKILLS TESTS

1. Organising and Prioritising Test
   – Questions 239
   – Answers 251
2. Computer Literacy Tests
   – Questions 256
   – Answers 266
3. Accuracy Test
   – Questions 271
   – Answers 311

PART III: THE ASSESSMENT CENTRE FOR ASSISTANTS

1. About Assessment Centres and Exercises. 319
2. The Structured Interview 329
3. The In-Tray Exercise 346
4. Sample Assessment Centre Reports for Assistants 381

ABOUT THE AUTHORS

András Baneth wishes to express his appreciation to all those who made this book happen by contributing ideas and checking its content. Special thanks are due to Christine J. Ruzicka and Zoltán Arany-Szabó for their invaluable proof-reading and comments and to Delphine Galon for her advice on the exam process.

András BANETH is a trainer, consultant and senior partner at Arboreus Online EU Training dealing with strategy and online marketing. His bestselling Ultimate EU Test Book has helped thousands of candidates prepare for EPSO competitions. András has a wide knowledge of EU policies, institutions and communication, his career having included seven years' experience at the European Commission and the European Court of Justice, where his roles included coordinating briefings for Commission President Barroso and serving as member of the cabinet of Commissioner Kovács. Fluent in English, French and Spanish, he holds an M.A. in law and political sciences and the degree of Master of European Public Administration from the College of Europe, Bruges, Belgium. He is always open to invitations to speak about EPSO exams, EU communication or online entrepreneurship. His personal website is available at www.baneth.eu and his direct e-mail is andras@baneth.eu

Gábor MIKES is the managing director of Arboreus Online EU Training, Europe's leading training company for EPSO exam preparation, and an expert on successful methodologies, including both the theory and practice of passing pre-selection tests. With an M.A. in English Language and Literature and former Kellner Scholar at Trinity College in Hartford, Connecticut (USA), Gábor has worked at an NGO specialising in EU affairs communication and at Ericsson, the Swedish telecom giant. With a keen passion for psychometric tests, Gábor has held dozens of training courses for hundreds of people around Europe on verbal, abstract and numerical reasoning, many of whom are now working for various EU institutions.

Benjamin WILLIAMS is an HPC Registered Occupational Psychologist and a Chartered Associate Fellow of the British Psychological Society (BPS). Ben has led the design and implementation of Assessment Centres for over 300 public and private sector clients across Europe and the Middle East. Ben began his career reading Experimental Psychology at Oxford University followed by a Masters in Organisational and Occupational Psychology. After his studies, Ben joined SHL, the UK's largest Occupational Psychology firm, then began working for PSL as a Senior Consultant before launching his freelance career in 2006. Ben is an active member of the Division of Occupational Psychology within the BPS and has lectured at the Universities of Greenwich and Surrey on a range of assessment-related topics.

Thomas A. WILLIAMS, with over 20 years' experience teaching Writing, Translation and Business English, is currently involved in teacher education at the University of Szeged, Hungary. He has an MA from the University of Reading (UK) and is now working towards a PhD in English Applied Linguistics. He has published articles on a range of topics as well as a test prep book.

Disclaimer: Unless otherwise provided, all views expressed in this book are strictly those of the authors acting in their private capacity. Under no circumstance can these be partly or in full interpreted as representing or binding the European institutions, especially the European Personnel Selection Office (EPSO). None of the authors, the publisher or any other contributor has any connection to EPSO or its affiliates whatsoever. Despite the best efforts to provide up-to-date, practical and reliable information at the time of going to press (September 2011), neither the authors nor the publisher can take any responsibility for events or outcomes that may be linked to potentially obsolete or incorrect data contained in the book.

Any use of other copyright material is gratefully acknowledged.

FOREWORD

Purpose of the Book

The Ultimate EU Test Book is published to help you, as a candidate, prepare and practise for the European Personnel Selection Office (EPSO) recruitment competitions for jobs in the EU institutions. This 2012 edition is specifically designed for those who intend to compete in the competitions for Assistant (AST) posts and it fully reflects the major reform and overhaul of the competitions launched by EPSO in 2010.

The book's main purpose is to help you prepare for the competition, combined with information on the qualities and behaviours the examiners are seeking to identify in candidates so that it will stand you in good stead to be "operational from Day One" when starting to work in an EU institution or body.

The Three Parts

The Ultimate EU Test Book Assistant Edition begins with an introductory step-by-step guide with timeline describing each stage of the current EU recruitment process. Including dozens of useful tips and hints, it signposts you to all the areas covered in greater detail later in the book.

PART I deals with the **psychometric tests** (reasoning tests) encountered in the so-called pre-selection phase of the competitions, which is the stage where candidates face the most competition. These tests involve computer-based testing of verbal, numerical and abstract reasoning skills and situational judgement tests. Many candidates find verbal, numerical and abstract reasoning tests difficult and intimidating and the aim is to help you gain the technical skills and confidence to achieve the best you are capable of. With this in mind, individual chapters are devoted to detailed methodologies for succeeding in each of these test types, followed by comprehensive test exercises which include explanatory answers so you can learn lessons from your performance.

PART II covers the **professional skills** tests that will also be encountered at pre-selection. Individual chapters allow you to practise your skills in organisation and prioritisation, accuracy tests with icons and computer literacy – all vital areas in AST job profiles. As with the psychometric tests, explanatory answers are provided to enable you to learn from your mistakes. In addition, wherever possible, the realism of the exercises is increased by simulating real-world tasks and situations that might be encountered while working in EU institutions.

Candidates who do not reach the required level in the pre-selection psychometric and professional skills tests will not be offered the chance to proceed further in the competition. It is therefore vital to study carefully the methodology to learn the principles and shortcuts involved and then make sure to practise to increase your speed, accuracy and ratio of correct answers.

PART III deals with the second stage of the testing system, the **Assessment Centre**. It explains how Assessment Centres work and the exercises Assistants are likely to face. Included are individual chapters dedicated to the structured interview and the in-tray exercise, the latter including a full-scale simulation based around an imaginary EU body. It should be noted that professional skills, the subject of Part II, will also be further tested at the Assessment Centre, while the interview will explore your personal strengths and weaknesses. To round the book off, Part III ends with sample Assessment Centre reports, based on current best practice, which will help you get an idea of how assessors will approach their task and what they will be looking for.

Keep up-to-date!

Despite my and the contributing authors' best efforts to be thorough and up-to-date to the fullest possible extent, the reformed EPSO recruitment system put into effect in 2010 is still at a relatively early stage. Make sure therefore that you keep up-to-date with the EPSO website and other EU news sources including the Ultimate EU Test Book and Online EU Training facebook pages.

The task that lies ahead of anyone seeking to pass an EPSO recruitment competition is undoubtedly very challenging. Each competition brings many good candidates contesting for a finite number of places. I hope that this edition of *The Ultimate EU Test Book* will be an ever-useful guide to help you on the road ahead.

András Baneth

Brussels, September 2011

For the latest news and critical updates about The Ultimate EU Test Book and EPSO competitions, visit us at **www.eu-testbook.com** *and follow The Ultimate EU Test Book on Facebook*

Introduction: The EU Personnel Selection and Recruitment Process for Assistants

Introduction

There are thousands of applicants, including trainees and those already working for the EU with a fixed term contract, who attempt to pass the open competitions knowing that this is the only way to become a permanent official of the European Union institutions and bodies. EPSO, being aware of the high interest from candidates and also from its "clients", the EU institutions and bodies, realised the need for strategic and transparent planning. It consequently in 2010 made radical changes to the competitions by introducing annual (therefore regular) cycles.

The reform launched in 2010 resulted in significant changes being introduced for all job profiles compared to the previous system that had been in place for decades with only minor adjustments over the years. In this chapter, I provide a detailed overview of the system, the candidates, the eligibility criteria, the exam steps and other relevant information with numerous practical tips and hints that I hope may improve your chances of success.

The Recruitment Procedure since 2010

Applications in General

Owing to the exclusive nature of open competitions, EPSO cannot consider any applications or CVs that are submitted outside the framework of an official competition. On the other hand, vacancies for non-permanent posts or a limited number of senior positions that do not require the selection procedure described below are regularly posted on the EPSO website with links to the given Agency or body where applications should be submitted directly.

Planning and Transparency

Further reinforced by the European Ombudsman and the European Court of Auditors' analysis, EPSO in 2008 adopted a Development Programme[1] that outlined a number of improvements and changes to the selection procedure. One of the key elements was to make recruitment as transparent as possible by giving more information to candidates about the stages and methodology of recruitment, along with detailed and timely feedback about the applicants' very own performance in the tests.

It is in this framework that strategic human resource planning is being introduced in all institutions, meaning that each Directorate General or high-level administrative unit must signal a forecast of its staffing needs for the upcoming three or so years. This is to help EPSO to plan competitions and it should also help to decrease frustrations that occured when a successful laureate received no job offer for months or even years. Planning is further reinforced by analysing employee fluctuations, political developments (e.g. the recent creation of the European External Action Service after the Treaty of Lisbon entered into force on 1 December 2009) or other factors affecting staff turnover or intake.

Increasing transparency is an ongoing effort that includes detailed information about the flagging system (see below), disclosing the names of Selection Board members, the aim to communicate test results and Assessment Centre reports to candidates and help candidates plan their preparation efforts by knowing a relatively precise timeline of exam schedules. This trend is certainly highly appreciated by all applicants.

Skills vs. Knowledge

The most significant change in the new recruitment system is a shift from primarily knowledge-based testing to a greater emphasis on competencies (meaning that multiple choice tests and essays focused on memorising facts such as the infamous "How many women Commissioners are there in the Barroso Commission?" type of question are completely phased out).

EPSO has instead created a competency framework against which candidates are evaluated. This way EU-specific and domain-specific knowledge is only of secondary importance and these aspects are only tested to evaluate a candidate's final suitability for the job provided they possess all the required basic skills.

While this may look like a radically novel approach to recruitment, it has in fact been demonstrated by numerous studies that job performance predictability is best provided by a unique mix of skill and knowledge testing, jointly called "competency testing". While not contradicting the above, EPSO nonetheless wishes to recruit candidates who are "operational from day one"; therefore, items such as professional skills tests or in-tray exercises for Assistants, which are the items most closely related to the specific knowledge required for the job, are of considerable importance, being the main elements of testing on-the-job suitability.

Core Competencies

According to EPSO[2], the following are considered as core competencies (which are required for all profiles independent of the competition though the relative weight of each differs depending on whether it is an Administrator or Assistant profile these are measured against):

- **Analysis and Problem Solving** – Identifies the critical facts in complex issues and develops creative and practical solutions
- **Communicating** – Communicates clearly and precisely both orally and in writing
- **Delivering Quality and Results** – Takes personal responsibility and initiative for delivering work to a high standard of quality within set procedures
- **Learning and Development** – Develops and improves personal skills and knowledge of the organisation and its environment
- **Prioritising and Organising** – Prioritises the most important tasks, works flexibly and organises own workload efficiently
- **Resilience** – Remains effective under a heavy workload, handles organisational frustrations positively and adapts to a changing work environment
- **Working with Others** – Works co-operatively with others in teams and across organisational boundaries and respects differences between people

A further competency, but only for Administrator grades, is:

- **Leadership** – Manages, develops and motivates people to achieve results

One or two further competencies may be identified for specific job profiles or competitions, depending on the analysis of the given position. The above general competencies are always tested by two different exercises to ensure their validity and reliability as organisational psychologists and human resource experts have created a specific method to ensure the above quality criteria. For more details on what each competency means, how it is measured and how to best improve your performance on them, please refer to the relevant chapters on the Assessment phase in Part III.

Duration

Given candidates' frustration with the extremely long recruitment process under the previous system (where it could easily take two years or more from the exam announcement until actual recruitment), EPSO has radically cut down the recruitment cycle by streamlining and professionalizing it. This in practice means that instead of ad hoc competitions, exams are now announced each year on a regular, cyclical basis, complemented by exams for Specialists based on resource needs. The cycles start with announcement of Administrator exams in March, linguists in July and Assistants in November (or December), but it is essential to check the EPSO website for the latest information on the schedule as this is subject to minor changes.

The duration of each cycle is planned to be not above 9 months from announcement until the publication of the reserve list, which still means however that the actual recruitment may take longer despite the efforts of the new system. In any case, it is now possible to plan ahead your preparation as it is clear what type of competition is to be announced and when. On a related note, it is advisable to focus your efforts only on preparing for the given upcoming exam phase (pre-selection or Assessment Centre) and not the entire procedure as such.

Soon-to-be Graduates Welcome

A significant improvement in the new system is that the so-called "cut-off date" – meaning the date by which a candidate must meet all eligibility criteria, especially those of possessing a diploma or vocational school qualification or job experience – has in many cases been moved beyond the application deadline. This is not always the case for Assistant exams, however, and it is important to always check the requirements in the Notice of Competition.

Take a practical example. EPSO announces the cycle of AST competitions in November. The change means that if you are a graduating student and would expect to receive your diploma in the following January but the exam, where a recognised vocational school degree is a pre-requisite, has its application deadline in December, you can still apply as long as the diploma is obtained by the time of the date specified for the competition. The rationale behind this change is to offer soon-to-be graduates the opportunity to apply in their last year of studies, thus broadening the scope of the candidate pool – a great step forward.

Candidates with Special Needs

European Union institutions have always been keen to respect the principles of equal access and non-discrimination given this policy's pivotal place in the EU Member States' legislation and obviously inside the institutions themselves. Therefore in the EU recruitment procedure candidates with special needs, such as seriously limited eyesight, physical disability or other issues that require adaptation in the test centres, should notify

EPSO well in advance to make sure that both their access to the testing and the scoring of their exams are adapted to their condition. In its Development Programme, EPSO has also referred to the possibility of introducing supervised one-on-one tests or other measures to encourage such candidates to apply.

Chances of Succeeding

The total number of applications per year is very high and it reached 40,000 for the 2011 Administrator exam alone. This should, however, not discourage anyone from applying as this figure is far better once put into perspective. Consider that about 10% of these applicants never actually show up at the test centre (they change their minds, were not really serious about sitting the exam, could not make it due to personal reasons etc.) and thus your chances are already higher.

Further, the pre-selection phase is very challenging for those who see verbal, numerical and abstract reasoning and professional skills questions for the first time at the exam centre. Those having done their "homework" to prepare well are therefore immediately at an advantage. This is the stage at which most will drop out.

EPSO estimates[3] that for the Assessment Centre stage of the exams 1200 Administrators, 600 Linguists and 300 Specialists are to be tested each year; in addition 900 Assistant candidates will be assessed. This means that the chance of passing the pre-selection phase and proceeding further is about 1:15 (varying largely among the profiles of course, as more specialised profiles such as financial management or IT tend to offer far better chances of success). This is tough but certainly not impossible. On the other hand, it also means that it is not enough to just pass – you have to aim for the highest possible score. This is mostly true for the pre-selection phase as those candidates who win through to the Assessment Centre are measured more against the pre-established competencies and less against each other.

Competition and Sifting-in

In the EPSO system, the concept of "sifting-in" is used: this means that after looking at the overall results and the number of candidates, the Selection Board determines the threshold score above which all candidates are *considered* for the next phase. This does not mean that all those having scored above this limit will be admitted to the assessment phase or Assessment Centre; however the Selection Board will examine their formal qualifications, eligibility and CVs, and only invite a certain pre-determined number of them for the upcoming stage of recruitment.

This also means that you must consider carefully which exam profile to apply for. For example, if you have a qualification in human resource management and relevant professional experience, you can sit an Assistant exam and maybe also an Administrator exam (if your qualification is a diploma), and may also be eligible for a Specialist exam if that fits your profile. Similarly, if you are an economist who considers that, based on the earmarked figures disclosed in the Notice of Competition (published on EPSO's website and in the Official Journal), you have more chances in the Economist profile than in the Public Administration segment, you are free to choose either one as long as your diploma and other formal criteria make you eligible for both.

Let's consider an imaginary but practical example. Depending on your profile, you may look at the Notice of Competition and discover that EPSO plans to create a reserve list of Assistants, within which there would be 500 Secretary profiles and 280 Human Resources profiles in the framework of the Assistant (AST) competition. If you have a human resources background and secretarial experience, you would thus be eligible to compete in either of the two categories.

While at first glance it might seem logical to apply for the one where more people are taken and thus your chances seem higher, practice shows that far more candidates apply in the "generalist" Secretary profile – which changes the equation. If we assume that 9,000 people apply in the Secretary profile and 3,000 people apply for the Human Resources one, your chances are 500:9,000 compared to 280:3000 for the Human Resources, therefore the latter is the smarter choice. The only problem in this logic is the lack of actual statistics: the number of applicants is only shown once you start your application, which may be helpful, though it is quite risky to wait until the last moment to evaluate your chances accordingly. In any case, this is a unique mix of logical reasoning and chance.

Another aspect to consider is the long-term repercussions of your choice: not only will your exam profile determine the required professional knowledge but it will also affect your recruitment prospects once placed on the reserve list. It is for obvious reasons that EPSO creates sub-profiles and specialist profiles in the recruitment: if an Assistant on research grants and financial management is sought, those on a Financial Management reserve list have far better chances of being offered a job than those on a Secretary list (though this is not a formal rule of course).

Deciding on which exam profile to sit is therefore a tough decision for many, given its repercussions on the chances to succeed. Nevertheless, as long as you are aware of these aspects, you can evaluate the position better for yourself – this will, in fact, be your first numerical reasoning practice exercise!

Feedback and Complaints

When discussing feedback and complaints, it must be borne in mind that given the significant number of candidates, both are handled in an automated way in the first place until human intervention is required.

Feedback (on test results) is only available in an automated format for the pre-selection phase while those who take part in an Assessment Centre are to be offered more comprehensive feedback in the form of a written report (see a sample of a detailed positive and negative report in Part III, Chapter 4). For complaints, only well founded and serious ones can be taken into account by the Selection Board, for the above reasons.

In the previous system, the Notice of Competition set out which steps candidates could take if they were not satisfied by the procedure or the way their application was treated, as follows:

• Submit a request for review (appeal directly to the Selection Board);

• Bring a case before the EU Civil Service Tribunal;

• Lodge a complaint under Article 90(2) of the Staff Regulations;

• Submit a complaint to the Ombudsman.

As EPSO outlined in its Development Plan, this system had been rather confusing for candidates unfamiliar with the competencies of each body. As it happens, many candidates are unaware that the Ombudsman can only deal with "maladministration" (which refers to exam rules or proceedings that fail to respect certain principles or best practices and affect individual candidates as a consequence – as opposed to individual exam results or evaluations of the selection board). This is obviously different from filing a request for review of your in-tray exercise's scoring.

Lodging a complaint and, in case of rejection, initiating its review by the Civil Service Tribunal, are long and cumbersome procedures that are only worth the effort if you are truly and reasonably convinced that you have been discriminated against or that your application's treatment can be challenged on legal grounds (e.g. your relevant diploma was not accepted even though the issuing university is accredited and recognized by your Member State).

EPSO also acknowledged this in the above document and foresaw the following changes:

> "... good practice shows that bodies can limit the number of appeals by providing comprehensive feedback on request. For this reason, EPSO will introduce a feedback mechanism for both successful and unsuccessful candidates which will become an integral part of the assessment procedure. Candidates will be informed in advance that they may obtain their feedback report after the close of competition.

> The availability of the feedback report should answer follow-up queries from candidates and obviate the need for the Selection Board to undertake reviews. In the light of this, EPSO will abolish the option for candidates to make requests for review of their marks directly to the Selection Board. It will be clear in the Notice of Competition that the decision of the Selection Board is final and that no review mechanism is provided for within the terms of the competition. Any legal route will be limited to cases where a Selection Board has failed to respect the provisions laid out in the Notice of Competition."

On a positive note, the best thing about feedback is that it opens the way to identifying areas where you may need to improve. Should you not succeed, try to honestly analyse and work on the issues that the assessors pointed out as weaknesses. This will not only help in a subsequent application but, given the nature of such reports, can help in your own personal development as well, independent of EU competitions.

Another important aspect is that regardless of any failed efforts to pass the exams you can apply for new ones without limitations. Unlike other tests, EPSO does not retain your scores or keep a file on your results, therefore you can start with a "clean slate" if you decide to re-attempt passing the exams.

The Selection Boards

Selection Boards have traditionally been composed of EU officials who volunteer to take part in such tasks. Their background, motivation and interests vary greatly which ensures an objective and fair treatment based on strict guidelines that each of them must follow. Selection Boards, including most assessors, are still going to be chosen from among volunteering active and even retired personnel, though some expertise may be provided by external contractors. EPSO has also ensured the professionalizing of the Selection Boards by extending the scope of their members' assignment for several months or even years instead of using them on an ad hoc basis, thus ensuring the accumulation of more insight and knowledge on their part.

Members of the Selection Boards generally perform the full administration of an exam on behalf of EPSO, such as preparing the tests, admitting candidates on the basis of their files or marking the exercises. You, of course, may never approach a Selection Board member for any additional information other than that formally communicated to you even though the board members' names are always made public on EPSO's website for reasons of transparency. Some candidates think that a quick online search to find the professional background of board members could help identify their favourite topics though this is not the case, especially since the introduction of the Assessment Centre where the procedure and content is pre-determined.

Venues and Costs

The pre-selection exams take place all over Europe and in several other locations around the world, and in the event that an open competition is related to the EU's recent or upcoming enlargement or when several Member States' citizens are eligible (e.g. in the case of an EU-10 or EU-27 competition), the capital city of the affected Member States or to-be Member State all host an exam centre. As almost all exams under the new EPSO system are administered on computers, exams being held over a certain period of time at the designated centres, the list of which is found on EPSO's website.

Candidates are required to pick and book a date and venue online that suits them most within this period, though you must be very careful in your first choice as revisions or changes are almost never allowed after the booking period is over (the very few exceptions may include issues such as childbirth or medical events).

When the booking is made available, be careful when to sign up: the sooner you do, the sooner you must sit the pre-selection tests. However, if you sign up towards the end of the application period, you can risk having less choice of dates as most people tend to put off preparation until the last moment. Another reason why last minute applications are to be avoided is potential internet blackouts or server crashes that may prevent you from securing your place in time (though if such problems happen at EPSO's end, they tend to extend the deadline). For the assessment phase, you will most likely be given a specific date some time in advance with limited or no option to amend it unless compelling events prevent you from attending and you can duly justify the reason.

As a rule, no contribution is made towards any travelling or subsistence expenses associated with the pre-selection phase of the exam. As these exams take place in the exam centres located in the capital of each Member State and in case of larger countries, also in other large cities, and also in selected capitals around the world, travelling from your home to these centres is always on your own budget.

In the new system the Assessment Centre is located centrally in Brussels. Candidates who need to travel there will be reimbursed for their travel costs and also given a daily subsistence allowance. The specific rules are always communicated in advance either as early as the Notice of Competition or later to those who actually make it through to the assessment phase. The underlying principle is that nobody should suffer any disadvantage in attending the competitions due to budgetary issues. The same rule of equal opportunities applies for those flying in or travelling to a specific job interview unless a telephone or videoconference is a feasible alternative.

Motivation

Before applying, and also because it is now part of the application questionnaire, it is useful to reflect on what factors motivate you in wanting to work for an EU institution. Usually it is a mixture of various considerations – such as the desire to work on international affairs, the opportunity to travel, getting an attractive salary and benefits, having an interesting and varied job, speaking and learning foreign languages, job security etc. Realising which factors are the most important for you can help better identify which profile to apply for and it should also help in the structured interview when assessors try to find out more about your personality. "Being part of something larger than yourself" is a vital aspect that you may also emphasize if asked why you applied to become an EU official.

The Candidates

It is very hard, if not impossible, to outline a "typical" candidate profile given the large number and diverse backgrounds of applicants. However, I have formed the impression that most of the serious applicants have five things in common. They:

- Are interested in EU affairs, committed to European integration and wish to work for a "good cause"

- Have a solid knowledge of at least two foreign languages

- Are flexible and willing to work abroad in a multi-cultural environment

- Have strong motivation to study for and pass the exams to get into the EU institutions

- Understand that EU institutions are different from the private sector inasmuch as they are a hybrid of a diplomatic corps, an international organisation and a government administration that is based on a hierarchic model

The above qualities will also be looked at by assessors if only on an indirect or informal level. Should you feel that any of the above features does not relate to you, you may wish to divert your attention to the other sorts of EU-related jobs described in the previous chapter. In any case, EU institutions deal with such a wide variety of issues that you can certainly find the job that best suits your interests and personality if your motivation is right.

Age

There is no limitation on an applicant's age as long as it is not overly close to the retirement age (minimum age is determined by the requirement of a diploma or work experience, therefore this age is never formally spelled out). Obviously the EU is keen on ensuring a level playing field in terms of candidates' backgrounds, ensuring equal opportunities for all based on merit, regardless of whether they belong to any particular religious, sexual, ethnic or other minority, social segment or age group.

Whatever your age, you will be required to pass a medical check that will serve as a benchmark for your social security and health insurance file before taking up an EU job. This also serves to ensure that you are physically capable of doing the job you are to be required to perform.

Quotas

It is frequently asked whether EU institutions apply a quota system for allocating posts to a certain number of officials from each Member State. In fact the Staff Regulations provides that officials are to be "recruited on the broadest possible geographical basis from among nationals of Member States of the Communities"[4], which explains the special treatment of so-called EU-10 and EU-2 candidates (nationals of EU Member States that joined in 2004 and 2007, namely Central and Eastern European countries, Malta and Cyprus; later Romania and Bulgaria) and explains why some niche competitions aimed at a limited number of nationalities (including to-be Member States such as Croatia or exams aimed only at Polish and Czech candidates) are announced from time to time.

Apart from the above, this provision in practice means an ongoing effort to maintain a proportional allocation of posts that more-or-less reflects the ratio of each Member State's population and size in the EU, both for ASTs and ADs, including those for senior management. Yet, despite the above principle, there are no hard-coded quotas for Irish or Cypriot citizens given the merit-based competition system. Natural imbalances therefore always exist and they could only be challenged by the introduction of specific staff allocations, which would then likely infringe upon the principle of non-discrimination based on nationality. This is certainly not an easy issue to handle politically as it touches on the very essence of the principles guiding European integration.

Language Rules

One of the most common misunderstandings regarding EU competitions is the language regime: what is the exact meaning of the so-called first and second language? In fact the first language refers to your mother tongue, as long as it is an official EU language. The reason why this needs to be specified is because, for example, a Latvian candidate may have Russian as their mother tongue but that cannot be considered as their first language since it is not an official EU language.

In some cases, especially for enlargement-related exams, the candidate's citizenship automatically determines the first language (e.g. exams for Croatian candidates will require the first language to be Croatian), whereas in other instances you are free to choose your first language as long as the above rules on citizenship and the official EU language requirements are respected (for instance if you have Luxembourgish citizenship, your first language may just as well be French or German; Luxembourgish is not an official EU language).

The second language is in fact your *first foreign language* and in most cases it must be English, French or German. However, for linguist exams the second language is usually the one for which candidates are sought. For example, if EPSO announces a linguist exam for Bulgarian translators, the first language is required to be Bulgarian, the second language may be English, French or German or a certain number of other EU official languages, and there may be a third language (in fact, second foreign language) requirement as well. Note that I did not mention any Bulgarian citizenship requirement here as the goal is the perfect command of a language regardless of which EU citizenship you may have.

An important development is that from 2011 onwards, EPSO provides for pre-selection tests (abstract reasoning, verbal reasoning and numerical reasoning) to be taken in your first language. This shows that the aim of the pre-selection is not to test your linguistic knowledge but to assess your psychometric reasoning skills, which can best be done in your "EU mother tongue". Situational judgement tests and certain other tests (including Assessment Centre exams) are, however, in English, French or German.

Formal Criteria

As a candidate applying for EU exams, you must meet certain formal (objective) criteria. These, as a general rule, say you must:

- Be a citizen of a Member State of the European Union (though exceptions occur as in the case of enlargement-related competitions)

- Be entitled to full rights as such a citizen (e.g. no legal limitations as a result of criminal acts or other issues) and meet the character requirements for the duties involved.

- Have fulfilled any obligations imposed by the laws on military service (only relevant for those Member States where such service is compulsory, and even there you may prove that you were exempted from the service)

- Have a thorough knowledge of one of the official languages of the European Union and a satisfactory knowledge of a second (this is the minimum requirement but further linguistic prerequisites may be set out in the given Notice of Competition)

- Have the sufficient minimum education[5] and/or work experience[6] as set out in the Notice of Competition

These formal criteria are required for all profiles, regardless of the specific provisions of an exam announcement; meeting these does not lead to passing any stage but their lack certainly leads to non-eligibility or if discovered later, disqualification from the exam.

The Four Profiles

The EPSO system comprises four main segments generally referred to as profiles. These can be summarised in the following table:

	Administrators (AD)	Linguists (AD)	Assistants (AST)	Specialists (AD or AST)
Minimum Qualification	Diploma (min. 3 years, EPSO may require it to be related to the chosen sub-profile, e.g. Audit)	Diploma (min. 3 years)	High school degree or post-secondary degree	Same as for ASTs and ADs
Work Experience	None (AD5) 6 years (AD7) 12 years (AD9)	None (AD5) 6 years (AD7) 12 years (AD9)	None or 3 years, depending on the qualification and exam (AST1-3)	Same as for ASTs and ADs (with possible exceptions, e.g. AD7 lawyer-linguists may need only 3 years of work experience instead of 6)
Type of Qualification (in many cases, though not always, qualifications are eliminatory, so make sure to read EPSO's Notice of Competition carefully)	Arts, Law, Economics, Political Science etc.	Language Studies, Interpreting	Clerical Studies, Arts, Finances, Technical skills etc.	Lawyers, Linguists, Engineers, Scientists, Doctors, Veterinaries

Please note that the above table is for information purposes only and the actual requirements may differ; please always consult EPSO's official communications for up-to-date information. Examples of actual job tasks for each profile can be found in the previous chapter.

Choosing a profile is determined by both objective and subjective reasons: depending on your qualifications and work experience (which are "objective" facts you cannot change overnight), you may be limited to only one "choice"; it may nevertheless happen that you are formally eligible for multiple profiles and it remains your individual choice which one to sit for (e.g. a lawyer with three years' experience and fluent knowledge of three languages might be eligible for all the above profiles, including Specialists [lawyer-linguists]).

Multiple Applications

A general approach taken by many candidates is to apply for all competitions they are eligible for, this way increasing their chances. This is in fact a highly recommended strategy though you should be very careful not to apply for two exams in parallel that are mutually exclusive.

Such rules are usually indicated in the Notice of Competition and are limited to the sub-profiles of a given exam: an Administrator (AD5) or Assistant (AST) competition in the annual cycle may have 4-5 domains such as Public Administration, Law, Economics, Audit and Information-Communication Technologies where candidates are required to pick only one of these options. Apart from the risk of being disqualified from both, it is also technically impossible to choose two domains at the same time given the features of the online application form. If in doubt whether you may run parallel applications for different competitions (for example an AST exam and a Specialist exam), better to ask EPSO than lose out on both counts.

The Exam Procedure Step-by-Step

Having overviewed the above general principles and hints, below are the elements and possible pitfalls of the new EPSO system.

The EPSO system comprises the following elements for the four main profiles:

As seen in the table below, the new exam system comprises essentially four main phases:

1. Notice of Competition, Self-Assessment, Registration

2. Pre-selection Phase

3. Assessment Centre

4. Reserve List, Recruitment

Month(s)	Administrators	Assistants	Linguists	Specialists
0	Notice of competition + self-assessment	Notice of competition + self-assessment	Notice of competition + self-assessment	Notice of competition + self-assessment
1	Online registration	Online registration	Online registration	Online registration
2-4	Pre-selection: verbal/numerical/abstract reasoning tests + situational judgement tests	Pre-selection: verbal + numerical + abstract reasoning tests + situational judgement tests (for AST3) + accuracy tests + prioritising and organising tests + computer literacy tests	Pre-selection: verbal (in 2 or 3 languages) + numerical + abstract reasoning tests	CV sift and "Talent Screener" (if the No. of candidates exceeds a specified threshold, abstract + verbal + numerical reasoning tests are also used in this phase)
5-7	Admission + Assessment Centre: case study + group exercise + oral presentation + structured interview	Admission + professional skills test + structured interview	Admission + Assessment Centre: practical linguistic tests (translation from the source language/s) + structured interview + oral presentation + group exercise	Admission + detailed case study and/or domain specific interview +structured interview + group exercise (+verbal + numerical + abstract reasoning tests, if not yet used in the pre-selection tests)
8-9	Reserve lists/recruitment	Reserve lists/recruitment	Reserve lists/recruitment	Reserve lists/recruitment

Below I have tried to provide an introduction to each of the stages and tests, along with some practical advice. Later chapters in this book provide sample tests with detailed answer keys on these components.

Phase 1: Notice of Competition, Self-Assessment, Registration

The Notice of Competition

As mentioned earlier, the Notice of Competition (NoC) is a special administrative notice addressed to all EU citizens and it is therefore published in the Official Journal of the EU both in print and online. It is important to underline that the NoC is the *only* official source of information, therefore if you see any contradicting or different interpretation in the press or on a website, make sure to check the original authentic source which is always referenced on EPSO's website.

The NoC is a rather extensive document that sets out all the formal eligibility criteria, language requirements, deadlines and other practical arrangements linked to the exam. Even more importantly, the NoC contains a wealth of information that you can use to your benefit by reading it attentively, such as the size of the reserve list (so you can estimate your chances and thus decide which sub-profile or domain to apply for after analysing the earmarked number of applicants to be accepted for the assessment phase and how many people are to be placed on the reserve list).

The job description, also detailed in the NoC, is particularly interesting as it is not only an indication of what sort of tasks you would need to carry out once inside but you can deduce lots of hints about the topics to cover when preparing for the domain-specific parts of the assessment phase.

Below is a sample extract of a Public Administration/Human Resources competition's NoC[7]. The comments I have added indicate what type of documents and information sources you could research and focus on if you were preparing for this exam. I suggest using the same method for your specific NoC once the exam you wish to apply for has been published.

It is therefore crucial to understand and analyse every detail provided in the NoC to make sure you can gain valuable insights. This also helps you avoid seemingly evident pitfalls that might lead to disqualification (such as a requirement to submit a certain cer-

---

Field 1: European Public Administration/Human Resources

— preparing, developing and implementing Community initiatives, including working on case studies, producing reports, drafting Community legislation, and taking part in consultations and negotiations within the institution and, if necessary, with business and other interest groups in the Member States and with the other Community institutions;

[Meaning: You will need to be familiar with the EU institutional structure, the main principles of stakeholder consultation, transparency rules, major EU policies currently on the political agenda, legislative procedures including impact assessment and decision-making procedures, be familiar with distinguishing shared and exclusive EU competencies]

— taking part in international negotiations, implementing bilateral and multilateral agreements, and managing commercial or development policy instruments;

[Meaning: You will most likely need to read about EU competencies in concluding international agreements, trade agreements, commercial and development policy instruments and main institutions involved in formulating, implementing and controlling these policies]

— administration and implementation of Community policies and action programmes in various fields of activity, including the single market, external relations, social affairs, agriculture, structural policies, transport, the environment and information;

[Meaning: The main elements of all the above policies should be revised, including prospective changes in the next five years]

— communication and information policy;

[Meaning: What are the EU's efforts to improve its communication, which are the flagship proposals of information and communication policy, be familiar with initiatives, communications and policy papers in this field]

— specifically for the European Parliament: assisting MEPs, by means of written and oral briefings, and taking an active part in organising the work of different parliamentary bodies;

[Meaning: Understand the main organs, bodies and structure of the European Parliament, be familiar with the key elements of its internal operations]

— formulating and implementing human resources policies, including recruitment and selection techniques, equal opportunities, training and career development, appraisal, promotion and reward systems, advisory, managerial and mentoring skills, employment law and employment relations.

[Meaning: Know the EU Staff Regulations' main provisions on staff rights and obligations, its principles and key formal rules related to the above issues; research some general, non-EU human resources concepts regarding employee satisfaction, training needs, equal opportunities and promotion]

tificate or sign a submitted document) – you would be surprised to know how many people get rejected on formal grounds by accidentally overlooking a date, a provision or a prerequisite.

Self-Assessment

Self-assessment as a tool is widely used in international organisations and multinational private companies (such as the Canadian civil service, universities, pharmaceutical companies etc.) and EPSO also decided to introduce it from 2010 onwards. Its goal is to make candidates realise what EU jobs are really about and dispel misconceptions or misperceptions at the earliest stage. This is hoped to result in decreasing non-eligible applications and thus lead to decreasing overhead expenses related to the organisation of exams caused by registered applicants not showing up or refusing job offers because they had a very different idea of what working for the EU means.

Self-assessment is non-eliminatory, meaning that you cannot pass or fail based on your answers. Expect questions about your willingness to relocate to Brussels, Luxembourg or elsewhere if you are successful in the competition; your interest in working in a multi-cultural environment; your capacity to handle complex tasks, and various other issues related to values. This latter group of questions may include a check on whether your personal values (such as integrity, hard-work, ethics and others) and personality (flexible, self-driven, confident, autonomous etc.) match those honoured by the EU institutions (working for a public administration, serving the public interest, involvement in policy making, travelling, reward etc.).

This exercise serves both to raise awareness about the rights and obligations that come with an EU job and also to sift out those who may not be so serious about sitting the exam after all. When filling out the self-assessment, there is no real trick to it – simply be honest, think carefully about the issues and bear in mind the above comments on candidate profiles.

Registration

Registration is done exclusively online on the EPSO (EU Career) website at the start of the procedure, which also means that you will not need to hand in any proof, paper or document at this stage. The first step is to create an EPSO account, which is an online personal profile where your correspondence with EPSO will take place. If you change your postal or e-mail address during the procedure or any other contact information becomes obsolete, make sure to update your online account immediately.

If, after registration, the confirmation e-mail does not arrive in your inbox within a few hours, check your spam or bulk mail folder as it may have been misfiled by your e-mail application; should you still not receive anything, ask EPSO for technical assistance. Make sure, however, that you do not register twice as it may lead to confusion or even to potential disqualification if other signs show you had second thoughts when doing so.

As in all other steps of the exam, make sure to re-read all input you provide as a wrong click with your mouse can lead to sitting the exam in a different language or location than intended or an error in choosing your citizenship from a drop-down menu may even result in you being refused for the pre-selection. Lastly, never leave anything for the final moment as many candidates may rush to complete their account in the last few days of application and it may cause service interruptions or outages and prevent you from securing your place – which is every candidate's worst nightmare!

Phase 2: Pre-Selection

Having taken the above steps and provided that you meet all formal eligibility criteria, you should receive an official invitation to the pre-selection phase, communicated to you in your online EPSO profile. Once this eagerly awaited message arrives, you should start planning seriously your preparation as the booking period will open shortly and the exam is imminent. Once the booking starts, you can choose a venue and a time from the available exam centres and time slots but bear in mind that the later you finalise your application, the later you can sit the exam. If you live outside Europe, you can choose an exam centre outside the Member States; EPSO has extended the reach of exam centres to other continents via international test centres, which is a welcome development.

When choosing an exam centre, make sure you are fully aware of the logistical issues: print the map of its location, find out which public transport goes there on the exam day, make sure that no strike or service interruption is foreseen for that day, and have a fall-back plan in case you are running late, such as the phone number of a reliable taxi company.

My general advice for test-takers is to start practicing as early as you can; preferably straight after *deciding* to sit for an EPSO exam. Though in the new system you will not need any EU knowledge in the pre-selection phase, competition is still fierce and you must achieve the highest possible score. For those who have not dealt with maths since high school (as is the case for most of us), some refreshing courses or online research can always help for the psychometric tests.

As also detailed in the relevant chapters, I strongly advise creating a concrete study plan where you allocate sufficient time for the upcoming weeks and months for practice, revision, simulation and preparation. Simply saying "I'll find the time whenever I have nothing else to do" will not lead to tangible results as watching the next episode of *Desperate Housewives* always seems more fun than dealing with rhombuses in abstract reasoning quizzes.

Scoring

In the new EPSO system, and depending on the exam you are taking, some of the multiple choice tests may have as many as six answer options, thus reducing your guessing chances from 25% (in the case of four options) to a bit more than 16% in cases where you are unsure of the answer and need to randomly pick one from six. In any event, as opposed to the system commonly used in French competitions and exams, there is only one correct answer for any given test except for Situational Judgement Tests (see below), though a few examples of alternative formats for verbal reasoning are given below.

A small but very important piece of advice is to read the question extremely carefully to avoid overlooking words such as "not" in a question that reads "Which of the following is not an EU policy?" I have been told more than a dozen times that a certain question in the previous editions of this book was wrong when it turned out that the readers had misread the question. This of course relates to verbal and numerical reasoning tests as much as other multiple choice questions.

Another important aspect to note is that EPSO is going to evaluate your scores separately for each exercise, which means that you must reach at least 50% (or whatever pass mark is required by the NoC) in each of the tests; in some exams, however, verbal reasoning and abstract reasoning tests may be considered as one, therefore the threshold needs to be reached as if these were a single test – which makes it slightly easier to pass. Apart from passing the individual thresholds, it will be your overall score that is going to decide whether or not you make it to the next round. Note, however, that verbal and numerical reasoning is no longer considered a "single" test, therefore the minimum threshold must be reached in both of them and not just in aggregate.

Computer Screens

As all tests in the pre-selection phase are administered on computers located in accredited exam centres, you should be prepared for the difficulties this entails. Reading a text is always slower on a computer screen than on paper, speed being also influenced by the font size and screen resolution. Highlighting, underlining or adding comments on screen is technically not available, therefore you need to take notes on the scrap paper or erasable slate the exam centres provide. Even though an on-screen calculator is usually available, handling it is less easy than using a physical one, especially if you could not practice such operations beforehand.

Computer-based exams do have a few advantages however. The display of the available time (which is not meant to put pressure on you but rather to help time management); the automatic registration of answered and unanswered questions (which should help you keep track of the questions); the flexibility of choosing a convenient exam day (as opposed to having a single exam day); and the faster (and more reliable) correction of your answers given the electronic evaluation, are among the advantages of computer based exams.

Verbal and Numerical Reasoning Tests

The verbal and numerical reasoning tests, along with abstract reasoning, are commonly known as psychometric tests. These are one of the most popular methods to evaluate cognitive skills and the intelligence of prospective employees. They are widely used by multinational companies and civil service recruiters around the world given their flexible application, cost-effectiveness and proven relevance to gauge candidates' skills. The relevant chapters of this book provide a full methodology and hundreds of practice exercises: what follows here is more of a description of how these tests are administered along with some general advice on how to tackle them.

Verbal reasoning tests are essentially reading comprehension tests where you are required to choose the "true" or "false" statement or answer a question based on an 8-15 line-long text. A fundamental rule is to only consider information contained in the text and ignore all prior knowledge you may have of a given topic unless it is a law of nature or common knowledge (e.g. that the Earth revolves around the Sun).

Numerical reasoning, on the other hand, is a calculation exercise based on statistical charts and graphs based on which you are required to find a certain percentage, figure, or decide on relative values (e.g. "Based on the table, which country had the highest relative birth rate in 2008?"). Questions can be tricky as in many cases no calculation is required given that you can simplify the riddle by applying calculation methods and short-cuts. A comprehensive toolkit is offered in the relevant chapter of this book regarding the above.

EPSO has been using verbal and numerical reasoning tests for several years in its competitions and they have proven to be one of the most challenging parts of the exam procedure. The likely reason is that while EU knowledge could be memorised by dedicating sufficient time to this end, succeeding in verbal and numerical reasoning requires a completely different approach. Extensive practice is only part of the solution as applying a few fundamental principles and understanding the methodology are essential to succeed.

It is relevant to note that the level of difficulty of psychometric questions for Assistants and Administrators differs; the questions in this edition of the book have been specifically selected to match AST level.

As a piece of general advice, work as hard as you can to improve your overall vocabulary in the exam's language by reading quality newspapers, boost your spelling skills for complex words, your understanding of measurement units (billions vs. millions, how many litres is one m³ etc.) and revise basic mathematical operations. You can also find dozens of further hints and resources in this book.

Abstract Reasoning Tests

A new element in the reformed competition system is the abstract reasoning, which is another test type that various international employers commonly use; it is a common feature of popular IQ tests as well. Abstract reasoning is different from the other two tests as it requires no linguistic skills: there is only one main question for all tasks, namely "Which figure is the next in the series?"

Using these questions for personnel selection is practical for EPSO given that there is no need to translate the exercise into any language and also because abstract reasoning tests have been scientifically proven to be culture-neutral while effectively testing candidates' so-called "fluid intelligence". This latter term refers to the capability to solve new problems and understand the relationship between various concepts, independent of any acquired knowledge.

The main skill you need to efficiently resolve abstract reasoning tests is "imagination", that is, the ability to mentally rotate, flip or turn certain figures according to a certain logic or rule. This rule is one of the main challenges of this question type as you should be able to "dissect" a figure and identify its component elements. Those capable of performing such tasks are likely to be able to cope with unknown or new situations in the workplace: this skill therefore does have more practical value for predicting actual job performance than may seem at first glance. You can find a large number of abstract reasoning tests in the relevant chapter of this book, along with an in-depth methodology that is highly practical and applicable.

Professional Skills Tests

These types of tests are widely used by assessors and recruiters around the world to gauge candidates' ability to concentrate, attention to detail and computer literacy skills. The skills tests used by EPSO for AST exams are the following: prioritising and organising (planning skills involving allocation of limited resources); accuracy tests with icons (spotting typos, misquotes or spelling errors in a large set of data, table or chart); IT literacy tests (your knowledge of Microsoft Office and other computer and information technology tools); and e-tray simulations (a series of emails coming in to a simulated interface where you need to process and understand them).

Situational Judgement Tests

Situational judgement tests (or SJTs for short), although a new element since 2010 in EPSO pre-selection exams and which are used for many profiles (but not necessarily AST), have been employed for decades by different organisations, such as the FBI of the United States, and companies that have wished to measure potential candidates in real-life work scenarios. The objective of SJTs is to create realistic work-related scenarios in which you must determine the proper course of action given the parameters and situation. In other words, the test basically asks what you would do in a particular circumstance.

An important element of SJTs is that there are no qualitatively right or wrong answers when testing your judgement. Rather, judgement is about your ability to assess a given situation and make clearly defined decisions on how to proceed from there, based on your own unique set of experiences in life, understanding of the EU institutions' culture and ethical rules, while applying a certain common sense to workplace situations.

For example, given a sample question about witnessing malpractice in your unit committed by a colleague, your reaction or response may be to confront that person first while another person may feel it is most appropriate to let your head of unit know about what has happened. This is therefore closely linked to the competencies that EPSO is seeking to find in future EU officials.

Since there are no right or wrong answers, the decision whether one answer is better than another would have to be in the hands of the test administrators; however, the benchmark for deciding the value of each answer is the competency list that EPSO has established (see above) and against which it evaluates candidates. SJTs therefore have the potential to measure various issues such as your organisation or team working skills, or your ability to prioritise.

It is important to point out that while real world situations can certainly be summarised into brief sentences or paragraphs, rarely do we come across situations in life that resemble these questions precisely. As in the above example, you may be confronted with a colleague who may be stealing but is also your friend, or someone with whom you are in direct competition for a promotion. This would certainly affect your judgement and response.

For further background details on SJTs, and how they are created, including a full sample that covers all competencies EPSO has determined for the Assistant profiles, please refer to Part I Chapter 8.

Notification of Results

After the pre-selection phase, or in the case of Specialist profiles, after the successful sifting-in of their CV, candidates are notified both of their positive or negative results. The scores and the answers you had given are communicated to you in all cases though for practical reasons EPSO cannot disclose the multiple choice questions themselves, only the answers you had marked.

Should you not make it to the structured interview in the assessment phase, your situational judgement tests are "lost" in the sense that your competency profile is not established. Otherwise a special algorithm interprets your SJT answers, which is then forwarded to the assessors for follow-up in the assessment phase.

Since the number of applicants in the pre-selection phase runs into the tens of thousands, EPSO decided some time ago to require the submission of supporting documents only for those who have passed the pre-selection or were "short-listed" Specialists based on their CV. This means that even those who have already cleared the first hurdle may not take their eligibility for the assessment phase for granted: EPSO will first of all require you to send in a completed and signed application form along with annexes listing your educational qualifications and if necessary, documents attesting your professional experience or other required information.

As soon as the above documents are validated and accepted, you receive an official notification in your EPSO profile that you have been admitted to the assessment phase. Shortly afterwards you will be required to confirm your presence at a given venue and date to undergo the assessment exams.

Phase 3: Assessment Centre for Assistants

The assessment phase is a generic term to describe the second round of the EPSO recruitment competition: it refers to the Assessment Centre (or AC for short) for all profiles including Administrators, Linguists, Assistants and Specialists.

An Assessment Centre consists of a standardized evaluation of behaviour based on multiple inputs[8]. This in practice means that several trained observers called "assessors" evaluate your performance throughout half a day or a full day of exercises that have been developed specifically for this purpose. EPSO is using multiple types of exercises based on their competency framework: the idea is that each competency (listed above such as "Delivering quality and results") will be tested by two types of exercises to make sure that the observations are valid.

The reason why different competencies are tested by using various exercises for various profiles is that EPSO has linked certain competencies to each profile and therefore only wishes to test you on those that are relevant for your field. Accordingly, Assistants are not required to give an oral presentation as their job roles will not include giving presentations; similarly, a case study is used for Administrators and Specialists as it is a highly complex drafting/analytical exercise that other profiles do not need to be tested on.

Based on the above, EPSO uses the following exercises in the Assessment Centre phase of the recruitment competition for Assistants:

Assistants' Professional Skills Tests

– *Professional Knowledge in your chosen Sub-profile* (secretary, human resources or other). This test is in a case study format to assess your knowledge of the given sub-profile mentioned above. It usually lasts 90 minutes and you are requested to process multiple documents, such as emails, newsletters, legal texts and other types in order to answer questions such as "Provide a background note for your superior on the various approaches outlined in the background files", or "Draft a letter on behalf of your Head of Unit to the European Parliament's relevant committee on the practical steps to be taken for the public hearing they are proposing to organise with your Unit". Knowledge of your field and the EU context is crucial to achieve a high score in the case study. This is the only exercise where your domain specific knowledge is in fact evaluated.

– *E-Tray Exercise* (also called In-tray Exercise). This type of test is a complex one using a computer and you can expect such an exercise in the assessment phase of the recruitment competition. The chief goal is to evaluate your skills to prioritise and organise: this is a business simulation exercise in which you will skim through a large number of items such as internal and external memos, telephone and fax messages, e-mails, reports and correspondence, together with information about the structure of the organisation and your role therein. The e-tray exercise is the electronic (computer-based) version of the classic in-tray exercise; you can find a full sample of the latter in the Part III Chapter 3 of this book with a detailed report and hints for preparation.

The most important thing in these exercises is to quickly get a full overview of the actors and relations between them; identify urgent/non-urgent and important/unimportant issues and act on them accordingly; look out for conflicts between items in the file such as appointment requests for the same time slots, personal issues that you can identify from the items or other practical/legal conflicts such as e.g. a budget ceiling set out in a contract and a provider's invoice exceeding that amount; finally, to extract relevant information from the data you are provided with. For further tips and hints, please refer to the sample exercise and its evaluation.

– *Structured Interview.* This type of interview is very different from a job interview as the latter focuses on meeting specific job requirements and maybe your CV, whereas a structured interview tries to gauge your competencies by asking you to recall certain situations ("Give me an example from your previous experience when you efficiently delegated a task to a colleague") and events that assessors can connect to various skills that are being evaluated. A detailed description and tips can be found in Part III, Chapter 2.

EU and Domain-Specific Knowledge

In the previous system, this knowledge used to be tested in the second (written) phase of the exams in the form of multiple choice tests and an essay; in the current system this type of domain specific knowledge is tested in the assessment phase mainly in the form of a practical exercise or in the framework of the case study. This latter is closely related to the exam profile and the sub-profile or domain that you had chosen at the time of application.

In any case, specialist knowledge is going to be tested for all profiles as no capable candidate who otherwise lacks the proper knowledge of the chosen field can be recruited, given EPSO's wish that all new officials should be "operational from day one". Moreover, even financial or human resources specialists need a basic understanding of EU institutions, procedures and stakeholders, which can add valuable points to your performance in the assessment phase of the exam.

For instance, if you are familiar with the overall context of the EU's procedures, know which institutions and agencies are involved, which are the formal rules to enact policy in the main fields, which European associations and NGOs are taking an active part in influencing decision-makers and what the strategic thinking is on a policy's future, you are immediately in a position to make more out of the Assessment Centre.

Assessment Report

After both the Assessment Centre and other forms of assessment, a report will be drawn up by the assessors to evaluate you against the pre-established competencies. This also means that first and foremost you will not be judged against other candidates but rather against the objective behavioural criteria EPSO seeks in candidates. The ranking of suitable candidates will come afterwards and will be largely influenced by your performance in professional knowledge metrics.

Based on a streamlined and structured methodology, assessors draw up a report that summarises your performance, along with your strengths and weaknesses (see Part III Chapter 4). Upon request or even automatically, EPSO plans to reveal this report to all candidates regardless of whether or not they were successful in the assessment phase. This report can add a lot to your self-development as it provides a comprehensive analysis of your personality traits as observed during the assessment. It can also be very helpful in deciding which of your skills or competencies may need to be developed.

Phase 4: Reserve List, Recruitment

For those candidates who successfully passed both stages and survived other potential pitfalls in the exam procedure, a notification starting with the words "we are happy to inform you" arrives in their virtual EPSO account's mailbox. This also means that your name will be published in the reserve lists that appear in the EU's Official Journal and on EPSO's website (unless you explicitly request anonymity) and your competency passport, based on the above assessment, will be added to your profile once you take up employment. Those who did not succeed this time should not despair as they can re-apply for any later exam with the advantage of being familiar with the working methods of the system.

Validity of the Reserve List

Once a reserve list is published, it is always clearly indicated when it is going to expire, meaning until which date can you be recruited from it. However, EPSO has regularly extended the validity period of a reserve list to make sure that all available candidates are recruited from it. In the new system, the idea is to have the Administrator (AD) and AST competitions' reserve list valid until the next annual cycle results in a new list; for linguists it is the same approach but instead of the next annual cycle, it will be the next competition in the same language that replaces the previous list; for Specialists, the lists are valid as long as they still contain recruitable (available) laureates.

Flagging

Once on the reserve list, candidates (or as they are called at this stage, "laureates") are "flagged" by the institutions. This means that your profile listed in the "E-laureates" database can be assigned different statuses (marked in colours) as follows:

- **Green**: Any institution may recruit the candidate; they are not reserved for any specific EU institution or body

- **Yellow**: A specific institution or EU body has a keen interest in the candidate or the candidate passed an exam which was specific for a given institution (e.g. a lawyer-linguist exam to recruit officials for the European Parliament); as a general rule, this reservation is valid for three months, after which the candidate regains a "green" flag

- **Orange**: It is similar to the yellow flag but an interview has already been scheduled with the laureate or an extension of the above 3-month rule has been requested

- **Blue**: It is again similar to the yellow flag but it also shows that the laureate is already employed by an EU institution (e.g. an Assistant who is working for DG SANCO has passed an AD5 exam)

- **Red**: The laureate has already been recruited or their recruitment is happening right now

- **Grey**: The laureate is temporarily not available (e.g. the person is interested in taking up a job but currently cannot do so due to family or work reasons)

- **No Flag**: The candidate is no longer available for an EU job despite having passed the competition and being on the reserve list

Job Interview

Once on the reserve list, you can try to lobby for yourself by indicating your exam's reference number and presenting your CV to targeted heads of unit. This, however, is of mixed effectiveness; while it works for some, it may yield no result at all for others. EPSO much rather recommends that you wait to be contacted by interested institutions or if you wish to get in touch with them yourself, they provide a candidate contact service list on their website[9].

Any time between a few weeks and several months, you may receive a phone call or e-mail asking whether you would be interested in an interview for a position at x or y EU institution. Always make sure your contact data is up-to-date and that you regularly check your EPSO profile as well in order not to miss such important events.

Once offered the chance to attend a job interview, it is highly recommended to participate even if the job itself may not be the most appealing. You can always decide to decline and wait for a better or different offer, but it is better to have such options than decline flatly in the first place. You can also gain useful interview experience and find out more about the position; you might even realize that the job is in fact meant for you.

The job interview itself is different from other parts of the recruitment competition as it is focused on your suitability for the specific position and it does not include any general EU questions. If you apply for an Assistant position at a consumer health unit, you may expect technical questions on this specific topic and how your clerical skills would fit in, but nothing on e.g. the Treaty of Lisbon.

Your interviewers will most likely speak in English, French or German, unless you are applying for an Assistant post in the field of translation or interpretation where your second language may be tested (if different from the above three). Be aware, however, that questions may be put to you in any other language specified in your CV. Should you feel that you need to further clarify matters, take care not to patronise the interviewer and that your body language is also entirely respectful. It is very much recommended to review the hints and tips described in detail in the structured interview chapter of this book as it contains dozens of practical bits of advice for this stage as well.

Medical Check

A medical check is required for all new recruits; it may take place even before you know the result of your job interview. Should you not be chosen, the medical check results are valid for a few months so you will not need to re-take it if you attend another interview and you are accepted for another post. In any case, avoid the temptation of having that delicious-looking ham-and-eggs for breakfast or you risk further check-ups due to an excessive cholesterol level.

Travelling

You will most likely need to travel to Brussels or Luxembourg for the interview unless a video- or phone-conference call can be arranged at the EU representation or delegation office of your country of residence. Should you need to travel, all costs will be reimbursed and you will be given a modest daily subsistence allowance as well (based on strict formal conditions), but be prepared to receive the reimbursement only several weeks later.

Recruitment

If your interview was successful, you will be offered a job first by phone or e-mail, then formally by letter. Should this not arrive in time, make sure you ask your future EU institution's HR department or the unit in which you will work to send it to you. Generally you can agree on the starting date of employment with your future boss, so you can look for accommodation (if in Belgium, try www.immoweb.be) and arrange paperwork in due course.

Moving costs are paid for unless you have lived in the country where you were recruited to for more than a certain period of time (e.g. if you had done an EU traineeship at the Commission in Brussels right before you got recruited, this may prevent you from having your moving costs paid or being granted a so-called "expatriation allowance"). The detailed rules can be found in the EU officials' Staff Regulations, listed in the section below on further resources.

Preparation Methods

Preparing for EPSO tests is far from being an easy exercise and experience has shown that most test takers have had feelings of apprehension as they prepared. The way of preparing for the tests is really an individual choice. You may find that simply looking at the tests' objectives and preparing on your own makes you feel confident; conversely, you may want to read text books, take web-based training, or actually go through instructor-led preparatory classes offered by a training centre. Another great way of preparing is forming a study group where you can evaluate each other's written and oral expression skills based on the guidelines of this book.

Whatever method you choose, know that timing and motivation is the linchpin. As you prepare for your test, make sure to start soon enough and take it very seriously all the way. Knowing when to begin your preparation process is critical to having enough time without feeling rushed. The change in EPSO's communication, where the timelines of subsequent exam phases are transparently published, will make the planning much easier than it has been in the past, and it is strongly advised to start preparation at least two months before the exam day.

The important thing that you must remember is that tests are not written with the intention of catching you out. In fact they are only meant to probe your skills and competencies in various "reasoning" exercises and assess whether you have a concise understanding of the chosen field while ensuring that you possess the right competencies at the same time.

What to Study About the EU

For Assistants, EU knowledge is less relevant than for Administrators, nevertheless it is always useful to have a core understanding of the main issues, including the "Treaties" (the Treaty on European Union and the Treaty on the Functioning of the European Union). This is something that can add greatly to your performance and potentially impress the assessors (as long as you get all the other items right).

Try to acquire a good basic knowledge of how EU institutions and decision-making procedures work and what the key priorities of the European Commission and Parliament are; an idea about some milestones in EU history; and familiarity with the latest European Council Presidency Conclusions, basic notions of the legal system, basic Eurostat data, and the main proposals or papers in the specialist field that you applied for. These are also useful for learning the specific character and vocabulary of the EU. In addition, reading EU news on a daily or weekly basis can help you understand how a seemingly abstract or complex piece of legislation works in real life.

Preparation Resources

For the pre-selection phase, I recommend reading through this book's concise methodology chapters and practicing the exercises multiple times. You can find further resources online such as www.eutraining.eu. EU specialist bookshops such as www.eubookshop.com, www.libeurop.be and www.eurobookshop.be also offer a wide range of books as well. For the assessment phase, several YouTube videos can help you see real life examples and tips for each exercise (see relevant chapter for specific links), and this book should also help in identifying the key concepts to be aware of.

Browsing the Commission Directorates-Generals' websites for "hot" issues and checking the relevant Commissioner's website and speeches on your topic will help you understand where to focus your attention; having a look at the European Parliament website can also serve as a time-saving and efficient tool.

Having reviewed the above rules and general advice, let's get started with the preparation!

Endnotes

1   *http://europa.eu/epso/doc/epso_development_plan.pdf*

2   *http://europa.eu/epso/discover/selection_proced/selection/index_en.htm*

3   *http://ted.europa.eu/Exec?DataFlow=N_one_doc_access.dfl&Template=TED/*
     N_one_result_detail_curr.htm&docnumber=58794-2009&docId=58794-2009&StatLang=EN

4   The wording "Communities" is likely to be changed soon to "Union" according to the changes introduced by the Treaty of Lisbon.

5   For the official list of diploma types accepted by EPSO, please refer to *http://europa.eu/epso/doc/diplomasfortheweb.pdf*

6   Regarding work experience, generally a copy of references from the current and previous employers is sufficient to demonstrate that the required level and length of professional experience have been attained

7   Even though this particular competition was announced under the previous EPSO system, this section still serves as a good example. Extract taken from *http://eurlex.europa.eu/LexUriServ/LexUriServ.do?uri=OJ:C:2006:172A:0003:0023:EN:PDF*

8 *http://www.assessmentcenters.org/pdf/00guidelines.pdf*

9 *http://europa.eu/epso/success/recru/contacts/index_en.htm*

Further General Resources (see other specific resources in the relevant chapters)

Europa: *http://europa.eu*

EU Legislation Summaries: *http://europa.eu/legislation_summaries/index_en.htm*

EU CV Registration for Temporary Jobs:

http://ec.europa.eu/civil_service/job/cvonline/index_en.htm

European Parliament Fact Sheets:

http://www.europarl.europa.eu/parliament/expert/displayFtu.do?language=EN&id=73&ftuId=t heme.html

European Court of Justice: *http://www.curia.europa.eu*

Council of the European Union: *http://www.consilium.europa.eu*

Presidency Conclusions: *http://european-council.europa.eu/council-meetings.aspx?lang=en*

European Court of Auditors: *http://www.eca.europa.eu*

European Environment Agency glossary: *http://www.eea.europa.eu/maps/ozone/resources/ glossary*

Eur-lex: *http://eur-lex.europa.eu*

Treaties: *http:/eur-lex.europa.eu/en/treaties*

European Personnel Selection Office: *http://europa.eu/epso/*

EU Official Directory: *http://europa.eu/whoiswho/*

Staff Regulations: *http://ec.europa.eu/civil_service/docs/toc100_en.pdf*

Citizens' Europe: *http://ec.europa.eu/citizenship/ index_en.htm*

Multilingual Terminology: *http://iate.europa.eu/iatediff/*

EU Financial Regulation: *http://europa.eu/legislation_summaries/budget/l34015_en.htm*

DG Translation Aids: *http://ec.europa.eu/translation/index_en.htm*

Wikipedia: *http://www.wikipedia.org*

Euractiv: *http://www.euractiv.com*

EU Observer: *http://www.euobserver.com*

EU Politix: *http://www.eupolitix.com*

Language self assessment tool: *http://europass.cedefop.europa.eu/LanguageSelfAssessmentGrid/en*

To find this list with updated information, visit ***www.eu-testbook.com***

PART I

PRE-SELECTION – PSYCHOMETRIC TESTS

PART I covers the PSYCHOMETRIC tests you will face in the EPSO recruitment pre-selection phase. Professional skills tests are covered in Part II.

We can group these tests into two main types: classic psychometric tests (verbal reasoning, numerical reasoning and abstract reasoning) and situational judgement tests. While the first group of tests gauges candidates' skills in an indirect manner, situational judgement tests relate closely to real-life work situations while measuring competencies against a pre-established framework that EPSO has determined for each job profile.

Although situational judgement tests are described as "non-eliminatory" at pre-assessment, and may therefore seem less important at this stage, how well you do in them will be taken into account and "validated" in hands-on exercises when it comes to the assessment phase, so they also need to be taken seriously from the beginning.

We start Part I with a general overview of what verbal, numerical and abstract reasoning tests involve and how to approach them. These are tests that often strike alarm in candidates and a sound understanding of how they should be tackled is essential. For each of these test types methodological guidance is given, followed by plenty of practice questions designed to resemble AST level tests. In each case, answers are provided to help you understand where you may have gone wrong and so to improve your performance.

1. Verbal, Numerical and Abstract Reasoning Tests in EPSO Assistant Exams

Introduction

EPSO has, since its inception, used verbal reasoning and numerical reasoning tests in the so-called pre-selection or admission phase of open competitions (while for some Specialist profiles these are required in the assessment phase). Although it is often said that taking such tests does not require specific knowledge and they are therefore "easy" to pass, they have been dreaded by many candidates – and for good reasons.

From 2010 onwards, a new component, the so-called abstract reasoning test also became part of the pre-selection stage of the competitions. While this is a new test type that has never been administered to candidates before, it is expected to trigger the same kinds of mixed feelings in test-takers as the other two test types.

When it comes to abstract, verbal and numerical reasoning tests (commonly referred to as "psychometric tests"), it is important to answer the following questions:

- *What exactly are these tests like?*
- *What do they measure?*
- *What is the concept behind their design?*
- *What is the rationale for their use?*
- *What are the factors determining success?*
- *How are these tests scored?*
- *And finally: how to prepare and practice for them?*

An Overview of the Three Test Types

Each test type will be described in detail in the relevant upcoming chapters, but it is important to first get a sense of what these tests are like in general terms.

Format

All three test types, verbal, numerical and abstract reasoning, are in multiple-choice format. Based on EPSO's practice, all three "reasoning" tests have either four or five answer options for each question or text passage. In any case, there is always only one correct answer.

Verbal Reasoning

Verbal reasoning tests are designed to measure a candidate's ability to comprehend complex texts on various topics. These may vary from the description of an EU policy through current news, culture, history, or even natural sciences – in other words, the topic can be almost anything.

The length of the text is usually not more than 200 words (e.g. a similar length to the above "Introduction" section), and it is usually followed by one of the following two questions:

"Which of the following statements is correct?" (the most common format in AST competitions)
"Which of the following statements is incorrect?" (an alternative but less common format)

The four (or more) answer options will then measure whether you:

- *...understood key concepts?*
- *...have the necessary vocabulary to comprehend a wide range of topics?* (Believe it or not, this may be an issue in your native language as well.)
- *...are able to deduce arguments from the text?*
- *...can accurately interpret key indicators (such as chronology, causality, quantities) in the text?*

For more information and practice tests, turn to the chapters on "Verbal Reasoning".

Numerical Reasoning

Numerical reasoning tests are designed to measure a candidate's ability to interpret data and numbers, with a special emphasis on the relationship between various data sets and on performing quick calculations based on intuitive insight. This means in practice that the focus is not on complex mathematics but on identifying how one can arrive at the figure in question in the most efficient way.

The data on which the test question is based is usually a table with several rows and columns. The rows usually indicate various groups (countries, age groups, regions, industries, and so on), while the columns often contain various metrics (GDP, average income, amount transported, percentages, and so on). Alternatively, the data can also be presented in the form of a chart or several charts (pie chart, bar chart, etc.), or any combination of the above-mentioned items.

The test question usually seeks either a figure ("200", "0.3", "45%", "1/5", etc.) or one of the groups in the data set ("France", "People aged between 15-64", "Europe", "Agriculture", etc.) as the answer.

By arriving at the answer in a timely manner, you can demonstrate your ability to:

- *identify relevant data*
- *understand the relationship between various metrics*
- *determine the level of accuracy needed to answer the question*
- *perform quick mental calculations, and*
- *make fast but relatively accurate estimates*

For more information and practice tests, turn to the chapters on "Numerical Reasoning".

Abstract Reasoning

Abstract reasoning tests always involve geometric shapes. Although there are test types where the shapes are three-dimensional, EPSO decided against using such tests and therefore candidates will only be given questions with two-dimensional objects.

The drawings in the questions can be geometrical ones, such as circles, rectangles, triangles, lines, and combinations of these, but they can also be the simplified representations of real-life objects, for example bodies, faces, vehicles, animals, and so on. Another important aspect is to avoid any gender, nationality or other bias regarding candidates' abilities to solve them; EPSO also made sure that those with visual challenges are not being discriminated against either.

The tests are designed so that there is some kind of relationship among the items in the set of illustrations included with the question. In general, such relationships in abstract reasoning tests can take several forms: one item can be the odd-one-out, the items in the set can form a meaningful series, and they can even be the visual representation of mathematical concepts like addition or subtraction. EPSO, however, decided to limit its test database to test items where the figures form a series and the test-taker is expected to select which of the five answer options would come next in the series.

Abstract reasoning tests measure your ability to:

- *interpret abstract concepts that do not carry actual real-life meaning*

- *draw conclusions in new and unfamiliar scenarios*

- *discover relationships between seemingly "unrelated" concepts, and*

- *use your so-called "fluid intelligence" and apply it to any intellectual problem*

For more information and practice tests, turn to the chapters on "Abstract Reasoning".

Why these Tests are Used

When someone first looks at verbal or numerical reasoning test questions, and especially in the case of abstract reasoning, a thought that often comes to mind is *"How is this related to my potential performance as an Assistant in the European Commission?"* It is a fair question and one which deserves a good answer.

According to one approach, these tests are generic indicators of intelligence. Their results are standardized and are simply good predictors of performance in any work situation where intelligence, creativity and independent thinking is required. While this is certainly true, it is also easy to identify much more concrete work scenarios where the "skills" measured by these tests can actually be put to good use.

As mentioned above, verbal reasoning tests measure a general ability to interpret texts, regardless of the topic. One can easily imagine the wide array of topics, formats and styles an Assistant at the European Commission or the Committee of the Regions will be expected to read about and make sense of in the course of their career. One day you might be reading about some new internal procedures to follow, the next day you might be asked by your superior to skim through a report on the effects of the increasing price of fertilizers on the Latvian farmers' standard of living. Regardless of the topic, one thing is certain: you will need to be able to make sense of the text in a timely manner, draw the right conclusions, avoid common misunderstandings and eventually summarize your findings. Sounds familiar? Hopefully it does as this is exactly what you will be expected to do in the verbal reasoning test as well.

You might also be given a statistical report one day at work. It may contain a mind-numbingly large number of tables and charts, and although you are looking for one single figure or piece of data, it's just not in there. There may be a wealth of other (irrelevant) data, but not the bit you are looking for though you are expected to come up with an answer based on that report and nothing else. What you will need to do is sort through all the data, disregard everything you do not need and find a way to "extract" the useful information. Again, this is exactly what you will do when taking the numerical reasoning tests.

When it comes to abstract reasoning, the above analogy will of course not work. Not even in an institution with as widespread responsibilities as the EU will you face a situation where you need to select a shape with four circles and one rectangle (as opposed to two rectangles) in order to get through the day. You do, however, stand a good chance of going to your office one Monday morning and facing a situation or being given a task that will be completely unfamiliar; it might be about something you have never even heard about. Situations like this are the ones where the above-mentioned "fluid intelligence", the ability to manage the "unfamiliar" and apply logic, patterns and common sense becomes useful and that is exactly what abstract reasoning tests measure, as proven by various psychological experiments.

The Factors Determining Success

Just as is the case with any other test, success and good performance in EPSO's pre-selection exam is determined by several factors. We will now briefly discuss the four most important ones:

- *Motivation*
- *Habits and hobbies*
- *Educational background*
- *Preparation and practice*

Motivation

EPSO's pre-selection exam is certainly an event that one must prepare for and set aside significant amounts of time for this purpose: expect to experience a lot of stress both in the process of preparing and in the exam itself. In short, it takes time and effort, and it is easy to be distracted or discouraged on the way. This is exactly why having a clear and strong motivation is so important.

I always found that one essential component of motivating myself is to know why am I expected to carry out a given task and how I can benefit from the effort that must be dedicated to it. Even if performing well at these tests is just a means to an end, it is still much easier to put in the required effort if we have a clear sense of why we are expected to do it and understand its objective benefits such as the potential of getting an EU job or performing much better in job tasks requiring psychometric skills.

The above section on how these test types can be related to actual work situations may be thought of as one component of the motivation needed to succeed – knowing why you are expected to do this at the exam, and not something else.

Motivation is also about setting clear and attainable goals. There is an acronym that nicely sums up this challenge: being SMART.

A SMART strategy is one that includes goals that are:

$\mathbf{S}$pecific – "I will practice X hours a day for X days a week in order to get the job I have always wanted. Each week I will do X number of tests and revise X previous tests. I will also start reading about EU affairs to familiarise myself with the institutions."

$\mathbf{M}$easureable – "I will improve this or that much every week, and will be able to get X per cent at these tests by the time of the exam. I will do a benchmark test against which I can measure my progress."

$\mathbf{A}$chievable – "I have never been particularly good with numbers so I will not try to score 100% at numerical reasoning, but I will make sure to score as much as possible above the 50% threshold and to make it up in the other test types."

$\mathbf{R}$elevant – "I will do all of the above because my goal is to work in the Directorate General for Development of the European Commission. I would also like to get this job so I will have the financial means to pursue my long-time dream of visiting a friend in Australia. Even if I find these tests challenging or tedious at times, I understand that they are required for the exam and in any case I can improve my skills too."

Time-bound – "I will set aside this amount of time for the next X months to achieve this or that goal. I will have a clear timetable for the next two months where I indicate the days and hours I plan to spend on practicing. I will be able to stick to my schedule because I see the end of the tunnel."

Educational Background

Educational background is another important factor in success. In addition to the obvious fact that the quality of education one received can make a huge difference, there are various fields of study that provide a more relevant background for performing well at these tests than others. Mathematics or other disciplines that make use of logic and deduction may help in solving the test questions better under time pressure.

Obviously, your educational background is not something you can change at the time you decide to participate in an EPSO Assistant competition. If you have a more relevant background, so much the better – though if you do not, there is certainly no reason for despair either: there are numerous important factors in success, all of which you can improve significantly (see relevant tips below and in each consequent chapter).

Habits and Hobbies

Before turning to the "controllable" factors mentioned above, we must also mention that there are certain hobbies and activities that, if you are a fan of them, may provide some temporary advantage. When it comes to verbal, numerical and abstract reasoning, people who have done crossword puzzles, Sudoku and other mind games might be at some advantage.

Preparation and Practice

The factor, however, that is the single most important one is what this book is all about: *the quality and quantity of preparation and practice you complete in the run-up to the exam*.

In the following chapters, we will introduce in detail:

- *the three test types and how they are designed*
- *the typical problems and challenges they pose*
- *the methods and tricks that can greatly improve your performance*
- *the best ways to approach and interpret the test questions, and*
- *the optimal way to prepare and practice for these tests*

With a clear grasp of the methods that can be used to efficiently take these tests and with the right amount of focused practice, powered by the correct motivation, even those candidates who feel that such tests are not their strong suit can improve significantly and pass this stage of the exam.

How these Tests are Scored

When you are preparing for the exam, you might often wonder exactly how well you are expected to perform in order to succeed. To answer this question, let us overview the marking system for these tests. The score candidates receive will have to satisfy two conditions:

Pass Mark – this is a simple "objective" barrier, usually 50% of the overall score in the test that must be reached in each test separately, to be considered for the shortlist. It is also possible that EPSO will set a pass mark for two or more tests combined (e.g. they will consider your numerical and abstract reasoning test scores as one and establish a 50% pass mark for the global score of these two tests) – this would be an easier situation because you can compensate for poorer performance in one test by excelling in the other one(s).

The Best X –   this is a "relative" barrier, meaning that in addition to scoring higher than the objective pass mark, you must also be among a given number of best-performing candidates in all tests collectively.

Mixed Version –   EPSO may also use the "pass mark" approach to create a larger pool of potential candidates and then "sift in" a certain number whose qualifications match various objective, pre-determined criteria, though the "best X" may also be factored in the decision.

In Practice

- *Although you can count on compensating your weakness in one test type by performing stronger in another and thus still reaching a relatively high overall score, this option is limited by the requirement to reach the pass mark in each test separately*

- *A "good" score in the context of one group of candidates (e.g. those who sit AST exams for the human resources sub-profile) might be an insufficient score in another group (e.g. those who have chosen the financial management sub-profile) – so examples of "successful scores" from the past are not really relevant*

The figure below shows what is known as a "bell curve". Although it is just an illustration and it is not based on statistics, it quite accurately shows the typical distribution of scores candidates get at such tests. As we can see, there are few candidates with very low scores and very high scores. Most of the candidates will get scores in a very narrow range, for example between 60% and 70%, or 70% and 80%.

If "successful" candidates are selected by the best X number of participants in the exam, you must certainly score higher than others. *Looking at the bell curve, it is easy to see that only a few percentage points of improvement can mean that you have beaten a large number of additional candidates!*

Why is this important? The way we must approach this information is that the goals you set when you start preparing and practicing for these tests do not have to be unrealistic or unattainable. Also, you can take comfort in the fact that every small improvement will make a huge difference at the exam and will improve your chances exponentially – all thanks to the bell curve.

In the following chapters, we will see what the best methods and tricks to achieve success are, accompanied by a large number of quality practice tests.

After all, the best way of learning things is by doing them.

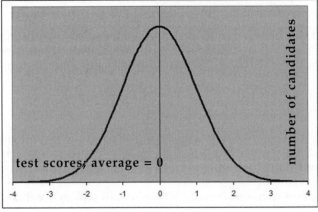

2. Succeeding in Verbal Reasoning Tests

In the world of standardized testing, the term "verbal reasoning" is often used to designate various test types relating to the interpretation and comprehension of texts. Although EPSO is currently administering only one of these verbal reasoning test types, some of the models below are being considered for checking Assistants' spelling or linguistic skills. It is therefore worth taking a quick look at each of them:

- **Spelling tests** are designed to test a person's ability to spell words correctly and also to differentiate between words with similar spellings yet completely or partially different meanings (for example, "their" and "there" or the correct spelling of "conscientious")

- **Word meaning tests** measure a person's vocabulary and their ability to select the best definition for words that have complex meanings (for example, to correctly identify the meaning of "preposterous" or "spill-over effect")

- **Word relationship tests** are designed to test a person's ability to determine the relationship between two concepts based on the analogy of another pair of concepts (for example, "what apple is to pear, a horse is to a ...")

- **Comprehension tests** measure a person's ability to comprehend complex texts and determine whether statements about a text are correct, incorrect, or impossible to tell (this is the "classical" type used by EPSO)

- **Verbal deduction tests** are the most advanced form of verbal reasoning exercises – they measure the reader's ability to make correct and logical conclusions based on the information provided (for example, a text describing Dubai's financial troubles followed by various questions such as "Who is the main investor in the country?", "Why did construction stall last year?" etc; this is a somewhat different approach from the "Which of the following statements is false?" question)

EPSO's verbal reasoning tests are closest in design to the comprehension test type. It is, however, easy to see how good performance in a comprehension test is based on the candidate's ability to identify correct spelling, the meaning of complex expressions and the relationship between various concepts. In this respect, this type of test is at the top in a hierarchy where success in comprehension depends on skills stemming from good performance on each of the lower levels.

We must also mention another particular feature of the way EPSO has implemented verbal reasoning tests. It is important to note that verbal reasoning tests are, by design, not language tests. They were not conceived to measure a candidate's command of or vocabulary in a second language (that is, the candidate's first foreign language). This is true even though up until 2010, likely due to various technical and organizational challenges, EPSO only offered verbal reasoning tests in three of the EU official languages: English, French and German. This is no longer the case – since 2011 candidates have been able to take the verbal reasoning test (along with abstract and numerical reasoning tests) in their main (native) language, as long as it is one of the 23 official EU languages.

In the following, we will overview several issues to look out for in a text, as well as a

number of methods and tricks that, once mastered, can greatly improve your performance.
These include:

- *How verbal reasoning tests are designed*

- *The role of familiar and unfamiliar topics*

- *Sources of information*

- *Assumptions*

- *Correct versus incorrect statements*

- *Near-equivalent versus identical concepts*

- *Omission of information*

- *General versus particular*

- *Determiners and quantities*

- *Frequency*

- *Verbs: time and mode*

- *Causality versus chronology*

We will also discuss the best way to deal with each test question, the suggested order of
reading the various components of the test (the text, the question and the answer
options) and the recommended methods to practice for the test.

The sample test below is representative of the type of test questions EPSO currently
uses (though you might be given for example five instead of four options) as well as the
expected level of difficulty at an Assistant competition. It consists of:

- *A passage of text of between 100 and 200 words*

- *A standard question asking which of the supplied statements is correct*

- *Four statements as answer options, one being the correct answer, that is, the only correct statement*

A Sample Test

Rebuilt after an earthquake in 1963 wiped out most of the city, Skopje, the capital of the ex-Yugoslav
republic of Macedonia, was for years characterised by ugly concrete blocks and strange empty spaces.
But earlier this year Nikola Gruevski's conservative government produced a video that revealed the full
ambition of "Skopje 2014", its plan for a radical reinvention of the city centre. Supporters of the plans
said that, after decades of stagnation, Skopje would at last get the regeneration it deserves, its heroes
commemorated in marble and bronze. Sceptical critics, used to a city where nothing much happens, sarcastically asked which triumph the proposed triumphal arch would be celebrating. Yet it is happening.
New buildings are sprouting up along the banks of the Vardar river and a fresh statue is unveiled every
few weeks (*The Economist*, Aug 26th 2010).

Which of the following statements is correct?

A Promoted by a conservative government, the "Skopje 2014" project has a nationalistic tone to it.

B Critics of Skopje's city regeneration plans have had their predictions of inaction come true.

C The Vardar river runs through Skopje, the capital of the former Yugoslav republic of Macedonia.

D Skopje's concrete blocks represent the legacy of rebuilding after the destruction of World War II.

We will now consider the factors and methods listed above one by one. Before we do that, however, I believe that it is essential to gain some insight into how verbal reasoning tests are designed by their authors – if you understand the concepts and strategies behind the creation of verbal reasoning tests, taking those tests will become incomparably easier.

How are verbal reasoning tests designed?

When psychologists whose specialty is the creation of psychometric tests design verbal reasoning items, they essentially follow two design steps:

1.   Selecting an appropriate piece of text.

2.   Authoring appropriate answer options.

Let us see what considerations go into each of these two steps.

1. Selecting an appropriate piece of text

When selecting excerpts for a verbal reasoning text, several factors are considered, such as:

Does the text include a good variety of verbs, nouns, adjectives, and so on?

Is the difficulty of vocabulary appropriate for the purposes of the test (e.g. for assessing Assistant candidates for an EU job?)

Is the text free of jargon?

Are abbreviations explained at least once in the text?

Is the text free of topics that might be objectionable from a political, moral or ethical point of view?

The difficulty of the text and its vocabulary is a complex issue, suffice it to say that such things are considered as the length of the sentences (in number of words) or the length and complexity of the words themselves.

2. Authoring appropriate answer options

The creation of the answer options is the most difficult and most important task in the design of verbal reasoning tests. Let us overview what kind of answer options exist – being aware of the types of answer options that you might face will be highly useful in the EPSO pre-selection as well.

Patently true statements: Such statements are clearly and demonstrably correct based on the information in the text. No outside knowledge is required to prove their correctness; it is possible to determine that on the basis of the excerpt and by drawing well-founded conclusions. Obviously, each verbal reasoning test item features only one such statement, and that statement will be the correct answer. It is worth noting that the difficulty of the test item can be greatly influenced by how this statement is formulated:

• Does the correct answer use similar expressions to those found in the text? The more similar the wording, the easier it is to spot that it is the correct statement.

• Is the correct answer simply a reworded version of a statement in the passage, or is it a conclusion that can be drawn by utilizing several pieces of information from various parts of the excerpt?

Patently false statements: Such statements are clearly and demonstrably incorrect based on the information in the text passage. It is important to point out that these statements are not simply unfounded (that is, no evidence exists as to whether they are correct or incorrect) but can be clearly disproved by utilizing information in the text. The difficulty of spotting such statements is, again, dependent on several factors:

- Is part of the statement correct? If so, it may be more difficult to realize that it is an incorrect statement, because only part of the information contained in it makes it so.

- Is the topic of the text expected to be familiar to test-takers? If so, it is much easier to decide a statement is incorrect, because you know it to be false and it will immediately "stand out".

You may now think that the above two statement types are all there is to verbal reasoning tests, but we will see very soon that there is one more statement type which makes the whole thing much more complicated. Nevertheless, we can already see that the difficulty of test items that utilize only these two statement types can also vary greatly in difficulty based on the factors listed above.

"Insufficient information" statements: This is the statement which usually causes the greatest confusion and represents the most dangerous trap when taking a verbal reasoning test. "Insufficient information" statements can belong to one of two categories:

- Statements that are *incorrect* if assessed using outside knowledge: such statements are easier to handle, because they will "feel" incorrect – you might know the statement to be incorrect based on your knowledge of facts, but it is impossible to classify the statement as incorrect based solely in information in the test passage. Fortunately, you are not expected to do that – just remember that **any statement which cannot be clearly proven by information in the excerpt is "incorrect"** in the context of a verbal reasoning test

- Statements that are *correct* if assessed using outside knowledge: such statements are the hardest to spot because they will "feel" correct upon first reading. The reason they are dangerous is exactly because you instinctively want to agree with the statement you know to be true. The important thing to remember here is that the **only correct statement in a verbal reasoning test is one that is fully supported and proven by information in the text passage**.

We can now easily realize that verbal reasoning tests can be designed using any mixture of the above statement types.
Here are a few:

- 1 patently true statement, 3 patently false statements: this is probably the easiest type, as patently true and false statements are easier to spot

- 1 patently true statement, 2 patently false statements, 1 "insufficient information" statement: this test would be a bit harder, because in addition to the correct answer, one additional answer option might at first "feel" correct – remember the tips above and you will be able to easily avoid this trap

- 1 patently true statement, 3 "insufficient information" statements: this is the "crown jewel" of verbal reasoning tests – the most difficult type. This is because due to the nature of the statement types used, you might feel that *all four statements* are correct upon first reading, but, again, you can discard those with insufficient information by remembering the principles described above

Based on experience and consulting with occupational psychologists, I expect that the overwhelming majority of verbal reasoning test questions that you will encounter at an EPSO Assistant competition will feature only one "insufficient information" statement.

You should, however, be aware of the existence of the other combinations listed above as well – better safe than sorry, as the saying goes.

Let us now consider a concrete example and return to the sample test item at the beginning of this chapter. Let us analyze the answer options based on the criteria we established.

A. Promoted by a conservative government, the "Skopje 2014" project has a nationalistic tone to it.

This is a typical "insufficient information" statement that is made even more difficult because it might "feel" correct. For many people, "conservative" might seem synonymous with "nationalistic", and the theme of the sculptures mentioned in the text (commemorating heroes) also could create the impression that the project has a nationalistic tone. Considering this statement correct, however, violates two important principles:

- we make unfounded assumptions about the nature of the project that are not supported by the text

- we also consider a subjective opinion to be patently true – a real correct statement will never be subjective unless the text passage itself is also subjective (which in this case it is not)

B. Critics of Skopje's city regeneration plans have had their predictions of inaction come true.

This is a *patently false* statement. Although the text does state that critics are used to inaction in the city, we also know that "[the project] is happening" and that new buildings are being erected in the city.

C. The Vardar river runs through Skopje, the capital of the former Yugoslav republic of Macedonia.

This is a *patently true* statement:

- the text passage states that Skopje is the capital of Macedonia

- the text passage states that the project involves new building and statues in the centre of Skopje

- the text passage states that these new buildings are erected along the banks of the Vardar river

- we can draw the well-supported conclusion that the Vardar river runs through Skopje

Consequently, this will be the correct answer.

D. Skopje's concrete blocks represent the legacy of rebuilding after the destruction of World War II.

This is a *patently false* statement. The text passage clearly establishes that the current state of the city is due to reconstruction after a devastating earthquake that occurred in 1963.

Now that we have analyzed the above four statements, we can see that our sample test item contains one patently true statement (the correct answer), one "insufficient information" statement, and two patently false statements. From a design perspective, the above test item is of medium difficulty, and I expect that the EPSO verbal reasoning test for Assistants will include items of comparable or lower difficulty.

Let us now turn our attention to the factors listed a few pages earlier – familiarity with such techniques as verb time and mode or generalizations will help you quickly determine which category each statement in a test belongs to, allowing you to find the correct answer in record time.

The Role of Familiar and Unfamiliar Topics

The topics of the texts in the verbal reasoning test can be varied. They may be closely EU-related (descriptions of policies, EU news) or they may be completely unrelated, dealing with history, art, nature, science and technology, music, and so on. Based on their interests or hobbies, most candidates have one or several preferred topics; however, the topic of the text should be completely irrelevant from the point of view of performing well in the test. While it is troubling to be faced with a topic that is completely alien to you, a familiar topic has its own dangers, because you must only use the information in the text, not your own knowledge.

Let us consider the pros and cons of familiar and unfamiliar topics.

Familiar Topic (e.g. EU-related)		Unfamiliar Topic (e.g. molecular biology)	
Pros	*Cons*	*Pros*	*Cons*
Mainstream vocabulary	*Bias*	*No bias*	*May be colloquial*
Familiarity	*Technical vocabulary*	*May be everyday topic*	*May include exotic vocabulary*
No colloquialisms	*Assumptions*	*No assumptions*	*Not familiar*

As we can see, there is no significant argument either for or against wishing for familiar topics. Each has its distinct pitfalls and advantages.

As an example, if a candidate is very up to date in EU issues and reads a text on a topic she knows a lot about, for instance the Services Directive, it may seem a comfortable situation but may also backfire. Having a deep knowledge of a topic may make it hard to separate the information in the text from the information we already have about the subject – and, as we will see, it is one of the main mistakes test takers commit. In the above example, the candidate may be familiar with the regulations on cross-border healthcare services and "project" this into the text even if it does not mention this particular aspect at all.

On the other hand, many candidates panic when faced with a text about a subject they have never been interested in. There may even be several words and expressions that they have never even heard of. Yet it often happens that it is exactly the distance from the topic and "objectivity" that allows us to consider only the information in the text and select the correct answer quickly and correctly.

Sources of Information

When we discussed the familiarity of the subject, we touched upon the fact that it is crucial to always keep in mind what information we use when assessing whether statements in the answer options are correct.

Let us consider the following sentence from an imaginary verbal reasoning text passage: "*small businesses employ almost half of all US workers.*"

If the reader of this passage happens to have an encyclopaedic knowledge about the United States and knows the exact figure for how many workers there are in the country, he might unconsciously use that information when assessing whether a certain statement is correct. Let's see a theoretical answer option where this could cause a problem:

"*Almost 100 million US workers are employed by small businesses.*" If the reader happens to know that there are approximately 200 million workers in the US and uses that assumption when taking the test, he might end up selecting the above answer option as correct – and lose a point, because the above answer cannot be correct if the text does not contain information about the actual number of people employed by small businesses.

It is thus crucial to remember that statements in the answer options must be assessed based solely on the information in both the main text and the answer itself.

Assumptions

In the previous example, we saw a situation where an assumption (regardless of whether correct or incorrect) was made about a statement based on "outside" knowledge. Let us consider another example.

"Consuming small amounts of healthy nuts improves the speed at which certain cognitive tasks can be performed."

A possible answer option:

"Consuming small amounts of peanuts improves, for example, performance in verbal and numerical reasoning tasks."

One might be tempted to select the above answer option as correct. If we do so, we make two assumptions:

1. Peanuts are a type of healthy nuts.

2. Verbal and numerical reasoning belongs to those types of cognitive tasks whose performance is boosted by consuming healthy nuts.

Whether the above answer option is indeed the correct one depends entirely on what other information regarding healthy nuts and the types of cognitive tasks is included in the text on which the answer options are based. For example, if there is no mention of peanuts in the text, considering them as healthy nuts will be a false assumption which will cause us to lose a valuable point in the test. Also, it is merely our interpretation (assumption) that verbal and numerical reasoning tests belong under "cognitive tasks" unless the text itself gives that information.

Correct versus Incorrect Statement

Although the verbal reasoning test in Assistant competitions almost exclusively includes items where the question is *"Which of the following statements is correct?"*, I believe it is important to mention another possibility – when the question is *"Which of the following statements is incorrect?"*

The same principles that we discussed apply in this situation as well, but we will need to look for the patently false statement – that will be the "correct" answer. It is also important to point out that if the question is seeking the incorrect statement, we can still encounter "insufficient information" statements – in this case, however, such statements will often be designed to "feel" incorrect - thereby leading you to think that they indeed are. Just remember: if you are expected to pick the incorrect answer option, look for a statement that can be clearly and unambiguously disproved based on the information in the text passage.

As a final point, I would like to mention something that may seem so trivial that some readers will wonder whether it was even worth mentioning. Yet it is crucial to always carefully read the question (the one immediately after the text) and keep in mind whether you are supposed to look for the correct or incorrect statement. As simple as this may sound, hundreds of candidates have lost points in verbal reasoning tests by not taking the extra two seconds to read the question, especially under the stress and time pressure of the exam. This inattention happens more often than you would think and leads to the unnecessary loss of valuable points.

Near Equivalent versus Identical Statements

Consider the following example:

> *"Not many inventions last for more than 100 years without major modifications. One of these is the barometer."*

A possible answer option:

> *"Since it was invented, the barometer has not been modified in any way."*

The statement in the answer option is very similar to the information in the excerpt. It uses many of the same words and expressions, and it essentially conveys the same meaning. We could say that the two statements are nearly equivalent. Yet in the context of a verbal reasoning test, we cannot infer that "without major modifications" is equivalent to "not been modified in any way".

It is always dangerous to look for similar words and expressions in the answer option. Similarity can hide small but important differences in meaning and can prevent the reader from reading on and seriously considering other answer options among which the correct one can be found.

Another piece of advice is to always look for prefixes or adjectives that change the meaning or the scope of a statement, such as "some", "hardly", "almost", "not always", "any", "completely", "at all", "partially", "to some extent", "mostly", "generally", "exclusively", "sometimes", "largely", "arguably", "seemingly" and others (see more examples below).

Although since 2011 this problem has eased as you are now able to take the verbal reasoning test in your native (official EU) language, it is still worth taking some time to think about words and expressions in your own language that slightly modify the meaning of the sentence in which they are included. This is especially true because we use our native language much less consciously than a second language and slight shifts in meaning are often overlooked in everyday speech.

Omission of Information

Here is an excerpt from another text:

> *"Verdi's operas continue to be extremely popular. This year, over 50 opera houses have staged Verdi's various works with great success all over the world."*

A possible answer option:

> *"Verdi's operas are still being played in a number of theatres."*

Note that the above answer option has a completely different approach than the excerpt from the text. Having read the text, readers might be inclined to look for answer options that emphasize how extremely popular Verdi's operas still are. Our example answer option does not do that, it simply states that Verdi's operas are still being played in certain places.

At first reading, the statement in the answer option seems to be in conflict with the excerpt by not conveying the extreme popularity of these operas. Yet it is a perfectly valid and correct statement.

We must, then, remember that the fact that a statement fails to convey all the information that was included in the text about something does not mean that it is an incorrect statement. In short and all other factors being equal, omission of information is not necessarily disagreement or contradiction.

General versus Particular

Another typical mistake many candidates make has to do with the difference between general categories and particular instances. This mistake can take one of two forms:

- *Generalisation*

- *Over-specification*

Let us consider an example.

"Deserts are the driest habitats on Earth. Average precipitation in deserts is 5% of the amount we are used to in Western Europe. Some deserts in Central America do not experience rain for several years in a row."

A possible answer option:

"Deserts do not experience rain for several years in a row."

The above statement is an example of a generalisation where a statement made about certain instances of a category (in this case, Central American deserts) is assumed to be correct about the entire category (that is, deserts).

Let us consider another example.

"Some deserts do not support any plant life whatsoever; others, such as those that get limited rainfall every year, support some plant life."

A possible answer option:

"Some deserts support some plant life, depending on the season."

The above answer option is correct in stating that some deserts support some plant life, but it is overly specific in stating that the supported plant life depends on the season – this is unfounded information not included in the text which makes the statement incorrect.

Determiners and Quantities

We now come to more language-specific problems. While most of the points raised so far are valid in all languages the test is administered in, there are always language-specific issues to consider. If the test is administered in English, these tips will be directly useful to your preparation.

If you take your test in another language, the following few sections can serve as a guideline along which you can consider the peculiarities of your own language and come up with a list of things to look out for. A good way of doing this is to read newspaper articles with higher than usual attention – professional journalists are always careful about how they formulate their statements and use many of the linguistic devices demonstrated here to make their statements more accurate.

Determiners and words expressing certain or uncertain quantities can be hard to notice; many candidates tend not to attribute much meaning to them in everyday situations even though they may greatly alter the meaning of a statement in the context of a verbal reasoning test.

Be mindful of the exact meaning of some of the most common determiners:

- "the" usually signifies one concrete object or person, or one concrete group: "the girl", "the Member States", "the books [on the table]", and so on.

- "a/an" and nouns without any determiner usually refer to one unspecified object or person, or an unspecified group of objects or persons, "a girl", "a Member State", "Countries around the world", and so on.

When the answer option lacks the determiner found in the text or features a different one, we must always be suspicious and consider whether this distinction changes the meaning of the statement.

A similar pattern can be observed when it comes to quantities: "some", "many", "several", "a number of" refer to an unspecified number of objects of persons. "All", "the entire", "every", and "each" signifies that the statement is about every single member of a group, or an object in its entirety, without exception.

It is important to bear in mind that these determiners of quantity are not interchangeable and if the text mentions "many countries", an answer option that extends that claim to "all countries" will not be correct.

Frequency

A very similar situation can be created by the use of adverbs signifying the frequency at which an action takes place. Always pay special attention to the use of the adverbs "sometimes", "often", "usually", "frequently", "never", "hardly ever", "occasionally", "always" and so on.

Although the only two concrete indicators are "never" and "always", and it is very hard to define the difference between "sometimes" and "occasionally", we must be mindful of the fact that they do carry meaning and can significantly change the meaning of a statement.

The same also can be said about adjectives and adverbs expressing chronology:

- "before", "previously", "earlier", "prior to that" are hints that one event took place sooner than another one

- "meanwhile", "concurrently", "simultaneously", and others indicate that two events occured at the same time

- "after", "subsequently", "followed by", "later", and similar words help us establish that one event followed another event in time

Think of the following statements: "He copied the document and left the office; subsequently he talked to the press." and "After he talked to the press, he copied the document and left the office." – the implied actions are very different in the two scenarios. Another example is "Birds have colourful feathers" versus "Birds occasionally have colourful feathers": the scope and extent are very different.

Verbs: Time and Mode

Closely related to the previous point, the tense of verbs also plays a crucial role in re-creating a series of events. Take an example:

"Prior to her sister Anne's marriage to King Henry VIII of England, Mary Boleyn was the most renowned member of her family due to her adulterous affair with the King."

A possible answer option:

"Mary is the most famous member of the Boleyn family."

The above option is incorrect because according to the text, she had been the most famous member of the family only until her sister became the wife of the King. This fact is indicated by the use of the expression "prior to" and also the past tense.

Verb mode also plays an important part in determining whether a statement is correct:

- Probability – "would happen" does not necessarily mean that something "will happen"; "would have happened" certainly means that that event did not in fact happen at all

- "Could happen" indicates that a certain event is only one of several possible outcomes

- "Should do something" indicates that a certain course of action is recommended or likely, but not necessarily unavoidable or mandatory

- "About to happen" shows that an event was going to take place but may or may not have actually happened

- "Was about to" (e.g. "he was about to go home when") refers to an intention or plan that was likely to take place when a certain event interrupted it or took place

Causality versus Chronology

As a last point, we must mention two phenomena that are frequently confused. Let us look at an example.

"Café Vian has been frequently visited by Hollywood celebrities since 2003 [...] In 2008, it finally received the highest rating in one of the world's most respected restaurant review guides."

A possible answer option:

"Hollywood celebrities frequently dine at Café Vian, which led to the restaurant receiving the highest rating in a respected restaurant review guide."

The statement in the above answer option incorrectly makes the assumption that there is a cause-and-effect relationship between the patronage of Hollywood celebrities and the rating the restaurant received in the review guide a few years after celebrities started going there. The relationship between the celebrity visits and the high rating is, in this case, merely chronological (one event happened before the other one), but there is no evidence that the earlier event led to the second event mentioned in the text.

It is often very easy to mistake a merely chronological relationship for a cause-and-effect one, but one thing that will help decide is the verbal clues mentioned above. Since test-makers tend not to include ambiguous information in tests, we can always count on indicators of a cause-and-effect relationship ("led to", "consequently", "resulted in") or a mere chronological relationship to appear in the text.

Methods for Approaching the Test Questions

Let us return to our sample text:

Rebuilt after an earthquake in 1963 wiped out most of the city, Skopje, the capital of the ex-Yugoslav republic of Macedonia, was for years characterised by ugly concrete blocks and strange empty spaces. But earlier this year Nikola Gruevski's conservative government produced a video that revealed the full ambition of "Skopje 2014", its plan for a radical reinvention of the city centre. Supporters of the plans said that, after decades of stagnation, Skopje would at last get the regeneration it deserves, its heroes commemorated in marble and bronze. Sceptical critics, used to a city where nothing much happens, sarcastically asked which triumph the proposed triumphal arch would be celebrating. Yet it is happening. New buildings are sprouting up along the banks of the Vardar river and a fresh statue is unveiled every few weeks (The Economist, Aug 26th 2010).

Which of the following statements is correct?

A Promoted by a conservative government, the "Skopje 2014" project has a nationalistic tone to it.

B Critics of Skopje's city regeneration plans have had their predictions of inaction come true.

C The Vardar river runs through Skopje, the capital of the former Yugoslav republic of Macedonia.

D Skopje's concrete blocks represent the legacy of rebuilding after the destruction of World War II.

When somebody first looks at a verbal reasoning test like the one above, the natural instinct is to start reading the text, then read the question, and finally read the four or more answer options. If we wish to consider all the factors we discussed in this chapter and make mental "notes" of them by underlining the key expressions in the text using the above method, it would look like this:

Rebuilt <u>after</u> an earthquake in 1963 wiped out <u>most</u> of the city, Skopje, the capital of the ex-Yugoslav republic of Macedonia, <u>was for years</u> characterised by ugly concrete blocks and strange empty spaces. But <u>earlier</u> this year Nikola Gruevski's conservative government produced a video that revealed the full ambition of "Skopje 2014", its plan for a radical reinvention of the city centre. Supporters of the plans said that, <u>after decades</u> of stagnation, Skopje <u>would at last</u> get the regeneration it deserves, its heroes commemorated in marble and bronze. Sceptical critics, <u>used to</u> a city where <u>nothing much</u> happens, sarcastically asked which triumph the proposed triumphal arch would be celebrating. Yet <u>it is happening</u>. New buildings are sprouting up along the banks of the Vardar river and a fresh statue is unveiled <u>every few weeks</u>.

Which of the following statements is correct?

A Promoted by a conservative government, the "Skopje 2014" project has a nationalistic tone to it.

B Critics of Skopje's city regeneration plans <u>have had</u> their predictions of inaction come true.

C The Vardar river runs through Skopje, the capital of the former Yugoslav republic of Macedonia.

D Skopje's concrete blocks represent the legacy of rebuilding <u>after the destruction</u> of World War II.

The underlined expressions are "suspect phrases" because of the various factors we discussed.

But what if most of the factors that we concentrated on when reading the text for the first time later turn out to be completely irrelevant because the answer options do not relate to those bits of the text? In order to avoid wasting time on irrelevant information, it is a good idea to *read the question and the answer options first*, looking for keywords and key concepts, and *then read the text*, already focusing on and searching for those bits that we know we need to answer the question.

Our mental notes using this recommended method would therefore look like this:

Rebuilt after an <u>earthquake in 1963</u> wiped out most of the city, Skopje, <u>the capital of the ex-Yugoslav republic of Macedonia</u>, was for years characterised by ugly concrete blocks and strange empty spaces. But earlier this year Nikola Gruevski's <u>conservative government</u> produced a video that revealed the full ambition of "Skopje 2014", its plan for a radical reinvention of the city centre. Supporters of the plans said that, after decades of stagnation, Skopje would at last get the regeneration it deserves, its heroes commemorated in marble and bronze. Sceptical critics, <u>used to a city where nothing much happens</u>, sarcastically asked which triumph the proposed triumphal arch would be celebrating. <u>Yet it is happening</u>. New buildings are sprouting up <u>along the banks of the Vardar river</u> and a fresh statue is unveiled every few weeks".

Using this method, answer option D can be discarded the moment we read "rebuilt after an earthquake in 1963", answer option B rejected the moment we read "Yet it is happening", and answer option A immediately after having read the entire text passage if we realize that the excerpt makes no characterizations about the tone of the project. Even if we are not entirely confident in the conclusion that the Vardar river must run through Skopje, we are quite simply left with that answer option as the only correct answer possible.

Let us summarize the above method in a few points:

1. Read the question first – are we looking for the correct or incorrect statement?

2. Read the answer options and make a mental note of the important keywords and themes included in those statements.

3. Read the text by focusing on the themes and keywords we made a mental note of when reading the answer options.

4. If you encounter a statement in the text that is clearly in agreement with an answer option (or in clear disagreement, if we are looking for the incorrect statement), and you are sure about your assessment, you can even stop reading and move on, thereby saving precious time.

5. If you are not sure about your assessment, you can continue reading and then eliminate the answer options one by one. This is where your knowledge of the possible statement types (patently false, insufficient information, etc.) will prove extremely useful – if you apply this knowledge right, and factor in the methods we discussed in this chapter, no amount of "witchcraft" on the part of the test item's author will confuse you.

Practice Methods

As a last point, it might be useful to make a few suggestions as to what the best methods are for preparing for the verbal reasoning test.

• Start practicing by taking your time, reading all kinds of high level texts, making mental notes of the "suspect phrases" we covered in this chapter

• Continue by doing the same, this time with actual test questions, for example the ones in this book (for the sake of practicing, you may wish to underline or outline these concepts and also write down in your own words why a certain answer option is wrong)

• Once you have established the necessary routine in identifying the key phrases and concepts, you can start timing yourself – start by simply measuring how much time it takes for you to answer one test question

• Check how much time you will have at the exam, and how many questions you will need to answer (as a general rule, you will have 30 minutes for 20 questions, i.e. 90 seconds per question)

• Start decreasing the amount of time you let yourself use for answering one question – ideally, by the time of the exam, you should be able to answer more questions in the given time than required in the exam (this is necessary because you cannot re-create the stress of the exam, which can decrease performance, not to mention the slower pace when reading texts on a computer screen for the pre-selection exams)

• Try to re-create as much of the atmosphere and infrastructure of the exam as you can – do not interrupt the test, go to a quiet place, use an alarm clock, and so on

• If you have access to such a service, practice tests online – the EPSO exam will also be computer-based, and it is a good idea to get used to the "interface" before going to the exam

• Try to read as much as possible on screen and measure the time it takes to read texts of comparable length (e.g. one page copied into Word) so you can measure and improve your performance.

In the following chapter you will find 150 verbal reasoning questions that you can use to start practicing straight away.

When you have completed the verbal reasoning test in the next chapter, why not try practicing verbal reasoning questions on line?

Online EU Training offers 1600+ verbal reasoning test questions where you can simulate an EPSO exam in real time, with the benefit of statistics on your performance and progress.

Readers of *The Ultimate EU Test Book* can claim a 12% discount.

For full details *see* page 387 of this book.

3. Verbal Reasoning Test

150 QUESTIONS – ANSWERS follow questions

In each question below, which statement is correct or can be best derived from the question text?
Please note that each question should be considered independently and no further information or knowledge should be considered when answering.

1. The European Council welcomed the fact that, following the opening session of the Intergovernmental Conference in Rome, work in the Conference was now underway. It recalled its support for the approach and timetable put forward by the Presidency in line with the conclusions of the European Council meeting in Thessaloniki. The European Council invited ministers to continue the political discussions.
   (Presidency Conclusions, Brussels European Council, 2003)

A. The Intergovernmental Conference was launched in Rome

B. The Thessaloniki European Council is due to follow the Intergovernmental Conference

C. The European Council consists of ministers of Member States

D. The timetable put forward by the Presidency is supported by the Intergovernmental Conference

2. The foreign occupation of Lebanon began in 1976, when Syria's dictator, Hafez Assad, sent his army to intervene in Lebanon's brutal three-cornered civil war between Maronite Christians, Muslims and Palestinians. The mass protests that forced Lebanon's pro-Syrian government to resign this week would probably not have happened but for a powerful shock: last month's murder of Rafik Hariri, the country's former prime minister and most popular politician. This was the catalyst for a chain reaction.
   (The Economist, 3 March 2005)

A. Lebanon's government had always been against supporting Syria

B. Lebanon had suffered a civil war in which Syria intervened

C.   Rafik Hariri was Lebanon's president in 1976 but he was overthrown by Maronite Christians

D.   Lebanon has had widespread relations with Arab nations in the Middle East

3.   Belgian chocolates and pralines (chocolate with creamy or nutty fillings) need no introduction, but Brussels and Liege waffles are appreciated just as much. The country's bakeries offer a great variety of different kinds of bread and a number of regional specialities. They include couque (sugary, spicy bread from Brussels and hard spiced bread with honey from Dinant), craquelin (sugar-filled brioche or enriched bread), noeud (butter biscuit with brown sugar), cramique (milk bread with raisins), pistolet (small round loaf), and mastel (rusk bread with aniseed). (*Michelin Guide*)

A.   Liege is mostly famous for its waffles, whereas Brussels is more known for chocolate and pralines

B.   Craquelin and pistolet are both Belgian specialities that are like a small cake or loaf

C.   The noeud is mainly sold in the Liege area and occasionally in other regions as well

D.   Craquelin is a rusk bread with aniseed and a sugar topping

4.   Iraqis now have their first democratically elected government in 50 years – appointed, as it happens, on Saddam Hussein's 68th birthday. Even so, five cabinet jobs, including that of defence minister, are still being disputed, and will be filled temporarily until final agreement is reached. One of the main hold-ups had been the demands by the Shia-led party of Iyad Allawi, the outgoing, interim prime minister, for a large share of the cabinet seats. Mr Allawi and his allies will not now take part in the government, and are likely to form the main opposition block in the Parliament. (The Economist, 29 April 2005)

A.   Iyad Allawi is an extrovert person who heads the Shia-led party

B.   Until recently, Iyad Allawi was Iraq's prime minister

C.   The interim, democratically elected Iraqi government was appointed on the same day when Saddam Hussein took power

D.   Iyad Allawi's allies will take part in the government only at a later stage and until then they will form the main opposition block

5.   In 1986 the Community received fresh impetus from the third round of enlargement to include Spain and Portugal and later the conclusion of the Single Act, a Community Treaty setting new targets for the enlarged Community (single market, economic and social cohesion etc.) with the result that a radical reform of the Community's financial system on a sound policy footing was envisaged. In February 1987, the reform was presented by the Commission as an overall proposal in the "Delors package". (*ScadPlus*)

A.   The Single European Act was initiated by Portugal and aimed at setting new targets for the Community

B.   Jacques Delors served two terms as the president of the European Commission

C.   The Delors package, aiming at higher spending on regional policy, was fostered by the accession of Spain and Portugal to the Community

D.   There had been two enlargements before the accession of Spain and Portugal to the European Community

6.   According to projections by the United Nations, on present trends the median age of Americans, now 35, will rise by only five years by 2050, and the population will grow by over 40%. Japan's median age, on the other hand, will rise by 12 years to 53, and its population will fall by 14%. Germany's is due to drop by 4% and Italy's by 22%. Falling and ageing populations will make it harder to boost demand. As people age and their children grow up, they tend to save more and spend less, though usually after retirement a prolonged period of dissaving sets in. (*The Economist, 18 September 2003*)

A.   The current median age in Japan is higher than that of the USA

B.   Germany's population is expected to fall by 22%, whereas Italy's is likely to fall by 14%

C.   According to the United Nations, the median age of Americans is expected to rise by more than 40% by 2050

D.   People tend to spend more than before once their children have grown up

7.   The first independent Slovene state dates back much further: when the Romans had been driven out by Mongolian Avars, who had in turn been driven out by Slavs, it was in AD 623 that king Samo established a kingdom (tribal confederation) stretching from Lake Balaton (now in

Hungary) to the Mediterranean, which had its centre in the present Czech Republic. The territory fell under the Frankish Empire late in the 8th century, and in the 10th century it became the independent duchy of Carantania under Holy Roman Emperor Otto I. From this period onwards, until 1414, a special ceremony of the enthronement of princes, conducted in Slovene, took place. *(DG Enlargement)*

A.   Otto I ruled in the 15th century as the Emperor of Rome

B.   King Samo's country stretched to areas that today belong to Hungary and the Czech Republic

C.   The Mongolian Avars destroyed the Frankish Empire late in the 8th century

D.   The special ceremony conducted for princes in the Slovene language first took place in 1414

8.   The protection of intellectual property is, of course, governed by many international conventions. The World Intellectual Property Organisation (WIPO) and, more recently, the World Trade Organisation (WTO) are responsible for implementing numerous international conventions and treaties. The first convention, the Paris Convention for the Protection of Industrial Property, dates back to 1883, and since then several conventions and treaties have been signed which cover various aspects of the protection of intellectual property, such as the protection of literary and artistic works (Berne Convention) and the protection of performers, producers of phonograms and broadcasting organisations (the Rome Convention). *(ScadPlus)*

A.   Artistic works and broadcasting organisations are protected by the Berne Convention

B.   The first convention to protect industrial property was the Paris Convention

C.   The World Intellectual Property Organisation and the World Trade Organisation have their headquarters in Paris and Rome

D.   Performers are generally protected by the Paris Convention and, in some special cases, the Rome Convention

9.   Nintendo's quirky game console, the Wii, will go on sale in the United States on Nov. 19 for USD 250 – much less than Sony's PlayStation 3, which launches just two days earlier with USD 500 and USD 600 models. In an unusual move for the launch of a Japanese product, the Wii (pronounced "wee") will go on sale in Japan two

weeks after the U.S. launch. "The release date is clearly a stab at Sony," said Ricardo Torres, editor at GameSpot.com. The Wii, which is about the size of a large paperback book, is the successor to Nintendo's GameCube, the third-best selling console of its generation after the PlayStation 2 and Microsoft Corp.'s Xbox. Nintendo Co.'s Game Boy and DS are dominant in the market for portable game machines, but the company hasn't been a market leader in consoles since the early 1990s. The company had promised to launch the Wii sometime in the last quarter of this year. By bringing it out on time, it's avoiding Sony Corp.'s embarrassing PlayStation 3 delays. *(CBS)*

A.   Sony PlayStation 3 is being launched with USD 500 and USD 600 models on Nov. 17

B.   Nintendo's Wii is the third best selling console of its generation

C.   The Nintendo Co. company has been a market leader in portable game machines since the early 1990s

D.   The Wii, as a standard move for the launch of most Japanese products, will go on sale in Japan two weeks after the U.S. launch

10.   The annual allocation to Romania under ISPA is between EUR 208-270 million for the period 2000-2006. The sectors benefiting from ISPA are transport and the environment, with both sectors receiving around half of the annual allocation. The ISPA programme is designed principally to support municipalities in the field of the environment and the central authorities in the field of transport. In order to bring Romania up to EU standards, ISPA will concentrate on the "heavy investment" directives (mainly drinking water, treatment of wastewater, solid-waste management and air pollution). *(DG Enlargement)*

A.   The ISPA programme for the period 2000-2006 mainly concerns the transport and energy sectors

B.   Romania is due to become a member of the European Union in 2007

C.   Romania is receiving around 104-135 million euros from ISPA for the period 2000-2006 to improve its environment sector

D.   Wastewater treatment is not included in the "heavy investment" issues tackled by the ISPA programme

11.   In the past decade, the effects budget for a typical blockbuster has ballooned from $5 million to $50 million. As digital effects (DFX) have become more complex and accessible, the barriers

between fanciful computer-animated films and ostensibly realistic ones have crumbled. DFX now allow filmmakers to not only manipulate reality, but to build it from scratch. *(Popular Science)*

A. Digital effects have become more complex but fewer filmmakers can afford their application

B. There is a limit to the extent digital effects can change "reality" in a movie

C. Movie effects have seen a tenfold increase in terms of their budget over the last ten years

D. There is still a huge difference between computer-animated movies and real ones

12. **Both man and machine are approaching the future at an ever-accelerating clip. Almost every year, our vehicles break speed records. This past fall, the X-43A scramjet-powered aircraft reached a speed of nearly Mach 10, beating a record of Mach 6.8 set only six months before. Today's fastest supercomputer, IBM's Blue Gene, is about 450,000 times as speedy as the ruling machine of 30 years ago and twice as fleet as the fastest machine of just one year ago. We build passenger trains that travel 267 miles an hour and rocket cars that break the speed of sound. *(Society of Broadcast Engineers)***

A. The fastest aircraft reached a speed more than three times higher than six months before

B. Today, the fastest computer is made by IBM and it is twice as fast as the fastest model a year ago

C. Aircraft, computers and trains have undergone an incredible development that is soon coming to an end

D. Passenger trains have managed to break the speed of sound

13. **Madonna will not be sent into space, despite a lawmaker's proposal to book a seat for the pop star on a Russian flight to the international space station, news agencies reported Wednesday. State Duma member Alexei Mitrofanov, referring to Madonna's reported expression of desire to become a "space tourist," proposed that the lower house of parliament send a formal inquiry to the Russian space agency about organizing a space trip for her in 2008. "Because of the television possibilities, it would be a pretty serious event in the year of elections in the United States and Russia," he was quoted as saying by the RIA-Novosti news agency. The Duma turned down the proposal, agencies reported without specify-**

ing the vote tally. Later, space agency spokesman Igor Panarin was quoted by RIA-Novosti as saying no seats on the Soyuz spacecraft would be available until 2009. *CBS*

A. RIA-Novosti is the agency which organizes the "space trip"

B. Igor Panarin announced that all seats should be booked until 2009 as no seats would be available on the Soyuz spacecraft afterwards

C. Madonna will not be sent into space on a Russian flight to the international space station because of a lawmaker's proposal

D. Alexei Mitrofanov is the State Duma member who proposed that a formal inquiry should be sent to the Russian space agency about arranging a space trip for Madonna

14. **Qori Kalis, a glacier that lies at above 18,000 feet in the Peruvian Andes, is melting at a rate of nearly 700 feet a year. In 2002, Ohio State University paleoclimatologist Lonnie Thompson discovered a perfectly preserved Distichia muscoides, a moss-type plant that carbon dating measured as 5,200 years old, on the Qori Kalis. "The find is remarkable," he says. "This tells us the glacier hasn't been this small for more than 5,000 years." *(Impact Lab)***

A. Qori Kalis is a paleo-climatologist at Ohio State University who made a discovery about a moss-type plant

B. Carbon dating is generally used to determine the size of glaciers

C. Half of the Peruvian Andes is covered by snow all year long

D. The Ohio State University professor based his conclusion about the size of the glacier on a moss-type plant

15. **Freedom of movement for persons was not brought about only in the context of the European Communities. In 1985, Germany, France and the Benelux countries (Belgium, Luxembourg and the Netherlands) signed the Schengen Agreement on an intergovernmental basis. That Agreement, which was supplemented by an implementing convention in 1990, was to introduce genuine freedom of movement for all citizens of the European Communities within the Schengen area and to deal with visa, immigration and asylum issues. *(Commission)***

A. The village of Schengen, where the Agreement was

signed in 1985, is on the Luxembourgish-German border

B.   The Schengen Agreement aimed to introduce freedom of movement for all citizens of the European Communities

C.   In 1990, the Schengen Agreement was replaced by what is known as an implementing convention

D.   The Schengen Agreement was originally signed by five countries

16.   The transport industry occupies an important position in the Community, accounting for 7% of its GNP, 7% of its total employment, 40% of Member States' investment and 30% of Community energy consumption. Demand, particularly in intra-Community traffic, has grown more or less constantly for the last 20 years, by 2.3% a year for goods and 3.1% for passengers. *(DG Transport)*

A.   The transport industry accounts for a higher percentage of the Community's GNP than it does of the Community's total employment

B.   The transport industry accounts for one-third of the Community's energy consumption and more than half of Member States' investment

C.   Demand for transport services has grown more dynamically for passengers than goods in the last twenty years

D.   Each Member State spends about 7% of its gross national product on transport services

17.   In 2002, English track star Paula Radcliffe won the Chicago Marathon with a world-record-breaking time of two hours, 17 minutes and 18 seconds. Then, less than a year later, she ran the 2003 Flora London Marathon and finished in 2:15:25 – beating her own record by nearly two minutes and slicing an unprecedented three minutes off her closest competitor. In a sport where speed improvements are marked in seconds, not minutes, Radcliffe redefines the rate of human performance gains. Prior to her record-smashing run, it had taken 16 years for women to knock a minute and 20 seconds off the world record. *(Popular Science)*

A.   Paula Radcliffe had managed to keep her record for 16 years

B.   Paula Radcliffe won the London Marathon in 2002 and 2003 as well

C.   The Chicago Marathon was held after the London Marathon

D.   Paula Radcliffe broke the world record twice

18.   Over the next few months two reports on Kosovo are due to be presented to the UN Security Council. If they paint a generally positive picture, Kofi Annan, the UN secretary-general, will appoint a "status envoy" to shuttle between Belgrade and Pristina, talking over what is now being dubbed Kosovo's "future", not its "final status". The envoy will probably be a former politician well acquainted with the Balkans. One possibility is Giuliano Amato, a former Italian prime minister who chaired an international commission on the Balkans that released its report this week. The report advocates Kosovo's independence, to be achieved in four stages. *(The Economist, 14 April 2005)*

A.   Kosovo's independence is one of the principal issues in the United Nations Security Council and on Kofi Annan's agenda

B.   Once Kosovo's final status has been resolved, talks will turn to its "future"

C.   The former Italian prime minister may become a special representative commissioned by the United Nations

D.   There have been severe tensions between Kosovo and Pristina in recent years

19.   Doc Ock, the tentacled villain at the heart of the movie Spider-Man 2, nearly succeeded where thousands of scientists and 50 years of work have so far failed: in building a nuclear fusion reactor. But non-villainous scientists may be about to save their reputation. This year a multinational team is scheduled to begin constructing ITER, the International Thermonuclear Experimental Reactor, a project designed to demonstrate that fusion can generate almost limitless amounts of electricity without the risks and long-lived radioactive waste linked with nuclear fission reactors. *(Popular Science)*

A.   Doc Ock is the chief scientist leading the project on the International Thermonuclear Experimental Reactor

B.   Scientists were inspired by the movie Spider Man 2 to create a new alternative energy source

C.   Researchers may succeed in achieving what the scientist in Spider Man 2 was about to create: a fusion reactor

D.   The ITER project may be very beneficial for generating electricity but it also leaves radioactive waste behind

20.   **One vital exercise of preventive "soft power" over the past decade has been the spending of more than $7 billion by the United States to secure nuclear and other weapons materials and know-how in the countries of the former Soviet Union. Although the problem is on their doorstep, the Europeans collectively have mustered less than $1 billion. America has committed itself to another $10 billion over the next decade; Europeans, alongside the rest of the G8, including Canada and Japan, have promised to find a matching amount, but the pledges do not yet add up.**
      (The Economist, 21 November 2002)

A.   Europeans have given or pledged less than 15% of what the USA has spent on securing nuclear weapons

B.   Canada and Japan do not take part in the G8 but they wish to participate in the prevention efforts

C.   America plans to spend a further 7 billion dollars on halting the proliferation of nuclear weapons

D.   Almost all countries of the former Soviet Union have bought nuclear and other weapons as well as the know-how

21.   **To the average EU insider the big concerns at the moment are as follows: referendums on the European constitution, the success or failure of the new European Commission and the future of EU budget negotiations. Back in Britain, however, it seemed that everyone from taxi-drivers to middle-class housewives had only one thought about Brussels. And this is that the whole place is a massive sink-hole of corruption, a funnel into which British taxpayers' money is poured, to be sprayed liberally about by corrupt bureaucrats on a variety of undeserving causes. In Brussels, the reaction to all this is often to dismiss it as typical British Euroscepticism, stoked up by its malign American-owned press. But the image of the European Union as corrupt is not confined to Britain, as any Danish, Dutch or German politician will know. So is it true?**
      (The Economist, 7 April 2005)

A.   Only the British think the European Union is badly affected by corruption

B.   Insiders dealing with European issues tend to have

a different view on what is an important issue than the average citizen

C.   Brussels based officials tend to attribute British Euroscepticism to the fact that television channels are owned by Americans

D.   All European taxpayers are concerned by the negotiations on the European Union's budget

22.   **In the dimly lit cyber-café at Sciences-Po, hothouse of the French elite, no Gauloise smoke fills the air, no dog-eared copies of Sartre lie on the tables. French students are doing what all students do: surfing the web via Google. Now President Jacques Chirac wants to stop this American cultural invasion by setting up a rival French search-engine. The idea was prompted by Google's plan to put online millions of texts from American and British university libraries.** *(The Economist, 31 March 2005)*

A.   French students are doing the same thing as most other students in the world, i.e. surfing the web

B.   Mr. Chirac would like to put French texts online as Google has done with English language texts

C.   Sartre used to be the most popular French philosopher among students but very few read his works now

D.   American and British university libraries are strongly opposing Google's plan to put their texts on the web

23.   **Most people require about 8 hours sleep a night, but some lucky oddballs function well on 4 hours or even less. A new study in fruit flies provides evidence that genetics plays a strong role in determining who can get by with little rest. A single mutation in a gene that's also found in people can reduce the insects' sleep needs by about two-thirds. Although researchers have been studying sleep for decades, they've made little progress in teasing out the genetic components that control this phenomenon. A sleeping fly simply sits motionless, usually for many hours a day.**
      (Science News)

A.   Everybody needs at least four hours' sleep every day

B.   A sleeping fly, as a recent study has found, does not move for more than 8 hours

C.   Those who require four hours' sleep a night are likely to have a mutation in the same gene that also reduces the sleep needs of insects

D. Scientists have been researching insects' sleep needs for decades

24. Although vitamin pills can provide much or all of the U.S. recommended daily intake (RDI) of vitamin D for children and adults – 200 to 600 International Unit (IU), depending on age – bone and mineral researchers have lately been recommending that people get much, much more. In fact, some scientists have advised the federal government to boost the vitamin D RDI up to at least 1,000 IU and to bump up the certified-safe limit beyond the current 2,000 IU.

A. The maximum certified vitamin D intake is currently 600 international units

B. Scientists have proposed to increase the recommended level of vitamin D intake per day to at least a thousand international units

C. According to mineral researchers, only sun can provide sufficient levels of vitamin D

D. Children usually get less vitamin D than adults because of unhealthy nutrition

25. As SANCO Commissioner Markos Kyprianou underlined at the launch of the EU Platform, "Today's overweight teenagers are tomorrow's middle aged heart attack victims". Tackling this serious public health issue will also have an impact on the EU's economy and health care services. Obesity, poor nutrition and lack of exercise and associated health problems such as cardiovascular disease, type 2 diabetes, respiratory problems and an increased risk of cancer are already linked to 2-8% of EU health care costs. *(Commission en Direct, no. 358, p. 4)*

A. Obesity and malnutrition not only cause serious health risks but also increased spending on health care

B. The Commissioner for Health and Consumer protection is of Greek nationality

C. Overweight teenagers usually suffer from cardiovascular diseases which entail a higher risk of cancer

D. The EU spends 2-8% of its budget on health care costs

26. As inhabitants of rugged shores, mussels have an amazing capacity to stick to rocks, despite the constant pounding of waves. These organisms are also notorious for sticking to ships, glass, and, well, just about anything – even Teflon. Researchers at Purdue University in West Lafayette say they have uncovered the secret to what makes mussel glue so strong. It's iron. Once they understand the glue's chemistry, researchers might develop more effective antifouling paints to prevent mussels, barnacles, and other hangers-on from sticking to ships. Another payoff could be stronger biomaterials, particularly sutures and other wound-closing products. *(Science News)*

A. Teflon is the only material a mussel is unable to stick itself to

B. Barnacles are posing a real danger to the safety of maritime shipping

C. The fact that scientists have managed to reveal the chemistry of mussels' glue may help in developing special paints to prevent them from sticking to ships

D. Mussels can glue themselves to anything with a special kind of iron web

27. The decline of newspapers predates the internet. But the second – broadband – generation of the internet is not only accelerating it but is also changing the business in a way that the previous rivals to newspapers – radio and TV – never did. Older people, whom Mr Murdoch calls "digital immigrants", may not have noticed, but young "digital natives" increasingly get their news from web portals such as Yahoo! or Google, and from newer web media such as blogs. Short for "web logs", these are online journal entries of thoughts and web links that anybody can post. Whereas 56% of Americans haven't heard of blogs, and only 3% read them daily, among the young they are standard fare, with 44% of online Americans aged 18-29 reading them often, according to a poll by CNN/USA Today/Gallup. *(The Economist, 21 April 2005)*

A. Newspapers started to decline when the internet became more and more widespread

B. The internet changes journalism the same way as radio and TV once did

C. More than half of Americans have never heard of web logs, or "blogs"

D. Older people increasingly tend to get their news from web portals

28. Beethoven first joined Prince Lichnowsky's household and studied under Haydn, Albrechtsberger, and possibly Salieri. His music is usually divided into three periods. In the first (1792–1802), which includes the first two symphonies, the first six quartets, and the 'Pathétique' and 'Moonlight' sonatas, his style gradually develops its own individ-

uality. His second period (1803–12) begins with the 'Eroica' symphony (1803), and includes his next five symphonies, the difficult 'Kreutzer' sonata (1803), the Violin Concerto, the 'Archduke' trio (1811), and the 'Razumovsky' quartets. His third great period begins in 1813, and includes the Mass, the 'Choral' symphony (1823), and the last five quartets. *(Biography.com)*

A.   Beethoven was born in 1770

B.   The second period of Beethoven's music began with the Kreutzer sonata

C.   Salieri had most probably died before Beethoven was born

D.   Beethoven composed the Moonlight sonata in the first period of his musical life

29.   Certain cells lining the lungs and other membrane-covered areas make and store mucus. These cells, called goblet cells, routinely release small amounts of the slippery substance. But the cells also secrete bursts of mucus in response to irritants. The mechanism behind the switch from healthy burst to aberrant secretion, as seen in people with asthma, remains unknown. *(Science News)*

A.   Goblet cells in the lungs release mucus

B.   Aberrant secretion of mucus has recently been discovered by scientists

C.   Goblet cells are the only ones that do not release any slippery substance

D.   The cause and mechanism of asthma are not yet known

30.   Early in the history of the planet, when only single-celled life forms such as bacteria were around, there was little oxygen in the air. About halfway through Earth's 4.6 billion years, oxygen began to rapidly accumulate in the atmosphere. The first eukaryotes with several different types of cells emerged at the same time. *(Science News)*

A.   In the very beginning of Earth's history, little else but bacteria were present

B.   The age of the Earth is 4.6 million years

C.   Oxygen started to accumulate "only" a billion years ago

D.   Eukaryotes, like bacteria, have only one cell

31.   The EU has from the outset taken a pro-active role in the negotiations and unreservedly supported the implementation of the Doha Declaration. The recently adopted reform of the CAP (Common Agricultural Policy) and proposals for reform in other sectors are the best proof that for the EU the path towards less trade-distorting support need not be an external constraint, but a desired policy orientation. Internally, the path chosen meets the domestic challenges of promoting competitiveness for EU agriculture while at the same time meeting the highest environmental, quality and animal welfare standards that our citizens expect. *(Reviving the DDA Negotiations – the EU Perspective, 2003)*

A.   According to the Doha Declaration, EU agriculture is not competitive enough

B.   The Common Agricultural Policy (CAP) had undergone several reforms in the past

C.   Regarding agriculture, the EU did not have any substantial objection to the implementation of the Doha Declaration

D.   The EU considers that less trade-distorting support is indeed nothing else but an external constraint

32.   Picasso studied at Barcelona and Madrid, and in 1901 set up a studio in Montmartre, Paris. His 'blue period' (1902-4), a series of striking studies of the poor in haunting attitudes of despair and gloom, gave way to the gay, life-affirming 'pink period' (1904-6), full of harlequins, acrobats, and the incidents of circus life. He then turned to brown, and began to work in sculpture. His break with tradition came with 'Les Demoiselles d'Avignon' (1906-7, New York), the first exemplar of analytical Cubism, a movement which he developed with Braque (1909-14). *(Biography.com)*

A.   Picasso painted 'Les Demoiselles d'Avignon' in 1904 in Paris

B.   Picasso had blue, pink and brown periods of painting

C.   Cubism was a brand new style of painting and architecture Picasso had invented

D.   Picasso had lived in Paris before pursuing his studies in Spain

33.   Many of the European Union's most ardent supporters still see the EU as a crucial bulwark against the return of war to Europe. In pressing the case for monetary union, Mr

Kohl argued that adopting the euro was ultimately a question of war and peace in Europe. When efforts to write a European constitution looked like stalling, Elmar Brok, a prominent German member of the EU's constitutional convention (and confidant of Mr Kohl), gave warning that if Europe failed to agree on a constitution, it risked sliding back into the kind of national rivalries that had led to the outbreak of the first world war. *(The Economist, 23 September 2004)*

A.   Mr. Kohl was the federal chancellor of Germany for several years

B.   Pro-EU politicians often see the European Union as a means to prevent a return of war to the continent

C.   The constitutional convention was co-chaired by Mr. Elmar Brok

D.   The euro was the first tangible sign of European monetary union

34.   At first glance, Kentlands, Md. looks like a snapshot of an old-fashioned city or small town neighborhood: a mix of houses, schools, shops and cafes, all within an easy stroll. Just like the old days, some of those neighbors even reside above the store. But this town is not an old established area. Twenty years ago, none of it was here. Kentlands is a town built from scratch, according to town architect Mike Watkins. "The main street's the heart of the community. It's where neighbors hang out," he told. "Kentlands is 352 acres, 2200 residential units, about a third multi-family, a third townhouses and a third singles in rough numbers." There are rental apartments, too, and lots of shared green space. The governing principal is simple. "Many of us prefer walking to driving, so it was deliberately designed as a place as a counterpoint to that – to offer an alternative to driving absolutely everywhere," Watkins said. In fact, Kentlands is just one example of a movement that's been dubbed "new urbanism." "Well, essentially the suburbs have crashed," said Andres Duany, who with his wife, Elizabeth Plater-Zyberk, is leading the new urban movement. "The promise of suburban living was not fulfilled. You don't get nature, you get a little lawn. You don't get the freedom to drive everywhere, you get traffic congestion." *(CBS)*

A.   The creation of Kentlands two decades ago started a movement that's been dubbed the "new urbanism".

B.   Since everything in Kentlands is within strolling distance, it is possible to drive anywhere in the town without getting caught up in traffic congestion

C.   Kentlands is an old-established city, which has been successfully preserved, despite the creation of new suburbs

D.   The new urban movement believes that the suburbs have proved a failure

35.   Since the first one was built 60 years ago, Ferrari has defined Italian style, reports CBS News correspondent Allen Pizzey. Ferraris have also been called the ultimate status symbol, a rich man's toy, an answer to a mid-life crisis, a proof of more money than brains – and the finest cars in the world. Depending on whether one is speaking out of envy, disdain or admiration, a Ferrari is all of those and more, according to product development manager Massimo Fumarola. "You don't have actually any need to buy a Ferrari," Fumarola says. "It's not a product that brings you from A to B. You can do it more efficiently with any other car. It's much more about a self-realization – a dream. And like all dreams, a Ferrari takes a while to come true. The assembly line produces a mere 27 cars a day – a little over five thousand a year. Every one is unique with the exception of the engine. They are handcrafted under hospital-like hygienic conditions, but no matter how rich you are, there are no optional extras available. "If a customer is looking for more horsepower, we always say no," Fumarola says. "Apart from that, we can really match any kind of expectation from our customers." One of those expectations is color. From Formula One racecars to sleek street models, Ferrari is a synonym for red. But in fact there are three shades of "Ferrari Red": the brilliant racing one, a slightly less bright more common to street models, and a deeper hue for the luxury end of the spectrum. But you can order almost any color imaginable. One customer wanted a paint job to match his wife's eyes – obviously a man who knew how to have an expensive toy and a peaceful life. *(CBS)*

A.   Ferraris have been called nearly everything – the ultimate status symbol, a rich man's toy, an answer to a mid-life crisis and a proof of more money than brains – except the finest cars in the world

B.   No matter who, or how rich the customer is, the engine always stays the same in all Ferrari cars

C.   A custom paint job was done on one of the cars, so that it would match the eyes of Mr Fumarola's wife

D.   Ferrari, being a synonym for red, is the only colour that these cars are available in, though in almost any shade imaginable

36. A full-size granite Mercedes-Benz is the pride of
a New York cemetery. It's one of the more eccen-
tric tombstones that try to tell people more than
just name, date of birth and date of death. We
long ago forgot about John Matthews, the soda
fountain king, but we can be reminded of him in
Green-Wood cemetery in Brooklyn, N.Y., by star-
ing for all eternity at his achievements in the car-
bonated drink world – carved in marble. But
Green-Wood didn't get to be a national historic
landmark because of this sort of thing. Rather, it's
because of the who's who of famous people
buried here. Among them is the tomb of amateur
Egyptologist Albert Parsons. "We start off with
the Old Testament on the far left there, Moses
and his mother and then Christian imagery here –
you see the lamb which is symbol of the inno-
cence of a child, and then you see the Egyptian
god responsible for safeguarding tombs and mau-
soleums," said Green-Wood historian Jeffrey
Richman as he showed off Parsons' very own
Sphinx tombstone. Richman says the cemetery
reflects what was going on in the world at the
time. In fact cemeteries are like a social history of
the United States. Dutch Gravestones from the
18th century were plain and severe, which indicate the harshness of life in colonial America.
"This is about a hostile nature, this is about death
constantly stalking the person, the living,"
Richman said. (*CBS*)

A. What actually got Green-Wood to national historic
landmark status, is the freshly added full-size granite Mercedes-Benz

B. According to a Green-Wood historian, cemeteries
provide a social history of the United States

C. Richman says that all the graves in the cemetery
reflect the hostility of nature, and are about death
constantly stalking people

D. The pride of Green-Wood cemetery is a tombstone
that tells the person's name, date of birth and date of
death and nothing more

37. The iPhone doesn't go on sale until Friday
evening but, thanks to Apple's full-court press
advertising and media campaign, some people
are already standing in line to get one. Ed Baig,
personal technology columnist for USA Today,
has tried one, and offered his thoughts on its pros
and cons. Basically, says Baig, it's very good, but
not perfect. Its hype though, he told co-anchor
Hannah Storm, is "remarkable. I've been covering tech for more years than I can remember, and
this product has had such a mania and attraction
that I've never seen it with any other product."
Storm wondered if the iPhone make other prod-

ucts obsolete. "I don't know about that," Baig
replied. "If you have a Blackberry or a Trio, don't
throw them away just yet, but it's pretty cool."
Apple says the iPhone – which combines the
functions of a cell phone, iPod media player and
Web-surfing device – will be easier to use than
other smart phones because of its unique touch-
screen display and intuitive software that allows
for easy access to voice mail messages, the
Internet, and video and music libraries. But skep-
tics question whether even the most innovative
product can live up to the iPhone's lofty expectations. AT&T is its exclusive carrier, and Baig calls
the network AT&T is using for the iPhone the
device's "biggest drawback." The iPhone is on
AT&T's Edge data network, and Baig says Edge is
slow compared to other "third generation" or
"3G" networks. (*CBS*)

A. Until Friday, the iPhone will not be tried by anyone,
so even Ed Baig can only take guesses

B. Baig remarked on a disadvantage too, which is
regarding the speed of the iPhone's current data network

C. Later on, a unique touch-screen display will also be
added

D. The iPhone was designed to be perfect in all aspects

38. Fireworks and the Fourth of July go hand and
hand, but the Consumer Product Safety
Commission estimates there were 9,200 emergency room-treated injuries associated with all
fireworks last year – 6,400 fireworks-related
injuries occurred between June 16 and July 16,
2006, alone. The CPSC found that three times as
many males were injured as females and between
2000 and 2006, an average of seven people died a
year because of accidents with fireworks. Almost
1/3 of those deaths involved professional fireworks the consumers had obtained illegally.
"They're often referred to as fireworks – truly,
they're explosives," said Julie Vallese of the
CPSC. Vallese demonstrated how illegal fireworks or fireworks intended for professional use
can cause severe injuries. Demonstration No. 1:
M1000 illegal firework in a watermelon. The
watermelon was completely blown up. "We do
see amputations of fingers and even limbs,"
Vallese said. "There are eye injuries and permanent scarring. So the devastation and the injuries
really are permanent to consumers."
Demonstration No. 2: Mannequin and professional fireworks. The mannequin was positioned
leaning slightly forward, as if to light the firework, which then exploded in its face.
"Professional-grade fireworks have very long

fuses but they burn very quickly," Vallese said. "Oftentimes, consumers just don't have the kind of time they need to get away with a professional-grade firework." (*CBS*)

A. According to Julie Vallese of the CPSC professional standard fireworks pose no danger, only true explosives

B. Demonstration No. 2 was to show that even professional-rated fireworks are only dangerous if they explode in one's face

C. In a period of only one month in 2006, there were more than six thousand fireworks-related injuries

D. The problem is that professional-grade fireworks are being sold legally to the public

39. On a mission to fight AIDS and malaria, first lady Laura Bush is on her third trip to Africa. Her trip includes visits to Senegal, Mozambique, Zambia and Mali. The first lady spoke from Maputo, Mozambique on Wednesday. Bush expressed her excitement over a new grant set forth by the president as part of his malaria initiative, which targets the most affected countries in Africa. The USD2 million grant was given to an inter-religious group made of Catholic priests, imams and ministers who represent 10 different religious groups. These religious representatives met in Mozambique to go into rural communities to teach people how to use insecticide treated nets and show other ways to help eradicate malaria within their villages. The initiative should reach almost 2 million people. As part of her visit to Maputo, Mrs. Bush also visited a pediatric hospital that holds a program for mothers and children infected with AIDS. She was very encouraged by the progress of the program called Positive Tea. Positive Tea is a support group, which helps mothers overcome the stigma associated with the disease. In addition to her work with AIDS and malaria, Mrs. Bush also hopes to raise awareness about women's issues in Africa. She had lunch with several African and American women leaders in Mozambique, including members of the Peace Corps. They discussed how important education is for women. "If girls and women are educated, they are much less likely to get HIV," Mrs. Bush said. "They are much more likely to know how to protect themselves. They have a chance to contribute to their society." (*CBS*)

A. Positive Tea is a possible vaccine to cure AIDS and malaria

B. On Wednesday, Laura Bush managed to speak with the first lady of Mozambique

C. Laura Bush has been to Africa twice before

D. Getting African women leaders to understand how important education is for women was Mrs. Bush's primary objective

40. There is water on the Moon, scientists stated unequivocally on Friday. The confirmation of scientists' suspicions is welcome news to explorers who might set up home on the lunar surface and to scientists who hope that the water, in the form of ice accumulated over billions of years, holds a record of the solar system's history. The satellite, known as LCROSS, crashed into a crater near the Moon's south pole a month ago. The 9,000-kilometres-per-hour impact carved out a hole 20 to 30 meters wide and kicked up at least 90 litres of water. The LCROSS mission, intended to look for water, was made up of two pieces — an empty rocket stage to slam into the floor of Cabeus, a crater 96 kilometres wide and 3 kilometres deep, and a small spacecraft to measure what was kicked up. (*New York Times*)

A. Scientists now suspect that there might be water on the moon

B. When the LCROSS mission hit the south pole of the moon, the impact carved out a crater 96 kilometres wide and 3 kilometres deep on the lunar surface

C. The LCROSS mission confirms that there is at least 90 litres of water on the Moon

D. The water on the Moon has accumulated over billions of years in a liquid form

41. Herman Melville was born Aug. 1, 1819, in New York City, into a family that had declined in the world. In 1837 he shipped to Liverpool as a cabin boy. Upon returning to the U.S. he taught school and then sailed for the South Seas in 1841 on the whaler Acushnet. After an 18-month voyage he deserted the ship in the Marquesas Islands and with a companion lived for a month among the natives, who were cannibals. He escaped aboard an Australian trader, leaving it at Papeete, Tahiti, where he was imprisoned temporarily. He worked as a field labourer and then shipped to Honolulu, Hawaii, where in 1843 he enlisted as a seaman on the U.S. Navy frigate United States. After his discharge in 1844 he began to create novels out of his experiences and to take part in the literary life of Boston and New York City. (*History Channel*)

A. Many of Melville's voyages took place between the age of 18 and 25

B.   Between 1841 and 1844, Melville visited Liverpool, the Marquesas Islands, Tahiti and Hawaii

C.   Melville lived alone for a month among cannibals

D.   Melville spent the entire time on Tahiti in prison

42.   **Tundra are among Earth's coldest, harshest biomes. Tundra ecosystems are treeless regions found in the Arctic and on the tops of mountains, where the climate is cold and windy and rainfall is scant. Tundra lands are snow-covered for much of the year, until summer brings a burst of wild-flowers. Mountain goats, sheep, marmots, and birds live in mountain, or alpine, tundra and feed on the low-lying plants and insects. Hardy flora like cushion plants survive on these mountain plains by growing in rock depressions where it is warmer and they are sheltered from the wind. The Arctic tundra, where the average temperature is -12 to -6 degrees Celsius, supports a variety of animal species, including Arctic foxes, polar bears, gray wolves, caribou, snow geese and musk-oxen. The summer growing season is just 50 to 60 days, when the sun shines 24 hours a day. (National Geographic)**

A.   Rainfall is abundant in Tundra ecosystems

B.   Tundra lands are snow-covered for around 300 days a year

C.   Mountain goats as well as snow geese and musk-oxen live in alpine tundra areas

D.   The average temperature in the Arctic tundra is -12 to -6 degrees Celsius, so it does not support any animal life

43.   **William III of England (1650–1702) was the Prince of Orange, Stadtholder of the main provinces of the Dutch Republic, and King of England, Scotland, and Ireland. Born a member of the House of Orange-Nassau, William III won the English, Scottish and Irish crowns following the Glorious Revolution, in which his uncle and father-in-law, James II, was deposed. In England, Scotland and Ireland, William ruled jointly with his wife, Mary II, until her death in 1694. A Protestant, William participated in several wars against the powerful Catholic King Louis XIV of France in coalition with Protestant and Catholic powers in Europe. Many Protestants heralded him as a champion of their faith. Largely due to that reputation, William was able to take the British crowns where many were fearful of a revival of Catholicism under James. William's vic-tory over James II at the Battle of the Boyne in 1690 is commemorated by the Orange Institution**

in Northern Ireland to this day. (*Wikipedia*)

A.   William III defeated his wife's father in the Battle of the Boyne

B.   William III fought several wars against Louis XIV as part of a Protestant coalition

C.   James II was fearful of a Catholic revival in England

D.   Protestants viewed William III as their champion until he entered a coalition with Catholic powers against Louis XIV

44.   **During Mozart's formative years, his family made several European journeys in which he and Nannerl were shown as child prodigies. These began with an exhibition in 1762 at the court of the Prince-elector Maximilian III of Bavaria in Munich, then in the same year at the Imperial Court in Vienna and Prague. A long concert tour spanning three and a half years followed, taking the family to the courts of Munich, Mannheim, Paris, London, The Hague, again to Paris, and back home via Zürich, Donaueschingen, and Munich. During this trip Mozart met a great number of musicians and acquainted himself with the works of other composers. A particularly important influence was Johann Christian Bach, whom Mozart visited in London in 1764 and 1765. The family again went to Vienna in late 1767 and remained there until December 1768.** (*Wikipedia*)

A.   During his three-and-a-half-year concert tour, Mozart visited Zürich last before heading home

B.   Johann Christian Bach visited Mozart twice

C.   Mozart was first shown as a child prodigy in the Imperial Court in 1763

D.   Mozart's three-and-a-half-year concert tour included 9 stops, and they visited 7 locations

45.   **The wind-whipped tip of South America, Patagonia occupies a pristine, 673,000-square-kilo-metre expanse of southern Argentina and Chile. Never precisely defined, the dry, desolate region extends from the Río Colorado south to the tip of the continent. From the dramatic peaks of the Andes and the grinding ice fields of Glaciers National Park to the arid steppes of the east, Patagonia is South America's frontier—harsh, unspoiled, raw. Portuguese explorer Ferdinand Magellan was the first European to discover the region when he arrived in 1520. Subsequent explorers called the area's Tehuelche Indian inhabitants Patagones, from which the region's name evolved. Today, Patagonia is a sparsely pop-ulated area rich in natural resources and wildlife,**

including herons, condors, pumas, tortoises, and guanacos. Sheep herding, oil, mining, agriculture, and tourism make up Patagonia's economy. (*National Geographic*)

A. Ferdinand Magellan was the first person ever to lay eyes on what we know today as Patagonia

B. Patagonia today is heavily populated due to its flourishing mining, agriculture and tourism industries

C. One of the natural resources found in Patagonia is oil

D. Río Colorado is in the heart of the Patagonia region

46. **The ecosystems surrounding us are the lifeblood of the planet, providing us with everything from the water we drink to the food we eat and the fibre we use for clothing, paper or lumber. Historically, agricultural production was stepped up by increasing land use and employing the best technologies available. Densely populated parts of the world, such as in China, India, Egypt and some regions of Europe, reached the limits of arable land expansion many years ago. Intensification of production has therefore become a key strategy — obtaining more from the same amount of land. Until recently, food output kept up with global population growth: in 1997 agriculture provided (on average) 24% more food per person than in 1961, despite the population growing by 89%.** (*European Group on Ethics in Science and New Technologies to the European Commission*)

A. Agricultural production increased by only 24% between 1961 and 1997, while population grew by 89%

B. Global population almost doubled between 1961 and 1997

C. In China, increasing land use is still the best option for boosting production

D. In the past, agricultural production was increased solely by expanding land use

47. **The Empire State Building is a 102-story land-mark Art Deco skyscraper in New York City at the intersection of Fifth Avenue and West 34th Street. Construction on the building started on March 17, 1930. The project involved 3,400 work-ers, mostly immigrants from Europe, along with hundreds of Mohawk iron workers, many from the Kahnawake reserve near Montreal. According to official accounts, five workers died during the construction. Governor Smith's grandchildren cut**

the ribbon on May 1, 1931. The construction was part of an intense competition in New York for the title of "world's tallest building". Two other projects fighting for the title, 40 Wall Street and the Chrysler Building, were still under construc-tion when work began on the Empire State Building. Each held the title for less than a year, as the Empire State Building surpassed them upon its completion, just 410 days after construc-tion commenced. The building was officially opened when United States President Herbert Hoover turned on the building's lights with the push of a button from Washington, D.C. (*Wikipedia*)

A. The Chrysler Building was finished more than a year earlier than the Empire State Building

B. The 3,400 workers took only about four days on average to finish one story

C. 40 Wall Street was finished before construction began on the Empire State Building

D. All 3,400 workers were from Europe

48. **Switzerland's privacy watchdog is preparing to battle Google over its Street View service, which shows panoramic street-level pictures of 100 cities globally, with people, cars and businesses clearly visible in many shots. According to The Daily Mail the Swiss data protection commissioner, Hanspeter Thuer, has demanded that Google ensures all faces and car plates are blurred to pro-tect people's privacy, and that enclosed areas such as walled gardens and private roads are removed from the images. He also wants the California firm to declare at least one week in advance which Swiss towns and cities it plans to send its teams to, so residents are informed before they are unwittingly photographed and their pictures posted online. The service has also proved contro-versial in Britain, Germany, Japan and elsewhere for allowing individuals to be identified without their knowledge or consent.** (*The Daily Telegraph*)

A. Hanspeter Thuer, the Swiss data protection com-missioner has not said whether or not he wants to ban Google Street View from Switzerland

B. Google's Street View service has already been banned in Germany, Britain, Japan, and elsewhere

C. Switzerland's privacy watchdog demands that all people and cars be removed from the images

D. Google has undertaken to declare one week in advance which cities it will photograph

49. The economy of the EU has returned to growth after five consecutive quarters of contraction, according to preliminary figures published today by Eurostat, the European Commission's statistical office. Eurostat estimated that the EU's gross domestic product (GDP) grew by 0.2% in the third quarter of 2009 compared to the previous quarter. In the eurozone, growth was 0.4%. Germany, the EU's largest national economy, was among the best performers, with growth of 0.7% compared to the previous quarter. France, however, disappointed economists by recording growth of only 0.3%, identical to the amount of growth it achieved in quarter two. Experts had predicted results of 0.5-0.6%. The highest percentage growth was achieved by Austria and Portugal, whose economies both grew by 0.9% of GDP. The economies of Estonia, Greece, Spain, Cyprus, Hungary, Romania and the UK all contracted in the third quarter. The largest contraction recorded was in Estonia, whose economy shrank by 2.8% compared to the previous three-month period. (*European Voice*)

A. Germany's growth in the third quarter of 2009 was the greatest in the EU

B. The economy of the EU shrank continuously for over a year

C. France's GDP figure disappointed economists, because it grew less than in the second quarter of 2009

D. The eurozone performed worse than the EU as a whole

50. According to the rules of parliamentary debate, a debate round has two teams with two debaters each and a Speaker. The Speaker serves as both the judge and arbiter of the rules during the round. One team represents the Government, while the other represents the Opposition. The Government team is composed of a Prime Minister, who speaks twice, and a Member of Government, who speaks once. The Opposition team is composed of a Leader of the Opposition, who speaks twice, and a Member of the Opposition, who speaks once. The Government proposes a specific case statement, which the government team must demonstrate to be correct. The Opposition does not have to propose anything, but must demonstrate that the case statement is not correct. The Speaker decides at the end of the round, based on the arguments made in the round, whether the Government has proved its case or whether the Opposition has disproved it. The team which met its burden more convincingly wins. (*American Parliamentary Debate Association*)

A. The Speaker decides at the end of the round whether the Government or the Opposition has proved its proposed case

B. The person who speaks at any given time during a parliamentary debate changes five times during one round

C. The Opposition team starts the debate round

D. There are altogether four people involved in a parliamentary debate round

51. Norman Borlaug was a plant breeder who for most of the past five decades lived in developing nations, teaching the techniques of high-yield agriculture. He received the Nobel in 1970, primarily for his work in reversing the food shortages that haunted India and Pakistan in the 1960s. The form of agriculture that Borlaug preached may have prevented a billion deaths. Borlaug's leading research achievement was to hasten the perfection of dwarf spring wheat. Though it is conventionally assumed that farmers want a tall, impressive-looking harvest, shrinking wheat and other crops has often proved beneficial. Bred for short stalks, plants expend less energy on growing inedible column sections and more on growing valuable grain. Stout, short-stalked wheat also neatly supports its kernels, whereas tall-stalked wheat may bend over at maturity, complicating reaping. Nature has favoured genes for tall stalks, because in nature plants must compete for access to sunlight. In high-yield agriculture equally short-stalked plants will receive equal sunlight. (*The Atlantic Monthly*)

A. It takes less energy to grow the column sections of plants than it does to grow grain.

B. Less sunlight is enough for short-stalked plants bred by Borlaug.

C. Nature prefers plants with long stalks because they are exposed to more sunlight.

D. Tall-stalked wheat is easier to reap.

52. The giant panda is the rarest member of the bear family and among the world's most threatened animals. Today, the giant panda's future remains uncertain. As China's economy continues rapidly developing, this bamboo-eating member of the bear family faces a number of threats. Its forest habitat, in the mountainous areas of southwest China, is increasingly fragmented by roads and railroads. Habitat loss continues to occur outside of protected areas, while poaching remains an ever-present threat. Great strides have been made in recent years to conserve the giant pandas. By

2005, the Chinese government had established over 50 panda reserves, protecting more than 2.5 million acres - over 45 percent of remaining giant panda habitat – protecting more than 60 percent of the population. (*World Wildlife Fund*)

A. The giant panda is the world's most threatened animal

B. In 2005, the remaining giant panda habitat covered more than 5 million acres

C. The most serious threat facing the giant panda is poaching

D. More than 40 percent of the giant panda population is still in danger

53. The No. 2 killer in Africa by parasite, after malaria, is an organism called Entamoeba histolytica – or "Eh" for short. It was discovered in 1873, the year it took the life of missionary-explorer David Livingstone. I know this because, when I returned home from reporting in the sub-Sahara, the same pathogen was drilling through the walls of my gut. It would colonize there for months, unbeknownst to me, absorbing my nutrients and spewing its toxins, as I grew weak and emaciated. A skilful intruder, Eh can produce a population explosion in a very short time. It tricks human defence mechanisms into thinking all is well in the homeland by killing local immune cells, then hiding the evidence by eating the cells' corpses. Unfortunately, the more virulent the strain, the more the parasite risks killing the host – sometimes by invading the brain. (*Fast Company Magazine*)

A. In Africa after malaria, Eh is the No. 2 killer by parasite

B. "Dead" immune cells in the human body are evidence of an intruder present

C. The presence of the Eh parasite in the human body can be noticed immediately

D. The author did not personally experience the illness caused by the parasite

54. Below its icy crust Jupiter's moon Europa is believed to host a global ocean up to 160 kilometres deep, with no land to speak of at the surface. And the extraterrestrial ocean is currently being fed more than a hundred times more oxygen than previous models had suggested, according to provocative new research. That amount of oxygen would be enough to support more than just microscopic life-forms: At least three million tons of fishlike creatures could theoretically live and breathe on Europa, said study author Richard Greenberg of the University of Arizona in Tucson. "There's nothing saying there is life there now," said Greenberg, who presented his work last month at a meeting of the American Astronomical Society's Division for Planetary Sciences. "But we do know there are the physical conditions to support it." In fact, based on what we know about the Jovian moon, parts of Europa's seafloor should greatly resemble the environments around Earth's deep-ocean hydrothermal vents, said deep-sea molecular ecologist Timothy Shank. (*National Geographic*)

A. Europa supports at least three million tons of fish-like creatures in its global ocean

B. Microscopic life forms have been known to exist on Europa

C. There is no evidence that life exists on Jupiter's moon Europa

D. Jupiter has several moons

55. Bustling modern-day Phnom Penh in Cambodia is a city rich with the legacies of kings and conquerors, both foreign and Khmer. Legend has it that Phnom Penh was founded when a woman called Penh discovered five images of Buddha inside a log washed up on the bank of the Mekong River. In 1373, Wat Phnom was built to house them. The town that grew around it became known as Phnom Penh. With phnom in Khmer meaning hill, the name literally means Hill of Penh. Oudong, 40 kilometres north, usurped Phnom Penh as the capital between 1618 and the mid-19th century, but it was Phnom Penh that was the seat of government when the French arrived in 1863. Their influence is obvious in many of the grand colonial buildings that dot the city, especially in the French Quarter around the Old Market. Colonial rule brought stability. During this prosperous time, in 1892, King Norodom constructed the stunning Wat Preah Keo (Silver Pagoda), paved with 5,000 blocks of silver. (*Travel Channel*)

A. A woman called Penh found a log near the Mekong River with images of Buddha carved into it

B. The last time Phnom Penh was the seat of government was in 1618

C. Oudong today is still the seat of government in Cambodia

D. Phnom Penh is south of the city that was the capital of Cambodia for more than 200 years after 1618

56. The rich cultural diversity of New Mexico has created a culinary melting pot. Finding something to eat is easy, but choosing from all of the options may take awhile. There are a variety of ethnic restaurants in Albuquerque, and for every one of these, there are at least three restaurants offering New Mexican cuisine. In the Old Town, offering the finest New Mexico beef, wild game and poultry, the High Noon Restaurant and Saloon serves gourmet meals in a casual atmosphere. No trip to this area of town would be complete without a stop at one of the restaurants on the plaza. Casa de Fiesta Mexican Grill offers fine New Mexican dining with a full view of the plaza. Old Town's bars and pubs reflect the quiet atmosphere of this historical district and rowdier nightlife needs to be sought in another part of town. (*Travel Channel*)

A. Many different cuisines have mixed in New Mexico.

B. New Mexico's culinary specialty is food cooked in a so-called melting pot.

C. The High Noon Restaurant and Saloon offers gourmet food and visitors can also play exciting games.

D. Albuquerque does not have a bustling night life.

57. "It is a fact of life that people give dinner parties, and when they invite you, you have to turn around and invite them back," Laurie Colwin wrote in her bite-size masterpiece, "Home Cooking," published in 1988. "Often they retaliate by inviting you again, and you must then extend another invitation. Back and forth you go, like Ping-Pong balls, and what you end up with is called social life." Colwin wasn't complaining, exactly. She liked dinner parties. But she would also have liked Margaret Visser's observation, in her new book, "The Gift of Thanks," that the word "host" is related through Indo-European roots to the words "hostile" and "hostage." Dinner parties are complicated things, where obligation and gratitude collide and overlap — and sometimes crash and burn. Ms. Visser writes with as much scholarly wit about dinner and dinner parties — what we put in our mouths, and why and with whom — as any writer alive. (*The New York Times Book Review*)

A. Dinner parties are always a burden for both the host and the guests.

B. Laurie Colwin observes that the word "host" is related to the words "hostile" and "hostage".

C. Laurie Colwin likens dinner party invitations to revenge.

D. A dinner party can be ruined by burning the food.

58. Mention global health, and everybody thinks of HIV, malaria, and a host of other infectious diseases rampant in developing countries. But a group of research institutes says it's time that chronic, non-infectious diseases that afflict people in poor countries get a more prominent place on the global scientific agenda—and yesterday they announced three new priorities for their own research. The targets are hypertension, tobacco use, and the crude stoves polluting indoor air in developing countries. For hypertension, effective and inexpensive drugs exist but they reach few people in low- and middle-income countries, so research will need to focus on new ways to deliver them, says Alliance chair Abdallah Daar, a public health expert at the University of Toronto in Canada. The problem of open fires and primitive stoves for cooking—which WHO estimates cause 1.5 million deaths annually—requires more engineering studies to come up with clean, cheap alternatives. Research on how to curtail tobacco use is often highly country-specific: What works in the United States for instance, may not work in India, where many smoke bidi, hand-rolled, high-nicotine cigarettes that are unregulated. (*Science*)

A. Tobacco use, hypertension and other chronic diseases kill more people than HIV, malaria and other infectious diseases.

B. Cheap and successful medication for hypertension already exists, but more efficient ways need to be found to get them to the people who need it.

C. According to the WHO, 1.5 million people die in fires each year caused by primitive stoves.

D. Methods used in the United States to curtail tobacco use will not work in India.

59. You smell the oil in the creeks and farmland of Ogoniland and the Niger delta long before you see it. Nigerian crude is a sweet oil which barely needs refining but in the sweltering tropical heat, it stinks of garage forecourts and rotting vegetation. We tried to find the source of one spill in a creek near the fishing village of Otuegwe. The further we swam into the warm shallow waters the more we became covered in a sheen of grease. The light brown and yellow liquid was coming from a buried, rusty pipeline. That was Ogoniland nearly 10 years ago. These days the 400 sq mile, densely-populated delta which provided Shell and the Nigerian government with some $100bn (£64bn) of oil between its discovery in 1958 and the company being expelled by the community in 1994, is still badly polluted (*The Guardian*, Aug. 22, 2010).

A. Shell has offered to return to Ogoniland to repair the oil spills there, but the local community will not hear of it.

B. Oil had polluted Ogoniland and the Niger river delta ten years ago, but by now the area has been cleaned up.

C. Oil in Ogoniland had earned Shell and the Nigerian state a great deal of money, but the environmental impact is still being felt there.

D. Nigerian crude is full of impurities and must therefore undergo a relatively complex and expensive refining process.

60. **Symbolic gestures come in all shapes and sizes, but few as imposing as that of the USS George Washington, a ship more than three football-pitches long, and capable of carrying 85 aircraft and more than 6,200 people. But even symbols of such massive heft can be interpreted in various ways. The George Washington has just been in the South China Sea, off the coast of Danang, once home to one of the American army's biggest bases in Vietnam. Fifteen years after the opening of diplomatic relations, and 35 years since the end of the Vietnam war, the carrier's visit, and the joint naval exercises that followed, were striking tokens of reconciliation. But observers in China saw a different sort of gesture: not so much a handshake with a former enemy; more a brandished fist towards a potential one, their own country (*The Economist*, Aug. 12, 2010).**

A. The US's warming military relations with a former enemy are a matter of great concern for China.

B. Diplomatic relations between China and Vietnam were only established fifteen years ago.

C. The US currently maintains one of its largest army bases in Vietnam at Danang.

D. The US sent an impressively large aircraft carrier to Vietnam in a show of defensive strength.

61. **China has become the world's second biggest economy according to data released on Monday August 16th. Japan's economy fell behind China's at market exchange rates in the second quarter (it has been number three in purchasing power parity – PPP – terms for some time). These numbers are not strictly comparable: Japan's data have been seasonally adjusted while those for China have not. Quibbles aside, Japan will surely be eclipsed soon, if it has not been already. Data compiled by Angus Maddison, an economist who died earlier this year, suggest that China and India were the biggest economies in the world for**

almost all of the past 2000 years. Why they fell so far behind may be more of a mystery than why they are currently flourishing (*The Economist*, Aug. 16, 2010).

A. By all of the various standard economic measures, America's economy is larger than that of both China and Japan.

B. As China's economy grows and overtakes Japan's, tensions between the two neighbours have been growing.

C. China's flourishing economy seems to be in line with its economic performance over most of the last two millennia.

D. When measured according to PPP, China has been the third largest economy for a relatively long time.

62. **There is a strong Asterix atmosphere in the annual cork oak harvest of the Alentejo in Portugal. Deep into one of the 350 remaining cork oak forests (in my case Herdade dos Fidalgos, near Lisbon) sometime between June and August you'll suddenly come across a team of about 20 men, ranging in ages from 16 to 70, striking huge twisted trees with axes. Then, with a sensitivity you would not associate with an axe, they prise the juicy bark from the tree and it is levered from the trunk in great, satisfying pieces. From the base, right up to the beginning of the branches, it is peeled away to reveal the oak's red, nude surface underneath. When the tree is completely harvested, the axe man takes a swig from his water barrel and moves on to the next (*The Guardian*, Aug. 22, 2010).**

A. Herdade dos Fidalgos near Lisbon represents one of only 350 cork oak forests left in Portugal.

B. Come summertime, a group of men, old and young alike, harvest cork in the Alentejo in Portugal.

C. Cork is harvested by chopping out large pieces of the red wood from tall oak trees with an axe.

D. Cork is harvested twice a year in Portugal by pulling off long pieces of bark from oak trees.

63. **Huge dust storms, like the ones that blanketed Sydney twice last week, hit Queensland yesterday and turned the air red across much of eastern Australia, are spreading lethal epidemics around the world. However, they can also absorb climate change emissions, say researchers studying the little understood but growing phenomenon. The Sydney storm, which left millions of people choking on some of the worst air pollution in 70 years, was a consequence of the 10-year drought**

that has turned parts of Australia's interior into a giant dust bowl, providing perfect conditions for high winds to whip loose soil into the air and carry it thousands of miles across the continent. It followed major dust storms this year in northern China, Iraq and Iran, Pakistan, Saudi Arabia, Afghanistan, east Africa, Arizona and other arid areas. Most of the storms are also linked to droughts, but are believed to have been exacerbated by deforestation, overgrazing of pastures and climate change (*The Guardian*, Sept. 27, 2009).

A. Climate change is responsible for the droughts that are the exclusive cause of dust storms.

B. The primary causes of dust storms is the fact that too many trees are being cut down.

C. Dust storms in Australia and elsewhere are carrying not only loose soil, but also deadly diseases.

D. Parts of Australia have been suffering from a drought for much of the past 70 years.

64. Without anyone quite realising it, live performance has experienced a revolution. From being a unique experience shared by one group of people, it has become a form of mass participation. How has that come about? Is it even a good thing? And what about the work itself? I am mulling over these questions while sitting on the floor of a rehearsal room in Edinburgh's dockyard district of Leith. Four actors, a director and her assistant are earnestly discussing the script with the playwright. But it isn't just me watching. Everywhere there are video cameras and lapel microphones; next door, a sound engineer listens patiently. The cast may be here to run through Quartet, a subtle, heart-tugging love story by Marina Carr – but it feels rather like the Big Brother house. The cameras are recording every second of the rehearsal for later use, and experimenting with shots for the live broadcast (*The Guardian*, Aug. 22, 2010).

A. Seven people are talking over a play in preparation for a theatre performance to be aired live.

B. The writer is watching a TV program of a cast and crew rehearsing a revolutionary kind of play.

C. Seven people are being recorded discussing a new kind of play about reality television.

D. The video cameras are only being used to try various shots in advance of a live broadcast.

65. The book has sold extremely well (nearly 40,000 copies so far), earned glowing reviews and has been long-listed for this year's Booker prize. But the fascination that The Slap has engendered is about more than sales, hype or even its frankly dubious literary merits. Its zeitgeist-capturing qualities can be summed up in a single sentence: more than any other recent work of fiction, it is a novel about the failings of middle-class life – and one that points to wider concerns about the durability of liberal values in a multicultural society. I use the phrase "middle class" here advisedly. I don't mean to conjure up the familiar British stereotypes. The Slap is a long way from being an Australian version of Ian McEwan's Saturday. Set in the suburbs, it centres on a close-knit, affluent community made up of predominantly second-generation Greek Australians, but also including white Australians, descendants of Aborigines and ethnic Indians (*The Guardian*, Aug. 22, 2010).

A. The Slap makes great use of humour to point out the failings of middle-class life.

B. Having sold well and earned strong reviews, The Slap is the latest novel by Ian McEwan.

C. The Slap focuses on a wealthy community made up of several different ethnic groups.

D. Capturing the spirit of the times very handily, The Slap tells a story of life in a British suburb.

66. Donor conception involves having a baby or babies after undergoing fertility treatment using someone else's eggs, or sperm, or both, or another woman's embryo. In 2008 a total of 1,600 children were born in the UK as a result of donated sperm (977), eggs (541) or embryos (82). That represented 11% of the total of 15,237 births that year due to either in vitro fertilisation (IVF) or donor insemination (DI) – the highest number ever. In 2008 Britain's Human Fertilisation and Embryology Authority (HFEA) registered just 396 sperm donors – far fewer than experts say is needed to help women conceive. Although it was the highest since 1996, fewer men donate sperm than previously, mainly because donors lost their right to anonymity in 2005. Children born as a result of a donation are allowed to find out who their biological father is when turning 18 (*The Guardian*, Aug. 22, 2010).

A. In 2008 more children were born in Britain because of donated sperm than because of donated embryos.

B. In 2008 more babies were born in the UK due to in vitro fertilisation (IVF) than to donor insemination (DI).

C. Experts generally agree that about 400 sperm donors are sufficient in the UK to assist women in conceiving.

D. Changes in anonymity rules in 2005 have had little effect on the number of men who donate sperm.

67. **You are what you remember. It's difficult to imagine being you without some access to your remembered life story. But the new science of memory tells us that remembering is just that: a story. Memories are not stashed away, fully formed, in the vaults of the brain; they are constructed, when needed, according to the demands of the present. And they are soberingly fragile as a result. You can have vivid memories of things that never happened, and yet you can come away with the sketchiest recollections of events that actually did.**

Memories of childhood are particularly suspect. When I recall my first day at school, I know I'm not remembering the event itself, but more my last act of remembering it. The brain stores autobiographical information in many different systems, and the sensory qualities of early experiences are likely stored accurately. It's the mental home movie into which they're assembled that may not bear much resemblance to reality (*The Guardian*, Aug. 22, 2010).

A. Our minds probably create a precise store of what our senses have picked up in our earliest days.

B. Normally, we can neatly and accurately call to mind most experiences from our past.

C. With special training, we can have far greater control over our memories than we normally do.

D. Even for someone with an active imagination, it is impossible to remember events that never happened.

68. **Most of us, even the most ardent food lover, have at least one food that they just can't bear. Offal is a common culprit (though I suspect a lot of that is about the idea of it, rather than the taste), as well as fish that's too fishy and the much-maligned sprout.**

The flavour and fragrance of coriander is disliked to such an extent by some that it is capable of turning otherwise gastronomically adventurous types into overgrown toddlers, clamping their mouths shut and making scrunched up faces at the very thought of a sprinkling on their chilli con carne.

Neuroscientist Jay Gottfried recently put forward his theory that the specific disgust coriander can inspire is linked to its smell, which many people find soapy. He believes that our brains fit food smells into patterns of already known foodstuffs, and if something is perceived as belonging
to a different group – cleaning products, in this case – the brain will reject it as being something we should not eat. Evolutionary biology at work on a basic level (The Guardian, Aug. 23, 2010).

A. Certain smells tend to trigger dislikes based on what we feel are unacceptable smells for food.

B. Foods that smell like cleaning products appeal to us because our brains tell us they are safe to eat.

C. Certain colours in foods tend to stimulate dislikes, the green in coriander being common.

D. Flavour and smell are actually never interrelated with regard to food likes and dislikes.

69. **After responsibility for security is handed over to Afghan police and soldiers in 2014, German police trainers will continue to teach local recruits. "That seems to me to be in tune with the sustainability of our current engagement," German Interior Minister Thomas de Maiziere told the DPA news agency. "But whether three, five, twenty or another number of police trainers will stay in Afghanistan, I can't yet say."**

In July, Afghan President Harmid Karzai told international diplomats at a conference that 2014 was the date when Afghans "will be responsible for all military and law enforcement operations throughout our country." It is a non-binding date, but has been seized upon by Western politicians facing electorates at home who are increasingly opposed to sending soldiers to fight an increasingly powerful Taliban insurgency for a national government plagued by high levels of corruption (*Deutsche Welle World*, Aug. 22, 2010).

A. Afghan President Harmid Karzai has announced that he will expel all foreign troops from his country in 2014.

B. It has become expedient for Western politicians to refer to the statement made by the Afghan president.

C. Soldiers and law enforcement trainers from Germany will all pull out of Afghanistan in 2014.

D. Voters in Western countries increasingly back the fight against the Taliban because of their human rights abuses.

70 **Last month, a small Islamic terrorist group named al Qaeda in the Islamic Maghreb (AQIM) made headlines when it executed Michel Germaneau, a French aid worker. He was not the first hostage to be executed by AQIM, but his death provoked France to declare war on al Qaeda. While Western nations like France are just starting to escalate**

their engagement against terrorist organizations in Africa, the Tuareg people of Niger – where Germaneau was kidnapped – have long been victims of the underdevelopment that nourishes fundamentalism. Often pretending to fight for communities like the Tuareg, groups like AQIM operate in the ungoverned regions of a continent that is struggling to establish centralized states and the rule of law. From the Sahel to the Horn of Africa, they thrive off of the symptoms of state collapse: drugs, weapons and grinding poverty (*Deutsche Welle World*, Aug. 23, 2010).

A. AQIM wish to create their own state to fill the void left in the ungoverned regions of Africa.

B. Where there are many poor people, organisations like AQIM tend to flourish.

C. Victimized people like the Tuareg have staunch allies in organisations like AQIM.

D. AQIM drew international attention when they killed their first hostage, Michel Germaneau.

71. After the earthquake which hit Haiti in January this year, a number of European officials called on the EU to create a European emergency force to react as a single body in international crisis situations. The EU came under fire for its lack of cohesion with critics lamenting the missed opportunity for the bloc to show its solidarity and project its image as a major player on the world stage. Eight months on from Haiti, the EU has yet to create a single emergency reaction force or aid fund and as such is running the risk of being labelled weak and inefficient again. Over the weekend, French President Nicolas Sarkozy called for the establishment of an EU disasters rapid reaction force in a letter to EU Commission President Jose Manuel Barroso (*Deutsche Welle World*, Aug. 16, 2010).

A. The Union has been criticised for not cooperating effectively in dealing with the crisis in Haiti.

B. The EU has established an office in Brussels to coordinate the Union's emergency relief efforts.

C. The EU set up an emergency force to assist in disaster relief after the Haitian earthquake in January.

D. Mr Sarkozy praised Mr Barroso for his efforts in setting up an EU disasters rapid reaction force.

72. After months of haggling over its involvement in the unprecedented European Union bailout to save Greece from defaulting, Germany finds itself at the centre of another financial tangle with the debt-ridden Mediterranean nation – this time involving defence contracts Greece could ill afford and the shadowy deals behind them. At the same time that German Chancellor Angela Merkel's cabinet was approving 22.4 billion euros ($29.7 billion) in aid to Greece, prosecutors in Germany began investigating whether defence contractors had paid millions of euros in bribes to Greek officials in connection with the sale of two German submarines in a deal worth more than a billion euros (*Deutsche Welle World*, Aug. 12, 2010).

A. Germany's government is accused of corruption in connection with money given to Greece to help pay its debt.

B. Germany gave away two submarines worth over a billion euros to improve Greece's defensive posture.

C. Military contractors are suspected of having paid government officials in Greece to sweeten a procurement deal.

D. After the German government voted to give financial aid to Greece, investigators launched a corruption probe.

73. Every year, the Stockholm International Peace Research Institute (SIPRI) issues a report surveying international military expenditure. And if anyone thought that, this time, the financial crisis would have dampened the world's enthusiasm for bringing death and destruction upon their neighbours, they'll be disappointed. Military expenditure went up substantially. A SIPRI report released on Wednesday estimates expenditure in 2009 amounted globally to 1.5 trillion dollars, 5.9 percent more than in the previous year. In fact the crisis may have been one of the reasons for the increase. Dr Sam Perlo-Freeman, Head of the Military Expenditure Project at SIPRI, says that many countries increased public spending generally in 2009 as a way of boosting demand to combat the recession: "Although military spending hasn't been a big part of economic stimulus packages, public spending hasn't been cut yet," he said (*Deutsche Welle World*, June 2, 2010).

A. Despite the tough economy, many governments may have increased defence spending partly in an effort to increase demand.

B. A survey on global military expenditure has found that many countries are causing more death and destruction than before.

C. The Stockholm International Peace Research Institute (SIPRI) publishes a biannual report on defence outlay.

D. Each surveyed country spent more money on

weapons and equipment in 2009 than they did the year before.

74. Last year, a group of young Moroccans campaigning to change the law banning eating in public during the Muslim Ramadan fast made plans for a picnic via social networking site Facebook. They organised to meet in Mohammedia near Casablanca for the public feast. It was a risky move because under Moroccan law, eating in public during daylight hours in the holy month is considered a crime. Sure enough, the authorities in Morocco monitored the Facebook group and cracked down before the demonstration could take off. "We were met by hundreds of police at the station in Mohammedia. They were like an army waiting for terrorists," Zineb Elghzaoui, one of the co-founders of the group called Alternative Movement for Individual Freedoms (MALI), remembered. "We were abused, forced back on the train and then we were arrested and interrogated for hours. It's only because the incident attracted international attention that the police finally closed our cases – for now," she said (*Deutsche Welle World*, Aug. 20, 2010).

A. Facebook made it possible for MALI to organise a demonstration, but it also enabled the police to stop it from taking place.

B. A group of young Moroccans called MALI fought in a battle against an army in Mohammedia near Casablanca.

C. In Morocco and many other Islamic countries, there are laws banning all eating in public places.

D. The Moroccan police consider MALI a terrorist organization and have detained many of their members indefinitely.

75. No news is good news, it seems, if it comes from the Democratic Republic of the Congo (DRC). The kind of Western headlines that make mention of the vast central African country focus on corruption, mineral conflicts, war, mass-scale rape and slavery of women, and most recently the ambush and brutal murder of three United Nations peacekeepers. There is a lot to report on, but as the DRC's low ranking in the press freedom index compiled by Reporters Without Borders underscores, it is not a place where journalists have the freedom to say and write what they want. In 2009, the African country stood at 146th place in the table of 175 nations. Ambroise Pierre, head of the Africa desk of the Paris-based Reporters Without Borders, told Deutsche Welle that journalists working in the DRC are fre-

quently silenced by intimidation and brutality, and sometimes even by murder (*Deutsche Welle World*, Aug. 21, 2010).

A. There is a great deal of news to report in the DRC and reporters there risk their lives covering it.

B. The DRC's low ranking in the press freedom index has shown a slight improvement recently.

C. Reporters Without Borders, which compiles a press freedom index, has its headquarters in Africa.

D. Three UN peacekeepers were recently killed in the DRC in a fire fight with Congolese rebels.

76. German director Christoph Schlingensief, who was also a renowned actor and artist, has died at the age of 49 after suffering from lung cancer for more than two years, according to a spokesman of the Ruhrtriennale festival. Mr Schlingensief directed numerous films, plays and operas, including an internationally recognised production of Parsifal for the Wagner summer festival in the southern German city of Bayreuth in 2004. Recently, he had been working on a project in the West African country of Burkina Faso, setting up a "village of opera" which was to combine video, live actors and music. His last major production was the Via Intolleranza II opera project in Brussels last year. He was engaged to curate Germany's pavilion at the Biennale in Venice next year (*Deutsche Welle World*, Aug. 21, 2010).

A. In 2004 Mr Schlingensief developed a "village of opera" project in Burkina Faso in West Africa.

B. German director and opera singer Christoph Schlingensief died of lung cancer at the age of 49.

C. Mr Schlingensief directed a critically acclaimed production at the Wagner festival in Bayreuth.

D. His opera production in Brussels in 2009 was very well received and won him several awards.

77. Egyptian police have arrested two Italians at Cairo airport suspected of stealing a famous van Gogh painting taken from a museum earlier on Saturday, August 21. The painting, Poppy Flowers, worth an estimated 39 million euros ($50 m), was stolen from the Mahmoud Khalil museum in the Egyptian capital after it was cut from its frame. Reports say the museum's surveillance system has been out of order for some time. "The cameras had not been working for a long time, and neither had the alarm system," a museum security official told news agency AFP. This was the second time the painting had been stolen from the museum. Thieves made off with

it in 1978, but it was returned a decade later. One year after that, a duplicate was sold for $43 m in London, sparking a debate in Egypt about whether the returned painting was, in fact, a fake (*Deutsche Welle World*, Aug. 22, 2010).

A. The painting was stolen in 1978 but was returned to the museum the very same year.

B. A duplicate of the painting was sold for 43 million dollars in London in 1989.

C. Worth an estimated €39 m ($50 m), van Gogh's Sunflowers has been snatched from a Cairo museum.

D. The museum's surveillance system was also out of order the first time the painting was taken.

78. Hasan Say's son, Ayhan, was one of a hundred soldiers in the Turkish army killed this summer in bombings, attacks and ambushes by the PKK Kurdish rebel group. Footage of the attack that killed Ayhan, broadcast live from an unmanned intelligence drone to army headquarters and 30 security units at the time, has been replayed over and over again on television and news websites. Families of the soldiers who died in the attack have had to watch as their sons were attacked, herded, cornered and killed by a group of PKK rebels, who ultimately escaped into the mountains. Many family members, including Hasan Say, wonder where the reinforcements the unit so desperately radioed for are, and why it took the first helicopter an hour to reach the scene (*Deutsche Welle World*, Aug. 22, 2010).

A. Mr Say wants some answers from the Turkish army regarding the deaths of his son and of the others in his unit.

B. The events that led up to the death of Ayhan and other soldiers were broadcast live on television and on the Internet.

C. Pilots flying overhead managed to film the tragic events of this summer when PKK rebels killed Turkish troops.

D. Ayhan and his fellow soldiers had no communication equipment to call for help as they were being attacked by the PKK.

79. Dutch teenager Laura Dekker has started her solo sailing trip around the world at the age of 14, with the intention of becoming the youngest person to sail solo around the world. There are conflicting reports on where she started her journey from on Saturday. Some reports say she sailed from Gibraltar, others say she set off from the south coast of Portugal. Ms Dekker ran into problems with Portuguese authorities, as it is against the law in Portugal for a minor to sail alone. Back home in the Netherlands, Ms Dekker had won a court case at the end of July that allowed her to make the trip alone. Dutch child welfare authorities had tried to prevent the voyage, insisting that it would stunt Ms Dekker's social and emotional development. The teenager wants to break the record currently held by Australia's Jessica Watson (*Deutsche Welle World*, Aug. 21, 2010).

A. Ms Dekker had some trouble with Portuguese authorities because she has no sailing licence.

B. Ms Dekker set out on her sailing trip from the Netherlands after winning a court case there.

C. In the end, Dutch child welfare officials voluntarily agreed to let Ms Dekker embark on her voyage.

D. Ms Watson is currently the youngest person to have sailed around the world on her own.

80. In its purchasing managers' index of 4,500 Eurozone companies, the London-based economic research group Markit Economics revealed a dip from 56.7 to 56.1 points on Monday, the third in four months. Although the figures indicate a new downward turn, Markit said the reading was "consistent with a robust rate of expansion," adding that combined manufacturing and service sector output had been rising for 13 consecutive months. ING Bank economist Martin van Vliet said that although economic recovery was slowing down, it still retained "significant forward momentum." There is concern, however, that growth is restricted to the bloc's power-houses, Germany and France. Markit head Chris Williamson said there was "little evidence" to suggest that "buoyant business conditions" in core economies were influencing weaker ones where austerity measures have been introduced to bring down budget deficits (*Deutsche Welle World*, Aug. 23, 2010).

A. According to Mr Williamson, positive developments in major European economies were also being felt in frailer ones.

B. Economic research group Markit's index shows an increase in Eurozone economies in line with 13 months of expansion.

C. Austerity measures taken to reduce budget deficits in certain Eurozone countries have significantly weakened those economies.

D. Mr van Vliet believes that the Eurozone economies

are recovering less quickly than before but recovering nonetheless.

81. A flagship European Earth observation satellite has been struck by a second computer glitch and cannot send its scientific data down to the ground. The Goce spacecraft is on a mission to make the most precise maps yet of how gravity varies across the globe. In February, a processor fault forced operators to switch the satellite over to its back-up computer system. This too has now developed a problem and engineers are toiling to make the spacecraft fully functional again. The European Space Agency (ESA) remains confident the situation can be recovered, however. "There's no doubt about it: we're in a difficult situation, but we are not without ideas," Goce mission manager Dr Rune Floberghagen told BBC News (*BBC News*, Aug. 21, 2010).

A. A European Earth observation satellite has suffered a malfunction due to the effect of gravity.

B. The European Space Agency (ESA) is confident that a problem with its Goce spacecraft can be resolved.

C. A satellite is no longer functioning since it experienced a processor error in its back-up computer.

D. A satellite is no longer able to transmit data to Earth since it was struck by space debris.

82. It has been a long hard year for those living beneath the crater of Eyjafjallajokull in Iceland. When the volcano erupted in March, air passengers faced chaos as their planes were grounded amid fears that the ash, thrown high into the atmosphere, would damage aircraft. But after little more than two weeks, and a safety all-clear, life started returning to normal for airlines and their customers. The people of Iceland living near the eruption site were not so lucky. The region of south Iceland where Eyjafjallajokull is situated has a significant farming industry. Floods, caused by lava melting glacial ice, swept down the side of the volcano and ruined farmland. Sixty hectares of the property Poula Kristin Buch farms with her husband was wiped away by the water (*BBC News*, Aug. 22, 2010).

A. An Icelandic volcano caused concerns for air passengers and devastated agricultural land.

B. Farmers in Iceland saw their fields completely destroyed by molten lava.

C. In March, an Icelandic volcano disrupted flights and caused damage to aircraft.

D. All of the land that Ms Buch works with her husband was swept away.

83. A Russian man suspected of selling arms to insurgent groups around the world is to be extradited to the United States, a court in Thailand has ruled. Viktor Bout, 43, is pleading not guilty on US charges of conspiracy to sell arms to Colombian rebels. Mr Bout – dubbed the Merchant of Death – was detained in a joint Thai-US sting operation in March 2008. Russia has condemned the decision and said it would work to secure his return. Russian Foreign Minister Sergei Lavrov described the ruling as "unlawful" and said his government believed it was made "under very strong external pressure". The ministry has summoned Thailand's ambassador to express its "extreme disappointment and bewilderment" at the verdict, the Agence France-Presse news agency reported. The US said it was "extremely pleased" at the news (*BBC News*, Aug. 20, 2010).

A. A Thai court has found Mr Bout guilty of conspiracy to sell weapons to Colombian insurgents.

B. Russia feels that Mr Bout must be brought to justice but that this should not be done in the US.

C. America and Thailand have worked together to capture a suspected Russian arms merchant.

D. Russia accepted a court decision on Mr Bout and will cooperate on the matter in future.

84. France has begun the first deportations of 700 members of the Roma Gypsy minority, to Romania and Bulgaria, as part of its controversial crackdown on communities officials hold responsible for criminal activity. The expulsions are set to be completed by the end of the month. Also affected by the law-and-order push are the nomadic 'travellers' group the Roma are a subset of; delinquents and their families in France's troubled suburban housing projects; and human traffickers and the illegal immigrants they smuggle into France. But the highly publicized targeting of Roma in particular has been criticized by opposition politicians as a cynical move by the conservative government of President Nicolas Sarkozy to seduce hard-right voters in the long march toward the President's 2012 re-election bid. It's also raising alarms from Romanian and European Union officials that France's drive may be fanning xenophobia and impinging on the rights of fellow EU citizens (*Time*, Aug. 19, 2010).

A. EU officials fear the possibility that France's crackdown on the Roma may be trampling on EU citizens' rights.

B.   Though both are targeted in France's crackdown, the Roma and the "travellers" are two different groups.

C.   Mr Sarkozy's political opponents in France cannot understand the motive behind carrying out the expulsions now.

D.   Human traffickers are among the groups being deported for their role in exploiting illegal immigrants through forced labour.

85.   **For most of the 105 years it's been in force, France's secularity law has endeavoured to segregate private religious belief from the strictly agnostic sphere of public life — usually without too much friction. But that relative harmony has given way to tension and conflict in recent years, as secularists have turned their attention to the spreading influence of Islam, now France's second largest faith.**

   Whereas secularism — or laïcité — traditionally sought to create a wall between religious expression and the public domain, critics claim its defenders have become far more militant. In some cases, that's creating a zero-sum showdown in which France's secularists, who dominate public life and debate, are exhibiting a quasi-evangelical zeal in imposing the values of laïcité on the private observance of religious minorities, particularly Muslims (*Time*, Aug. 23, 2010).

A.   France's secularity law has been key to the country's public life since it was passed during the French Revolution in 1789.

B .   Muslims in France do not seem to understand the importance of secularism, or laïcité, in French public life.

C.   Under the French secularity law, religious beliefs must not intrude into the conduct of public life.

D.   Secularism is being called into question in France by religious groups that now control public debate.

86.   **The water separating Iceland from the rest of Europe has been choppy these past few years. After Iceland's banks collapsed in 2008, the British government used anti-terrorism laws to force Reykjavik to agree to compensation for UK and Dutch account holders. When one of Iceland's many volcanoes spewed an ash cloud westwards in April, it grounded European air traffic for a week. Now there is a new feud between the two and this time it is about the sea itself: Iceland — along with the tiny Faroe Islands**

nearby — has started trawling for mackerel, a stock that Norway and the EU insist is overfished. After Iceland unilaterally raised its mackerel quota from 2,000 to 130,000 tons for the year in early August, and the Faroes raised their 25,000-ton quota to 85,000 tons, the outraged Scottish Fisheries Minister Richard Lochhead accused them of "hoovering up" stock, and warned that Iceland was jeopardizing its ambition to join the EU (*Time*, Aug. 27, 2010).

A.   Iceland negotiated with several other countries in the region before it increased its mackerel quota in early August.

B.   Norway and the Faroe Islands are at odds over the fishing of mackerel, with Norway arguing that the stock is shrinking.

C.   In its effort to maintain sustainable numbers of different fish species, the EU has always enforced fishing quotas consistently.

D.   Mr Lochhead is sympathetic to Icelandic ships needing to fish for more mackerel during difficult economic times.

87.   **Immigration has always been a contentious issue in Europe. But these days, with enduring economic turmoil further fuelling concerns over rising unemployment, European nations are especially sensitive about the prospect of foreigners taking jobs away from their citizens. So it's not difficult to understand why leaders in many European Union countries are displeased at seeing their peers in other member nations extend the promise of citizenship to millions of people — most of whom come from outside the EU, with its relatively high standards of living. It's a trend that's been growing since May, when Hungary decided to grant citizenship to any ethnic Hungarians in Slovakia, Ukraine, Romania and Serbia who apply for it. That followed Bucharest's move in April 2009 to vastly facilitate naturalization procedures for over a million people in Moldova with ethnic or linguistic ties to Romania, a simplification Bulgaria replicated earlier this year for nearly two million people in Macedonia and Turkey with Bulgarian roots (*Time*, Aug. 14, 2010).**

A.   The possibility of around three million immigrants entering the EU from Moldova, Macedonia and Turkey causes concern to many EU nations.

B.   European nations would be just as concerned about immigrants taking jobs even if there were no serious unemployment problems.

C.   After Hungary moved to grant citizenship to ethnic

Hungarians in Romania, Romania decided to aid its ethnic and linguistic cousins in Moldova.

D . The only European Union countries to promise citizenship to those outside the EU have been Hungary, Romania and Bulgaria.

88. **Official data released by European Union statistics agency Eurostat on Friday, Aug 13th, show that growth in the eurozone is chugging along at its fastest clip since 2006. And at the front of the European train is a German engine charging out of recession. Europe's largest economy accounted for about two-thirds of the eurozone GDP in the second quarter and is growing twice as fast as the rest of the bloc. Germany's economy, boosted by surging orders for its world-class machines, automobiles and other manufacturing products, expanded 2.2% in the second quarter over the previous quarter, pulling along behind it the rest of the eurozone, which posted growth of 1% in the same period. The German economy is now growing at its fastest rate since unification in 1990** (*Time*, Aug. 13, 2010).

A. The German economy has not grown as rapidly as it did in the second quarter of this year since 1990

B. Germany's expansion of 2.2% in the second quarter is principally due to an increased demand for its outstanding services.

C. Germany's economy grew faster than other eurozone countries in the second quarter, each of which also experienced some positive growth.

D. Leading the rest of the nations of the eurozone, Germany boasts a GDP that makes up around a third of that of the entire bloc.

89. **Britain's university Islamic societies have a reputation for fostering extremism among young male students, and have produced several alleged terrorists. Now, according to those who track extremist activities, they're targeting women, too, the BBC reports. The topic of Islamic extremism is fraught with scare stories, and it's important to note that the vast majority of Muslim students, like the vast majority of Muslims in general, are peaceful. Most condemn violence and extremism. But Britain's university Islamic societies have a track record for producing terrorists and sympathizers who help spread extremism around the world. Christmas Day bomber Umar Farouk Abdulmutallab, who tried to blow up a passenger jet in Detroit last year, was the head of the University College London Union Islamic Society, and organised controversial events**

designed to encourage anti-Western thinking (*Newsweek*, Aug. 5, 2010).

A. Christmas Day bomber Umar Farouk Abdulmutallab was the head of an Islamic Society at a university in Detroit.

B. According to CNN, Islamic societies at British universities are now encouraging extremist thinking among women.

C. Britain's university Islamic societies provide a social and intellectual forum for young Muslims often far away from home.

D. Islamic societies at British universities are known in part for creating sympathizers who help spread extremism internationally.

90. **During the 20th century, Switzerland appeared to combine deregulated low-tax economics with robust rule-of-law democracy. It was the first refuge for those fleeing communism after 1917 or Nazism after 1933 — just as it had offered safe haven to Voltaire, James Joyce and Lenin. Openness made Geneva a world capital, with the League of Nations, the International Red Cross, and then key U.N. agencies all settling there. The Alpine nation was an island of freedom during World War II. Churchill went to Zurich to appeal for European unity after 1945. Diplomats signed peace treaties in Switzerland in the 1950s and 1960s. The country sold itself as neutral, free of Cold War alignments and the snares of the European Union. Reagan and Gorbachev met there to begin ending the Cold War. Switzerland was where the world came to find solutions. Today, however, Switzerland's cities are grubby, its trains run late, its highways are always under repair, and its politicians often seem provincial** (*Newsweek*, Feb. 5, 2010).

A. As it did in the 20th century, Switzerland continues to demonstrate to the world a strong model on which other countries might build.

B. Like those fleeing Nazism after 1917, Voltaire, James Joyce and Lenin all sought refuge in Switzerland in the 20th century.

C. Reagan and Gorbachev were attracted to Switzerland as a neutral place where they could begin to resolve the problems of the Cold War.

D. In the 1900s, Switzerland's economy was characterised by high taxes, but the revenue was used to ensure a good life for all Swiss citizens.

91. In some ways, former British prime minister Tony Blair was Labour's most successful leader ever. No other Labour leader won three consecutive elections. After it had been 18 years in the wilderness he turned a reformed "New Labour" into a party of government. He played a significant role in bringing peace to Northern Ireland. His government devolved power to Scotland and Wales, giving them their own parliament and assembly. New Labour introduced a minimum wage and gave control of interest rates to the independent Bank of England. In an age of summitry he became one of the most recognisable leaders across the world. Mr Blair even forced changes on the Conservative party, driving its leaders to the centre ground of politics and to supporting significant public spending. But few ex-prime ministers are the butt of so many comedians' jokes, few have been so unpopular (*CNN*, Sept. 1, 2010).

A. Despite Mr Blair's successes, he is among Britain's most unpopular former prime ministers

B. Mr Blair's Labour government kept the power to raise or lower interest rates.

C. Though he had great influence on Labour, Mr Blair affected no other parties in Britain.

D. No British prime minister other than Tony Blair has ever won three elections in a row.

92. Religious leaders in Britain on Friday hit back at claims by leading physicist Stephen Hawking that God had no role in the creation of the universe. In his new book "The Grand Design," Britain's most famous scientist says that given the existence of gravity, "the universe can and will create itself from nothing," according to an excerpt published in The Times of London. "Spontaneous creation is the reason why there is something rather than nothing, why the universe exists, why we exist," he wrote.

"It is not necessary to invoke God to light the blue touch paper [fuse] and set the universe going."

But the head of the Church of England, the Archbishop of Canterbury Dr. Rowan Williams, told the Times that "physics on its own will not settle the question of why there is something rather than nothing" (*CNN*, Sept. 3, 2010).

A. The Archbishop of Canterbury wrote an opinion piece in the Times of London in which he argued against Stephen Hawking's ideas.

B. In a new book, Stephen Hawking states that the universe and even people came into being in a process known as spontaneous creation.

C. Stephen Hawking believes that God set the creation of the universe in motion and then allowed the universe to develop on its own.

D. Stephen Hawking has written controversially about God, yet the Archbishop of Canterbury is the only religious leader to respond to his claims.

93. Fires left at least four people dead and hundreds homeless in two regions of central Russia, government officials said on Friday. At least 18 people were injured and 957 people were moved to temporary homes, according to authorities. The blaze started after severe windstorms, coupled with hot weather, disrupted electricity transmission lines, causing short circuits that led to the fires, the Russian Emergency Situations Ministry said. More than 2,500 fire-fighters and rescuers are battling the blazes. The ministry said it is increasing its efforts to localize and put out the fires. Russian Prime Minister Vladimir Putin signed a decree on Friday allocating 1 billion roubles (almost \$33 million) in financial aid to the two regions. The funds will be used to replace houses lost in the fires and compensate for the loss of property. Families of those who died will receive a lump sum of 1 million roubles (almost \$33,000), according to the decree (*CNN*, Sept. 3, 2010).

A. Deadly wildfires that have struck two regions in Russia have also affected a third.

B. Russian Prime Minister Vladimir Putin has approved funds to assist victims of the disaster.

C. More than 2,500 fire-fighters and rescuers have aided victims and extinguished all the fires.

D. The blazes started in nearby forests, which are especially susceptible to fires in hot weather.

94. First there was the discovery of dozens of bottles of 200-year-old champagne, but now salvage divers have recovered what they believe to be the world's oldest beer, taking advertisers' notion of 'drinkability' to another level. Though the effort to lift the reserve of champagne had just ended, researchers uncovered a small collection of bottled beer on Wednesday from the same shipwreck south of the autonomous Aland Islands in the Baltic Sea. "At the moment, we believe that these are by far the world's oldest bottles of beer," Rainer Juslin, permanent secretary of the island's ministry of education, science and culture, told CNN on Friday via telephone from Mariehamn, the capital of the Aland Islands. "It seems that we have not only salvaged the oldest champagne in the world, but also the oldest still drinkable beer. The culture in the beer is still living." (*CNN*, Sept. 3, 2010).

A. Researchers first discovered bottles of champagne and then bottles of drinkable beer on a shipwreck in the Baltic Sea.

B. Champagne and beer were found on a ship that had sunk after leaving the port of Mariehamn in the Aland Islands 200 years ago.

C. Dozens of bottles of champagne had been lifted from one ship when a small collection of beer was found on another.

D. Having been bottled 200 years ago, the beer that was found under the sea would make one very ill if one were to drink it.

95. When a group of musicians in Guca, central Serbia, launched a competition in 1961 to determine the most accomplished trumpet band in the region, it's safe to assume they had little idea what the small rural town was in for. Just four bands took part in that first contest. Almost a half century later, Guca's trumpet festival is now synonymous with the wildest street party in the Balkans and a musical event with a burgeoning international reputation. Organisers say this year's 50th edition of the competition has been the biggest ever with an estimated 800,000 visitors and some 2,000 musicians taking part. But it's beyond the festival's formal programme that Guca really swings into life, with packed streets lined with beer stands and food stalls serving sizzling grilled meats, and entire farmyards of pigs and sheep slowly cooking on spit roasts (*CNN*, Aug. 23, 2010).

A. The competition was first organised by the state, but has grown since locals started running it.

B. Trumpet playing has grown in popularity over the past 50 years in what is today Serbia.

C. The trumpet festival in Guca, central Serbia, is a celebration of music, food and drink.

D. As a rule, no pork is served during the annual trumpet festival in Guca, central Serbia.

96. Former Colombian hostage Ingrid Betancourt tells the story of her six-year captivity in a book due to hit the shelves later this month, her publisher said on Friday. "Meme le Silence a un Fin," or "Even Silence Has an End," will go on sale around the world on September 21, the publishing house Gallimard said. Betancourt, a former presidential candidate in Colombia, was held for

more than six years by Marxist rebels before the Colombian military rescued her and 14 others in 2008. She now lives in France (*CNN*, Sept. 23, 2010).

A. Ms Betancourt describes her experience as a captive held by rebels in Colombia in a book written in French.

B. Held prisoner for over six years by Marxist rebels in Colombia, Ms Betancourt has since left that country.

C. Ms Betancourt was a French tourist on a brief tour of South America when she was captured and held hostage.

D. After holding Ms Betancourt for over six years, her captors released her as a sign of good will to the Colombian government.

97. This week, Catalonia took a huge step forward in ending the cruel "sport" of bullfighting. Its parliament voted in favour of amending the animal protection legislation to abolish bullfighting in the region. The vote, passed with 68 in favour of the ban and 55 against, is a historic victory for animal welfare. It is also a vindication for the thousands of Catalonians who called on their parliament to include bulls in their animal protection law. Back in December 2009, the organization PROU presented a "popular legislative initiative" to the Catalonian Parliament with more than 180,000 signatures supporting the end to bullfighting. This action initiated the nearly yearlong process that led up to this week's vote. Many pro-bullfighting activists have argued that the "sport" is an important part of the Spanish culture and should not be banned. But cultural heritage is no excuse for inflicting pain on a frightened and confused animal (*CNN*, July 30, 2010).

A. The vote is very important for anti-bullfighting activists because Catalonia is the bullfighting hub of Spain.

B. The push to have the Catalonian animal protection law cover bullfighting had clear popular support.

C. The anti-bullfighting vote was initiated by a parliamentarian who favours greater animal protection.

D. The vote to outlaw bullfighting in the Catalonian parliament won by a handy two-thirds majority.

98. West Nile Virus has killed 14 people in northern Greece and sickened 142, the Hellenic Centre for Disease Control and Prevention reported on Thursday. As of Wednesday, the health agency said, 32 people remained hospitalised, eight of them in intensive care. West Nile Virus is usually

transmitted by infected mosquitoes or blood transfusions. Severe symptoms can include high fever, headache, neck stiffness, stupor, disorientation, coma, tremors, convulsions, muscle weakness, vision loss, numbness and paralysis. About 80 per cent of people infected with the virus show no symptoms, health officials say. Authorities in central Macedonia, in northern Greece where most cases have been reported, said they would step up spraying programs in an attempt to ward off mosquitoes.

Authorities also said they are taking steps to prevent transmission by blood transfusions. Blood donations in regions at high risk for West Nile Virus have been cancelled and people leaving the area are encouraged not to donate blood for up to 28 days (*CNN*, Sept. 2, 2010.)

A. In a severe case of West Nile Virus, a victim may even lose movement in his arms or legs.

B. Stagnant waters in central Macedonia may account for the high number of mosquitoes there.

C. The West Nile Virus can generally only be contracted through an infected mosquito.

D. Only one-fifth of those infected by the West Nile Virus escape all the symptoms.

99. A dress made out of recycled waste; a collection of clothes composed of fresh flowers; a synthetic outfit that looks like a wave of water around the body. These unusual designs are the fruit of a novel collaboration between fashion designers and architects to look at the links between their disciplines.

The designs are being showcased in The Netherlands as part of an exhibition called Fashion & Architecture, currently on at ARCAM Amsterdam Centre for Architecture. The project is the brainchild of architect Wouter Valkenier and fashion designers Liza Koifman and Tomas Overtoom. They chose four teams comprising a fashion designer and an architect and tasked them with creating a wearable piece of architecture. Valkenier told CNN: "I think the way of design can be quite similar."

Both fashion designers and architects create inhabitable structures that protect people, he said. That function is as important a feature of the design process for both as aesthetics, he added (*CNN*, Aug. 30, 2010).

A. The designs on exhibit put a roof over one's head rather than give one something to wear.

B. Mr Valkenier, Ms Koifman and Mr Overtoom worked together to design the pieces on exhibition.

C. Mr Valkenier sees any kind of clothing that people might wear as merely a form of protection.

D. Mr Valkenier believes that aesthetics is common to the work of fashion designers and architects.

100. Proud of its title as a cultural capital, Paris boasts some of the world's most iconic monuments. Littered with ancient obelisks, Gothic churches, classical bridges and modern masterpieces, the city has for centuries cultivated an extraordinary array of artists, writers, philosophers and architects.

The end result makes for a city of unparalleled beauty, which revels in its cultural heritage. But with more than 400 parks, 134 museums, 143 theatres and 242 floodlit churches, statues, fountains and national buildings, it's virtually impossible to see all the cultural highlights Paris has to offer. So, for a quick fix of Europe's most fashionable, exclusive and elegant city, follow our 24-hour culture vulture guide. It's a whirlwind tour packed with the "must-dos" on the cultural trail – giving you a true taste of Paris' cultural life, past and present (*CNN*, Aug. 11, 2010).

A. The culture vulture guide offers an all-in exhaustive tour of all the significant cultural sights of Paris.

B. Paris boasts more churches than museums and many more parks than either of them.

C. Paris is a cultural hub at least partly because of the high number of theatres and museums.

D. Paris was once home to a range of creative talents, but now only their spirits live on.

101. Castle ruins invite you to ramble the ramparts and let your imagination roam. Climbing through waist-high weeds on rubble corralled by surviving walls, you can break off a spiky frond and live a sword-fern fantasy. In France's Dordogne region, I like to hike to Chateau de Commarque near Sarlat. The Chateau is a 20-minute walk through a forest of chestnut trees to a clearing, where the mostly ruined castle appears like a mirage. The owner, Hubert de Commarque, bought the castle in 1968 and has been digging it out of the forest ever since. Along Italy's Amalfi Coast in Ravello, the ruins of the 13th-century Villa Rufolo impressed Richard Wagner enough to place the second act of his opera "Parsifal" in a setting inspired by the villa's magical gardens. With its commanding coastline view, the ruins create an operatic experience that doesn't even need music (*CNN*, Aug. 5, 2010).

A. The writer of the piece appears to have visited the Chateau de Commarque and the Villa Rufolo as well, though this latter is not confirmed.

B. The Chateau de Commarque, which lies near Sarlat in France's Dordogne region, was passed down to Hubert de Commarque, its current owner.

C. Hubert de Commarque has regularly invited the writer to visit him at his chateau near Sarlat in France's Dordogne region.

D. Richard Wagner was so struck by an old villa along Italy's Amalfi Coast in Ravello that he set Act Two of the opera "Parsifal" there.

102. Nearly all nuclear power reactors in service around the world are fuelled with uranium; water is needed not only to cool the reactor, but also to slow the neutrons so fission will be effective. But dating back to the beginnings of nuclear power research, there have been efforts to deploy effective "fast" reactors, using a combination of plutonium and uranium. The neutrons were not cooled with water in these reactors; they remained "fast." The original idea was to create a chain reaction that would produce more fuel than the reactor consumed — a so-called "breeder" reactor. But the aim of the latest efforts in Integral Fast Reactor (IFR) technology is not to breed new fuel, but to fission the fuel as completely as possible — while producing a great deal of energy (*National Geographic*, Sept. 1, 2010).

A. The majority of nuclear power reactors today use a combination of plutonium and uranium.

B. The current purpose of the Integral Fast Reactor (IFR) technology is to create new fuel for later use.

C. Research has been conducted to develop nuclear power reactors that run on cold fusion.

D. The majority of nuclear power reactors today use water to slow down neutrons.

103. Along the warm coastal lowlands of New South Wales, the yellow-bellied three-toed skink lays eggs to reproduce. But individuals of the same species living in the state's higher, colder mountains are almost all giving birth to live young. Only two other modern reptiles — another skink species and a European lizard — use both types of reproduction. Evolutionary records shows that nearly a hundred reptile lineages have independently made the transition from egg-laying to live birth in the past, and today about 20 per cent of all living snakes and lizards give birth to live young only. But modern reptiles that have live young provide only a single snapshot on a long

evolutionary time line, said James Stewart, a biologist at East Tennessee State University. The dual behaviour of the yellow-bellied three-toed skink therefore offers scientists a rare opportunity to study this evolutionary change (*National Geographic*, Sept. 1, 2010).

A. The yellow-bellied three-toed skink is the only reptile that produces offspring in two ways.

B. Reptiles have become extinct on the warm coastal lowlands of New South Wales.

C. Around one-fifth of all living snakes and lizards give birth in order to live longer.

D. The yellow-bellied three-toed skink is important to science because of the stage it occupies in evolution.

104. Could we "terraform" Mars — that is, transform its frozen, thin-aired surface into something friendlier and Earth-like? Should we? The first question has a clear answer: Yes, we probably could. Spacecraft, including the ones now exploring Mars, have found evidence that it was warm in its youth, with rivers draining into vast seas. And right here on Earth, we've learned how to warm a planet: just add greenhouse gases to its atmosphere. Much of the carbon dioxide that once warmed Mars is probably still there, in frozen dirt and polar ice caps, and so is the water. Perfluorocarbons, potent greenhouse gases, could be synthesized from elements in Martian dirt and air and blown into the atmosphere; by warming the planet, they would release the frozen CO_2, which would amplify the warming and boost atmospheric pressure to the point where liquid water could flow (*National Geographic*, Jan. 15, 2010).

A. Scientists have found clear evidence of primitive life in the rivers and vast seas of Mars.

B. Since greenhouse gases harm Earth's environment, it is thought they should be prevented on Mars.

C. Laboratory experiments have been carried out to suggest that "terraforming" Mars is possible.

D. It is likely that both carbon dioxide and water can be found in frozen form on Mars.

105. There is something wonderfully unsettling about a plant that feasts on animals. Perhaps it is the way it shatters all expectation. Carl Linnaeus, the great 18th-century Swedish naturalist who devised our system for ordering life, rebelled at the idea. For Venus flytraps to actually eat insects, he declared, would go "against the order of nature as willed by God." The plants only catch

insects by accident, he reasoned, and once a hapless bug stopped struggling, the plant would surely open its leaves and let it go free. Charles Darwin knew better, and the topsy-turvy ways of carnivorous plants enthralled him. In 1860, soon after he encountered his first carnivorous plant — the sundew Drosera — on an English heath, the author of Origin of Species wrote, "I care more about Drosera than the origin of all the species in the world" (*National Geographic*, March 2010).

A.   Linnaeus and Darwin had heated debates on the various species of animals and plants.

B.   Darwin was known to have resented the Venus flytrap because of its unusual nature.

C.   Both Linnaeus and Darwin were interested in carnivorous plants, but disagreed about their nature.

D.   Darwin travelled the world in order to study the various species of animals and plants.

106.   Fewer than 200 rhinos were left in the north Indian state of Assam a century ago. Agriculture had taken over most of the fertile river valleys that the species depends on, and the survivors were under relentless assault by trophy hunters and poachers. Kaziranga was set aside in 1908 primarily to save the rhinos. It held maybe a dozen. Now Asia's premier rhino sanctuary and a reservoir for seeding other reserves, Kaziranga is the key to R. unicornis's future. A thundering conservation success story, the park also harbours almost 1,300 wild elephants; 1,800 Asiatic wild water buffalo, the largest remaining population anywhere; perhaps 9,000 hog deer; 800 barasinghs, or swamp deer (it's a main enclave of this vanishing species); scores of elk-like sambars; and hundreds of wild hogs (*National Geographic*, August 2010).

A.   With its animals regularly killed by trophy hunters and poachers, Kaziranga is viewed as a failure.

B.   Kaziranga's animals include nearly 1,300 wild elephants, 9,000 hog deer, and scores of wild goats.

C.   The spread of farming was once an important factor in the ever dwindling numbers of rhinos.

D.   Kaziranga is a nature preserve that was established in 1908 with only about 200 rhinos in it.

107.   The Middle Awash research project announced its greatest good fortune last October: the discovery, 15 years earlier, of the skeleton of a member of our family that had died 4.4 million years ago at a place called Aramis in Ethiopia. Belonging to the species Ardipithecus ramidus, the adult

female — "Ardi" for short — is more than a million years older than the famous Lucy skeleton and much more informative about one of evolution's holy grails: the nature of the common ancestor we share with chimpanzees. In the mediaphilic field of paleoanthropology, it has become almost a reflex to claim that one's new find "overturns all previous notions" of our origins. The research team despise such hyperbole. But in Ardi's case, it seems to be true (*National Geographic*, July 2010).

A.   The discovery of Ardi has actually cast doubt on the notion that human beings and chimpanzees are distantly related.

B.   Anxious to alert the media, the Middle Awash research team announced their discovery only a few days after it happened.

C.   Finding an example of Ardipithecus ramidus may truly "overturn all previous notions" of where human beings come from.

D.   One of the most important finds in paleoanthropology, the famous Lucy skeleton was uncovered in Ethiopia.

108.   A new computer program has quickly deciphered a written language last used in Biblical times — possibly opening the door to "resurrecting" ancient texts in other languages that are no longer understood, scientists announced last week. Created by a team at the Massachusetts Institute of Technology (MIT), the program automatically translates written Ugaritic, which consists of dots and wedge-shaped stylus marks on clay tablets. The script was last used around 1200 B.C. in western Syria. Written examples of this "lost language" were discovered by archaeologists excavating the port city of Ugarit in the late 1920s. It took until 1932 for language specialists to decode the writing. Since then, the script has helped shed light on ancient Israelite culture and Biblical texts. The new program compared symbol and word frequencies and patterns in Ugaritic with those of a known language, in this case, the closely related Hebrew (*National Geographic*, July 19, 2010).

A.   A computer program may one day translate texts in various long forgotten languages.

B.   Ugaritic is an ancient language that is closely related to Hebrew and Aramaic.

C.   Written Ugaritic has been translated for the first time using software developed at MIT.

D.   The Ugaritic script was last used 1200 years ago.

109. For years, the military and law enforcement agencies have used specialized robots to disarm bombs and carry out other dangerous missions. This summer, such systems helped seal a BP well a mile below the surface of the Gulf of Mexico. Now, with rapidly falling costs, the next frontiers are the office, the hospital and the home. Mobile robots are now being used in hundreds of hospitals nationwide as the eyes, ears and voices of doctors who cannot be there in person. They are being rolled out in workplaces, allowing employees in disparate locales to communicate more easily and letting managers supervise employees from afar. And they are being tested as caregivers in assisted-living centres. Sceptics say these machines do not represent a great improvement over video teleconferencing. But advocates say the experience is substantially better, shifting control of space and time to the remote user (*New York Times*, Sept. 4, 2010).

A. Specialized robots are routinely brought in to carry out dangerous missions for the military and law enforcement.

B. Advocates of specialized robots believe they represent a minor advance over video teleconferencing.

C. Specialized robots are regularly used to do repair and maintenance work on deepwater oil and gas equipment.

D. Specialized robots are now commonly used in many hospitals, places of work and assisted-living centres.

110. Make your password strong, with a unique jumble of letters, numbers and punctuation marks. But memorize it – never write it down. And, oh yes, change it every few months. These instructions are supposed to protect us. But they don't. Some computer security experts are advancing the heretical thought that passwords might not need to be "strong," or changed constantly. They say onerous requirements for passwords have given us a false sense of protection against potential attacks. In fact, they say, we aren't paying enough attention to more potent threats. Keylogging software, which is deposited on a PC by a virus, records all keystrokes – including the strongest passwords you can concoct – and then sends it surreptitiously to a remote location. Cormac Herley, who specializes in security-related topics, said antivirus software could detect and block many kinds of keyloggers, but "there's no guarantee that it gets everything" (*New York Times*, Sept. 4, 2010).

A. Some experts now argue that conventional wisdom on computer security is wrong since hackers have ways of detecting everything users key in.

B. Sceptics claim that the current password scare represents the latest cynical attempt to frighten computer users into spending more on their PC.

C. Mr Herley says that keylogging software may spot and stop a variety of hackers, but "there's no guarantee that it gets everything".

D. The standard view in computer security has been to create a unique password, keep it in a safe place in case you forget, and change it regularly.

111. Exporters in any country are susceptible to currency fluctuations, but in Switzerland the effect is particularly extreme. The strong franc, which has risen more than 10 per cent against the euro this year, has made Swiss chemicals, machinery and watches – the country's three most important exports – more expensive for foreign buyers. The strong franc, pushed upward by Switzerland's relatively healthy economic growth and its status as a haven from financial turmoil, has also had a negative effect on a sector most people don't think of as an export: tourism. In Switzerland, the tourism industry accounts for 3.4 per cent of gross domestic product (GDP), according to economists at UBS. But because tourism is labour intensive, it has an outsize effect on the job market. Tourism accounts for 6 per cent of employment in Switzerland, more than 200,000 full-time jobs or four times as many as watchmaking (*New York Times*, Aug. 20, 2010).

A. There is no clear link between the relative strength of the Swiss franc and the growth of Switzerland's economy.

B. Unlike machines sold abroad, tourism does not represent an export since no goods or services actually leave the country.

C. There is a clear connection between the relative strength of the Swiss franc and the level of full-time employment in Switzerland.

D. Accounting for around 100,000 jobs, watchmaking represents not only a key export, but also a significant employer.

112. Recent years at the Bregenz opera festival in Austria have trained the spotlight on seldom heard works by 20th-century composers such as Ernst Krenek and Karol Szymanowski, a process that continues this summer with two operas by the Russian composer of Polish birth Mieczyslaw Weinberg, most notably his Holocaust drama "The Passenger." Based on a novel by the

Auschwitz survivor Zofia Posmysz, the piece is set in the late 1950s aboard an ocean liner bound from Europe to Brazil, where Lisa and her husband, Walter, a West German diplomat, are headed so he can take a new post. But protagonist Martha's composure is shattered when she fears she recognizes a woman who, like herself, has an Auschwitz past, albeit a very different one: Martha, "the passenger," was an inmate, while Lisa was an SS overseer (unbeknownst to her husband, until now) (*The New York Times*, Aug. 3, 2010).

A.   Like the character Martha in Mieczyslaw Weinberg's opera "The Passenger", writer Zofia Posmysz was once an inmate at Auschwitz.

B.   Lisa, a former SS overseer at Auschwitz, is the main character in an opera by Mieczyslaw Weinberg being presented this summer in Austria.

C.   Walter is a character in "The Passenger" who learns that his wife was an SS overseer at Auschwitz, but who is also hiding his own Nazi past.

D.   Performed at the Bregenz opera festival, the Holocaust drama "The Passenger" is based on a work of nonfiction written by Zofia Posmysz.

113.   **Greek Prime Minister George Papandreou declared Saturday night that his government had won a "relentless and gruelling" battle to keep the country from going bankrupt, announced reforms to get the economy moving and sought to bolster the hopes of citizens whose salaries and pensions have been cut in an unprecedented austerity drive. In a concession to businesses that have suffered heavy losses amid a deepening recession, Mr Papandreou said that reductions in corporate taxes, due to drop in 2014 to 20 per cent from 24 per cent, would be introduced beginning next year. He also pledged to create at least 200,000 jobs by issuing licenses for wind farms and solar parks. The prime minister said that even more jobs would be created through the opening up of traditionally closed professions – a disparate group including truck drivers and pharmacists – that have restricted new entrants for decades. He also confirmed plans to streamline money-losing state enterprises, including the Greek railway organization (*The New York Times*, Sept. 11, 2010).**

A.   The prime minister announced that corporate taxes would begin dropping next year.

B.   The Papandreou government's belt-tightening measures have so far left retirement pay untouched.

C.   Members of restricted professions in Greece include lorry drivers, pharmacists and engineers.

D.   The prime minister will pump more state money into Greek railways in order to create more jobs.

114.   **Rebuilt after an earthquake in 1963 wiped out most of the city, Skopje, the capital of the ex-Yugoslav republic of Macedonia, was for years characterised by ugly concrete blocks and strange empty spaces. But earlier this year Nikola Gruevski's conservative government produced a video that revealed the full ambition of "Skopje 2014", its plan for a radical reinvention of the city centre. Supporters of the plans said that, after decades of stagnation, Skopje would at last get the regeneration it deserves, its heroes commemorated in marble and bronze. Sceptical critics, used to a city where nothing much happens, sarcastically asked which triumph the proposed triumphal arch would be celebrating. Yet it is happening. New buildings are sprouting up along the banks of the Vardar river and a fresh statue is unveiled every few weeks (*The Economist*, Aug. 26, 2010).**

A.   Promoted by a conservative government, the "Skopje 2014" project has a nationalistic tone to it.

B.   Critics of Skopje's city regeneration plans have had their predictions of inaction come true.

C.   The Vardar river runs through Skopje, the capital of the former Yugoslav republic of Macedonia.

D.   Skopje's concrete blocks represent the legacy of rebuilding after the destruction of World War II.

115.   **Among the Catholic nations of Europe, Poland stands out as the only place where seminaries are full and priests abound. The percentage of churchgoers remains high, though it peaked, at 55%, in 1987. But Catholicism has no monopoly over Poland's public square; the country played host this summer to a European gay pride march, and this year's musical hits include a song by a famous crooner, Olga Jackowska, in which she discloses that she was abused by a priest as a child. Nor is Polish Catholicism immune from social changes; a survey of Polish priests found that 54% said they would like to have a wife and family, and 12% said they already had a stable relationship with a woman (*The Economist*, Aug. 5, 2010).**

A.   A large percentage of people in Poland attend church whereas the number of Roman Catholic priests is relatively low there.

B. Poland is considered a Catholic nation; still, though Catholicism plays a very important role in Polish society, it does not control it.

C. Polish Catholicism has been affected by such social changes as priests wanting to get married and the formal approval of gay marriage.

D. Less than one out of every ten priests who wish to have a wife and family say they are currently in a relationship with a woman.

116. Conventional geothermal power exploits naturally occurring pockets of steam or hot water, close to the Earth's surface, to generate electricity. Because such conditions are rare, the majority of today's geothermal power plants are located in rift zones or volcanically active parts of the world, such as Iceland. Engineered geothermal systems (EGS) are based on a related principle, but they work even in parts of the world that are not volcanically active, by drilling thousands of metres underground to mimic the design of natural steam or hot-water reservoirs. Wells are bored and pathways are created inside hot rocks, into which cold water is injected. The water heats up as it circulates and is then brought back to the surface, where the heat is extracted to generate electricity. Because the Earth gets hotter the deeper you drill, EGS could expand the reach of geothermal power enormously and provide access to a virtually inexhaustible energy resource (*The Economist*, Sept. 2, 2010).

A. Some conventional geothermal power plants may also be situated outside of rift zones or volcanically active regions.

B. Engineered geothermal systems (EGS) will only be successful in rift zones or volcanically active regions.

C. Though the Earth is hotter deeper down it may not be cost-effective to drill beyond a certain depth.

D. Engineered geothermal systems (EGS) work by drilling deep to find pockets of steam or hot water.

117. Basque armed separatist group ETA's cease-fire declaration at the weekend was "insufficient," Spain's Interior Minister Alfredo Perez Rubalcaba said Monday. The Spanish government remains sceptical about ETA's true intentions and will leave its antiterrorist policy intact, Mr Rubalcaba said. "ETA needs to stop violence for good," he said. When it announced its last truce in March 2006, ETA used the word "permanent," which then raised hopes of negotiating a peaceful settlement to the conflict. ETA broke that cease-fire, however, in December 2006, with a bomb in a parking lot at Madrid's airport that killed two Ecuadorian immigrants. The new cease-fire would be the latest of many declared over the years. ETA is considered a terrorist organisation by the European Union and the US, and is held responsible for the deaths of 829 people in more than 40 years of a violent campaign for the independence of the Basque region in northern Spain and southwest France (*Wall Street Journal*, Sept. 6, 2010).

A. The Basque region is situated entirely within Spain and is thus seen primarily as a Spanish internal matter.

B. ETA announced a truce at the weekend, though authorities are sceptical; indeed, ETA had violated its last cease-fire.

C. ETA has claimed responsibility for 829 deaths in over 40 years of violent struggle to free the Basque region.

D. ETA announced a cease-fire at the weekend, only the second it has made in its 40-year history of armed struggle.

118. The European Commission has long struggled to break the public's perception that it is a dry, bureaucratic ivory tower. It would rather be seen as a bold leader in vital policy debates throughout the world. To that end, as reported by Euractiv, the commission is trying to build up the brand of its president, Jose Manuel Barroso. Mr Barroso's first opportunity will come on Tuesday, 9 a.m., at the European Parliament's second home in Strasbourg, France. He will make a speech, followed by a debate. There's a hitch: "Normally, these general debates attract only a few dozen MEPs," says a parliament official. "They'd rather spend that time in their office or having meetings." To stop MEPs from checking in, then leaving – a common practice among MEPs keen to assure their €298 daily living allowance – the leaders have ordered three electronic attendance checks during the three-hour speech and debate (*Wall Street Journal*, Sept. 6, 2010).

A. Mr Barroso has arranged electronic attendance checks to ensure that MEPs remain throughout his speech.

B. According to a parliament official, the European Commission is attempting to develop its president's brand.

C. MEPs will be gathering for a speech and debate in Strasbourg, but this is not the only city in which they meet.

D.   MEPs' only source of income is their living allowance of €298 per day which they do not receive if they do not turn up in parliament.

119.   A former spy with the UK Secret Intelligence Service, or MI6, was sentenced on Friday to one year in prison for trying to sell top-secret information to Dutch agents. Daniel Houghton admitted violating Britain's secrecy act by trying to sell the files. The Dutch agents told their British counterparts about the approach, leading to Mr Houghton's arrest at a London hotel in March. Prosecutors said the information he was peddling included staff lists and personal details that could have endangered agents. MI6 is Britain's overseas intelligence service. Judge David Bean sentenced Mr Houghton on Friday, calling him "a strange young man" guilty of an "act of betrayal." He is expected to be released shortly because he has already served almost half of his prison time while awaiting sentencing (*Wall Street Journal*, Sept. 3, 2010).

A.   Mr Houghton has waited nearly six months for Judge Bean to pass sentence on him for violating the UK secrecy law.

B.   The UK Secret Intelligence Service, or MI6, is primarily responsible for gathering intelligence domestically.

C.   Mr Houghton approached Dutch agents with secret information, but they felt that it would be useless to them.

D.   Though Mr Houghton broke the law, the information he was attempting to sell never placed anyone at risk.

120.   Visiting Italy recently, Libyan leader Col. Moammar Gadhafi suggested that Europe pay his country €5 billion to staunch the flow of illegal immigrants across the Mediterranean. Many migrants use Libya as a jumping-off point for the dangerous trip to Sicily or Malta. The southern maritime border is a perennial source of frustration for Europe. Tens of thousands make the crossing each year. The countries where they land don't want them, and complain that inland countries are refusing to share the burden. Efforts to push back migrants at sea can violate international human rights law. The debate over what to do tests both Europe's commitment to human rights and its policy of tight borders. Many in Europe are convinced the solution is to stop migrants from leaving in the first place. That's where Col. Gadhafi comes in (*Wall Street Journal*, Sept. 1, 2010).

A.   European countries are within their rights under international human rights law to repel illegal migrants at sea.

B.   Every year, many thousands of migrants take the perilous voyage from northern Africa to Europe where they are not always welcome.

C.   Col. Gadhafi's visit drew attention to the fact that tens of thousands of Libyans migrate to Sicily or Malta and in this way gain entry to Europe.

D.   Col Gadhafi has proposed that Europeans pay his country €5 billion so that it can process migrants that are returned from Europe.

121.   As Poland marks the 30th anniversary of the Solidarity movement that tore a hole in the Iron Curtain and eventually helped topple the Berlin Wall, it's worth taking a look at how much the country has changed. Many Poles still feel dissatisfied with their quality of life, and some complain that life was better in the centrally planned economy that guaranteed employment for all, even if it didn't pay any real money. But as the daily Puls Biznesu shows today, compared to 30 years ago, Poles can afford bigger apartments, more cars and many household appliances. Over the past three decades, the average Polish consumer's buying power has increased six times. The currency is free floating and fully exchangeable, which means that in dollar terms Polish average salaries went up from a barely noticeable amount of sometimes as low as $20 during communism to more than $1,000 a month now. Average apartment space has risen by 14 square meters. (*Wall Street Journal*, Aug. 31, 2010).

A.   Compared to 30 years ago, Poles enjoy an average of 14 square meters more living space.

B.   The Polish currency is fixed to the US dollar and thus its value changes accordingly.

C.   Poland's Solidarity movement also played an active role in Berlin under communism.

D.   Since salaries have just kept pace with prices since 1980, Poles cannot afford more than before.

122.   The history of Anglo-French co-operation in naval matters is not an entirely happy one. France and Britain have fought each other at sea with explosive results on plenty of occasions – most famously at the Battle of Trafalgar in 1805. Then there was the British attempt to negotiate a surrender of the French fleet in July 1940. Churchill did not want it falling into German hands and was determined to send a signal that he intended to stay in the war. The resulting brutal engage-

ment cost more than 1,300 lives and resulted in the effective destruction of the French navy. Seventy years later a new tide of co-operation on defence is flowing back and forth between Paris and London. The UK government hopes to negotiate an arrangement by which the partners agree to co-ordinate refits of their carriers so that there is always at least one, either French or British, available from the European theatre (*Wall Street Journal*, Sept. 1, 2010).

A. As part of a new wave of defence co-operation, Britain wishes to enter into a deal with France to harmonize the timing on repair of certain of the two countries' ships.

B. The French are understandably reluctant to relinquish any of their navy's independence in the light of its sometimes turbulent history with British naval forces.

C. As part of a recent effort toward military partnership, Britain wishes to negotiate with France on co-ordinating naval exercises involving the two countries' aircraft carriers.

D. Since Churchill did not want Germany to get hold of France's naval ships, the British fought the Germans in a naval battle that led to over 1,300 deaths.

123. In late May this year, Dr. Stephane Huberty inserted a needle into his upper arm and injected himself with a cloudy white vaccine previously tested only on rats and dogs. Dr. Huberty, who suffered from myasthenia gravis for 14 years, has been taking medication for the disease that he and others developed. The reason for this desperate measure: Dr. Huberty suffers from myasthenia gravis, a rare neurological condition. It is one of more than 5,000 "orphan" diseases, so called because there are so few sufferers that most pharmaceutical companies are reluctant to invest in cures. The 48-year-old Belgian doctor, who has had the disease for 14 years, has been taking medication he and others developed, but he can't find investors to pay for a clinical trial. Pharmaceutical companies and other doctors say his product is unproven. So Dr. Huberty is taking a leaf out of 19th-century science and using himself as a guinea pig (*Wall Street Journal*, Sept. 2, 2010).

A. Before Dr Huberty gave himself an experimental vaccine against his rare neurological condition, he had only tested it on rats.

B. Like Dr. Huberty's work on myasthenia gravis, some scientists in the 1800s tested the results of their experiments on themselves.

C. Myasthenia gravis is known as an "orphan" disease due to the devastating effect it can have on the children of those who suffer from it.

D. Dr. Huberty has been in search of funds to assist him in paying for the medication he has needed to take for his condition.

124. A political ad rejected as hate speech by a Swedish television station has sparked tension between Sweden and neighbouring Denmark. Some Danish leaders have cried censorship, and even want to see election observers at Sweden's upcoming national poll. Danish politicians are in an uproar over democratic freedoms across the water in Sweden, ever since a Swedish TV station rejected a political ad on Friday because of alleged hate speech. The ad by the anti-immigrant Sweden Democrats (SD) party shows a retiree hobbling forward while Muslim women in burqas charge past to grab money from the national budget. "On Sept. 19," their ad declares, referring to the date of upcoming national elections, "you can choose to cut money from immigration budgets, or from pensions." Now leading politicians in Denmark are crying censorship. Some prominent Danes even want the Council of Europe to send election observers to Sweden (*Der Spiegel*, Sept. 1, 2010).

A. Danish politicians have criticised the Sweden Democrats (SD) party for an anti-immigrant election campaign ad broadcast on television.

B. Certain key figures in Denmark are so concerned about democratic freedoms in Sweden that they wish to act as election observers there.

C. Certain Danish politicians see an ad presenting a choice between funding for Muslim immigrants or vulnerable retirees as acceptable free speech.

D. A Swedish political commercial that some in Sweden consider inflammatory has been completely banned from television in that country.

125. It isn't difficult to describe the plenary hall of the state parliament building in Lower Saxony. It is hideous. Heinous. Revolting. A boxy concrete abomination whose ugliness stands out even amid the abundant architectural putrescence that Hanover has to offer. And soon, if state representatives have their way, the not-quite-50-year-old building is to be demolished. Good news, right? Not necessarily, say a growing number of architects. Germany, after all, is full of cringe-inducing concrete monoliths, monuments to the orgy of construction that swept the country in the hurry

to rebuild after the destruction of World War II. Getting rid of them all would amount to a vast, and expensive, re-reconstruction project. Instead, even as many city renewal projects are marked by a nostalgia for the homey, constricted city centres of old, an increasing number of architects are saying that ugliness has its virtues – and it is time to begin recognizing that fact (*Der Spiegel*, Aug. 20, 2010).

A. Despite the expense of replacing all of Germany's postwar concrete blocks, more and more architects see it as a necessary step.

B. The ugly legislative assembly building in the German Land of Lower Saxony outdoes Hanover's many other unsightly blocks.

C. Berlin is also filled with unattractive concrete buildings constructed quickly after the destruction caused by the Second World War.

D. Despite the wishes of Lower Saxony's state legislators, there is a plan afoot to tear down their parliament building.

126. In the difficult summer of 2010, the German-speaking Italian province of South Tyrol is like a small beacon of prosperity surrounded by doom and gloom. Despite the economic crisis, there is almost no unemployment in the area surrounding the capital Bolzano (known in German as Bozen), and the province is debt-free. By comparison, Italy as a whole has the highest government debt, as a percentage of the country's gross domestic product (GDP), in the entire eurozone. Within the last half-century, 19 prime ministers have been sworn in in Rome. In South Tyrol, on the other hand, there has been only one change in the province's top job during the same period – from its "über-father" Silvius Magnago to its current paternalistic governor since 1989, Luis Durnwalder (*Der Spiegel*, Aug. 25, 2010).

A. With heads of government serving under three years on average over the last 50 years, Italy shows less political continuity than South Tyrol.

B. Due in part to South Tyrol's economic situation, Italy suffers under the largest government debt in proportion to GDP in the eurozone.

C. Unlike northern neighbour Austria, the German-speaking Italian province of South Tyrol actually has no government debt.

D. Long-serving South Tyrol governor Luis Durnwalder has held the Italian province's top post for well over half of the last 50 years.

127. In 2007, it got a reprieve. A last-minute ruling by a judge saved the proud chestnut tree that Anne Frank had gazed at as she was hiding from the Nazis in her Amsterdam attic. It had been slated for felling due to an illness which had made it unsafe. On Monday, however, a storm knocked over the 150-year-old tree, weakened as it was by fungus and moths. "Someone yelled, 'It's falling. The tree is falling'." museum spokeswoman Maatje Mostart told the Associated Press. "Luckily, no one was hurt." The tree, which had offered comfort to Anne Frank and her family during their 25 months in hiding, did little damage as it fell, and the Anne Frank House museum was untouched. High winds and heavy rain have been blamed for the chestnut's demise (*Der Spiegel*, Aug. 23, 2010).

A. Hiding in an attic for over two years, Anne Frank and her family took daily comfort from the sight of an old chestnut tree nearby.

B. A judge ruled that a 150-year-old chestnut tree should be chopped down because it posed a hazard as it was sick from fungus and moths.

C. An old tree within sight of the house where Anne Frank had once lived caused only minor damage when it was knocked over in a storm.

D. An old chestnut tree associated with Anne Frank has been cut down owing to an illness that had made it potentially dangerous.

128. The Belgian media has been dominated by one dramatic statement after another from francophone politicians who now openly discuss the prospect of dividing the country in two. This comes in reaction to Friday's resignation by socialist francophone leader Elio Di Rupo as Wallonia's lead negotiator with Dutch-speaking Flemish rivals to form a coalition government. Belgium has been in political limbo ever since the inconclusive June elections. Among the central issues in this debate is the level of autonomy for regional governments. The Flemish north is seeking more regional authority from the central government in Brussels, but the financially weaker Walloons worry that such a move would harm their interests as they are net beneficiaries of federally funded programmes. King Albert II is moving quickly to get coalition talks back on track. He wasted little time after Mr Di Rupo's departure to appoint a pair of new negotiators in the hope of finally reaching a consensus to form a government (*France24*, Sept. 6, 2010).

A. The Dutch-speaking region of Belgium to the south

has been a net contributor to federal programmes that mostly benefit Wallonia.

B.   Talks between parties in Belgium have collapsed, but new negotiators have been charged with hammering out a coalition agreement.

C.   Efforts to form a coalition government collapsed after Mr Di Rupo said he would no longer represent the Flemish in negotiations.

D.   The single issue in the discussions between Walloon and Flemish politicians is the degree of autonomy enjoyed by regional governments.

129.   Gianfranco Fini, the former ally of Silvio Berlusconi turned bitter rival, made a fierce attack on the Italian prime minister on Sunday but said he would avoid steps that could trigger an early election. Mr Fini, the speaker of the lower house of parliament, was expelled in July from the People of Freedom (PDL) party he set up with Mr Berlusconi, leaving the government without a secure majority after months of increasing friction between the two. Denouncing his expulsion as an act of "Stalinism" by the prime minister's allies, he called for constitutional reform and urged the government to focus on economic issues and social justice, but rejected charges of disloyalty. The 58-year-old Mr Fini, who has the support of 34 lower house deputies and 10 senators, has the power to block legislation. His speech was the first declaration of the approach he will take when parliament resumes this week (*France24*, Sept. 6, 2010).

A.   Mr Fini decided to leave the government after months of growing tension between himself and his one-time ally, prime minister Silvio Berlusconi.

B.   Though accused of being disloyal, Mr Fini has stated that he would be careful not to do anything that might lead to an early election.

C.   Though he was recently kicked out of the PDL party, Mr Fini still enjoys the backing of some senators and a majority of lower house deputies.

D.   Though not speaking against the prime minister himself, Mr Fini is pushing the government to pay some attention to the economy and social issues.

130.   Romania's unpopular government plunged temporarily into turmoil Thursday after the prime minister fired five Cabinet ministers and named new ones, with the economy minister also saying he will quit. Romania is mired in recession and the government has slashed public sector wages by a quarter and hiked the sales tax from 19 to 24 per cent on July 1 to reduce the budget deficit –

measures derided by Romanians but requested by the International Monetary Fund. The cutbacks are aimed at meeting conditions for a €20 billion loan from the IMF, the European Union and the World Bank to bail the country out of serious financial difficulty it encountered last year, when its economy contracted by 7.1 per cent. Some of the money was used to pay pensions and wages (*France24*, Sept 2, 2010).

A.   The Romanian government increased the sales tax as part of an effort to raise state revenue and thus put the country's finances in order.

B.   The Romanian government cut public sector pay because it had generally been high and this had been unpopular among ordinary Romanians.

C.   Most of Romania's €20 billion loan was secured from the IMF so that the country could overcome financial problems that had struck last year.

D.   The Romanian prime minister sacked the economy minister for his inability to steer the country's economy safely out of rough waters.

131.   Police in the ex-Soviet republic of Moldova have seized 1.8 kg of radioactive uranium in a garage in the capital and have arrested several people, government officials said on Tuesday. The substance was sent for tests in the United States which showed it to be uranium-238, Igor Volnitchii, a top state adviser to the government, told Reuters. "A group of criminals involved in uranium smuggling planned to sell it abroad," Mr Volnitchii said. The seized uranium was valued at 9 million euros. He said three people had been arrested and several others were being sought. Two members of the group were former police officers. He said Moldovan authorities were now waiting for tests conducted in Germany to determine the country of origin of the uranium. EU officials say Moldova's territory, which covers the rebel area of Transdniestr bordering Ukraine, is vulnerable to all types of smuggling, including narcotics and human trafficking (*France24*, Aug. 24, 2010).

A.   A gang in Moldova caught attempting to smuggle 1.8 kg of radioactive uranium is probably also mixed up in narcotics trafficking.

B.   Tests carried out in Germany have determined that a radioactive substance found in a Moldovan garage was uranium-238.

C.   Once part of the former Soviet Union, today Moldova must contend with such problems as rebellion and drug smuggling.

D.   Worth 9 million euros, the radioactive uranium

uncovered in the Moldovan capital was found to have originated in neighbouring Ukraine.

132. Some 2,000 people on Sunday crammed into a Moscow square amid a heavy police presence for a banned rock concert to protest plans to build a motorway through a forest outside the Russian capital. The numbers were far higher than for past opposition rallies in Moscow but the concert failed to get off the ground after police refused to allow amplification gear through tight security, an AFP correspondent at the scene reported. Dozens of police vehicles and members of the feared OMON anti-riot police, equipped with helmets and bulletproof vests, thronged the square. The concert's aim was to buttress efforts by environmental activists to oppose the construction of a highway through Khimki forest outside Moscow, which has become a symbol for Russians fighting for their rights. While the demonstration on Pushkin Square against the construction of the road had been sanctioned by the Moscow authorities, they had explicitly banned the holding of a concert (*France24*, Aug. 23, 2010).

A. A public demonstration in a Moscow square has succeeded in stopping a controversial road building project.

B. Thousands showed up in a Moscow square for a rock concert that was ultimately stopped by the authorities.

C. An unauthorized protest was held in Moscow to halt the construction of a motorway outside of Moscow.

D. The purpose of a concert planned in Pushkin Square was to fight for rights that have been violated by the current regime.

133. China's remarkable growth is as apparent in beer consumption as it is in more formal economic indicators. In the space of a couple of decades the country has gone from barely touching a drop to becoming the world's biggest beer market, a considerable distance ahead of America. And beer drinking in China is growing fast, by nearly 10% a year according to Credit Suisse's World Map of Beer. This might seem like good news for the four big firms that dominate global brewing. Between them ABI, SABMiller, Carlsberg and Heineken have nearly half the world market. But unlike America and other hugely profitable mature markets where beer drinking has levelled off or is in decline, China's drinkers provide slender profits. Still it remains a market with huge

potential, though foreign brewers must now be rather tired of hearing that (*The Economist*, Aug. 17, 2010).

A. The Chinese beer market is expanding quickly, yet beer makers' profits are relatively low.

B. America's beer market is lucrative and growing, but it is not expanding as quickly as China's.

C. China has long been a beer-drinking nation, but new wealth has led to a demand for imported beer.

D. ABI is the largest of the four brewing companies that dominate the world's beer market.

134. As rulings go, Judge Vaughn Walker's verdict on August 4th in San Francisco was relentless. The state of California, he wrote, cannot ban, even by popular vote, gays and lesbians from marrying because this would violate America's constitution by denying some couples "a fundamental right without a legitimate (much less compelling) reason." His decision is certain to be appealed, and most watchers think it will end up before the Supreme Court. But whatever happens there, it represents a huge leap forward in America's long struggle over the civil rights of homosexuals (*The Economist*, Aug. 5, 2010).

A. The judge made his decision in response to a California referendum on gay marriage.

B. Even if the judge's verdict is not upheld in the Supreme Court, it is an important advance for gays.

C. Since most people agree with the wisdom of the judge's ruling, it will probably not be appealed.

D. The issue of civil rights for gays and lesbians is a relatively new one in the United States.

135. The nota roja, a section reporting the previous day's murders and car crashes in all their blood-stained detail, is an established feature of Mexican newspapers. It is also an expanding one, as fighting over the drug trail to the United States inspires ever-greater feats of violence. Last month in the northern state of Durango, a group of prisoners was apparently released from jail for the night to murder 18 partygoers in a next-door state. A few days later, 14 inmates were murdered in a prison in Tamaulipas. In all, since Felipe Calderón sent the army against the drug gangs when he took office as president almost four years ago, some 28,000 people have been killed, the government says. There is no sign of a let-up, on either side (*The Economist*, Aug. 12, 2010).

A. Though the death toll has been high, the army

appears to be winning the battle with the drug gangs.

B. 28,000 people have been killed in Mexico in clashes between the Mexican Army and drug gangs.

C. The nota roja is a section in Mexican newspapers containing readers' opinions about the violent drug wars.

D. An increasing number of people are dying in Mexico in incidents related to drug-smuggling to the United States.

136. Hanna Nasir, the head of Palestine's Central Elections Commission, is not prone to expletives. But the Christian nuclear physicist and former dean of Palestine's leading university was full of them when the cabinet of the Palestinian prime minister, Salam Fayyad, who runs the West Bank, recently cancelled the municipal elections he was organising. If anything, his rival prime minister in Gaza, Ismail Haniyeh of Hamas, is even less keen to put his movement's popularity to the test. It was the third election the Palestinian Authority (PA) has annulled in less than a year. The terms of the PA's presidency, parliament and municipalities have all now expired. With no date for fresh polls and in constitutionally uncharted waters, officials increasingly rule by fiat. How far, bemoans Mr Nasir, has Palestine fallen from the heights of 2005 and 2006, when he ran elections that international observers hailed as being among the fairest in the Middle East. Instead of building a democratic state, the PA is fast on its way to creating just another Arab autocracy (*The Economist*, Aug. 12, 2010).

A. The Palestinian Authority (PA) looks as if it is rapidly forming an autocracy like that of its neighbour Egypt.

B. Mr Nasir takes it with resignation that one election after another has been cancelled in Palestine recently.

C. A Palestinian scientist and one-time university administrator, Mr Nasir also has experience organising elections in his country.

D. The most recently cancelled elections would have had Mr Fayyad running against Mr Haniyeh for the office of prime minister.

137. This February, inventor Nathan Myhrvold of the investment firm Intellectual Ventures unveiled a Star Wars-inspired mosquito killer: a laser death ray. Mr Myhrvold mounts LED lamps on a fence post and uses a sensor called a charge-coupled device to monitor the field of light they create.

When a disturbance in the field indicates the presence of an insect, a non-lethal laser beam is fired to determine how quickly the insect's wings beat – a trait that reliably distinguishes one species from another. Only female, malaria-bearing mosquitoes get zapped with the powerful kill laser (their wings beat at a low frequency); other insects are allowed to escape unharmed. "This is the first example of a smart insecticide," Mr Myhrvold says. "If you sprayed, you'd kill all kinds of bugs" (*Scientific American*, Aug. 19, 2010).

A. Mr Myhrvold's device can be adjusted to kill mosquitoes with other potentially harmful diseases.

B. Mr Myhrvold has invented a device that selectively destroys a potentially deadly insect.

C. A non-lethal laser beam on Mr Myhrvold's device is able to determine the size of a passing insect.

D. Mr Myhrvold has developed a device which kills all mosquitoes that pass a sensor on a fence post.

138. A farm chemical with an infamous history – causing the worst known outbreak of pesticide poisoning in North America – is being phased out under an agreement announced on Tuesday by the US Environmental Protection Agency (EPA). Manufacturer Bayer CropScience agreed to stop producing aldicarb, a highly toxic insecticide used to kill pests on cotton and several food crops, by 2015 in all world markets. Use on citrus and potatoes will be prohibited after next year. Tuesday's announcement comes 25 years after a highly publicized outbreak of aldicarb poisoning sickened more than 2,000 people who had eaten California watermelons. New EPA documents show that babies and children under five can ingest levels of the insecticide through food and water that exceed levels the agency considers safe. "Aldicarb no longer meets our rigorous food safety standards and may pose unacceptable dietary risks, especially to infants and young children," the EPA said in announcing the agreement (*Scientific American*, Aug. 18, 2010).

A. Aldicarb once may have satisfied the EPA's food safety standards, but that is no longer the case.

B. The producer of Aldicarb has consented to stop manufacturing the insecticide immediately.

C. Aldicarb has been used only on citrus fruits such as oranges, lemons and grapefruit.

D. The potential dangers of Aldicarb to human beings have only come to light recently.

139. Poliomyelitis – a viral disease that wreaks havoc on motor neurons, often paralysing sufferers for life – was supposed to be banished from the planet a long time ago. When Jonas Salk unveiled his famed vaccine to the world in 1955, and Albert Sabin introduced an oral version shortly thereafter, inoculations began in earnest in many parts of the world, drastically lowering incidence numbers. Polio was completely eradicated in North and South America by 1994; in Australia and China by 2000; and in Europe by 2002. Even so, cultural animosities in isolated pockets of the world have conspired to keep global health authorities from stamping out the disease altogether. In 2003, for instance, the World Health Organisation's Global Polio Eradication Initiative mounted a Herculean effort to vaccinate 15 million Nigerian children. But prominent leaders from the country's Islamic community tarred and feathered the campaign, warning citizens that the vaccine was part of an imperialist US plan to keep Nigeria's population down (*Scientific American*, Aug. 18, 2010).

A. Jonas Salk discovered a vaccine against polio that did not have any significant side-effects.

B. Leaders from Nigeria's Islamic community fought a vaccination campaign in that country based on religious doctrines.

C. Soon after Jonas Salk discovered a polio vaccine, inoculation campaigns dramatically cut the number of polio cases.

D. Over 50 years since a polio vaccine was developed, the disease has been completely eliminated.

140. Scientific misconduct is defined as "fabrication, falsification or plagiarism in proposing, performing or reviewing research or in reporting research results," according to the US Office of Research Integrity (ORI). A 2009 meta-analysis of misconduct studies found that about 14 per cent of responding scientists reported having witnessed falsification by others – and 2 per cent confessed (anonymously) to having been involved in fabrication, falsification or modification of data themselves.
     An inquiry into scientific misconduct often leads to research disruption, evidence confiscation and lengthy meetings, all of which can add up quickly in terms of expenses such as faculty and staff labour. A typical case might run in the neighbourhood of half a million dollars, concluded the authors of the new case study, led by Arthur Michalek of the Roswell Park Cancer Institute in Buffalo, NY. Taking as an example a real case from their own institution, they esti-

mated the direct costs of that instance of misconduct to be about $525,000 (*Scientific American*, Aug. 17, 2010).

A. According to the US Office of Research Integrity (ORI), plagiarism in research is a form of scientific misconduct.

B. When suspected scientific misconduct is under investigation, as a rule, all evidence is seized.

C. A 2009 study found that 14 per cent of scientists had been involved in some form of scientific misconduct.

D. Research headed by Arthur Michalek received approximately half a million dollars in funding.

141. Fisheries agreements with countries outside the EU and negotiations within regional and international fisheries organisations ensure that not only the waters of the EU, but those of the whole world, are not over-fished. At the same time, they give EU fishermen access to fish in distant waters. With developing countries, the EU pays for access rights. The money raised in this way is largely invested in the fisheries industries of these countries and in building up their fish stocks. (*Europa policy*)

A. International fisheries agreements aim to keep fish populations steady off the shores of Europe and throughout the world.

B. The EU tends not to enter into talks within regional fisheries organisations, preferring instead the clout of international ones.

C. Through international fishing agreements, the EU and other wealthy nations pay developing countries to use their waters for fishing.

D. Most of the EU fisheries' money that developing countries receive is used to diversify the economy in fishing communities.

142. Each EU country is free to decide on the health policies best suited to national circumstances and traditions, but they all share common values. These include the right of everyone to the same high standards of public health and equity in access to quality health care. So it makes sense to work together on common challenges, ranging from ageing populations to obesity. The EU is also committed to taking the implications for health into account in all its policies. Moreover, diseases know no borders, particularly in a globalised world where many of us travel widely. Joint action adds value when facing potential threats such as influenza epidemics or bioterror-

ism. It is also equally logical that the EU has common standards on safe food and nutrition labelling, the safety of medical equipment, blood products and organs, and the quality of air and water. (*Europa policy*)

A.   Due to varying degrees of budgetary strength and of commitment among policy makers in different countries, the standard of health care is uneven in the EU.

B.   While health policies may vary within the Union, all EU citizens should enjoy the right to gain access to quality health care.

C.   The EU has long had common standards in such areas as safe food and nutrition labelling and the quality of air and water.

D.   While the EU takes such potential dangers as bioterrorism seriously, it has not yet made health concerns a part of other areas of policy making.

143.   To meet the common challenges, the EU is spending more than €50m annually on activities to improve our health security, to promote good health – including reducing inequalities, and to provide more information and knowledge on health. The money goes to a wide range of issues, including planning for health emergencies, patient safety and reducing injuries and accidents. There is also funding to promote better nutrition and safe consumption of alcohol, healthy lifestyles and healthy ageing, to combat consumption of tobacco and drugs, to prevent major diseases including HIV/AIDS and tuberculosis, and to exchange knowledge in areas such as gender issues, children's health and rare diseases. Activities to combat drug use can draw on the expertise of the European Monitoring Centre for Drugs and Drug Addiction in Lisbon. This provides the EU and its Member States with objective, reliable and comparable information on drugs and drug addiction. (*Europa policy*)

A.   Even today, tuberculosis is still considered a major disease whose prevention is a priority.

B.   The EU finances an effort to encourage the safe consumption of alcohol and tobacco.

C.   The annual health care budget in the EU stands at approximately €50 million.

D.   Though certainly considered important, no funding is yet set aside for specific women's health issues.

144.   Large differences in prosperity levels exist both between and within EU countries. The most prosperous regions in terms of GDP per capita (the

standard measure of well-being) are all urban – London, Brussels and Hamburg. The wealthiest country, Luxembourg, is more than seven times richer than Romania and Bulgaria, the poorest and newest EU members. The dynamic effects of EU membership, coupled with a vigorous and targeted regional policy, can bring results. The case of Ireland is particularly heartening. Its GDP, which was 64% of the EU average when it joined in 1973, is now one of the highest in the Union. One priority of regional policy is to bring living standards in the countries which have joined the EU since 2004 up to the EU average as quickly as possible. (*Europa policy*)

A.   In terms of levels of prosperity among EU Member States, Luxembourg is even richer than Ireland.

B.   Annual total GDP is the standard measure of well-being in comparing the relative wealth of countries and regions within the Union.

C.   EU membership and a strong regional policy have already had a positive effect on living standards in Romania and Bulgaria.

D.   One aim of regional policy is to help emulate the strategies of Ireland in the countries that have joined the EU since 2004.

145.   Regional inequalities have various causes. They may result from longstanding handicaps imposed by geographic remoteness or by more recent social and economic change, or a combination of both. The impact of these disadvantages is frequently evident in social deprivation, poor quality schools, higher joblessness and inadequate infrastructures. In the case of some EU states, part of the handicap is a legacy of their former centrally-planned economic systems. The EU has used the entry of these countries to reorganise and restructure its regional spending. In the period from 2007 to 2013, regional spending will account for 36% of the EU budget. In cash terms, this represents spending over the seven years of nearly €350 billion. The effort focuses on three objectives: convergence, competitiveness and co-operation, which are grouped together in what is now termed Cohesion Policy. (*Europa policy*)

A.   A centrally-planned economic system has represented no serious handicap in the rise of the relatively new Member State Slovenia.

B.   Cohesion Policy addresses a number of key aspects of regional inequalities, including higher unemployment and inadequate education.

C.   The EU budget for the 2007-2013 period amounts to

almost €350 billion, 36% of which will go to resolving regional inequalities.

D. There is no connection between the accession of the poorest new members and the EU's reorganised and restructured regional spending.

146. The 12 countries which have joined the EU since 2004 will receive 51% of total regional spending between 2007 and 2013, although they represent less than one quarter of the total EU population. The money comes from three difference sources, according to the nature of the assistance and the type of beneficiary. The European Regional Development Fund (ERDF) covers programmes involving general infrastructure, innovation, and investments. Money from the ERDF is available to the poorest regions across the EU. The European Social Fund (ESF) pays for vocational training projects and other kinds of employment assistance, and job-creation programmes. As with the ERDF, all EU countries are eligible for ESF assistance. The Cohesion Fund covers environmental and transport infrastructure projects as well as the development of renewable energy. Funding from this source is reserved for countries whose living standards are less than 90% of the EU average. This means the 12 recent newcomers plus Portugal and Greece. (*Europa policy*)

A. The Cohesion Fund pays for efforts to develop sources of renewable energy.

B. EU money available for projects in the poorest Member States comes exclusively from the Cohesion Fund.

C. The poorest regions in the EU are not necessarily part of the poorest countries.

D. The European Regional Development Fund (ERDF) finances schemes that create jobs.

147. The bulk of regional spending is reserved for regions with a per capita GDP below 75% of the Union average to help improve their infrastructures and develop their economic and human potential. This concerns 17 of the 27 EU countries. On the other hand, all 27 are eligible for funding to support innovation and research, sustainable development, and job training in their less advanced regions. A small amount goes to cross-border and inter-regional co-operation projects. The idea is for regional policy to dovetail with the EU's so-called Lisbon agenda to promote growth and jobs by making countries and regions more attractive for investments by improving accessibility, providing quality services and pre-

serving environmental potential; encouraging innovation, entrepreneurship and the knowledge economy through the development of information and communications technologies; and creating more and better jobs by attracting more people into employment, improving workers' adaptability and increasing investment in human capital. (*Europa policy*)

A. A total of 17 of the 27 Member States have a GDP less than 75% of the Union average.

B. All 27 Member States have regions with a GDP lower than 75% of the EU average.

C. 17 of the EU's 27 Member States have at least one region with a per capita GDP below 75% of the EU average.

D. EU spending on less advanced regions has no connection to the Lisbon agenda.

148. To remain competitive, the EU needs to spend more on research and development (R&D), matching investment R&D by major competitors. In particular, EU industry needs to close the spending gap between itself and counterparts in the US and Japan to remain competitive at the cutting edge of technology and innovation. The EU is likely to fall short of its goal to close this gap by investing 3% of GDP in research by 2010. The EU must also improve its record of translating scientific knowledge into patented processes and products for use in high-tech industries. The new European Institute for Innovation and Technology will support this process by promoting partnerships which link the three sides of the 'knowledge triangle': education, innovation and research. (*Europa policy*)

A. Closing the R&D spending gap between the EU and its competitors (the US and Japan) depends on the private sector as well as on the EU itself.

B. The EU has improved on its already strong trend of applying scientific findings in high-tech industries.

C. The complicated and expensive process of obtaining a patent in the EU holds back progress in R&D.

D. The European Institute for Innovation and Technology has long promoted R&D in the Union.

149. Space has its own research budget for the first time in the Seventh Framework Programme 2007-2013 (FP7), marking the increasing importance the EU attaches to playing an independent role in space. The Global Monitoring for Environment and Security project will make it easier to use observations from space to anticipate or deal with

environmental and security crises. The EU is also leading the Galileo project for the next generation of satellite global positioning systems (GPS), another area where the EU wants to develop its own technology rather than rely on other countries. The systems of the future will have a much broader range of applications than the common GPS used to reach a destination on car journeys, such as more efficient traffic management and a feature to support search-and-rescue operations. (*Europa policy*)

A. The EU currently relies almost entirely on American satellites to serve GPS devices in Europe.

B. The EU wishes to establish a more independent role in space generally and in GPS technology in particular.

C. The Global Monitoring for Environment and Security Project aims primarily to develop defensive weapons in space.

D. While the current positioning systems are widely used for search and rescue purposes, the Galileo system is purely aimed at navigation and traffic management purposes.

150. It is our governments which set tax rates on company profits and personal incomes, savings and capital gains. The EU as a whole merely keeps an eye on these decisions to see they are fair to the EU as a whole. It pays particular attention to company taxation because of a risk that taxes could create obstacles to the smooth movement of goods, services and capital around the EU's single market. Member countries are bound by a code of conduct to prevent them from providing tax breaks which unfairly distort investment decisions, for example. (*Europa policy*)

A. The EU does not set tax rates, but it does monitor member countries' taxation policies for the good of the single market.

B. Countries in the Union are entirely free to tax individuals and business organisations at their discretion.

C. The EU encourages Member States to keep taxes on individuals low to boost consumer spending and thus stimulate the economy.

D. The EU encourages especially less advanced members to use lower or no taxes as an incentive to attract foreign-owned companies.

THE VERBAL REASONING ANSWERS FOLLOW ON THE NEXT PAGE

1:   A

A.   Correct. The opening session was in Rome and that work is now underway.

B.   Wrong. The current conference is referencing the conclusions of the European Council meeting in Thessaloniki.

C.   Wrong. While this may be true, we are only told that ministers were asked to do something. It doesn't say they were on the Council or that they were from Member States.

D.   Wrong. The body which gave its support was the European Council and not the Intergovernmental Conference.

2:   B

A.   Wrong. The text states precisely the opposite, "…Lebanon's pro-Syrian government…"

B.   Correct. The text clearly states that Syria intervened in Lebanon's three-cornered civil war.

C.   Wrong. The text states that Rafik Hariri was a former prime minister not the president.

D.   Wrong. This may be true but the text does not reveal it.

3:   B

A.   Wrong. Both Brussels and Liege are famous for their waffles. It is Belgium as a whole that is famous for its chocolate and pralines.

B.   Correct. The country referred to is Belgium as a whole, while craquelin and pistolet, which are like a small cake or loaf, are listed among its specialties.

C.   Wrong. There is no evidence to support this statement at all.

D.   Wrong. It is mastel that is described as rusk bread with aniseed.

4:   B

A.   Wrong. The text does not explicitly say that he heads the Shia-led party (even though it is quite likely as he was interim prime minister).

B.   Correct. Because a new government had been elected, the interim (temporary) government (in which Iyad Allawi was prime minister), has recently had to step down.

C.   Wrong. The text says it was appointed on his birthday not the anniversary of his taking power.

D.   Wrong. There is no evidence to suggest that his party will take power at a later date.

5:   D

A.   Wrong. There is nothing stated that suggests Portugal initiated anything.

B.   Wrong. He may well have done but it doesn't say so here.

C.   Wrong. There is no mention of the Delors package advocating higher spending or being about regional policy.

D.   Correct.

6:   A

A.   Correct. It states that America's median age is 35 and Japan's will grow by 12 years to 53 which means it must currently be 41.

B.   Wrong. It states Germany's population will fall by 4% not 22% and Italy's will fall by 22% not 14%.

C.   Wrong. It is the population that will rise by 40% by 2050.

D.   Wrong. The text says that when people's children have grown up then they tend to save more not spend more.

7:   B

A.   Wrong. It was in the 10th century that Otto I ruled.

B.   Correct. The text states that King Samo's country stretched from present day Hungary and centred on the Czech Republic.

C.   Wrong. The Avars were driven out by the Slavs much earlier and it was the Frankish empire which took the country in the 8th century.

D.   Wrong. The ceremony took place until 1414.

8:   B

A.   Wrong. It is the Rome Convention which protects broadcasting organisations.

B.   Correct.

C. Wrong. There is no indication where these organisations have their headquarters.

D. Wrong. There is no indication that the Paris Convention affords any protection to performers but it is explicitly stated for the Rome Convention.

9:   A

A. Correct. The Play Station 3 is being launched two days before the Wii, which is being launched on Nov. 19

B. Wrong. It is the Game Boy which is the third-best selling console.

C. Wrong. On the contrary, Nintendo hasn't been a market leader since the 1990s.

D. Wrong. It is an unusual move for launching a Japanese product.

10:   C

A. Wrong. It is the transport and environment sectors that are mentioned.

B. Wrong. It may well be due to become a member but it doesn't say so here.

C. Correct. Half the money is due to go to each of the two sectors, transport and environment, which is 104-135m euro.

D. Wrong. Wastewater is specifically mentioned as being included in the heavy investment issues.

11:   C

A. Wrong. Effects have become more complex but they have become more accessible.

B. Wrong. Effects can now build "reality" in any way they see fit.

C. Correct. In the last decade their budget has gone from $5m to $50m.

D. Wrong. The barriers between the types of film have now crumbled.

12:   B

A. Wrong. We are not told how the Mach scale works, but if it is linear and not logarithmic (like the Richter scale) then it is only about 50% faster than 6 months before.

B. Correct.

C. Wrong. There is no indication in the text that the trend is likely to come to an end, soon or otherwise.

B. Wrong. It is rocket powered cars that are breaking the sound barrier.

13:   D

A. Wrong. RIA-Novosti is a news agency not a space agency.

B. Wrong. He said that there would be no seats available until 2009.

C. Wrong. It was the lawmaker's proposal which suggested sending Madonna into space.

D. Correct.

14:   D

A. Wrong. Qori Kalis is the name of the glacier not the scientist.

B. Wrong. Although used indirectly on this occasion, there is nothing to suggest this is a general method or happening.

C. Wrong. This may well be true but we can't tell from the text.

D. Correct.

15:   D

A. Wrong. It doesn't say in the text where Schengen is.

B. Wrong. It aimed to provide freedom of movement for citizens in the Schengen area.

C. Wrong. The agreement was added to, not replaced, in 1990.

D. Correct. France, Germany and the 3 Benelux countries.

16:   C

A. Wrong. The transport industry's contribution to GNP and employment are both 7%.

B. Wrong. The transport industry's contribution to Member States' investment is 40% which is not more than a half.

C. Correct. Passenger transport has grown 3.1% per year whereas goods have increased 2.3% per year.

D.   Wrong. The average is 7% but each Member State's spending could vary wildly.

in the countries of the former Soviet Union mainly by the US.

17:   D

A.   Wrong. The 16 years refers to the time taken to reduce the record by 1minute 20seconds.

B.   Wrong. Maybe she did. Maybe she didn't. It doesn't say.

C.   Wrong. We are told that the Chicago marathon was held in 2002 and the London marathon in 2003.

D.   Correct. Paula broke the record at both the 2002 Chicago marathon and the 2003 London marathon.

18:   C

A.   Wrong. Although it may be true, there is nothing to indicate this in the text.

B.   Wrong. The talks are being called to discuss its future rather than its final status.

C.   Correct.

D.   Wrong. This information is not given in the text.

19:   C

A.   Wrong. Doc Ock is a fictitious character from a film not a scientist from ITER.

B.   Wrong. On the contrary. Scientists have already been working for 50 years toward this goal.

C.   Correct. According to the text, Doc Ock nearly succeeded and now real scientists may succeed.

D.   Wrong. A benefit of fusion is that it doesn't leave behind radioactive waste.

20:   A

A.   Correct. Europe has pledged or spent less than $1bn which is 1/7 or 14% of the American spending.

B.   Wrong. The G8 includes Canada and Japan as non-European members.

C.   Wrong. America intends to spend a further $10bn not $7bn.

D.   Wrong. The weapons were bought or secured

21:   B

A.   Wrong. It states that the Danish, Dutch and Germans do too.

B.   Correct.

C.   Wrong. They blame it on the American-owned press not the TV.

D.   Wrong. It is the EU insiders who are concerned by this.

22:   A

A.   Correct.

B.   Wrong. He wants to set up a French search engine.

C.   Wrong. There is no mention of how often people read Sartre now. They could be reading him online.

D.   Wrong. There is no mention of the reaction by any university to Google's plan.

23:   C

A.   Wrong. Some people ("lucky oddballs") function on 4 hours sleep or even less.

B.   Wrong. The text states that the flies remain motionless for many hours a day, not 8.

C.   Correct. A mutation in an insect's gene which is shared by humans has been identified.

D.   Wrong. The reference in the text is to scientists studying sleep for decades, not the specific issue of insect sleep.

24:   B

A.   Wrong. The current limit is 2000 IU ("certified-safe limit").

B.   Correct.

C.   Wrong. This may well be true but the sun isn't even mentioned.

D.   Wrong. The text never mentions nutrition.

25:   A

A.   Correct. It says obesity and poor nutrition will

have an impact on the EU's economy and health care services.

B. Wrong. The text does not say that Markos Kyprianou is Greek or Greek Cypriot.

C. Wrong. Obesity may be linked to cardio-vascular disease and cancer in later life, but there is no suggestion that it is usual for overweight teenagers to suffer from these illnesses.

D. Wrong. It is 2-8% of the health care budget which is spent on obesity-related problems.

26: C

A. Wrong. Mussels are able to stick to Teflon along with ships, glass and just about anything.

B. Wrong. It does mention that barnacles stick to ships but there is no mention of whether this poses a danger.

C. Correct. The crux of the text is that scientists may develop antifouling paints because of this discovery.

D. Wrong. There is no mention of a web. It is an iron-based glue that is used.

27: C

A. Wrong. It states that the decline of the newspapers pre-dates the internet.

B. Wrong. It states that the internet is changing the business in a way that TV and radio never did.

C. Correct. 56% of Americans have never heard of blogs, which is more than half.

D. Wrong. There is no mention of trends among older people.

28: D

A. Wrong. The text gives no indication of when he was born.

B. Wrong. His second period started with Eroica not Kreutzer.

C. Wrong. As Beethoven possibly studied under Salieri then Salieri could not have died before Beethoven was born.

D. Correct.

29: A

A. Correct. "Mucus" in the first sentence is "the slippery substance" referred to in the next sentence.

B. Wrong. There is no mention of when this discovery was made.

C. Wrong. On the contrary, they do secrete slippery substances.

D. Wrong. It is the cause of the aberrant secretion which remains unknown.

30: A

A. Correct.

B. Wrong. The Earth is 4.6 billion years old not 4.6 million.

C. Wrong. Oxygen started to accumulate about 2.3 billion years ago.

D. Wrong. Eukaryotes are multi-cellular life forms with several different types of cells.

31: C

A. Wrong. Whilst the CAP is moving towards promoting competitiveness, there is no indication that the Doha Declaration states that it isn't competitive enough.

B. Wrong. There is no indication in the text that this is so.

C. Correct. It states that from the outset it has been pro-active and unreservedly supports the Declaration.

D. Wrong. It states that less trade-distorting support need not be a constraint.

32: B

A. Wrong. He painted "Les Demoiselles d'Avignon" in 1906-7.

B. Correct. His blue period was 1902-4, pink was 1904-6 and then he turned to brown.

C. Wrong. It doesn't say that Picasso invented cubism nor does it mention architecture.

D. Wrong. On the contrary. He studied in Spain before moving to Paris.

33:   B

A.   Wrong. There is no mention of Mr Kohl's role in Germany.

B.   Correct. This is the view of the European Union's most ardent supporters.

C.   Wrong. It only states that Elmar Brok was a member of the constitutional convention.

D.   Wrong. It only states that Mr Kohl argued that adopting the euro is a question of war and peace.

34:   D

A.   Wrong. Kentlands is just one example of "new urbanism".

B.   Wrong. While everything is within walking distance, it doesn't mention anything about the traffic congestion.

C.   Wrong. Kentlands is not an old established city; it is only 20 years old.

D.   Correct.

35:   B

A.   Wrong. They have also been called the finest cars in the world.

B.   Correct. It states that every car is unique with the exception of the engine.

C.   Wrong. It is an unnamed customer's wife's eyes that were being matched.

D.   Wrong. It states that you can order in any colour imaginable.

36:   B

A.   Wrong. Its claim to fame is the who's who of famous people buried there.

B.   Correct. Richman says the cemetery reflects what was going on in the world at the time.

C.   Wrong. He says that only about Dutch gravestones from the 18th century.

D.   Wrong. The pride of the cemetery is a Mercedes-Benz tombstone that tells more than name and dates.

37:   B

A.   Wrong. Ed Baig has already tried one.

B.   Correct. Baig says Edge, which the iPhone uses, is slow compared to other 3G networks.

C.   Wrong. The touch-screen display is already on it.

D.   Wrong. Apple is not reported to have made this claim.

38:   C

A.   Wrong. Julie Vallese calls all professional fireworks explosives.

B.   Wrong. The demonstration showed one of the dangers posed by these fireworks.

C.   Correct. 6400 injuries were recorded during a one-month period in 2006.

D.   Wrong. It states that consumers had obtained professional fireworks illegally.

39:   C

A.   Wrong. Positive Tea is a support group not a vaccine.

B.   Wrong. Laura Bush is the first lady referred to in the text and was speaking in Maputo on Wednesday.

C.   Correct. It was Laura Bush's third trip to Africa.

D.   Wrong. Although this was extolled by Laura Bush, there is no indication that this was her primary objective.

40:   C

A.   Wrong. Scientists have long suspected this. They now know it to be a fact.

B.   Wrong. The probe crashed into a crater of this size. It wasn't the cause of the crater.

C.   Correct. There could, of course, be more but only 90 litres has been confirmed.

D.   Wrong. It has accumulated over billions of years but in ice form

41:   A

A.   Correct. He started sailing in 1837 at age 18 and in 1844, aged 25, he settled down to writing.

B.   Wrong. He visited Liverpool in 1837 and there is no reference to a later visit.

C. Wrong. He lived amongst the cannibals with a companion.

D. Wrong. He was only temporarily imprisoned on Tahiti.

42:   B

A. Wrong. The text states that rainfall is scant.

B. Correct. It says it is snow-covered for much of the year until summer and summer lasts 50 to 60 days.

C. Wrong. Musk-oxen are listed as living in arctic tundra areas.

D. Wrong. The stated temperature is correct but it supports a variety of animal species.

43:   A

A. Correct. James II was Mary's father whom he defeated in the Battle of the Boyne.

B. Wrong. It was a Protestant and Catholic coalition.

C. Wrong. It states that many were fearful of a Catholic revival.

D. Wrong. He was viewed as a champion while he was in the Protestant-Catholic coalition.

44:   D

A. Wrong. He visited Donaueschingen and Munich after Zurich.

B. Wrong. It was Mozart who visited Bach.

C. Wrong. It was 1762 when he was first shown to be a prodigy.

D. Correct. There were nine stops but two in each of Munich and Paris.

45:   C

A. Wrong. Magellan was the first European not the first person ever.

B. Wrong. Patagonia is sparsely populated.

C. Correct. Oil is one of the natural resources listed.

D. Wrong. Patagonia stretches from Rio Colorado so it must be at the edge of the area.

46:   B

A. Wrong. The text states that agricultural production increased by 24% per capita, but the population increased by 89% in the period.

B. Correct. It states that the world population increased by 89% between these years which is fairly close to double.

C. Wrong. It cites China as a country that reached the limits of increasing arable land use "many years ago".

D. Wrong. The text states that in the past agricultural production was improved by increasing land use AND employing the best technologies available.

47:   B

A. Wrong. The Chrysler Building held the record of tallest building for less than a year.

B. Correct. 102 storeys were built in 410 days which is about 4 days per story. [NB: Story is the US spelling of storey.]

C. Wrong. 40 Wall Street, like the Chrysler Building, was still under construction when work began on the Empire State Building.

D. Wrong. They were "mostly" from Europe.

48:   A

A. Correct. There is no mention of Mr. Thuer wanting to ban Google Street View.

B. Wrong. It has been controversial but it hasn't been banned.

C. Wrong. The watchdogs want people and cars to be blurred out not removed.

D. Wrong. Google have been asked to do this; they haven't declared that they will.

49:   B

A. Wrong. Although Germany was among the best performers, it was Austria and Portugal who were the best.

B. Correct. The economy shrank for 5 consecutive quarters which is over a year.

C. Wrong. It grew by 0.3% which was the same as Q2.

D. Wrong. The eurozone performed better than the EU as a whole.

50:   B

A.   Wrong. The Opposition does not propose a case.

B.   Correct. There are four who speak, two of whom speak twice, so there will be five changes of person speaking.

C.   Wrong. The Government must propose something first otherwise there is nothing to oppose.

D.   Wrong. Two proposers, two opponents and a the Speaker (judge and arbiter) making five in total.

51:   C

A.   Wrong. We cannot tell from the text. It tells us that short stalk varieties waste less energy growing a stalk than long varieties.

B.   Wrong. The text tells us that short stalk varieties will receive less sunlight amongst other longer-stalked varieties.

C.   Correct.

D.   Wrong. Because tall varieties tend to bend it complicates the reaping process.

52:   B

A.   Wrong. It is "among" the world's most threatened anuimals..

B.   Correct. 2.5 million acres protected are just under half of the remaining habitat. Therefore there must be over 5 million acres in total.

C.   Wrong. Poaching is a threat but so is habitat loss and fragmentation. No order is ascribed to these threats.

D.   Wrong. More than 60% are now protected so less than 40% remain in danger.

53:   A

A.   Correct.

B.   Wrong. The parasite kills the immune cells and then hides the evidence by eating the corpses.

C.   Wrong. The text states that it can colonize for months without the host knowing.

D.   Wrong. The author clearly states that he had the same pathogen in his gut when he returned home from the sub-Sahara.

54:   C

A.   Wrong. It is theorized that Europa could support this quantity of life, not that it does.

B.   Wrong. There is no evidence in the text that any form of life has ever existed on Europa.

C.   Correct. Greenberg said that there was nothing saying there is life there now.

D.   Wrong. Jupiter has many moons but it doesn't say it here.

55:   D

A.   Wrong. There is nothing in the text about the images being carved into the wood.

B.   Wrong. Phnom Penh was the seat of government when the French arrived in 1863.

C.   Wrong. Oudong was the seat of government from 1618 until the mid 19th century.

D.   Correct. Phnom Penh is 40km south of Oudong.

56:   A

A.   Correct. It says that the cultural diversity has produced a culinary melting pot.

B.   Wrong. A melting pot is a mixing of multiple cultures and not a cooking vessel.

C.   Wrong. There is no mention of the opportunity chance to play games at the restaurant.

D.   Wrong. The old town may be quiet; other parts of town are rowdier.

57:   C

A.   Wrong. The author is merely using a satirical metaphor to define social life.

B.   Wrong. It is Margaret Visser who makes this observation.

C.   Correct. Revenge that seems to escalate with each invitation.

D.   Wrong. Although this may well be true, the text states that it is obligation and gratitude which may crash and burn.

58:   B

A.   Wrong. There is no mention of how many these diseases kill relative to others.

B.   Correct. According to Abdallah Daar, chair of Alliance.

C.   Wrong. 1.5 million people die due to primitive stoves but not necessarily by fire.

D.   Wrong. It says that what works in the US may not work in India.

59:   C

A.   Insufficient information. Although it mentions that Shell was expelled by the community, there is no mention of Shell attempting to return to clear up the pollution.

B.   Wrong. It states: "These days the 400 sq mile delta ... is still badly polluted".

C.   Correct. It states that Shell and the government have earned $100bn (a substantial amount by any yardstick) and that it is still badly polluted.

D.   Wrong. On the contrary, it states that it "barely needs refining".

60:   A

A.   Correct. China sees this gesture as "brandishing a fist at a potential [enemy]".

B.   Wrong. It was diplomatic relations between America and Vietnam that were established 15 years ago.

C.   Wrong. Danang was ONCE home to one of America's largest army bases in Vietnam.

D.   Wrong. The large aircraft carrier was intended as a "striking token of reconciliation".

61:   C

A.   Insufficient information. This is probably true but it doesn't say it in the article. It says China is second but doesn't say who is first.

B.   Insufficient information. There is no mention of any tension between the two neighbours, just quibbles about how the data are measured.

C.   Correct. It says that China's economy was one of the biggest for nearly 2000 years and has fallen back only briefly.

D.   Wrong. It is Japan's economy that has been the third largest for some time.

62:   B

A.   Insufficient information. It does state that

there are only 350 cork oak forests left but it doesn't specify how many are in Portugal.

B.   Correct.

C.   Wrong. The cork is stripped from the tree exposing the inner red wood.

D.   Insufficient information. There is no mention of this being done twice each year.

63:   C

A.   Wrong. Climate change is cited as a possible cause but not the only one.

B.   Wrong. Deforestation is cited as a possible cause but not the only one.

C.   Correct. It states that they are "spreading lethal epidemics around the world".

D.   Wrong. It is a 10-year drought which has caused the worst air pollution in 70 years.

64:   A

A.   Correct. There are 4 actors, a director, an assistant and the playwright.

B.   Wrong. The writer is present in the rehearsal room.

C.   Wrong. It is a "heart-tugging love story" but it feels more like reality TV.

D.   Wrong. That is only part of their function.

65:   C

A.   Insufficient information. There is no mention of humour being used at all.

B.   Wrong. The Slap is not written by Ian McEwan; it is compared to Ian McEwan's book Saturday.

C.   Correct. It is a close-knit, affluent society made up from many ethnic backgrounds.

D.   Wrong. It is telling a story of life in an Australian suburb.

66:   A

A.   Correct. There were 977 babies born from donated sperm and 82 from donated embryos.

B.   Insufficient information. This is not specified. We are only told that there were 15,237 births due to IVF and DI combined.

C.   Wrong. It says that 396 donors are far fewer that what is needed.

D.   Wrong. It says that fewer men donate mainly because of the loss of anonymity.

67:   A

A.   Correct. It says that sensory information from many systems is likely stored correctly.

B.   Wrong. It is the recollection and reassembly of memories that is so unreliable.

C.   Insufficient information. This may or may not be true; there is no mention of it in the text.

D.   Wrong. It states that you can have vivid memories of things that never happened.

68:   A

A.   Correct. The theory is that if it smells like soap then you shouldn't eat it.

B.   Wrong. On the contrary, if it smells like cleaning products then we usually don't want to eat it.

C.   Insufficient information. There is no mention of colour being a stimulus or otherwise.

D.   Wrong. It states that liking or disliking a food is linked to its smell.

69:   B

A.   Wrong. He has stated a desire to be self-sufficient by 2014, a date which is non-binding.

B.   Correct. It is being "seized upon" by politicians whose electorates are increasingly against keeping troops in Afghanistan.

C.   Wrong. It says that "German police trainers will continue to teach local recruits" after 2014.

D.   Insufficient information. It doesn't mention the views of voters about the Taliban, only about the corruption seen in the government.

70:   B

A.   Insufficient information. AQIM operate in their areas but there is no mention of them wanting to create their own state.

B.   Correct. This is the crux of the text.

C.   Wrong. AQIM only pretend to fight for people like the Tuareg.

D.   Wrong. It says: "He was not the first hostage to be executed by AQIM..."

71:   A

A.   Correct. "The EU came under fire for its lack of cohesion..."

B.   Insufficient information. There is no mention of establishing an office in Brussels or anywhere else.

C.   Wrong. It states that the EU has yet to create an emergency force.

D.   Wrong. Mr Sarkozy has called upon Mr Barroso to set up an EU disasters rapid reaction force.

72:   C

A.   Wrong. It is defence contractors who are suspected of corruption, not the government.

B.   Wrong. Germany is selling two submarines worth over a billion euros.

C.   Correct. Defence contractors are suspected of paying bribes worth more than a million euros.

D.   Wrong. It says that at the same time as the government approved aid for Greece, prosecutors began investigating.

73:   A

A.   Correct. This was the view of Dr Sam Perlo-Freeman.

B.   Wrong. The survey shows that many countries are spending more on military expenditure, not actually killing more people.

C.   Wrong. The report is issued every year.

D.   Insufficient information. The report merely says that spending was up 5.9% on the previous year. It makes no mention of how this is distributed.

74:   A

A.   Correct. The social networking site allowed the demonstrators to organise their picnic but it also allowed the authorities to monitor it as well.

B.   Wrong. MALI fought against the police who were described as being like an army waiting for terrorists.

C. Wrong. Eating in public places is only banned during daylight hours during Ramadan.

D. Wrong. The police have now closed all their cases – "for now".

75:   A

A. Correct. Journalists are often silenced by intimidation, brutality and murder.

B. Insufficient information. It is currently 146th out of 175 nations but there is no mention of whether this is improving or not.

C. Wrong. Reporters Without Borders is Paris-based.

D. Insufficient information. There is no mention of a fire fight or of Congolese rebels being involved.

76:   C

A. Wrong. The Wagner festival was in 2004 and the "village of opera" project is described as something he had been working on "recently". It can be inferred that this was not in 2004.

B. Wrong. Christoph Schlingensief is described as a director, actor and artist but not an opera singer.

C. Correct. He directed Parsifal at the Bayreuth festival.

D. Insufficient information. There is no mention of any awards being won for this production.

77:   B

A. Wrong. The painting was returned a decade later.

B. Correct. One year after its return in 1988 a duplicate was sold for $43m.

C. Wrong. It was Van Gogh's Poppy Flowers that was stolen.

D. Insufficient information. We are only told that the security systems have not been working "for a long time". There is no indication that this is for 32 years.

78:   A

A. Correct. Mr Say wondered where the reinforcements were and why the helicopter took so long.

B. Wrong. Just the attack was replayed several times on television and news websites.

C. Wrong. The drones filming the events were unmanned.

D. Wrong. It states that they had desperately radioed for help.

79:   D

A. Wrong. Her problems with the Portuguese authorities were due to her age.

B. Wrong. Having won her court case in the Netherlands she has set out from Portugal or Gibraltar.

C. Wrong. The Dutch welfare authorities lost their court case and so, could not stop her.

D. Correct.

80:   D

A. Wrong. Mr Williamson said that there was "little evidence" to suggest this.

B. Wrong. It showed a dip for the third time in four months.

C. Wrong. Weaker economies have introduced austerity measures. It is not the austerity measures that have weakened those economies.

D. Correct. He said that although economic recovery was slowing down, it still retained "significant forward momentum."

81:   B

A. Wrong. The satellite is mapping gravity and its malfunction has nothing to do with that.

B. Correct. They remain "confident the situation can be recovered..."

C. Insufficient information. It was the main computer which experienced a processor error. The fault on the back-up computer is unspecified.

D. Insufficient information. It was struck by a glitch which may, or may not, be space debris.

82:   A

A. Correct. There were fears that the ash might damage the aircraft.

B. Wrong. It was floods caused by lava melting glacial ice which ruined farmland.

C.   Insufficient information. There were fears it might damage aircraft but there is no report that it did.

D.   Insufficient information. It says that 60 hectares of her land was wiped away but it doesn't indicate if this was all of her land.

83:   C

A.   Wrong. The court has only agreed to his extradition to the US.

B.   Insufficient information. There is no indication how Russia intends to treat the man if he is returned.

C.   Correct. It was a joint Thai-US sting operation which caught Mr Bout.

D.   Wrong. It says that Russia will "work to secure his return".

84:   A

A.   Correct. It states that it may be impinging on the rights of EU citizens.

B.   Wrong. It states that the Roma are a subset of the nomadic "travellers" group.

C.   Wrong. It states that the opposition politicians see it as a cynical move to seduce voters.

D.   Insufficient information. It is true that human traffickers are being deported but there is no mention that they exploit the illegal immigrants through forced labour.

85:   C

A.   Wrong. The secularity law was passed 105 years ago in 1905. Moreover, there was no mention of the French Revolution.

B.   Insufficient information. There is no evidence to suggest any lack of understanding of laïcité on the part of Muslims.

C.   Correct. Secularism endeavours to segregate religious belief from the agnostic sphere of public life.

D.   Insufficient information. The text says that critics are attacking the defenders of laïcité but it doesn't say that they are religious groups.

86:   B

A.   Wrong. It states that Iceland "unilaterally raised its mackerel quota".

B.   Correct. The Faroe Islands have increased their quota and Norway, along with the EU, insists that it is already over-fished.

C.   Insufficient information. There is no mention of how, or how long, the EU has implemented or enforced its fishing quotas.

D.   Wrong. Mr Lochhead was "enraged".

87:   A

A.   Correct. Bucharest simplified naturalization procedure for over a million people and Bulgaria did the same for nearly 2 million people.

B.   Wrong. It says that European nations are especially sensitive because of the enduring economic turmoil which fuel concerns over rising unemployment.

C.   Wrong. The Hungarian move followed Bucharest's move.

D.   Insufficient information. These are the only countries specified in the article but it doesn't say that they are the only ones.

88:   A

A.   Correct. It is its fastest rate since unification in 1990.

B.   Wrong. It is for its world-class machines and manufacturing products.

C.   Insufficient information. The rest of the eurozone experienced a growth of 1% but there is no detail as to how this is distributed.

D.   Wrong. It is two-thirds not one third.

89:   D

A.   Wrong. He was the head of the Islamic society at UCL.

B.   Wrong. It is the BBC that is warning of this.

C.   Insufficient information. They may well do but it isn't detailed here.

D.   Correct. Britain's university Islamic societies have a track record of producing terrorists and sympathizers who help spread extremism around the world.

90:   C

A. Wrong. It states that today Switzerland is "grubby" and in need of repair.

B. Wrong. The text refers to those fleeing Nazism after 1933, not 1917.

C. Correct. They met there to begin ending the Cold War.

D. Wrong. They employed "deregulated low-tax economics", not high taxes.

91:   A

A. Correct. It says that "few have been so unpopular".

B. Wrong. It says that they "gave control of interest rates to the independent Bank of England."

C. Wrong. It states that "Mr Blair even forced changes on the Conservative party..."

D. Insufficient information. It only states that he is the only Labour leader to win three consecutive elections.

92:   B

A. Wrong. The Archbishop's comments in response to the article were carried by CNN not The Times.

B. Correct. He states that spontaneous creation is "why the universe exists, why we exist".

C. Wrong. He states that God isn't necessary to start the universe.

D. Insufficient information. The Archbishop is the only one quoted as speaking out about the theory but it doesn't say that he is the only one.

93:   B

A. Wrong. There is no mention or hint of any other regions being affected.

B. Correct. He has allocated 1 billion roubles for aid.

C. Wrong. They are still trying to put out the fires at the time of writing.

D. Insufficient information. There is no mention of the forest's susceptibility to fires.

94:   A

A. Correct.

B. Insufficient information. We are not told from where the ship originally sailed.

C. Wrong. The champagne and beer were found on the same ship.

D. Wrong. It is claimed that the beer is still drinkable.

95:   C

A. Wrong. It was originally organised by a group of musicians.

B. Insufficient information. The festival has grown in popularity but we have no information on the popularity of trumpet playing in general.

C. Correct. And lots of each.

D . Wrong. There are "entire farmyards of pigs" roasting on spits.

96:   B

A. Insufficient information. This is probably true but the only information we are given is that the title is in French.

B. Correct. Ms Betancourt now lives in France.

C. Wrong. She was a presidential candidate not a tourist.

D. Wrong. It was the Colombian military who rescued her.

97:   B

A. Insufficient information. We are not told anything about the importance of Catalonia to the bullfighting fraternity.

B. Correct. It had 180,000 signatures from the public.

C. Wrong. It was initiated by calls from thousands of Catalonians to include bulls in the animal protection legislation.

D. Wrong. 68 to 55 does not constitute a two-thirds majority.

98:   A

A. Correct. It is known to cause death and paralysis.

B. Insufficient information. There is no reason

given for any variation in mosquito populations.

C.   Wrong. It is usually transmitted by mosquito or blood transfusion.

D.   Wrong. It is only one-fifth of people who show any symptoms.

99:   D

A.   Wrong. The designs merely explore the overlap between the fashion world and the architectural world.

B.   Wrong. They thought up the idea for the exhibition but assigned the work to four teams.

C.   Wrong. He sees this function as just as important as aesthetics.

D.   Correct. He sees protection and aesthetics as common to both.

100:   C

A.   Wrong. The guide indicates only the "must-does" on the cultural trail but it doesn't mention anything that would imply it is an "all-in exhaustive tour".

B.   Insufficient information. We are only told that there are 242 churches, statues, fountains and buildings but not how many of them are churches.

C.   Correct.

D.   Wrong. It states that Paris has a cultural life "past and present".

101:   A

A.   Correct. He states that he likes to hike to the Chateau de Commarque and he talks of details at Villa Rufolo which imply he has been there as well though this is not stated explicitly.

B.   Wrong. The current owner bought the chateau in 1968.

C.   Insufficient information. The writer certainly seems to have visited many times but there is no information given as to whether he was invited or not.

D.   Wrong. He based the second act in a setting inspired by the Rufolo gardens.

102:   D

A.   Wrong. It states that "nearly all nuclear power reactors … are fuelled with uranium".

B.   Wrong. The IFR does not create new fuel but uses its existing fuel more completely.

C.   Insufficient information. There may well be research in this area but it isn't detailed here.

D.   Correct. They do this to make the fission more effective.

103:   D

A.   Wrong. It states there are two other modern reptiles that do this.

B.   Wrong. The skink in question is currently alive there.

C.   Insufficient information. While it is true that one-fifth of snakes bear live young, we are not told the benefit of this evolutionary change.

D.   Correct. It gives scientists a rare glimpse of this evolutionary stage.

104:   D

A.   Insufficient information. They have found evidence of former rivers and seas but it doesn't indicate whether signs of life have been detected.

B.   Wrong. Although greenhouse gasses harm the Earth by raising its temperature, this is seen as a benefit for Mars as it is so cold.

C.   Insufficient information. There is no mention of any laboratory experiments having been performed.

D.   Correct. Hopefully, this would be released by raising the temperature sufficiently to melt it.

105:   C

A.   Insufficient information. They certainly had contrary views but there is no indication that they ever debated this together, heatedly or otherwise.

B.   Wrong. It was Linnaeus who had a problem with the Venus Flytrap.

C.   Correct. They both saw them as special but had differing ideas on their adaptation.

D.   Insufficient information. Those familiar with

his life know that he did, but it doesn't say anything about it here.

106: C

A.   Wrong. Kaziranga is seen as a "thundering conservation success story".

B.   Insufficient information. It may or may not have scores of wild goats, we cannot tell from the text.

C.   Correct. "Agriculture had taken over most of the fertile river valleys that the species depends on".

D.   Wrong. When set up in 1908 there were about a dozen rhinos in it.

107: C

A.   Wrong. Ardi is "much more informative about … the nature of the common ancestor we share with chimpanzees."

B.   Wrong. The discovery was 15 years ago.

C.   Correct. They hate to use such hyperbole but they do it anyway.

D.   Insufficient information. Ardi was discovered in Ethiopia but we are not informed where Lucy was found.

108: A

A.   Correct. It raises the possibility of "resurrecting" ancient texts in other languages.

B.   Insufficient information. It is certainly closely related to Hebrew but we have no information on its similarity to Aramaic.

C.   Wrong. Specialists first decoded the language in 1932.

D.   Wrong. It was last used around 1200 B.C. which is around 3200 years ago.

109: A

A.   Correct.

B.   Wrong. It is the sceptics who say this; the advocates believe it is a great improvement.

C.   Insufficient information. It seems likely but there is no information to support this.

D.   Wrong. They are, at present, being tested in these environments.

110: A

A.   Correct. A strong password can be useless against keylogging software.

B.   Insufficient information. This is exactly what some sceptics would believe but it doesn't mention it here.

C.   Wrong. Mr Herley said this of antivirus software not keylogging software.

D.   Wrong. Received wisdom is not to store your password anywhere.

111: C

A.   Wrong. It states that the franc has been pushed upward by the relatively healthy growth.

B.   Wrong. It states that tourism is a sector most people don't think of as an export which implies that it really is.

C.   Correct. As the franc rises in value, exports become more expensive and so sales drop. This directly affects employment.

D.   Wrong. Watchmaking accounts for 50,000 jobs.

112: A

A.   Correct. We are told that Zofia Posmysz is an Auschwitz survivor.

B.   Wrong. We are told that Martha is the protagonist or main character.

C.   Insufficient information. Walter is the husband of Lisa who was an SS overseer but we are not told whether Walter hides a Nazi past.

D.   Wrong. We are told that the work is a novel which, by definition, is fictitious.

113: A

A.   Correct. They were due to drop in 2014 but it will now be next year.

B.   Wrong. It states that the reforms will benefit those whose pensions have been cut in the austerity drive.

C.   Insufficient information. The restricted professions certainly include lorry drivers and pharmacists but we cannot tell about engineers.

D.   Wrong. He will be streamlining the railways, which generally means job losses.

114:   C

A.   Insufficient information. There is no mention of a theme or tone for the project.

B.   Wrong. It says "...it is happening. New buildings are sprouting up..."

C.   Correct. We are told that Skopje is the capital of FYR Macedonia and that buildings are sprouting up along the banks of the Vardar.

D.   Wrong. It is the earthquake of 1963 that is responsible for the destruction.

115:   B

A.   Wrong. We are told that "priests abound" and so are plentiful.

B.   Correct. Demonstrations and marches against church teachings can take place freely.

C.   Insufficient information. There is nothing to indicate that the church would give formal approval to gay marriage.

D.   Wrong. 12% is more than one out of ten.

116:   A

A.   Correct. It states that the majority are in volcanically active regions, which implies that a few are not.

B.   Wrong. It states "they work even in parts of the world that are not volcanically active..."

C.   Insufficient information. There is no information about depth limits or cost-effectiveness.

D.   Wrong. Wells are bored into hot rocks and water is injected.

117:   B

A.   Wrong. The Basque region spans the Spanish-French border.

B.   Correct. The government remains sceptical and ETA did violate its last cease-fire after 9 months.

C.   Insufficient information. It is held responsible for 829 deaths but we are not informed as to whether they have claimed responsibility or not.

D.   Wrong. It states: "The new cease-fire would be the latest of many declared over the years."

118:   C

A.   Wrong. The attendance checks are to encourage MEPs to remain throughout the debate while there is nothing written in the text to suggest that Mr Barroso has arranged them.

B.   Wrong. This is according to Euractiv.

C.   Correct. It states that Strasbourg is the Parliament's second home.

D.   Insufficient information. It does not state whether or not this is the sole source of income for the MEPs.

119:   A

A.   Correct. He was sentenced to one year in prison but he has already served nearly half of that.

B.   Wrong. "MI6 is Britain's overseas intelligence service."

C.   Insufficient information. There is nothing said about the usefulness of the information to the Dutch agents.

D.   Wrong. It states: "...personal details that could have endangered agents."

120:   B

A.   Wrong. It says that pushing back migrants at sea can violate their human rights.

B.   Correct. Europe sees these migrants as a perennial problem.

C.   Insufficient information. We are only told that the migrants use Libya as a launch point but not where the migrants originate.

D.   Wrong. The money is for Libya to stop the migrants setting off in the first place.

121:   A

A.   Correct. Along with increased buying power.

B.   Wrong. The currency is free floating and fully exchangeable.

C.   Wrong. Solidarity helped topple the Berlin Wall.

D.   Wrong. The average consumer's buying power has increased six times.

122: A

A. Correct. The co-ordination will ensure that at least one British or French carrier is available at all times.

B. Insufficient information. There is no indication of the French attitude towards this proposal.

C. Insufficient information. There is no mention of co-ordinating exercises or aircraft, only the refits of the ships.

D. Wrong. The British sank the French ships to stop them falling into German hands.

123: B

A. Wrong. It had previously been tested on rats and dogs.

B. Correct. This was a known practice of 19th century scientists.

C. Wrong. It is called "orphan" because pharmaceutical companies don't want anything to do with it.

D. Insufficient information. There is no mention of whether Dr. Huberty needs funds to pay for his medication.

124: C

A. Wrong. The Danish politicians are criticising the TV company for banning the ad.

B. Wrong. The Danes are calling for observers to be sent from the Council of Europe.

C. Correct. They are criticising the TV company for banning the ad and call it censorship.

D. Insufficient information. It has been banned by one TV station but we are not informed whether or not all stations have done so.

125: B

A. Wrong. More and more architects are saying that ugliness has its virtues.

B. Correct. It stands out amid the architectural putrescence that Hanover has to offer.

C. Insufficient information. It may well be but it doesn't mention this here as it just mentions Germany in general, which might exclude Berlin as an exception.

D. Wrong. It is the state legislators who are pushing for its demolition.

126: A

A. Correct. 19 prime ministers in 50 years is less than 3 years each on average.

B. Insufficient information. We are not told whether South Tyrol's situation has affected the Italian situation as a whole.

C. Insufficient information. There is no mention of whether or not Austria has any government debt.

D. Wrong. He has held the post since 1989 which is 21 years, less than half of the last 50.

127: C

A. Insufficient information. We are told that it offered comfort to her and her family for 25 months but there is no mention of whether this was a daily comfort or not.

B. Wrong. It was the judge who gave the tree a reprieve.

C. Correct. It states that it did little damage as it fell.

D. Wrong. It was not cut down; it fell down in high winds.

128: B

A. Wrong. The Dutch speaking area of Belgium is in the north.

B. Correct. King Albert has already appointed new negotiators to thrash out an agreement.

C. Wrong. Mr. Di Rupo is the francophone leader not the Flemish leader.

D. Wrong. This is just one of the main issues.

129: B

A. Wrong. Mr Fini was expelled from the PDL party rather than leaving voluntarily.

B. Correct. It says "...he would avoid steps that could trigger an early election."

C. Insufficient information. We are told he has the backing of 34 lower house deputies but we cannot tell if this is a majority or not.

D. Insufficient information. We cannot tell whether he was speaking personally against the prime minister or not.

130:   A

A.   Correct. These measures were taken "to reduce the budget deficit".

B.   Wrong. The pay cuts were made to meet conditions for a loan from the IMF.

C.   Insufficient information. The loan was from the IMF, the EU and the World Bank but we are not told how much came from each source.

D.   Wrong. He sacked 5 ministers and the economy minister has said that he will quit.

131:   C

A.   Insufficient information. There is no information on whether they were also involved in narcotics trafficking.

B.   Wrong. The tests were done in the United States.

C.   Correct. It states that it is an ex-Soviet republic, it is a rebel area and prone to narcotics smuggling.

D.   Insufficient information. They are awaiting results of tests in Germany to determine its origin.

132:   B

A.   Insufficient information. There was a demonstration in Pushkin Square but there is no indication as to whether or not this was successful in getting the road building stopped.

B.   Correct. The police wouldn't allow the amplification gear through their security lines.

C.   Wrong. The protest had been sanctioned by the Moscow authorities.

D.   Wrong. The concert was to protest at the building of a motorway.

133:   A

A.   Correct. It states "... China is growing fast, by nearly 10% a year..." but also that "...China's drinkers provide slender profits."

B.   Wrong. It states that America's market has levelled off or is in decline.

C.   Wrong. We are told that the market has grown from virtually nothing in just 2 decades.

D.   Insufficient information. ABI is one of the 4 largest brewers but we are not told which is biggest.

134:   B

A.   Insufficient information. We are given no information as to why he gave this ruling.

B.   Correct. It represents a huge leap forward whatever happens in the Supreme Court.

C.   Wrong. It states that his decision is certain to be appealed.

D.   Wrong. It states that there has been a long struggle for civil rights for homosexuals.

135:   D

A.   Wrong. There is no sign of a let-up on either side.

B.   Insufficient information. There is no indication how or why the 28,000 people have been killed.

C.   Wrong. It is a section of the paper that details murders and violent accidents.

D.   Correct. The nota roja is expanding "as fighting over the drug trail to the United States inspires ever-greater feats of violence."

136:   C

A.   Insufficient information. There is no information on whether Egypt is an autocracy.

B.   Wrong. He was full of expletives.

C.   Correct. He ran elections in 2005 and 2006.

D.   Wrong. One runs the West bank and the other runs Gaza.

137:   B

A.   Insufficient information. It doesn't say whether the device can be adjusted in this way or not.

B.   Correct. It selectively kills the female mosquitoes which are malarial.

C.   Wrong. It determines the frequency of the insect's wing beat.

D.   Wrong. It only kills those with a low frequency wing beat which identifies them as female and carrying malaria.

138:   A

A.   Correct. It states that it "...no longer meets our rigorous food safety standards..."

B.   Wrong. It will stop producing it by 2015.

C.   Wrong. Potatoes and watermelons are also mentioned.

D.   Wrong. It was 25 years ago that more than 2000 people were poisoned by it.

139:   C

A.   Insufficient information. There is no information given about side-effects.

B.   Wrong. They fought the campaign because of anti-US sentiment.

C.   Correct. The incidence of the disease was "drastically reduced".

D.   Wrong. It states that the disease was supposed to have been eradicated long ago and the latest effort was sabotaged e.g. in Nigeria.

140:   A

A.   Correct. The definition of scientific misconduct includes plagiarism in research.

B.   Wrong. It states that it often leads to evidence confiscation.

C.   Wrong. It states that 14% reported having witnessed falsification by other people.

D.   Insufficient information. There is no mention of how much funding Mr. Michelek's research has received.

141:   A

A.   Correct. The agreements aim to ensure that waters are not over-fished.

B.   Wrong. It states that the EU makes agreements within regional and international organisations.

C.   Insufficient information. This is true of the EU but there is no information about other wealthy nations.

D.   Wrong. It is largely invested in the fishing industries.

142:   B

A.   Wrong. The reasons given for the current

inequity are "national circumstances and traditions".

B.   Correct. This is the basic premise of the text.

C.   Wrong. The text implies that these are goals to be achieved rather than a long standing situation.

D.   Insufficient information. It states that health needs to be taken into account with other polices but there is no evidence to suggest that it isn't yet so in some areas.

143:   A

A.   Correct. Tuberculosis is listed as a major disease and one of their priorities.

B.   Wrong. They finance an effort to combat consumption of tobacco.

C.   Wrong. This is merely the budget on promoting healthy living etc.

D.   Wrong. It states that there is already funding for gender issues.

144:   A

A.   Correct. Ireland is now one of the wealthiest countries but Luxembourg is the wealthiest.

B.   Wrong. It is GDP per capita that is the standard measure.

C.   Insufficient information. There is no mention of how much benefit Romania and Bulgaria have received since joining.

D.   Insufficient information. It is a goal to improve the wealth of the newer members but it doesn't state whether it should be done by emulating Ireland.

145:   B

A.   Insufficient information. There is no specific mention of Slovenia's circumstances.

B.   Correct. The Cohesion Policy focuses on convergence which means eliminating disadvantages such as "poor quality schools" and "higher joblessness".

C.   Wrong. The €350 billion is 36% of their total budget.

D.   Wrong. It states: "The EU has used the entry of these countries to reorganise and restructure its regional spending."

146:   A

1.   Correct. The Cohesion Fund is for, amongst other things, "the development of renewable energy".

2.   Wrong. The money comes from three different sources, the ERDF, the ESF and the Cohesion fund.

3.   Insufficient information. There is no specific information about the distribution of the poorer regions.

4.   Insufficient information. The ERDF cover various types of projects which may create jobs but it doesn't explicitly say so.

147:   C

1.   Insufficient information. We are told the 17 countries have at least one region with a GDP below 75% of the EU average be we cannot tell whether any or all of them are below 75% overall.

2.   Wrong. Only 17 do. The remaining 10 can only claim "...for funding to support innovation and research, sustainable development, and job training..."

3.   Correct. The fund reserved for regions with a GDP below 75% of the EU average concerns 17 of the 27 countries.

4.   Wrong. The policy is to dovetail with the Lisbon agenda.

148:   A

1.   Correct. The EU matches private investment so closing the gap is a joint effort.

2.   Wrong. It states that the EU must improve its record in this area.

3.   Insufficient information. There is no mention of how difficult the patent process is.

4.   Wrong. It talks of the "new European Institute" so it cannot have long promoted anything.

149:   B

A.   Insufficient information. It states that the EU currently relies on other countries but there is no indication which countries they may be.

B.   Correct. The EU does want to be less reliant on other countries and GPS is a key reason.

C.   Insufficient information. It does state that the Global Monitoring for Environment and Security wants to "deal with ... security crises" which could mean "develop defensive weapons in space" but there is no indication that this is one of the primary aims.

D.   Wrong. The current system has no support for search-and-rescue. This is a proposed addition for the new system.

150:   A

A.   Correct. It states that they keep an eye on the decisions of governments to see that they are fair.

B.   Wrong. It says that governments set the taxes but that the EU monitors them for fairness as these countries are bound by a code of conduct.

C.   Insufficient information. There is no information given of how the EU might encourage taxes on individuals.

D.   Wrong. A code of conduct prevents this kind of behaviour.

4.   Succeeding in Numerical Reasoning Tests

Introduction

It is often said that the difficulty in taking numerical reasoning tests lies not in finding the actual answer to the question but doing it within the limited time available. This observation is correct inasmuch as these tests do not require complex mathematical calculations but rather the ability to:

- *identify data relevant to answering the question from a larger set of information*

- *identify the quickest way to extract the answer from the relevant data*

- *discover one or several possible shortcuts that will allow us to arrive at the answer quickly*

- *determine the level of accuracy required to select the correct answer, and*

- *make quick mental calculations*

In order to be prepared for the above, there are certain aspects of numerical reasoning tests that we must be aware of.

First of all, the "alternative reality" of a numerical reasoning test is different from what we are used to in everyday life – relevant data is not provided in a clean format but is rather hidden among other pieces of information that we may call "noise". Our first task is to always identify what we will need to work with from the information provided and avoid getting bogged down in wondering why other data might also be present.

Secondly, such tests have a surprising tendency to reach back to basic mathematical skills that may in fact come naturally to a secondary school student but are often lost during later academic stages and at the workplace. It is essential to refresh our basic calculus (see for instance www.calculus.org or www.sosmath.com and other sites).

Also, many candidates dread the numerical reasoning test simply because it is based on mathematics and they have always considered this discipline their weakness. What we must realize here is that the "mathematical" aspect of numerical reasoning tests is rather basic – addition, subtraction, multiplication, division, fractions and percentages will always be sufficient to perform the necessary calculations. As we will see, in a large number of cases even such calculations are unnecessary and arriving at the correct answer is rather based on an intuitive insight or the realization of a relationship between figures that is in fact right in front of our eyes – we just need to learn to see it.

It is also useful to note here that, just like in the case of verbal reasoning, the broad term "numerical reasoning" may be used to designate various test types related to the handling of numbers, calculations and data, such as:

- **Computation tests** are basic tests that measure the speed at which the test-taker is able to make basic mental calculations such as addition, subtraction, multiplication and division (e.g. "how much is 45+19+52-38?").

- **Estimation tests** resemble computation tests in that the calculations to be made are very similar, but the numbers with which you have to work may be greater. The point of the test is not to measure ability to perform the actual calculation but rather the speed and accuracy at which candidates can approximate the result of the calculation. The aim is to select an answer option that will be close to what the result would be if the actual calculation was performed (e.g. 226 divided by 1000 is approximately 1/4).

- **Numerical reasoning tests** represent a higher level where the focus is not on the actual ability to make calculations but rather the insight required to find out which calculations need to be performed to arrive at the answer. In other words, applied reasoning is tested. These tests are usually text-based in which a certain scenario involving numbers is described – it is this situation that the test-taker is expected to interpret in mathematical terms. To take an example of such a scenario: "There are 300 people in a group. Each person in the group likes either coffee or tea. Five times as many people like coffee as tea. How many people in the group like tea?"

- **Data interpretation tests** are similar to the above but instead of using a text, a "scenario" or story as the input, the basis of the exercise is a data set presented in the form of a table, a chart, or any combination of these (e.g. "Based on the table's figures, how many more Spanish speaking people immigrated to Spain in 1990 than in 2000?")

EPSO's numerical reasoning tests are most closely modeled on the latter two test types. Yet it is easy to see how each subsequent test type in this "hierarchy" builds on skills and routine that is measured in a lower-level test type. Quick estimations can only be made if we can make quick calculations as well. When you are faced with text-based numerical reasoning tests and you need to find a way to arrive at the answer, once you have done that, you must actually perform the required calculations or estimations to end up with the correct figure. When it comes to data interpretation based on tables and charts, the task is very similar to those in a text-based numerical reasoning test, with the added twist of having the data presented in a tabular or graphical format.

Let's now turn our attention to a real numerical reasoning test item and see how the above skills come into play.

Mobile Phone Subscriptions in EU Member States (thousands)

	2005	2006	2007
Bulgaria	1594	1957	2451
Denmark	3799	4228	4982
Greece	5511	6824	9191
Poland	1759	1819	1928

What percentage of the mobile phone subscriptions shown did Denmark account for in 2005?

A.   10%;   B.   20%;   C.   30%;   D.   40%;   E.   50%.

Using the above sample test item, we can demonstrate how the above-described skills (data interpretation, numerical reasoning, estimation and computation) can be used to quickly and efficiently solve EPSO's numerical reasoning tests.

The first step is to interpret the data that we need to work with.

In the present case, the first step is to determine which figures from the table we actually need. The question concerns the number of mobile phone subscriptions in 2005, so we can concentrate on the 2005 column in the table knowing that all the other figures are irrelevant to the task.

Next, we need to figure out what calculations we actually need to perform – in other words, we apply our numerical reasoning skills to the task at hand. Since the question is about Denmark's share of the total number of mobile phone subscriptions in the four countries shown in the table, we need to calculate the total (by adding up the individual figures for the four countries), and then calculate Denmark's share in it (by dividing Denmark's share by the total). Finally, we need to convert the result of this division into a percentage figure (multiplying it by 100).

The next question we have to decide is whether we actually need to perform the exact above calculations at all. We can decide this by considering if there is any possibility of estimating certain results. Let's look at the four numbers we need to add up from this perspective:

1594

3799

5511

1759

Whenever making a decision about the use of estimation, we must take into account the answer options first. In our case, these are percentages which are quite far apart from one another: 10%, 20%, 30%, 40% and 50% - this will tell us that the level of accuracy required to answer the question is not too high and you can feel free to "guesstimate".

Looking at the numbers, we can see that they lend themselves quite nicely to rounding up and down. By doing this, we can arrive at some more "convenient" numbers:

1600 (rounded up)

3800 (rounded up)

5500 (rounded down)

1800 (rounded up)

Now that the numbers are easy to work with, we can perform some actual computation. Since all numbers end in 00, we can disregard those two digits and work with two-digit numbers as their relative proportions (percentages) will remain the same. Add up these four numbers to get to the total number of subscriptions:

16+38+55+18 = 127

Remember that we are looking for a percentage. This means that we do not need to add back the two zeroes – that would only be needed if we had to arrive at an actual value. Instead, we can just compare our total (127) with Denmark's number: 38.

38 / 127 = 0.296

To convert this to a percentage, simply multiply the number by 100:

0.296 x 100 = 29.6%

Remember at this point that we rounded all the numbers up and down a bit – this explains why our result is not exactly the same as any of the answer options provided. It is, however, overwhelmingly clear that it is closest to Answer C (30%), which will be the correct answer.

Let's take stock of what we did in solving this test problem:

1. We interpreted the data in the table.

2. We applied our reasoning to determine what calculations we needed to perform.

3. We made estimations to simplify our calculations.

4. Finally, we performed the actual calculations.

Hopefully, this example demonstrates how the various skills required for succeeding in numerical reasoning depend on one another. If you keep these simple principles in mind and follow the steps laid out above, you will gain a systematic approach to solving all numerical reasoning tests successfully. There are, of course, things to look out for in test items, traps to avoid and tactics to use and become accustomed to.

Based on the required skills and the aspects introduced above, we will provide an overview of the following:

- Mental calculus
- Order of magnitude
- Percentages and percentage points
- Estimation
- Equations
- Tables and charts

After reviewing these various methods and aspects, we will discuss how to approach numerical reasoning tests, what to focus on in each exercise and how to practice for the exam.

Mental Calculus

If you read through the information made available to candidates before the exam it will, based on recent data, be stated that an on-screen calculator may be used during the numerical reasoning test. EPSO may also make a physical calculator available for you to use at the exam centre. In light of this, you might be doubtful as to why it is so important to be able to perform quick mental calculations. There are several important reasons for this:

- The calculator provided may be quite slow to use and its layout may be unfamiliar to you, which might make its use counter-productive
- There are certain calculations that are always faster to perform in your head
- Overreliance on a calculator may make you less intuitive and prevent you from realizing whether certain calculations are really required to answer the question

It is therefore strongly advised to first practice as if no calculators were provided and start to use such devices only later when you have learned all the necessary ways of carrying out calculations.

Fractions

As mentioned above, certain types of calculations can quite simply be performed more efficiently without any "technical assistance". One such example is the handling of fractions (as in the illustration below).

Consider the following scenario. We are looking for the proportion of households with broadband access among all households in Estonia. Based on the data provided, you will

Numerator

$$\frac{3}{5} \times \frac{4}{6}$$

Denominator

realize that approximately three in five households in Estonia have an internet connection and among those, four in six have broadband access. One way of approaching this calculation would be to use the calculator to do the following:

$3 \div 5 = 0.6$ (proportion of households with internet access)

$4 \div 6 = 0.666$ (proportion of internet-connected households with broadband access, rounded to three decimal points)

$0.6 * 0.666 = 0.3996$ (proportion of households with broadband access among all households)

If we also have the total number of households, say 2,000,000, we then perform one additional calculation:

$0.3996 * 2,000,000 = 799200$

Let's see how this calculation would go without the use of a calculator, by using fractions:

$3/5 \times 4/6 = 12 / 30$ (fractions are multiplied by multiplying the first numerator by the second numerator and the first denominator by the second denominator)

$12 / 30 = 4 / 10$ (we can then simplify the fraction by finding a number that both the numerator and the denominator can be divided by)

It is easy to see that the above two calculations can be performed very quickly bymental arithmetic. Also, the final figure we arrive at is extremely convenient – now we know that four in ten households have broadband internet access.

If we consider that there are 2,000,000 households, the remaining calculation will also be very simple:

$2,000,000 / 10 = 200,000$ (by removing one decimal, we will get the number equal to one in ten households)

$200,000 \times 4 = 800,000$ (by multiplying that by 4, we get four-tenths of all households)

There are two observations to make here:

- We arrived at the required figure by making extremely simple calculations with easy, round numbers
- Using fractions is actually more accurate than the "calculator", because during the first method, we "truncated" one of the figures given its decimals

Calculations with Fractions

Multiplication: **Division:**   **Addition and subtraction:**

Lowest Common Multiple

$$\frac{3}{5} \times \frac{4}{6} = \frac{12}{30} \qquad \frac{4}{7} \div \frac{2}{3} = \frac{4}{7} \times \frac{3}{2} = \frac{12}{14} \qquad \frac{2}{3} + \frac{3}{7} = \frac{14}{21} + \frac{9}{21} = \frac{23}{21}$$

Multiplication

Method

If we need to multiply two fractions, we first multiply the two numerators (the numbers at the top) and then the two denominators (the numbers at the bottom).

Example of Application

Imagine that you are given a table showing Spain's population in millions. You are also given the following two pieces of information in the question text itself:

- one in five Spaniards considers sport to be their favourite hobby

- of those who consider sport as their favourite hobby, two out of three name football as their preferred choice

Your task is to calculate how many Spaniards consider football their favourite hobby. A quick answer to this question can be found using fractions.

"One in five can be described as $\frac{1}{5}$ and "two out of three" can be described as $\frac{2}{3}$. Based on this, the calculation would go as follows:

Number of Spaniards with Football as Favourite Hobby

= *Population x $\frac{1}{5}$ x $\frac{2}{3}$ = $\frac{2}{15}$ x Population*

Now we can perform a simple calculation with the data above. We divide Spain's population by 15 and multiply the result by 2, and our task is complete.

Division

Method

If we need to divide a fraction by another fraction, our first task is to turn the operation into multiplication. We do this by 'inverting' the numerator and the denominator in one of the fractions. This way, $\frac{2}{3}$ would become $\frac{3}{2}$, and so on.

Next, we multiply the two numerators and then the two denominators in the same way as we do when multiplying fractions.

Example of Application

Imagine that you are given the following information:

40% of Thailand's annual rice production is equal to half of China's annual rice consumption. If all of China's rice consumption would be covered by imports from Thailand, what percentage of Thailand's production would need to be imported?

We can transcribe the above information with fractions as follows.

$\frac{4}{10}$ x *Thailand's production = $\frac{1}{2}$ x China's consumption*

We are looking for China's total consumption in terms of Thailand's total production. This means that we want only China's total consumption on one side of the equation, so we need to divide both sides of the equation by $\frac{1}{2}$.

China's consumption = $\frac{4}{10} \div \frac{1}{2}$ x Thailand's production

We can now invert the numerator and the denominator (say, in the second fraction) and then perform the multiplication as described above.

China's consumption $= \frac{4}{10} \times \frac{2}{1} = \frac{8}{10} \times$ *Thailand's production*

The answer to the question is, then, that China's rice consumption is equal to 80% of Thailand's rice production.

Addition and Subtraction

Method

When adding or subtracting fractions, we need to make sure first that the denominators are the same in both fractions. We can achieve this by finding the smallest number that can be divided by both denominators. If our two denominators are 3 and 7, as in the illustration at the start of this section, that number will be 21. Once we have done that, we need to multiply the numerators by the same number as the one with which we had to multiply the denominator in the same fraction. In the illustration, the numerator in the left fraction needs to be multiplied by 7 and the numerator in the right fraction needs to be multiplied by 3.

The last step is to simply add up the two numerators.

Example of Application

Imagine that you have the following two pieces of information:

• three in ten Germans believe that the budget deficit needs to be reduced

• three in five Germans believe that the budget deficit needs to be kept at the current level

Based on the wording of the above, we can be sure that there is no overlap between the two groups – one group believes in reduction, the other in maintaining the current level.

We are looking for the following data:

What percentage of Germans believes that the budget deficit needs to be kept at the current level or reduced?

To answer the above question with fractions, we need to express "three in ten" and "three in five" in the form of fractions and then add up the two.

"three in ten" $= \frac{3}{10}$

"three in five" $= \frac{3}{5}$

The proportion we are looking for, then, is as follows:

$\frac{3}{10} + \frac{3}{5}$

We will notice that in this particular case, only the second fraction will need to be "converted". If we multiply both the numerator and the denominator of that fraction by 2, the two denominators will be identical and we can perform the addition.

$\frac{3}{10} + \frac{3}{5} = \frac{3}{10} + \frac{6}{10} = \frac{9}{10} = 90\%$

By using fractions, we can answer the question by saying that 90% of Germans believe the budget deficit needs to be reduced or at least kept at current levels.

When solving numerical reasoning tests, it is always worth considering for a second whether we can take advantage of fractions – they are an extremely powerful tool in reducing seemingly complex relationships into the simplest of calculations.

Order of Magnitude

	Nuclear Electricity Generation in the EU			
		Electricity Generated (millions MWh)		
	Population in 2005 (thousands)	*2005*	*2006*	*2007*
France	61013	452	446	440
Hungary	10078	163	158	150
Poland	38198	44	51	67
Ukraine	46936	87	90	93

How many MWh did France generate on average for each person in the country in 2005?

A.   0.74

B.   7.4

C.   74

D.   740

E.   7400

An order of magnitude is a scale of amounts where each amount is in a fixed ratio to the amount preceding it. The most common ratio is 1:10, which means that the next amount in a scale can be calculated by multiplying the previous figure by 10.

For example: 1, 10, 100, 1000, 10000 …and so on…

If we look at the above answer options, we can see that that is exactly the situation we have here:

0.74, 7.4, 74, 740, 7400

When we are faced with a set of numbers like the ones above, it gives us an important hint that the actual calculation of the figure may not really be necessary – all we need to figure out is the order of magnitude of the correct answer.

Let us consider the above sample test from the perspective of whether we can take advantage of this observation.

We have the following information:

•   The amount of nuclear energy France generated in 2005 – in million MWh – **452**

•   The population of France in thousands – **61013**

Since the answer options only differ in their order of magnitude, we can be quite flexible in rounding our number up or down to simplify our calculations.

Let us round 452 down to 450 and 61013 down to 60000. You can disregard the exact number of digits for a second. What is the relationship between the numbers 45 and 60? If you think for a second about time (45 minutes out of 60), you will realize that 45/60 is equal to three quarters. Expressed in decimal terms, this is 0.75. Our answer options include the digits 7 and 4 – this difference is caused by having rounded down the numbers.

Remember – we do not need to be particularly accurate in this case, all that we are looking for is the number of digits in the correct answer. Now turn your attention to those zeroes we disregarded so far.

Energy Production: 452 million MWh – we will need to add six zeroes here: **452,000,000 MWh**

Population: 61013 thousand – we will need to add three zeroes here: **61,013, 000**

If we turn back to our simplified figures, our calculation would look like this:

450 million divided by 60 million

We could use a calculator to obtain the result here, but let us recall what we said about time above – 45 minutes out of 60 minutes is three quarters, that is, 0.75. So, if the electricity generation was 45 million instead of 450 million, our two numbers would be:

45 million divided by 60 million – this would correspond to three quarters, that is, 0.75 – the closest answer option to this would be Answer A. We, however, removed one zero from the end of our electricity generation figure just now, which we need to add back. Adding a 'zero' to a figure is the equivalent of multiplying it by 10:

0.75 x 10 = 7.5

The above is closest to Answer B and that is the correct answer.

Percentages and Percentage points

The information in this section may seem trivial, yet mixing up two concepts (*percentage change* and *percentage point change*) can prove fatal when taking a numerical reasoning test.

Let us consider the following example (some lines are blocked out):

	European Airlines, 2009			
Airline	Turnover (in million €)	Number of passengers (in millions)	Number of airplanes	Average capacity utilization (in %)
Air France (FR)	1960	32	140	82

In many numerical reasoning tests, you will be faced with data where calculation of the correct answer will require working with percentages. A straightforward case is where one figure (for example the number of television sets in Italy) is an amount, and the other factor (for example the proportion of high-definition capable devices) is a percentage. In such cases, the calculation is obvious:

Number of television sets * Percentage of high-definition devices

Let us, however, consider another example. There are cases when both figures are proportions or percentages. What happens when the first piece of data (the capacity utilisation of Air France airplanes) and the second piece of data (the % change in capacity utilisation, for example) are both percentages?

Suppose that the question based on the above table is the following:

"How much was the capacity utilisation of Air France in 2008 if its capacity utilisation was 10% worse than in 2009?"

In the above example, where 82% capacity utilisation decreases by 10%, our natural instinct would be to perform the following calculation:

82% -10% = 72%, therefore the capacity utilisation in 2008 was 72%.

Not surprisingly, this would *not* be the correct answer. For comparison, keep in mind how we would calculate a 10% decrease of a regular amount, for example 550:

550 * (1 − 10%) = 550 * 90% = 550 * 0.9 = 495

Now apply the above logic to capacity utilisation:

82% * (1-10%) = 82% * 90% = 82% * 0.9 = 73.8%

We can see that the correct calculation yields a significantly different result from what our initial instinct suggested.

When it comes to percentage changes in values that are themselves percentages, what many people consider a 10 per cent change (for example 82% to 72%) is in fact a 10 *percentage point* change.

Through an intuitive example, we will be able to appreciate the fundamental difference between the two concepts.

Suppose that an imaginary central bank in the EU has an interest rate of 10%. Now let's take a look at possible changes to this interest rate:

- If the interest rate drops by 9 *percentage points*, the new interest rate will be 1%

- If the interest rate drops by 9 *percent*, the new interest rate will be 9.1%

- A 1% interest rate can decrease by a maximum of 1 percentage point, but it can decrease by as much as 100 per cent – both resulting in a 0% interest rate

Estimation

In a previous section, when calculating the per-capita electricity generation of France, we applied a sort of estimation to get to the correct answer. In that case, the estimation took the form of concentrating only on the number of digits in the correct answer. There are cases, however, where we need to be a little more precise than that.

Consider the following example:

	European Airlines, 2009			
Airline	Turnover (in million €)	Number of passengers (in millions)	Number of airplanes	Average capacity utilization (in %)
Air France (FR)	1960	32	140	82

"Based on the above table, how many passengers would Air France have transported in 2009 if its capacity utilisation had been 10% worse?"

a) 28.8 million

b) 23.6 million

c) 35.2 million

d) 35.9 million

Again, let us first consider the less innovative (and therefore more time-consuming) way of calculating the correct answer first.

The data we will work with are:

• Number of passengers in millions

• Capacity utilisation %

• The fact that capacity utilisation decreased by 10% as compared to the actual figure in the table

The first thing we would do is calculate the new capacity utilisation. An important point to mention here is the difference between percentage change and percentage point change, as discussed above.

New capacity utilisation = 82% * (1 − 10%) = 82% * 90% = 82% * 0.9 = 73.8%

One mistake we could make here is equating the figure for new number of passengers transported with the following:

32 million * 73.8% = 32 million * 0.738 = 23.616 million

Why is the above calculation incorrect? We must bear in mind that the number 32 million is actually equal to 82% of the total capacity of Air France, since its capacity utilisation according to the table was 82%.

We also know the new capacity utilisation figure (73.8%), but we must also calculate total capacity (X). We know the following:

X * 0.82 = 32 million (82% of the total capacity is 32 million passengers)

Let's solve the equation for X:

X = 32 million / 0.82 = 39.02 million

We can now calculate the number of passengers transported at 73.8% capacity utilisation:

39.02 * 0.738 = 28.8 million

Answer A is in fact the correct answer.

While the above series of calculations were all correct, we must always be suspicious when so many raw calculations are required to get to the correct answer. Do not forget that numerical reasoning is not a mathematical exercise in the first place so this might be a hint that an easier solution may exist.

We need to make two observations here:

• Some of the data is irrelevant

• The "distance" among the values in the answer options allows for estimation

Let's look at the first problem. As the question referred to average capacity utilisation, we immediately started to work with that number. However, we should reconsider the meaning of this term. If average capacity utilisation decreases by 10%, is this not the same as saying that Air France transported 10% fewer passengers?

This immediately simplifies our calculation:

32 million passengers - 10% = 32 million passengers * 90% = 32 million passengers * 0.9

`Now let us look at the answer options again:

a) 28.8 million

b) 23.6 million

c) 35.2 million

d) 35.9 million

`Answers C and D can be immediately ruled out because those numbers are larger than the 32 million in the table, which is impossible when the capacity utilisation decreases.

Answer B has a smaller number, but if we estimate 10% of 32 million (circa 0.3 million, or exactly 0.32 million) we will immediately see that Answer B's 2.36 million is too small an amount, which leaves only Answer A as a feasible option.

The correctness of Answer A can also be verified very quickly, with a simple subtraction:

3.2 million – 0.32 million = 3.2 million – (0.2 million + 0.12 million) = 3 million – 0.12 million = 2.88 million.

The above calculation also shows an example of how to make subtractions easier. In this example, we reformulated 0.32 million as 0.2 million + 0.12 million so it became much easier to first subtract 0.2 million from 3.2 million (leaving the round number of 3 million), and then deal with the rest.

Equations

Equations might sound too mathematical, yet they are a brilliantly inventive ways of dealing with problems where multiple calculations must be made. Consider this:

"There are 12,450 applicants for an exam. Out of them, 60% pass the first round, of these 40% pass the second round, of whom the last 500 performers are excluded. Eventually how many people get a job if only the best 25% of the remaining are selected?"

a)   747

b)   518

c)   622

d)   875

One way of approaching the problem would be to perform a series of calculations. First, we would calculate 60% of 12,450, then 40% of the resulting number, then we would subtract 500 from that number, and finally, we would calculate 25% of this last intermediate amount.

By denoting the number of people who get a job (which is the answer we are looking for) by X, we can create an equation which will make our lives much easier and the calculation significantly faster:

$X = (12450 * 0.6 * 0.4 – 500) * 0.25$ (where 0.6 equals 60%, 0.4 equal 40%, and 0.25 equals 25%)

We can further simplify the equation:

$X = (12450 * 0.24 – 500) * 0.25$

Since the answer options are quite far apart, we could also use some estimations and rounding up or down:

X ≈ (12000 / 4 – 500) / 4 (where 12450 is rounded down to 12000, 0.24 is rounded up to 1/4, and 0.25 is converted to 1/4 as well)

X ≈ (3000 – 500) / 4 = 2500 / 4 = 625

625 is closest to Answer C, so that will be the correct answer.

Tables and Charts

European Airlines, 2009				
Airline	Turnover (in million €)	Number of passengers (in millions)	Number of airplanes	Average capacity utilization (in %)
Swiss (CH)	1 570	19.7	93	72
British Airways (GBR)	2 600	36.8	13.7	84
Lufthansa (GER)	2 237	46.1	137	82
Air France (FR)	1960	32	140	82

"Based on the above table, how many passengers would Air France have transported in 2009 if its capacity utilisation had been 10% worse?"

a) 28.8 million

b) 23.6 million

c) 35.2 million

d) 35.9 million

The above table may seem familiar. This is because we previously used a version of this table with some rows "blacked out" for demonstrating certain methods. In real numerical tests, however, the table always contains lots of superfluous data that you will not need for your calculations – this is what I called "noise" in the introduction. When starting to solve a numerical reasoning question, it is always important to first decide which data is necessary for the calculation because the superfluous information will just confuse you and can take valuable time if you become distracted.

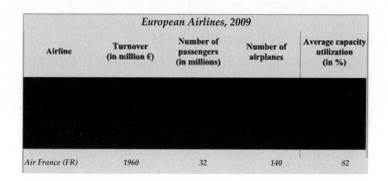

European Airlines, 2009				
Airline	Turnover (in million €)	Number of passengers (in millions)	Number of airplanes	Average capacity utilization (in %)
Air France (FR)	1960	32	140	82

For this reason, it is often suggested to mentally "black out" that data from the table which you will not need. In this instance, the first thing we will realize is that we can make no use of the data about the other three airlines (SWISS, Lufthansa, British Airways).

European Airlines, 2009				
Airline	Turnover (in million €)	Number of passengers (in millions)	Number of airplanes	Average capacity utilization (in %)
Air France (FR)	██	32	140	82

Since the question refers to the number of passengers transported, we will certainly not need turnover data to answer the question:

Based on our reasoning in the section on Estimation, we will also realize that the *number of airplanes* is a superfluous figure, as is *average capacity utilisation*:

If we systematically exclude all superfluous data, the task will seem significantly less

European Airlines, 2009				
Airline	Turnover (in million €)	Number of passengers (in millions)	Number of airplanes	Average capacity utilization (in %)
Air France (FR)	██	32	██	██

complicated. As it turns out, in our example, the table's only purpose is to tell us that Air France transported 32 million passengers in 2009. The other piece of information we will use (the 10% decrease in average capacity utilisation, and therefore 10% decrease in passengers transported) is supplied in the question, not the table.

How to Approach Numerical Reasoning Tests

The above sections demonstrated the number of factors we must consider to be able to efficiently solve the problems posed in numerical reasoning tests. Consider aspects such as the required level of accuracy, the relevance of data or the possibility of estimation, then decide the approach to take – whether to perform raw calculations, apply estimates, draw up an equation, or simply read a relationship or a trend off a chart.

As is true in the case of verbal and abstract reasoning tests, a systematic approach will make your test-taking experience much more efficient. Below, you will find a a summary of the recommended approach:

1. Read the question and the answer options first as carefully as possible.

2. The question will help you identify which data sets will be relevant and necessary for answering the question and know what to ignore.

3. Looking at the answer options will help you decide the level of accuracy required. If, for example, the values in the answer options are very far apart, you may consider estimation.

4. Based on the question, determine the relevant information and mentally "black out" the unnecessary data.

5. Having looked at the answer options and the data in the table, you can now make a final decision about whether to go for an exact figure or make an estimate, whether to use an equation, and so on.

6. Make sure you exclude all unrealistic answer options (for example numbers representing an increase when the question refers to a decrease).

7. Once you have performed your calculations, you can match the result against the remaining answer options. If you estimated, look for the answer option closest to your estimated result. If the result is significantly closer to one answer option than to all others, you were probably on the right track.

Practice Methods

Finally, a few suggestions for how to practice for the numerical reasoning test:

*   Start your practice by identifying your weaknesses. Percentages? Subtraction? Estimation? Equations? Calculus in general?

*   Once you have identified your weaknesses, you can pointedly practice these operations either by creating problems of your own or selecting practice tests where these calculations come into play

*   Once you have gained the necessary routine using all of these methods (and maybe further ones online), you can start practicing with tests that are similar to the real exam – for example the ones in this book

*   Check the available time at the real exam and the number of questions to be answered

*   Start without timing yourself at first but solve the same number of test questions as at the exam (usually around 20-30). Measure the average time you require.

*   Start decreasing the time needed to answer the questions so it gets closer to the time available at the exam

*   Ideally, by the time of the exam, you should be able to answer more questions in the time available than required at the exam, because you cannot account for stress and other outside factors are impossible to recreate at home

*   The EPSO test will be administered on a computer, which will make it much more challenging (and stranger) to take than a paper-based test where you can scribble on the paper and make quick calculations, write down equations, underline key concepts and so on – if you have access to such services, try to practice online

In the following chapter, you will find 150 numerical reasoning test questions that you can use to start practicing right away.

The answers may be found following question 150.

When you have completed the numerical reasoning test in the next chapter, why not try practicing numerical reasoning questions on line?

Online EU Training offers 1200+ numerical reasoning test questions where you can simulate an EPSO exam in real time, with the benefit of statistics on your performance and progress.

Readers of *The Ultimate EU Test Book* can claim a 12% discount.

For full details *see* page 387 of this book.

5. Numerical Reasoning Test

150 QUESTIONS – answers follow question 150

TABLE FOR QUESTIONS 1-4

	Total area (sq. km)	Population (1000 inhabitants)	GDP/ inhabitants	Inflation %
A	30 500	5 300	27 530	2.8
B	93 000	10 200	11 840	9.1
C	90 000	10 200	16 920	4.9
D	450 000	8 999	23 130	2.0
E	200 001	59 000	23 160	1.9

1. In which country is the density of population the lowest?

A. Country A

B. Country C

C. Country D

D. Country E

2. What is the average inflation rate in the five countries?

A. 2.5%

B. 4.1%

C. 5.1%

D. 6.3%

3. What percentage of the total population of the five countries live in country E?

A. 45%

B. 50%

C. Less than 60%

D. More than 60%

4. What is the ratio between the total area of country D and country C?

A. 1 : 4

B. 4 : 1

C. 5 : 1

D. 1 : 5

TABLE FOR QUESTIONS 5-7

PRODUCTION AND TRADE DATA IN NOVEMBER 2005
(WIRE & WIRE LTD.)

All lengths in metres (100s)	Bare copper wire	Tinned copper wire	PTFE silver plated copper cable	Gold plated copper wire
Production (100s)	100	150	30	20
Production costs per m in €	1	2	4	10
income per m in €	2	3	10	20
export (100s)	80	90	10	20

A.   19,000

B.   38,000

C.   30,000

D.   26,000

TABLE FOR QUESTIONS 8-10

INCOME FROM CERTAIN INDUSTRIAL PRODUCTS (in billion euros)

Products	2001	2002	2003	2004	2005
Cars	50	52	53	55	58
Buses	33	35	32	32	32
Trucks	40	44	45	46	49
Boats	8	12	11	15	14
Airplanes	40	40	30	40	50
Helicopters	20	22	20	22	20

5. How much income did Wire & Wire Ltd. generate from the export of bare copper wire and PTFE silver plated copper cable in November 2005?

A.   EUR 2,600

B.   EUR 26,000

C.   EUR 32,000

D.   EUR 320,000

6. What is the ratio between the total production of all types of wire and the quantity sold for export?

A.   3 : 2

B.   2 : 3

C.   4 : 3

D.   3 : 4

7. How much profit was made by Wire and Wire Ltd. from PTFE silver plated copper cable and gold plated copper wire in November 2005? (Profit is the

8. How much profit is made from the aircraft industry in 2003, if the production costs amount to 60% of the income received? (Profit is the difference between income and production costs.)

A.   EUR 10 billion

B.   EUR 15 billion

C.   EUR 20 billion

D.   EUR 25 billion

9. How many industries made a gain of 20% or more between 2002 and 2004?

A.   0

B.   1

C.   2

D.   3

10. Between which years does the production of any type of industry increase or decrease the most in absolute terms?

A. 2002 and 2003

B. 2003 and 2004

C. 2004 and 2005

D. Cannot say

TABLE FOR QUESTION 11

POPULATION DATA IN 2005

	Pop. in millions	Live births (per 1000 pop.)	Deaths (per 1000 pop.)	Under 18yrs (%)	65yrs or over (%)
Country A	40	12	10	20	19
Country B	22	4	5	22	18
Country C	35	6	5	25	20
Country D	80	20	18	18	22
Country E	100	30	28	20	20

11. Which country/countries has/have the largest elderly population?

A. Country A

B. Country D

C. Country E

D. Country D and Country E

12. How much money in million euros did Company B get in 2004 from pear juice if all juices are sold at the same price?

A. 80

B. 76

C. 120

D. 48

TABLE FOR QUESTIONS 12-14

Juices sold in 2004 (m. boxes)	Grapefruits	Orange	Pear
Company A	12	20	14
Company B	4	37	19
Company C	27	23	8

Income from all juices sold (millions in €)	2003	2004	2005
Company A	180	200	220
Company B	225	240	210
Company C	280	225	300

13. Which company had the highest income between 2003 and 2005?

A. Company C

B. Company A and B the same

C. Company B

D. Company A

14. Which company sold its juices at the lowest average price in 2004?

A. Company A

B. Company C

C. Company A and C the same

D. Company B

---

15. Based on the diagrams, what share did the European Union have of Hungary's exports in the period January-September 2008?

A. 20.4%

B. 43.5%

C. 57.5%

D. 77.9%

Increase in Hungary's exports by country group, 2008 (Q. 15-16)

■   Increase in the period January – September 2008 compared to the same period in 2007 (%)

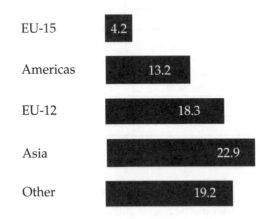

EU-15   4.2

Americas   13.2

EU-12   18.3

Asia   22.9

Other   19.2

(EU-15: member states of the EU before May 1, 2004)

(EU-12: the 12 newest member states of the EU)

16. By how much did the value of Hungarian exports to countries here referred to as "other countries" increase from the period January-September 2007 to the same period in 2008?

A.   840 million EUR

B.   1.23 billion EUR

C.   1.47 billion EUR

D.   1.92 billion EUR

Total advertising expenses in Russia (billion RUB), Q. 17-19

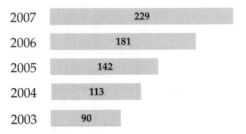

2007   229

2006   181

2005   142

2004   113

2003   90

Distribution of Hungary's exports by country group, 2008, Q. 15-16

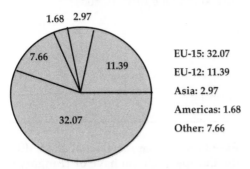

EU-15: 32.07

EU-12: 11.39

Asia: 2.97

Americas: 1.68

Other: 7.66

(January-September 2008, billion EUR)

(EU-15: member states of the EU before May 1, 2004)

(EU-12: the 12 newest member states of the EU)

(Source: Hungarian Central Statistical Office)

The Russian advertising market, first half of 2008 (shares in total advertising expenses, %), Q. 17-19

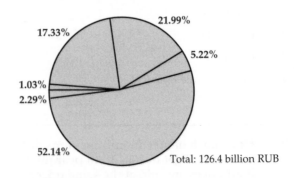

Total: 126.4 billion RUB

Television: 52.14%
Radio: 5.22%
Print media: 21.99%
Internet: 1.03%
Outdoor advertising: 17.33%
Other: 2.29%

(Source: Russian Association of Advertising Agencies)

17. Expenses on outdoor advertising in Russia increased by 13% from the first half of 2007 to the same period in 2008. By how much did they increase in absolute terms (in million RUB)?

A. 2062

B. 2520

C. 2848

D. 3273

18. Based on the diagrams and the fact that total advertising expenses in Russia increased by 12.8% from the first half of 2008 to the second half, by what percentage did this figure increase from 2007 to 2008?

A. 3.3%

B. 4.1%

C. 17.5%

D. 18.5%

19. How much more was spent on television advertising than on print media advertising and radio advertising together in Russia in the first half of 2008 (in billion RUB)?

A. 24.9

B. 31.5

C. 35.4

D. 38.1

20. Based on the diagram, in which of the four countries is the ratio of foreign exchange loans to GDP the lowest?

A. Czech Republic

B. Poland

C. Slovakia

D. Hungary

Indebtedness in the Visegrad countries, 2007, Q. 20-21

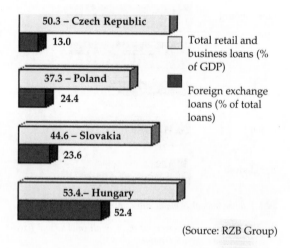

(Source: RZB Group)

21. Based on he fact that the GDP of the Czech Republic was 127 billion EUR in 2007, what was the amount of foreign exchange loans in the country?

A. 16.5 billion EUR

B. 80.4 billion EUR

C. 8,305 million EUR

D. 47,371 million EUR

22. Based on the diagram below and the fact that the population of the Czech Republic was about 20 times that of Luxembourg in 2007, approximately what proportion of the total number of mobile phone subscriptions in the Czech Republic did the same figure of Luxembourg account for?

A. 1/4

B. 1/5

C. 1/20

D. 1/25

Mobile phone subscriptions in various countries, 2007, Q. 22

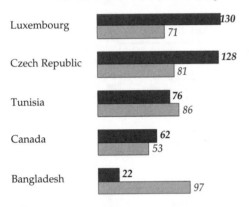

- ■ *Number of mobile phone subscriptions per 100 inhabitants*
- ▨ *Mobile phone subscriptions as % of all (mobile and fixed line) telephone subscriptions*

---

23. Based on the diagrams, how did the combined market share of the three leading PC manufacturers change between the second quarter of 2000 and the same period in 2008?

A. Decreased by 2.7 percentage points

B. Decreased by 7.7 percentage points

C. Increased by 10.7 percentage points

D. Increased by 13.1 percentage points

Worldwide PC sales by manufacturer, second quarter of 2000 (%), Q. 23-26

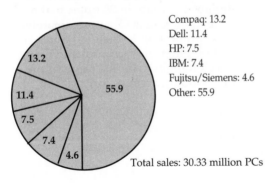

Compaq: 13.2
Dell: 11.4
HP: 7.5
IBM: 7.4
Fujitsu/Siemens: 4.6
Other: 55.9

Total sales: 30.33 million PCs

Worldwide PC sales by manufacturer, second quarter of 2008 (%), Q. 23-26

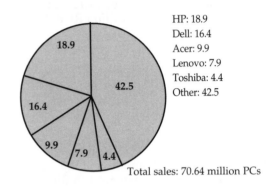

HP: 18.9
Dell: 16.4
Acer: 9.9
Lenovo: 7.9
Toshiba: 4.4
Other: 42.5

Total sales: 70.64 million PCs

24. Based on the diagrams, how many more PCs would HP have sold in the second quarter of 2008 than in the same period in 2000 if its market share had remained unchanged?

A. 3.023 million

B. 5.321 million

C. 8.053 million

D. 11.076 million

25 Based on the diagrams, by what percentage did the number of PCs sold by Dell increase between the second quarter of 2000 and the same period in 2008?

A. 35%

B. 135%

C. 235%

D. 335%

26. Based on the diagrams, what average quarterly increase took place in the total number of PCs sold worldwide between the second quarter of 2000 and the same period in 2008 in absolute terms?

A. An increase by 1.26 million

B. An increase by 2.52 million

C. An increase by 3.78 million

D. An increase by 5.04 million

100,000 EUR in 2001 on the Croatian coast (in square metres)?

A. 33

B. 47

C. 78

D. 83

Average property prices in Croatia (%, 1997 = 100%), Q. 27-28

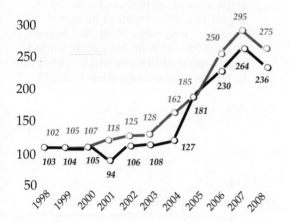

■ national average   ■ average of coastal properties

TABLE FOR QUESTIONS 29-31

GDP (US$ bn) and social expenditure (% of GDP) of various countries

	1990		2005	
	GDP	Soc.exp.	GDP	soc.exp.
Denmark	95.1	25.1%	179.9	26.9%
France	1007.4	25.1%	1869.4	29.2%
Germany	1462.8	22.3%	2586.5	26.7%
Ireland	45.7	14.9%	160.4	16.7%
Netherlands	264.1	25.6%	572.8	20.7%
Norway	76.0	22.3%	218.7	21.6%

Source: OECD

29. How many times greater was the absolute amount of social expenditure in France than in Denmark in 1990?

A. 9.7   B. 9.9

C. 10.6   D. 11.3

E. 11.7   F. 11.1

27. Based on the diagram, by what percentage did the average price of Croatian properties increase from 2005 to 2006?

A. 31%

B. 35%

C. 57%

D. 65%

30. In how many of the six countries did the GDP increase by more than 200% between 1990 and 2005?

A. one   B. two

C. three   D. four

E. five   F. six

28. Based on the diagram and the fact that the average price of coastal properties in Croatia was 3000 EUR per square metre in 2008, what size property could one expect to be able to buy with

31. By how much did social expenditure increase in Germany between 1990 and 2005?

A. 64.4 billion USD

B. 113.8 billion USD

C. 250.6 billion USD

D. 326.2 billion USD

E. 364.4 billion USD

F. 690.6 billion USD

TABLES FOR QUESTIONS 32-35

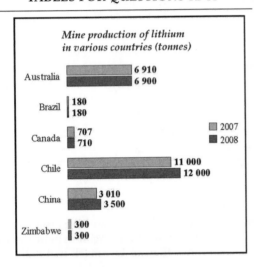

Mine production of lithium in various countries (tonnes)

Australia: 6 910 (2007), 6 900 (2008)
Brazil: 180 (2007), 180 (2008)
Canada: 707 (2007), 710 (2008)
Chile: 11 000 (2007), 12 000 (2008)
China: 3 010 (2007), 3 500 (2008)
Zimbabwe: 300 (2007), 300 (2008)

Proven lithium reserves in various countries, end of 2008 (thousand tonnes)

Australia	220	Brazil	910
Canada	360	Chile	3 000
China	1 100	Zimbabwe	27

Source: US Geological Survey

32. If the amount of lithium produced in Zimbabwe remains constant at the 2008 level, in how many years (starting from 2008) will the country's proven reserves be exhausted (assuming that no new reserves are discovered)?

A.　9

B.　11

C.　45

D.　81

E.　90

F.　111

33. How much did the world's total proven lithium reserves amount to at the end of 2008 given that the proven reserves of the six countries listed together accounted for 51.06% of the world total?

A.　8.5 million tonnes

B.　9.3 million tonnes

C.　10.2 million tonnes

D.　11.0 million tonnes

E.　11.4 million tonnes

F.　12.0 million tonnes

34. If the amount of lithium produced in the six countries together increases by the same percentage from 2008 to 2009 as from 2007 to 2008, how many thousand tonnes of lithium will be produced in the six countries together in 2009?

A.　20.9

B.　22.1

C.　23.6

D.　25.2

E.　26.4

F.　27.4

35. How many thousand tonnes did Chile's proven lithium reserves amount to at the end of 2006 (assuming that no new reserves were discovered in 2007 and 2008)?

A.　2,350

B.　2,600

C.　3,023

D.　3,730

E.　26,000

F.　29,770

36. According to the chart below, how many million hectolitres of wine were produced globally between 2005 and 2007 on a yearly average?

A.　242

B.　251

C.　260

D.　275

E.　278

F.　281

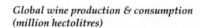

TABLE FOR QUESTIONS 36-37

Global wine production & consumption
(million hectolitres)

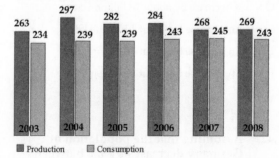

■ Production ☐ Consumption

(Source: OIV – International Organisation of Vine and Wine)

37. How much more wine (in million hectolitres) was produced globally between 2004 and 2008 than if annual production in this period had been the same as in 2003?

A.	18	B.	17
C.	280	D.	1,400
E.	34	F.	85

F. Decreased by 64.2 billion USD

38. By how many per cent did the gold reserves of the central bank of the United States decrease between March 1999 and March 2009?

A.	0.0006%	B.	0.006%
C.	0.06%	D.	0.61%
E.	6.14%	F.	61.43%

TABLE FOR QUESTIONS 38-39

Gold reserves of the world's central banks (tonnes)

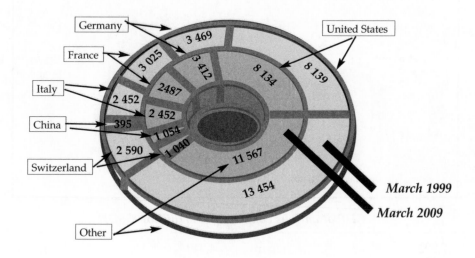

39. How many tonnes of gold did the world's central banks together sell on a yearly average between March 1999 and March 2008 given that they sold 345 tonnes between March 2008 and March 2009?

A.	303	B.	311
C.	337	D.	372
E.	384	F.	414

40. By what percentage is China's GDP projected to increase between 2008 and 2011?

A.	7.9%	B.	9.3%
C.	11.2%	D.	18.5%
E.	27.8%	F.	30.4%

41. What change is projected to take place in France's GDP between 2008 and 2010?

A. A decrease by about 20 billion USD

B. A decrease by about 49 billion USD

C. A decrease by about 78 billion USD

D. An increase by about 1 billion USD

E. An increase by about 16 billion USD

F. An increase by about 80 billion USD

42. Assuming that the population of Germany decreases by 1% between 2008 and 2010, by how many per cent is Germany's GDP per capita projected to decrease in this period?

A.	0.9%	B.	2.6%
C.	3.6%	D.	4.5%
E.	5.3%	F.	7.2%

TABLES FOR QUESTIONS 40-42

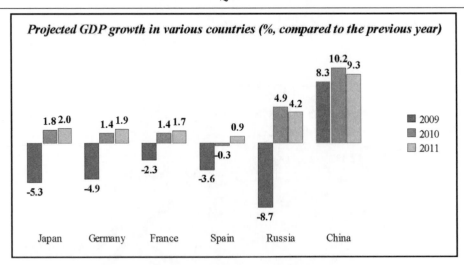

Projected GDP growth in various countries (%, compared to the previous year)

GDP of various countries, 2008 (billion USD)

China	7,992	Japan	4,340	Germany	2,925
Russia	2,271	France	2,133	Spain	1,402

TABLE FOR QUESTIONS 43-46

Total population and population projections (end of year, million inhabitants)

	2007	2020	2040	2060
EU 27	495.1	513.8	520.1	505.7
Belgium	10.6	11.3	12.0	12.3
Czech Republic	10.3	10.5	10.2	9.5
Poland	38.1	38.0	35.2	31.1
Romania	21.6	20.8	19.2	16.9
Sweden	9.1	9.9	10.5	10.9
United Kingdom	60.9	65.7	72.0	76.7

Source: Eurostat

---

43. **What is the projected population of Romania in 2040 expressed as a percentage of its population in 2007?**

A.   78.2%   B.   88.9%

C.   92.3%   D.   103.8%

E.   108.3%   F.   127.8%

44. **Assuming that the population of Sweden increases by the same amount every year between 2020 and 2040, in which year is it projected to exceed 10 million for the first time?**

A.   2024   B.   2027

C.   2029   D.   2031

E.   2033   F.   2036

45. **If the projected percentage decrease of the Czech Republic population between 2007 and 2060 was the same as that of Poland, how many inhabitants would the Czech Republic be**

projected to have in 2060?

A.   3.3 million   B.   5.4 million

C.   7.8 million   D.   8.4 million

E.   9.1 million   F.   12.6 million

46. **Approximately what proportion of the population of the EU-27 is projected to live in the six countries listed, in 2020?**

A.   Half   B.   One quarter

C.   One fifth   D.   Three sevenths

E.   Three eighths   F.   Three tenths

---

47. **What is the area of Portugal (in thousand square km)?**

A.   92.1   B.   97.1

C.   103.1   D.   109.5

E.   115.3   F.   122.5

TABLES FOR QUESTIONS 47-49

Average size of municipalities in various EU countries, 2008

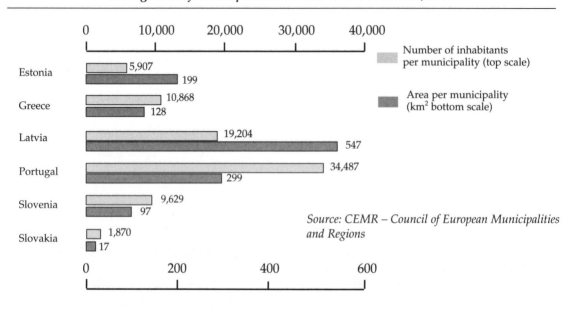

Source: CEMR – Council of European Municipalities and Regions

Population of various EU countries, 2008 (thousand inhabitants)

| Estonia | 1 341 | Greece | 11 237 | Latvia | 2 266 |
| Portugal | 10 622 | Slovenia | 2 022 | Slovakia | 5 406 |

48. Which of the six countries has the highest population density?

A.	Estonia	B.	Greece
C.	Latvia	D.	Portugal
E.	Slovenia	F.	Slovakia

49. Assuming that as a result of a territorial reform in 2010, the number of municipalities decreases by half in Greece, what will be the average area per municipality (in square km)?

A.	64	B.	85
C.	128	D.	170
E.	217	F.	256

EUROPEAN POPULATION STATISTICS (QUESTIONS 50-52)

	Population (%)			
	Population (thousands)	Urban	Over 60	Under 15
Country A	3140	47	13	24
Country B	7590	71	24	13
Country C	5120	81	27	16

50. How many people in country B are aged between 15 and 60?

A.	5.4 million	B.	1.82 million
C.	0.99 million	D.	4.78 million
E.	2.81 million		

51. How many people in country A live in outside urban areas?

A. 1.48 million   B. 1.66 million

C. 1.16 million   D. 1.98 million

E. 0.97 million

52. In country C 256,000 people are over the age of 75. What percentage of the population is this?

A. 5%   B. 10%

C. 15%   D. 20%

E. 25%

BRITISH BIRDS OF PREY POPULATIONS (QUESTIONS 53-55)

	2007	2008	2009
Buzzards	2200	2299	2296
Hawks	6140	6020	6090
Kestrels	450	470	517
Kites	790	792	707
Owls	1800	1850	1870
Totals	11380	11431	11480

53. By how much did the kestrel population grow between 2008 and 2009?

A. 47%   B. 15%

C. 9.1%   D. 10%

E. 12.5%

54. In 2009 what percentage of the birds of prey listed were buzzards?

A. 4%   B. 8%

C. 12%   D. 16%

E. 20%

55. By how many did the hawks outnumber the other birds of prey in 2007?

A. 6140   B. 5240

C. 900   D. 3

E. 300

SOLAR POWER GENERATION IN VARIOUS COUNTRIES (MILLONS OF KWH) (QUESTIONS 56-58)

	2006	2007	2008
France	12	16	24
Germany	36	38	42
Greece	33	36	44
Spain	23	27	34
UK	8	11	16

56. What is France's share of the total solar power generation in 2008?

A. 10%   B. 15%

C. 20%   D. 25%

E. 30%

57. What is the percentage increase in solar power generation for the UK between 2006 and 2008?

A. 8%   B. 50%

C. 45.45%   D. 100%

E. 129%

58. By how many million KWh did the overall generation of solar power increase between 2006 and 2007 across these five countries?

A. 4   B. 32

C. 12   D. 10

E. 16

INTERNET USAGE IN EUROPE (QUESTIONS 59-61)

	Population in 2005 (thousands)	Number of Internet Users (in thousands)		
		2004	2005	2006
Belgium	10415	7995	8020	8542
Bulgaria	7739	4392	4512	4902
Romania	21635	13450	13842	14660
Switzerland	7441	4942	5334	5892

EU ALCOHOL PRODUCTION IN 2005 (QUESTIONS 62-64)

	Population in 2005 (thousands)	Production (thousand hectolitres)		
		Wine	Spirits	Beer
France	61013	53440	1741	17200
Germany	82409	9450	4056	95000
Spain	43060	32430	1766	30200
Switzerland	7441	1000	57	3600

59. By how much did the number of internet users in Romania grow between 2004 and 2006?

A.   9%   B.   18%

C.   12%   D.   10%

E.   4%

62. If the Swiss drink half of the wine produced in their country what is the average amount consumed per person?

A.   0.067 litres   B.   0.67 litres

C.   6.7 litres   D.   67 litres

E.   670 litres

60. How many people in Romania and Switzerland combined did not use the internet in 2005?

A.   2.6m   B.   9.9m

C.   12.2m   D.   4.7m

E.   8.1m

63. What percentage of the total beer produced by the countries in this table is produced by Germany?

A.   65%   B.   29%

C.   73%   D.   38%

E.   95%

61. What percentage of the population of Belgium had access to the internet in 2005?

A.   25%   B.   43%

C.   57%   D.   68%

E.   77%

64. What is the volume of spirits produced per person in Spain?

A.   2.1 litres   B.   9.2 litres

C.   28.1 litres   D.   4.1 litres

E.   17.3 litres

MOBILE PHONE SUBSCRIPTIONS IN THE EU COUNTRIES (THOUSANDS)(QUESTIONS 65-67)

	2005	2006	2007
Bulgaria	1594	1957	2451
Denmark	3799	4228	4982
Greece	5511	6824	9191
Poland	1759	1819	1928

EU VACCINE TRADE IN 2008 (QUESTIONS 68-70)

	Trade US$ (millions)		Weight (tonnes)	
	Imports	Exports	Imports	Exports
France	506	1811	1019	3976
Italy	267	276	387	482
Spain	417	126	704	245
UK	1387	1132	14634	647

65. **What percentage of the mobile phone subscriptions shown did Denmark account for in 2005?**

A. 10%   B. 20%

C. 30%   D. 40%

E. 50%

66. **What was the growth in mobile phone subscriptions in Poland between 2006 and 2007?**

A. 4%   B. 6%

C. 8%   D. 10%

E. 12%

67. **If the population of Bulgaria in 2007 was 3.77million, how many mobile phone subscriptions were there per hundred people?**

A. 23   B. 31

C. 42   D. 55

E. 65

68. **What percentage of the shown exports by weight does Italy account for?**

A. 2.3%   B. 15%

C. 4.8%   D. 9%

E. 8%

69. **Which country has the largest trade deficit for vaccines?**

A. France   B. Italy

C. Spain   D. UK

E. Impossible to work out.

70. **What is the average price per gramme of vaccine exported from the UK?**

A. $1.75   B. $2.21

C. $0.23   D. $14.91

E. $6.23

NUCLEAR ELECTRICITY GENERATION IN THE EU (QUESTIONS 71-73)

	Population in 2005 (thousands)	Electricity Generated (millions MWh)		
		2005	2006	2007
France	61013	452	446	440
Hungary	10078	163	158	150
Poland	38198	44	51	67
Ukraine	46936	87	90	93

MUNICIPAL WASTE COLLECTION (THOUSAND TONNES) (QUESTIONS 74-76)

	2005	2006	2007
Austria	2713	2981	3002
Ireland	595	627	719
Norway	716	931	1014
Slovenia	1386	1326	1354

71. **How many MWh did France generate on average for each person in France in 2005?**

A.   0.74

B.   7.4

C.   74

D.   740

E.   7400

72. **What percentage of the total nuclear power generation did Hungary account for in 2007?**

A.   10%

B.   15%

C.   20%

D.   25%

E.   30%

73. **What is the percentage growth in nuclear power generation in the Ukraine between 2006 and 2007?**

A.   0.9%

B.   0.3%

C.   4.5%

D.   9.3%

E.   3.3%

74. **What percentage of waste collection did Ireland account for across these countries in 2005?**

A.   11%

B.   5.95%

C.   18%

D.   7%

E.   14%

75. **What was the growth in waste collection in Norway between 2005 and 2006?**

A.   10%

B.   15%

C.   20%

D.   25%

E.   30%

76. **If Slovenia had grown its waste collection by 5% between 2006 and 2007, how many more tonnes of waste would it have collected in 2007?**

A.   18100 tonnes

B.   27200 tonnes

C.   1392 tonnes

D.   38300 tonnes

E.   2289 tonnes

STUDENTS IN TERTIARY EDUCATION (QUESTIONS 77-79)

Female Proportion of Student Population (%)

	Student Population in 2007 (thousands)	2005	2006	2007
Austria	1090	55.2	55.3	55.3
Germany	2445	53.5	54.9	54.2
Luxembourg	171	50.9	51.7	52.4
Serbia	723	55.6	54.2	53.9

77. Assuming the population was constant, how many females were in tertiary education in Luxembourg in 2005?

A. 8700   B. 33600

C. 89600   D. 87000

E. 63200

78. How many more females than males were in tertiary education in Serbia in 2007?

A. 56400   B. 28200

C. 333000   D. 10600

E. 78000

79. What was the percentage growth in female student numbers in Germany between 2005 and 2006?

A. 1.4%   B. 0.2%

C. 10.6%   D. 5.2%

E. 2.6%

ACCIDENTAL DEATH RATES IN EUROPE (QUESTIONS 80-82)

Deaths Per 100,000 Population

	2006 Population (thousands)	2005	2006	2007
Belgium	10400	21	18	16
Italy	58645	49	37	39
Spain	43060	15	21	19
Slovakia	8187	21	23	26

80. How many more people died accidentally in Slovakia in 2006 than in Belgium in the same year?

A. 5   B. 11

C. 29   D. 35

E. 49

81. Assuming that the population remained unchanged, how many fewer people died accidentally in Italy in 2007 than in 2005?

A. 5   B. 59

C. 586   D. 5865

E. 58645

82. What was the percentage increase in the death rate in Spain between 2005 and 2006?

A. 20%   B. 30%

C. 40%   D. 50%

E. 60%

VIOLENT CRIME IN EUROPE
(QUESTIONS 83-85)

		Number of crimes committed		
	2005 Population (thousands)	2005	2006	2007
France	61013	58122	58595	59073
Ireland	4187	3105	3270	3532
Malta	403	305	316	357
Portugal	10529	11017	11256	11046

83. **Which country had the highest violent crime rate (i.e. per head of population) in 2005?**

A.   France   B.   Ireland

C.   Malta   D.   Portugal

E.   Impossible to tell from the data

84. **Assuming that the population remained unchanged, what was the percentage increase in the violent crime rate in Ireland between 2006 and 2007?**

A.   8%   B.   9%

C.   10%   D.   11%

E.   12%

85. **What was the average violent crime rate (the number of violent crimes per 100,000 of population) across these four countries in 2005?**

A.   0.02   B.   0.14

C.   3.7   D.   21

E.   95

SALES OF CHEESE IN EUROPE
(QUESTIONS 86-88)

	Cheese sold (thousand tonnes)		
	2005	2006	2007
Aldi	523	591	671
Carrefour	110	115	121
Lidl	618	581	570
Sainsbury's	294	327	348

86. **If 6 million people shopped at Carrefour during 2007, how much cheese did each person buy on average?**

A.   20 grammes   B. 200 grammes

C.   2 Kg   D.   20 Kg

E.   200 Kg

87. **What is the rate of growth of cheese sales in Aldi between 2005 and 2006?**

A.   9%   B.   10%

C.   11%   D.   12%

E.   13%

88. **What percentage of the total cheese sold in these supermarkets in 2005 was sold by Lidl?**

A.   40%   B.   38%

C.   36%   D.   34%

E.   32%

PATENT APPLICATIONS IN EUROPE
(QUESTIONS 89-91)

	2005	2006	2007
France	12471	12486	12508
Germany	32837	33936	33187
Italy	12601	12280	12984
Spain	8175	8155	8293
Total	66084	66857	66972

SPENDING ON OLD AGE BENEFITS
(QUESTIONS 92-94)

	Population in 2005 (thousands)	*Euros per inhabitant*		
		2005	2006	2007
Estonia	5346	1033	1055	1089
Georgia	4219	911	1059	1022
Latvia	2240	1008	1250	1297
Ukraine	45433	1096	1125	1296

89. What percentage of all the patents filed over the three years were filed by Germany?

A. 40%

B. 45%

C. 50%

D. 55%

E. 60%

92. Which country spent the most on old age benefits in 2005?

A. Estonia

B. Georgia

C. Latvia

D. Ukraine

E. Impossible to tell from the data

90. Which country had the greatest growth per capita in patent applications between 2005 and 2006?

A. France

B. Germany

C. Italy

D. Spain

E. Impossible to tell from the data

93. Assuming the population remained constant, how much did Latvia spend on old age benefits in 2006?

A. 28 million

B. 280 million

C. 2.8 billion

D. 28 billion

E. 280 billion

91. What was the overall growth in applications for patents between 2005 and 2006?

A. less than 1%

B. 1.17%

C. 1.34%

D. 1.72%

E. more than 2%

94. What is the percentage increase in spending per capita in Georgia between 2005 and 2007?

A. 12%

B. 15%

C. 9%

D. 7%

E. 19%

GLOBAL DISASTER AID IN 2009
(QUESTIONS 95-97)

	Population (thousands)	Local[1]	Indirect[2]	Direct[3]
Austria	9588	12504	1012	648
Czech Republic	10411	2321	6781	2901
Hungary	9973	6292	1019	871
Portugal	10732	9821	19223	561

Aid Donated (tonnes)

1. *Purchased in the country in need.*
2. *Purchased elsewhere and shipped.*
3. *Shipped directly from donating country.*

95. **What percentage of Portugal's aid contribution was purchased locally in the country in need?**

A. A half

B. A third

C. A quarter

D. Two fifths

E. Three fifths

96. **If the average cost of aid is $1219 per tonne, what was the average cost to the Hungarian public (per person) for their aid in 2009?**

A. $0.01

B. $0.10

C. $1

D. $10

E. $100

97. **What percentage of the total direct aid was funded by Austria?**

A. 25%

B. 22%

C. 19%

D. 16%

E. 13%

BIRTH RATES AROUND EUROPE
(QUESTIONS 98-100)

	Population in 2005 (thousands)	2000	2005	2010
Croatia	4443	15.4	14.1	12.1
Finland	5244	14.1	12.2	11.3
Ireland	4187	15.5	14.4	12.8
Slovakia	5386	13.1	11.9	11.1

Births per thousand population

98. **Which country had the most births in 2005?**

A. Croatia

B. Finland

C. Ireland

D. Slovakia

E. Impossible to tell from the data

99. **How many more children were born in Croatia in 2010 than in Ireland in the same year (assuming that both populations remained constant)?**

A. 166

B. 201

C. 23

D. 190

E. 82

100. **What is the percentage fall in birth rate in Finland between 2000 and 2010?**

A. 2.8%

B. 6.1%

C. 12.1%

D. 19.9%

E. 25%

CHURCH ATTENDANCE AROUND EUROPE (QUESTIONS 101-103)

		Churchgoers (%)	
	Population in 2005 (thousands)	2000	2005	2010
France	61013	18.4	16.2	15.6
Greece	11064	22.1	22.1	21.9
Italy	58645	16.8	16.7	15.9
Spain	43060	18.2	18.1	17.9

101. Which country had the most churchgoers in 2005?

A. France

B. Greece

C. Italy

D. Spain

E. Impossible to tell from the data

102. If the population of Greece increased by 351,000 between 2005 and 2010, how many churchgoers were there in Greece in 2010?

A. 2.7m

B. 2.5m

C. 2.3m

D. 2.1m

E. 1.9m

103. What was the percentage drop in church attendance in Italy between 2005 and 2010?

A. 2.3%

B. 7.1%

C. 4.8%

D. 6.2%

E. 8.1%

SALES OF WINE IN THE UK (QUESTIONS 104-106)

	Wine sold (million litres)		
	2007	2008	2009
Asda	470	478	490
Morrisons	210	215	221
Sainsbury's	525	516	529
Tesco	895	927	918

104. Which supermarket had the largest percentage growth in sales of wine between 2007 and 2009?

A. Asda

B. Morrisons

C. Sainsbury's

D. Tesco

E. Impossible to tell from the data

105. What percentage of all wine sales in 2007 by the supermarkets listed were made by Sainsbury's?

A. 25%

B. 20%

C. 52.6%

D. 13%

E. 31%

106. How much more wine would Asda have had to have sold in 2009 to have achieved a 10% rise in sales from 2007?

A. 2700 litres

B. 27 thousand litres

C. 270 thousand litres

D. 2.7 million litres

E. 27 million litres

SHOE SALES AROUND EUROPE
(QUESTIONS 107-109)

		Sales (million euro)		
	Population in 2005 (thousands)	2004	2005	2006
Belgium	7739	208	212	232
Greece	11064	222	231	233
Italy	58645	2280	2340	2771
Netherlands	16316	589	600	606

INSTALLED TELEPHONE LINES IN
EUROPE (QUESTIONS 110-112)

		Number of lines (thousands)		
	Population in 2005 (thousands)	2005	2006	2007
Andorra	80	35.4	36.5	37.2
Luxembourg	464	245	247	249
Malta	398	200	210	230
San Marino	30	20.8	21	21.1

107. How much did the average Italian spend on shoes in 2005?

A.   3.2 euro   B.   127 euro

C.   39.9 euro   D.   22.1 euro

E.   62.3 euro

108. How much extra did the average Greek spend on shoes in 2006 than in 2004 assuming the population remained constant? (Figures in the table should be rounded for ease of calculation)

A.   1 euro   B.   2 euro

C.   3 euro   D.   4 euro

E.   5 euro

109. If the population of the Netherlands increased by 163000 between 2005 and 2006, by how much did the per capita spending on shoes increase over the same period? (Figures in the table should be rounded for ease of calculation)

A.   1 euro   B.   0.61 euro

C.   0.37 euro   D.   0.1 euro

E.   It stayed the same.

110. Which country had the lowest number of telephone lines per head of population in 2005?

A.   Andorra   B.   Luxembourg

C.   Malta   D.   San Marino

E.   Impossible to tell from the data

111. What is the percentage rate of growth in the number of telephone lines in Malta between 2005 and 2007?

A.   23%   B.   13%

C.   30%   D.   15%

E.   4%

112. What percentage of telephone lines shown in the table were in Luxembourg in 2006?

A.   53%   B.   48%

C.   30%   D.   65%

E.   44%

NATURAL DEATH RATES ACROSS EUROPE (QUESTIONS 113-115)

	Number of Deaths (per hundred thousand)		
Population in 2005 (thousands)	1985	1995	2005
Latvia	2292	23.4	24.1	21.7
Liechtenstein	35	18.7	18.8	17.2
Lithuania	3416	27.1	26.9	24.1
Luxembourg	464	17.2	17.1	16.9

113. If the population of Latvia was the same in 2005 as in 1995, how many fewer deaths were there in Latvia in 2005 than in 1995?

A.   6   B.   12

C.   102   D.   41

E.   55

114. What was the decline in the natural death rate in Lithuania between 1985 and 2005?

A.   9%   B.   10%

C.   11%   D.   12%

E.   13%

115. How many people died of natural causes in Liechtenstein in 2005?

A.   6   B.   12

C.   102   D.   41

E.   55

EUROSTAR JOURNEY TIMES (HH:MM) (QUESTIONS 116-118)

From \ To->	Brussels	Geneva	London	Luxembourg	Paris
Brussels	-	X	01:56	X	01:22
Geneva	X	-	07:54	X	03:28
London	02:22	06:48	-	05:45	02:25
Luxembourg	X	X	05:45	-	02:16
Paris	01:20	03:33	02:15	02:39	-

116. What is the return journey time from Geneva to Paris?

A.   6:56   B.   6:01

C.   6:33   D.   7:06

E.   7:01

117. How much shorter is the Paris to London journey than the Paris to Luxembourg trip?

A.   5%   B.   10%

C.   15%   D.   20%

E.   25%

118. If you went from London to Paris then on to Brussels and returned home, how long would you spend travelling on the train (assuming the train runs to schedule)?

A.   5:41   B.   5:31

C.   5:33   D.   6:06

E.   6:08

OCTOGENERIANS IN EUROPE (%) (QUESTIONS 119-121)

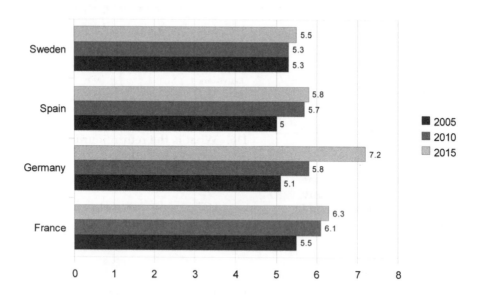

119. What is the growth rate of octogenarians in Spain between 2005 and 2015?

A. 5%   B. 5.8%

C. 0.8%   D. 16%

E. 13.8%

120. In 2010 the population of Germany is 82.1m and France is 62.6m. How many more octogenarians are there in Germany than in France?

A. 9.4m   B. 940000

C. 94000   D. 9400

E. 940

121. If the population of Sweden is 9.3 million and it remains constant, how many more octogenarians will there be in Sweden in 2015 than in 2005?

A. 18600   B. 12200

C. 1800   D. 21400

E. 9600

122. In 2003 Legoland, in Denmark, had 1.2 million visitors, half of which were from abroad. What proportion of Denmark's foreign visitors went to Legoland?

A. A half   B. A third

C. A quarter   D. A fifth

E. A sixth

VISITORS TO SCANDINAVIA (THOUSANDS) (QUESTIONS 122-124)

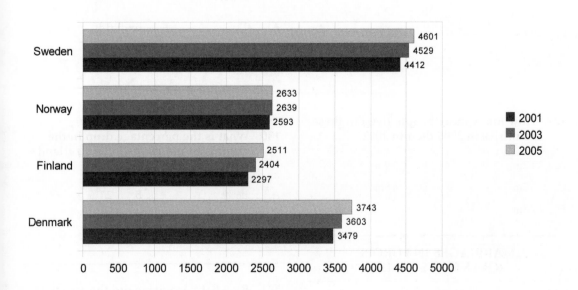

123. Which country had the greatest relative growth in visitors between 2001 and 2005?

A. Sweden B. Norway

C. Finland D. Denmark

E. Impossible to tell from the graph

124. If the population of Norway was 4.7m in 2005, how many visitors per head of population did Norway receive that year?

A. 0.33 B. 1.8

C. 1.3 D. 0.56

E. 2.37

POPULATIONS IN EUROPE (QUESTIONS 125-127)

		Population (thousands)		
	Area in km2 (thousands)	2002	2005	2008
Belgium	30	10310	10440	10667
France	540	61426	62773	63983
Portugal	91	10329	10529	10618
Spain	499	40970	43038	45067

125. What was the average population density, in people per square kilometre, in Belgium in 2005?

A. 0.348 B. 3.48

C. 34.8 D. 348

E. 3480

126. What was the growth in the population of Spain between 2002 and 2008?

A.   10%   B.   5.2%

C.   9.1%   D.   12.2%

E.   7.2%

127. How many more people lived in these countries in 2008 than in 2002?

A.   1.2m   B.   3.9m

C.   5.7m   D.   6.8m

E.   7.3m

MARRIAGES IN EUROPE
(QUESTIONS 128-130)

	Population in 2005 (thousands)	Number of Marriages		
		2004	2005	2006
Ireland	4187	20233	20209	19887
Italy	58645	234600	235200	233900
Slovakia	5386	15809	15628	15680
Switzerland	7441	18211	18202	17919

128. What is the largest percentage increase in marriages in any country on the table between any two years?

A.   0.11%   B.   0.22%

C.   0.33%   D.   0.44%

E.   0.55%

129. What is the difference in marriages per 1000 people in Ireland and Italy in 2005?

A.   0.1   B.   0.8

C.   1.4   D.   3.6

E.   5.2

130. What is the percentage drop in the number of marriages in Switzerland between 2004 and 2006?

A.   1.6%   B.   2.1%

C.   2.8%   D.   3.1%

E.   3.4%

---

131. By what percentage did the average spending on weddings rise in Poland between 1990 and 2010?

A.   10%   B.   20%

C.   30%   D.   40%

E.   50%

132. If there were 37,250 weddings in Sweden in 2000, what was the total spending on weddings that year in Euros?

A.   187000   B.   1.87m

C.   18.7m   D.   187m

E.   1870m

SPENDING ON WEDDINGS ACCROSS EUROPE (QUESTIONS 131-133)

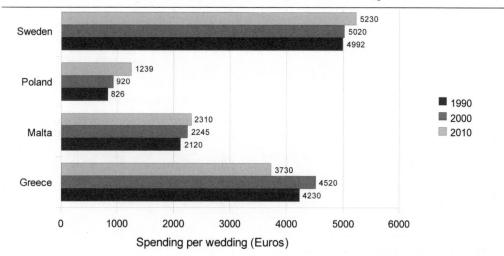

133. By what percentage did average spending on weddings drop in Greece between 2000 and 2010?

A. 6.4%

B. 17.5%

C. 21.2%

D. 11.8%

E. 14.4%

134. How many men in the UK wear shoes larger than size 9?

A. 9.25m

B. 15.18m

C. 9.83m

D. 15.75m

E. 12.8m

FREQUENCY OF MEN'S SHOE SIZE IN THE UK (QUESTIONS 134-136)

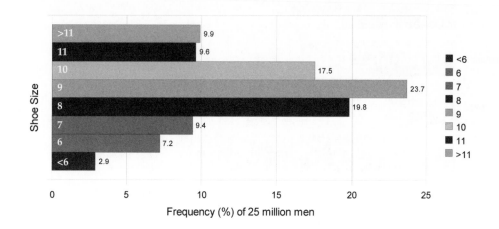

135. How many more men wear size 9 shoes than size 8 in the UK?

A.   1.55m   B.   1.15m

C.   975000   D.   823000

E.   735000

136. Which shoe size is worn by 2.4m men in the UK?

A.   7   B.   8

C.   9   D.   10

E.   11

UNEMPLOYMENT IN EUROPE IN 2008 (QUESTIONS 137-139)

	Population (thousands)	Unemployed (thousands)		Proportion of workforce (%)	
		Men	Women	Men	Women
France	61813	1163	1266	8	10
Italy	59545	902	987	6	10
Spain	44560	863	1050	7	12
UK	61260	817	580	5	4

137. What was the total size of the workforce in Italy in 2008?

A.   59.5m   B.   24.9m

C.   1.9m   D.   23.8m

E.   37.2m

138. How many women were in employment in Spain in 2008?

A.   9.5m   B.   4.9m

C.   7.7m   D.   3.8m

E.   7.2m

139. How many more women than men were unemployed across these four countries in 2008?

A.   22000   B.   39000

C.   64000   D.   97000

E.   138000

WIND POWER GENERATION (KWH MILLIONS) (QUESTIONS 140-142)

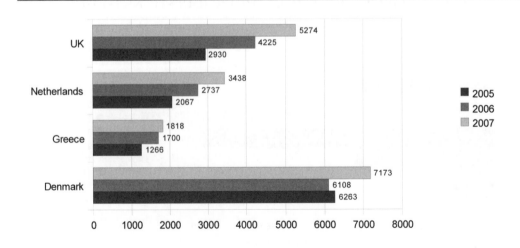

140. What is the percentage growth in wind power generation in the UK between 2005 and 2007?

A. 65%   B. 70%

C. 75%   D. 80%

E. 85%

141. How much more wind power than Greece did the Netherlands produce, as a percentage, in 2006?

A. 19%   B. 72%

C. 57%   D. 43%

E. 61%

142. What percentage of all the wind power generated in 2005 was generated by Denmark?

A. 45%   B. 50%

C. 55%   D. 60%

E. 65%

SPENDING ON EDUCATION IN EUROPE (QUESTIONS 143-145)

Amount spent in Euros (millions)

	Population in 2005 (thousands)	2004	2005	2006
Belgium	10415	12384	12394	12723
Estonia	1347	827	911	996
Norway	4635	4848	5012	5221
Slovakia	5386	6222	6318	6581

143. Which country had the highest growth (in %) in spending on education between 2004 and 2006?

A. Belgium   B. Estonia

C. Norway   D. Slovakia

E. Impossible to tell from the data

144. How much did Belgium spend per head of population on education in 2005?

A. 1190   B. 840

C. 1221   D. 1042

E. 1239

145. What is the overall growth in spending on education between 2005 and 2006?

A. 1.1%   B. 5.2%

C. 4.1%   D. 3.6%

E. 2.9%

SPENDING ON HEALTHCARE IN EUROPE (QUESTIONS 146-148)

Amount spent in Euros (millions)

	Population in 2005 (thousands)	2004	2005	2006
France	61013	175800	179200	181300
Ireland	4187	11398	11893	12302
Poland	38198	12671	15188	16872
Switzerland	7441	24281	24612	25010

146. Which country spent the least money per head of population on healthcare in 2005?

A. France   B. Ireland

C. Poland   D. Switzerland

E. Impossible to tell from the data

147. What is the growth in spending on healthcare in Switzerland between 2004 and 2006?

A. 3.5%   B. 3.0%

C. 2.5%   D. 2.0%

E. 1.5%

148. If the Irish had spent 2850 EUR per head of population on healthcare in 2005, how much extra would they have spent in total on healthcare that year?

A.   100m   B.   80m

C.   65m   D.   53m

E.   40m

EUROPEAN RAIL PASSENGERS (MILLIONS) (QUESTIONS 149-150)

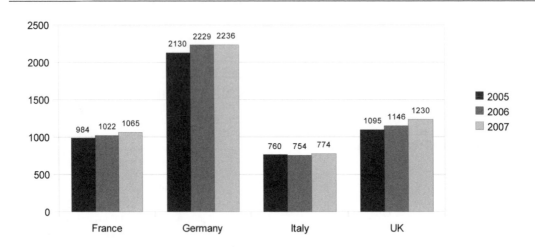

149. Which country had the lowest growth in rail passenger numbers between 2006 and 2007?

A.   France   B.   Germany

C.   Italy   D.   UK

E.   Impossible to tell from the data

150. How many passengers, on average, were carried each day on UK railways in 2005?

A.   0.03m   B.   0.3m

C.   3m   D.   30m

E.   300m

ANSWERS

The symbols used:

Plus or minus	+ –
Multiplication	*
Division	/

1.   C

Just look at the proportions.

Country A:	30.5 : 5.3 (roughly 30/5)
Country B:	93 : 10.2 (roughly 93/10)
Country C:	90 : 10.2 (roughly 90/10)
Country D:	450 : 8.9 (roughly 450/9)
Country E:	200 : 59 (roughly 20/6)

It is plain from the above that by having the biggest territory and one of the lowest number of inhabitants, Country D has the lowest density of population.

2.   B

Add the inflation rates and divide by the number of countries:
(2.8 + 9.1 + 4.9 + 2 + 1.9) / 5 = 4.14

3.   D

Divide the population of Country E by the total of the populations to get the percentage Country E represents in the total. You can calculate in 100s as in: 59 / (5.3 + 10.2 + 10.2 + 9 + 59) = 59 : 93.7 = 0.63 Approximately 63% of the total population lives in country E.

4.   C

The area ratio is 45 : 9, which equals 5:1.

5.   B

Bare copper wire income from export:
8,000 * 2 = 16,000 euros

PTFE wire income from export:
1,000 * 10 = 10,000 euros
The total = 26,000 euros.

6.   A

As we are looking for proportions, we can use the figures given in 00s:
Total wire produced = 100 + 150 + 30 + 20 = **300**
Total wire exported = 80 + 90 + 10 + 20 = **200**
Production : export = 300 : 200 = 3 : 2

7.   D

PTFE wire profit per metre:
10 – 4 = 6 euros;
Exported quantity: 1,000 m; total profit: **6,000** euros
Gold plated wire profit per metre:
20 – 10 = 10 euros;
Exported quantity: 2,000 m; total profit: **20,000**
Total profit: **26,000** euros

8.   C

Considering that production costs amount to 60% of the income, the profit is 40% of the income. The "aircraft industry" includes airplanes and helicopters. Therefore the total profit in 2003 is
(30 + 20) * 0.4 = 20 billion euros (as figures are in billion euros)

9.   B

Cars: gain of 3bn or 6% (3 / 52 = 0.06)
Buses: no gain in income
Trucks: gain of 2bn or 5% (2 / 44 = 0.05)
Boats: gain of 3bn or 25% (3 / 12 = 0.25)
Airplanes: no gain in income
Helicopters: no gain in income

10.   D

The question relates to "production", whereas the table only mentions income. Therefore no answer can be given to this question.

11.   C

The percentage of those 65 years or older is almost the same in every country, yet the population of country E is significantly higher than any other country's. Therefore it is obviously country E that has the highest number of elderly.

12.   B

Company B received 240 million euros for all juices sold in 2004. Pear juice represented a proportion of that, as in:
19 / (19 + 4 + 37) = 19 / 60
240 * (19 / 60) = (240 / 60) * 19 = 76 million euros

13.   A

Company A: 180 + 200 + 220 = **600**
Company B: 225 + 240 + 210 = **675**
Company C: 280 + 225 + 300 = **805**

14.   B

Company A had an income of 200 million euros from selling 46 million juices, or **4.3** euros per juice on average (as in 200 / 46 = 4.3).
Company B had an income of 240 million euros from selling 60 million juices, at **4** euros per juice on average (as in 240 / 60 = 4).
Company C had an income of 225 million euros from selling 58 million juices, at **3.8** euros per juice on average (as in 225 / 58 = 3.8).

15.   D

Looking at the pie chart, one might notice that the EU's share of Hungary's exports – which is equal to the combined share of the EU-15 and the EU-12 – is somewhere in the region of 3/4 = 75%, so 77.8% must be the correct answer. Alternatively, the share in question can be calculated as follows: (11.39 + 32.07) / (11.39 + 32.07 + 7.66 + 1.68 + 2.97) = 43.46 / 55.77 = 77.9%.

16.   B

The value of Hungarian exports to "other countries" was equal to 7.66 billion EUR (in 2008)/ 1.192 (in the period January-September 2007) = 6.43 billion EUR. Therefore, an increase by 7.66 billion EUR - 6.43 billion EUR = 1.23 billion EUR took place.

17.   B

According to the pie chart, the expenses on outdoor advertising equalled 126.4 * 0.1733 = 21.905 (billion RUB) in the first half of 2008 and 21.905 / 1.13 (which we arrive at by knowing there was an increase of 13%) = 19.385 (billion RUB) in the same period in 2007. Thus, an increase by 21.905 billion RUB - 19.385 billion RUB = 2.520 billion RUB = 2520 million RUB took place.

18.   C

Since total advertising expenses amounted to 126.4 * 1.128 = 142.6 (billion RUB) in the second half of 2008, the total for the whole year equalled 126.4 + 142.6 = 269 (billion RUB). Therefore, an increase by 269 / 229 - 1 = 17.5% took place compared to 2007.

19.   B

According to the pie chart, the expenses on television advertising equalled 126.4 * 0.5214 = 65.9 (billion RUB), while a total of 126.4 * 0.2199 + 126.4 * 0.0522 = 126.4 * (0.2199 + 0.0522) = 126.4 * 0.2721 = 34.4 (billion RUB) was spent on print media advertising and radio advertising together. The difference between the two figures is equal to 65.9 - 34.4 = 31.5 (billion RUB).

20.   A

The ratio of foreign exchange loans to the GDP in a given country is equal to the product of the two percentages shown in the diagram (total loans/GDP * foreign exchange loans/total loans = foreign exchange loans/GDP). One might notice that for each country, the length of the bottom bar represents exactly this ratio, and it is obviously the Czech Republic for which this length is the smallest.

21.   C

The ratio of foreign exchange loans to the GDP in a given country is equal to the product of the two percentages shown in the diagram (total loans/GDP * foreign exchange loans/total loans = foreign exchange loans/GDP). Multiplying this by the GDP we get the amount of foreign exchange loans. Thus, the figure in question equals 127 billion EUR * 0.503 * 0.13 = 8.305 billion EUR = 8305 million EUR.

22.   C

The total number of mobile phone subscriptions in a given country is equal to the product of the number of mobile phone subscriptions per inhabitant (which is 1/100 of the number of mobile phone subscriptions per 100 inhabitants) and the country's population. Comparing Luxembourg and the Czech Republic, it can be seen that the first factor of this product is almost the same for both countries, which means the proportion in question is approximately equal to the proportion of the second factors – the two population figures –, i. e. 1/20.

23.   D

In the second quarter of 2000, the three leading PC manufacturers were Compaq, Dell and HP with a combined market share of 13.2% + 11.4% + 7.5% = 32.1%; while in the second quarter of 2008, the top three consisted of HP, Dell and Acer, their market shares totalling 18.9% + 16.4% + 9.9% = 45.2%. Thus, the figure in question increased by 45.2% - 32.1% = 13.1 percentage points.

24.   A

If HP's market share had remained unchanged at 7.5%, the number of PCs it sold would have increased from 30.33 million * 0.075 to 70.64 million * 0.075, i. e. by (70.64 million - 30.33 million) * 0.075 = 40.31 million * 0.075 = 3.023 million.

25.   C

The number of PCs sold by Dell rose from 30.33

million * 0.114 = 3.458 million in the second quarter of 2000 to 70.64 million * 0.164 = 11.585 million in the second quarter of 2008. This corresponds to an increase by 11.585 / 3.458 – 1 = 235%.

26.   A

The total number of PCs sold worldwide rose from 30.33 million to 70.64 million between the second quarter of 2000 and the same period in 2008. This corresponds to an average quarterly increase by (70.64 million – 30.33 million) / (4 * (2008 – 2000)) = 40.31 million / 32 = 1.26 million (4 [quarters] * 8 [years] = 40.31 million).

27.   B

Denoting the 1997 average price by x, the same figure was equal to 1.85x in 2005 and 2.5x in 2006. Therefore, the average price increased by 2.5x / 1.85x - 1 = 2.5 / 1.85 - 1 = 35% from 2005 to 2006.

28.   D

Denoting the 1997 average price by x, the same figure was equal to 2.36x in 2008 and 0.94x in 2001. We also know that 2.36x = 3000, thus x = 3000 / 2.36 = 1271 and 0.94x = 0.94 * 1271 = 1195 (EUR per square metre). This means that in 2001, one could expect to be able to buy a 83-square metre property with 100,000 EUR since 100,000 / 1195 = 83.7.

29.   C

The absolute amount of social expenditure is the product of the GDP and the percentage of the GDP that social expenditure accounts for. Looking at the 1990 data, social expenditure amounted to 25.1% of the GDP in both Denmark and France; therefore, it is only the GDP figures of the two countries that need to be compared. Since France's GDP was 1,007.4 billion USD / 95.1 billion USD = 1 007.4 / 95.1 = 10.6 times greater than Denmark's in 1990, the absolute amount of social expenditure was also 10.6 times greater in France than in Denmark.

30.   A

If a figure increases by 200%, it is tripled (x + 200% = x + (200/100) * x = x + 2x = 3x); thus, we need to look for countries whose GDP more than tripled between 1990 and 2005. Taking a quick look at the data, we can see that Ireland is the only country which satisfies this condition (160.4 > 3 * 45.7, since 3 * 45.7 is less than 3 * 50 = 150; or more precisely, 160.4 / 45.7 = 3.51 > 3).

31.   E

Between 1990 and 2005, social expenditure in Germany increased from 22.3% of 1,462.8 billion USD = (22.3 / 100) * 1,462.8 billion USD = 0.223 * 1 462.8 billion USD = 326.2 billion USD) to 26.7% of 2,586.5 billion USD = (26.7 / 100) * 2,586.5 billion USD = 0.267 * 2,586.5 billion USD = 690.6 billion USD. This corresponds to an increase of 690.6 billion USD – 326.2 billion USD = 364.4 billion USD.

32.   E

Zimbabwe's lithium reserves were 27,000 tonnes at the end of 2008. If 300 tonnes are mined each year, Zimbabwe's reserves will be exhausted in 90 years (27 000 / 300 = 90).

33.   D

The total reserves of the six countries equalled 220 + 910 + 360 + 3 000 + 1 100 + 27 = 5 617 (thousand tonnes) at the end of 2008. This was 51.06% of the world total. One percent of the total reserves is 5 617 / 51.06 = 110 thousand tonnes. 110 * 100 (percent) = 11 000 (thousand tonnes), which is 11 million tonnes.

34.   D

The amount of lithium produced in the six countries together was equal to 6 910 + 180 + 707 + 11 000 + 3 010 + 300 = 22 107 (tonnes) in 2007 and 6 900 + 180 + 710 + 12 000 + 3500 + 300 = 23 590 (tonnes) in 2008. Since 23 590 / 22 107 = 1.067, an increase by (1.067 * 100) % – 100% = 106.7% – 100% = 6.7% took place in the production between 2007 and 2008. The amount of lithium produced in 2009 will thus equal 23 590

tonnes + 6.7% = 25 171 tonnes = 25.2 thousand tonnes.

35.   C

Looking at the table, at the end of 2008, Chile's proven lithium reserves amounted to 3 000 thousand tonnes. Add to this 11 000 tonnes and 12 000 tonnes mined in 2007 and 2008 and you get the total reserves at the end of 2006, or 3 000 thousand tonnes + 23 thousand tonnes = 3 023 thousand tonnes.

36.   E

The average annual wine production in this period was equal to (282 + 284 + 268) / 3 = 278 (million hectolitres).

37.   F

Global wine production in 2003 was 263 million hectolitres. The difference between the actual production in 2004-2008 period and what the figure would have been had production remained 263 million hectolitres each year equals (297 + 282 + 284 + 268 + 269) – 263 * 5 = 1,400 – 1,315 = 85.

38.   C

The gold reserves of the central bank of the United States decreased by 5 tonnes (from 8139 to 8134) between 1999 and 2009, giving a percentage decrease of 0.06% (5 / 8139 *100 = 0.06).

39.   C

The total gold reserves of the world's central banks decreased from 33,524 tonnes in March 1999 (8,139 + 3,469 + 3,025 + 2,452 + 395 + 2,590 + 13,454 = 33,524) to 30,146 tonnes in March 2009 (8,134 + 3,412 + 2,487 + 2,452 + 1,054 + 1,040 + 11,567 = 30,146). Since between March 2008 and March 2009 central banks sold a total of 345 tonnes, the reserves amounted to 30,491 tonnes (30,146 + 345 = 30,491) in March 2008. Thus, the total amount sold from the reserves between March 1999 and March 2008 is 3,033 tonnes (33,524 – 30,491 = 3,033), and so the yearly average for this period equals 3,033 / (2008 – 1999) = 3,033 / 9 = 337 (tonnes).

40.   F

China's GDP is projected to increase by 8.3% from 2008 to 2009. Thus, the 2009 GDP will be 108.3% of the 2008 GDP. If China's 2008 GDP is x, the 2009 GDP will equal x * 108.3 / 100 = 1.083x. The 2010 GDP is projected to be 110.2% of the 2009 GDP (= 1.083x), so it will equal 1.083x * (110.2 / 100) = 1.083x * 1.102. The 2011 GDP will be 109% of the projected 2010 GDP and thus equal (1.083x * 1.102) * 109.3% = 1.083x * 1.102 * 1.093 = 1.304x. This means China's 2011 GDP will be 1.304 times greater than the 2008 figure (= x) = 130.4% of the 2008 GDP; so between 2008 and 2011, the country's GDP is projected to increase by 130.4% – 100% = 30.4%.

41.   A

France's GDP is projected to decrease by 2.3% in 2009, therefore 2,133 * (100% – 2.3%) = 2,133 * 97.7% = 2,133 * (97.7 / 100) = (2,133 * 0.977) (billion USD). In 2010 it will increase by 1.4%, thus (2,133 * 0.977) + 1.4% = (2,133 * 0.977) * 101.4% = (2,133 * 0.977) * (101.4 / 100) = 2,133 * 0.977 * 1.014 = 2,113.1 (billion USD). Therefore, France's GDP will change by 2,113.1– 2,133 = –19.9 ≈ –20 (billion USD) between 2008 and 2010 approximately.

42.   B

Germany's 2009 projected GDP will decrease by 4.9% as in 2,925 * (100% – 4.9%) = 2,925 * 95.1% = 2,925 * (95.1 / 100) = (2,925 * 0.951) (billion USD). In 2010 it will increase by 1.4% from the projected 2009 figure, = 2,925 * 0.951 * 1.014 = 2,820.6 (billion USD). If the 2008 population of Germany is x (because we are not given the figure), the 2010 population will be equal to x – 1% = x * (100% – 1%) = x * (99 / 100) = 0.99x. As the country's GDP per capita was (2,925 / x) in 2008, it will equal 2,820.6 / 0.99x = 2 849.1 / x in 2010.The projected percentage of decrease from 2008 to 2010 is 2.6% because (2,849.1 / x) / (2,925 / x) = 2,849.1 / 2,925 = 0.974 = (0.974 * 100) % = 97.4% of the former one, a decrease by 100% – 97.4% = 2.6%.

43.   B

The population of Romania was 21.6 million in 2007, and it is projected to equal 19.2 million in 2040. The latter figure accounts for 19.2 million / 21.6 million = 19.2 / 21.6 = 0.889 = (0.889 * 100) % = 88.9% of the former one.

44.   A

Between 2020 and 2040, the population of Sweden is projected to increase from 9.9 million to 10.5 million, = 0.6 million, giving an annual increase of 0.6 million / (2040 – 2020) = 0.6 million / 20 = 0.03 million. In order to exceed 10 million, the population has to increase by at least 10 million – 9.9 million = 0.1 million compared to 2020, i.e. 0.1 million / 0.03 million = 0.1 / 0.03 = 10 / 3 = 3 1/3 years. Thus, the population will exceed 10 million in the course of the fourth year - i.e. 2024.

45.   D

Between 2007 and 2060, the population of Poland is projected to change from 38.1 million to 31.1 million = 31.1 / 38.1 = 0.816 = (0.816 * 100) % = 81.6% of the 2007 population, which means a decrease by 100% – 81.6% = 18.4% will take place. If the population of the Czech Republic decreased by this same percentage, it would equal 10.3 million * 81.6% = 10.3 million * (81.6 / 100) = 10.3 million * 0.816 = 8.4 million.

46.   F

In 2020, the population of the six countries together is projected to equal 11.3 + 10.5 + 38.0 + 20.8 + 9.9 + 65.7 = 156.2 (million), while the total population of the EU-27 will be 513.8 million. Thus, the proportion of the population of the EU-27 that will live in the six countries in 2020 is 156.2 million / 513.8 million = 156.2 / 513.8 = 0.304, which is approximately equal to 0.3 = 3/10, i. e. three tenths.

47.   A

The bar graph contains data on the area per municipality in each country, so in order to determine the total area of a country, first we need to know how many municipalities it has. This can be calculated by dividing the total population by the number of inhabitants per municipality, 10,622,000 / 34,487 = 308 municipalities. Therefore the area of the country is 308 municipalities * 299 square km / municipality = 92.1 thousand square km.

48.   D

The population density can be calculated by dividing the number of inhabitants per municipality by the area per municipality. When looking for the country with the highest population density, refering to the bar chart, Estonia and Latvia can be eliminated immediately since for these two countries the bar for the number of inhabitants per municipality is shorter than the one representing the area per municipality. As regards the rest, you might notice that in Greece and Slovenia, the quotient is below 100 (10 868 / 128 < 12,800 / 128 = 100 and 9,629 / 97 < 9,700 / 97 = 100), while in Portugal and Slovakia, it is above 100 (34,487 / 299 > 29,900 / 299 = 100 and 1,870 / 17 > 1,700 / 17 = 100). Thus, Greece and Slovenia are also eliminated, so we only need to exactly calculate the population densities of Portugal and Slovakia: the former equals 34,487 / 299 = 115.3, while the latter is equal to 1,870 / 17 = 110.

49.   F

If the number of municipalities decreases by half, the area per municipality will double to 2 * 128 square km = 256 square km.

50.   D

This is the total population (100%) minus those over 60 (24%) minus those under 15 (13%) which is 63%. We then need to multiply this by the population (7590 thousand and divide by 100 to convert the value from the percentage. 7590*63/100 = 4781.7 thousand = 4.78 million.

51.   B

The number of rural dwellers is the total (100%) minus the number of urban dwellers (47%) which is 53%. This is then multiplied by the population (3140 thousand) and divided by 100 to convert the value from percentage. 3140*53/100 = 1.66 million.

52.   A

256 (thousand) in a population of 5120 (thousand) is 256/5120 = 0.05. This is multiplied by 100 to make it a percentage which is 5%.

53.   D

The kestrel population grew by (517-470) = 47 during the year. To calculate the percentage we need to divide the increase by the starting value and multiply by 100. This is (100*47)/470 which is 10%.

54.   E

The number of buzzards in 2009 was 2296 out of a total population of 11480 birds. This is 2296/11480 = 0.2. Multiply by 100 to convert to a percentage which equals 20%.

55.   C

The number of hawks is 6140 so all the others total (11380-6140) = 5240 which is 900 fewer than the number of hawks.

56.   B

France generated 24MKWh out of a total of (24+42+44+34+16) = 160MKWh. This is a proportion of 24/160 = 0.15. To express this as a percentage, multiply by 100 which is 15%.

57.   D

In 2006 the UK generated 8MKWh which increased to 16 MKWh by 2008. This is an increase of (16-8) = 8. To express this as a percentage rise divide the increase (8) by the starting value (8) and multiply by 100. This gives 100%.

58.   E

The total generated in 2007 was (16+38+36+27+11) = 128 and the total generated in 2006 was (12+35+35+23+7) = 112. This is an increase of (128-112) = 16MKWh.

59.   A

In Romania the users grew from 13,450,000 to 14,660,000. This is an increase of 1,210,000. To express this as a percentage we divide the increase by the starting value and multiply by 100. So, 100*(1210000/13450000) = 9%.

60.   B

The total number of people in Romania and Switzerland is (21635+7441) = 29076 (thousand). The total number of internet users is (13842+5334) = 19176 (thousand). Therefore the number not using the internet is (29076-19176) = 9900 (thousand) or 9.9m.

61.   E

The proportion of the population using the internet is 8020/10415 = 0.77 (both numbers are in thousands so we can round to thousands). To make a percentage we multiply by 100 to get 77%.

62.   C

As the units for wine production and population are all in thousands then they can safely be ignored. The wine produced in Switzerland is 1000 hectolitres, half of which (50000 litres) is drunk by 7441 people. This is an average of 50000/7441 = 6.7 litres per person.

63.   A

The percentage produced by Germany is 95000 divided by the total amount produced which is (17200+95000+30200+3600) = 146000 and then multiplied by 100. This is 100*(95000/146000) = 65%.

64.   D

The production and population are both in thousands so can be rounded. The production is 176600 litres by 43060 people. This is 176600/43060 = 4.1 litres per person.

65.   C

The proportion of subscriptions accounted for by Denmark is 3799 divided by the total of all subscriptions for that year, (1594+3799+5511+1759) = 12663 which is 3799/12663 = 0.3. To make this a percentage then multiply by 100 which is 30%.

66.   B

The growth is the increase in subscriptions divided by the starting level and then multiplied by 100 to make it a percentage. The increase is (1928-1819) = 109. 100*(109/1818) = 6%.

67.   E

In 2007 there were 2451 (thousand) subscriptions in Bulgaria between 3770 (thousand) people. The (thousands) can be ignored. So there are 2451/3770 = 0.65 subscriptions per person or 65 per hundred people.

68.   D

The proportion of exports by weight accounted for by Italy is 482 divided by the total exports, (3976+482+245+647) = 5350. 482/5350 = 0.09 which is multiplied by 100 to make it a percentage, 9%.

69.   C

The trade balance is simply the difference between value of the exports and the value of the imports. If this is negative then it is a deficit. Only Spain and UK have imports larger than exports and thus, a deficit. Spain's is (126-417) = -291 and UK is (1132-1387) = -255.

70.   A

The UK exported 647 tonnes of vaccines for $1132m. One tonne is one million grammes and so the cost per gramme is simply 1132/647 = $1.75 per gramme.

71.   B

France generated 452 million MWh of electricity for 61.013 million people. This is an average of 452/61.013 = 7.4 MWh per person.

72.   C

Hungary generated 150 million MWh out of a total of (440+150+67+93) = 750 million MWh. This is 150/750 = 0.2 which is multiplied by 100 to make it a percentage, 20%.

73.   E

The growth is the increase in generation divided by the starting level which is then multiplied by 100 to make it a percentage. This is 100*(93-90)/90 = 3.3%.

74.   A

Ireland collected 595 (thousand) tonnes out of a total of (2812+595+716+1287) = 5410 (thousand) tonnes. This is a proportion of 595/5410 = 0.11 which is multiplied by 100 to make it a percentage of 11%.

75.   E

Norway increased its collection by (931-716) = 215 (thousand) tonnes. The growth is the increase divided by the starting level which is then multiplied by 100 to make it a percentage. Thus, 100*(215/716) = 30%.

76.   D

In 2006 Slovenia collected 1326 (thousand) tonnes of waste. If they collect 5% more in 2007 then they would have collected 1326*1.05 = 1392.3 (thousand) tonnes. They actually collected 1354 (thousand) tonnes which is a difference of 38.3 (thousand) tonnes.

77.   D

The student population in 2005 was 171000 of which 50.9% were female. So, we multiply these together

and divide by 100 to convert from a percentage to get 87000.

78.   A

The percentage of female students is 53.9% so the percentage of male students must be (100-53.9) = 46.1%. The difference is 7.8%. If we multiply this difference by the total student population and divide by 100 to convert from a percentage we get 56400.

79.   E

The female student proportion grew from 53.5% to 54.9% which is an increase of 1.4 percentage points. To calculate the percentage rise, divide the increase by the starting level and multiply by 100. So, 100*(1.4/53.5) = 2.6%.

80.   B

In Slovakia there were 23 deaths per 100,000 people so the total number of deaths is (8187 (thousand) * 23 / 100(thousand)) = 1883. In Belgium it was (10400*18/100) = 1872 which is a difference of 11.

81.   D

The death rate dropped from 49 to 39 per 100,000 population, a drop of 10 per 100,000 or 1 per 10000. So, the actual drop in deaths is 58645 (thousand) divided by 10000 or 58645/10 which is 5865.

82.   C

The death rate increased from 15 to 21 per 100,000 people. To calculate the percentage increase divide, the difference by the starting value and multiply by 100. So, 100*(21-15)/15 = 40%.

83.   D

The crime rate is the number of crimes divided by the population. From this it can clearly be seen that only Portugal will produce a number that is greater than 1 per thousand and must, therefore, be the highest.

84. A

The crime rate is the number of crimes divided by the population. However, if the population remains unchanged then it can be ignored. Hence the percentage change is simply the increase divided by the starting value and then multiplied by 100 to make it a percentage. Thus, 100*(3532-3270)/3270 = 8%.

85. E

The average rate is the total number of crimes (58122+3105+305+11017) = 72549 divided by the total population (61013+4187+403+10529) = 76132 which is 0.95 per thousand which is 95 per hundred thousand.

86. D

The average amount per customer is the total amount bought divided by the number of customers. This gives 121000 tonnes divided by 6 million which is 121Kg divided by 6 or 20 Kg per person.

87. E

The rate of growth is the increase in sales divided by the starting point and then multiplied by 100 to make it a percentage. The increase is (591-523) = 68. So, 100*68/523 = 13%.

88. A

Lidl sold 618 (thousand) tonnes out of a total of (523+110+618+294) = 1545 (thousand) tonnes. The percentage is then 100*618/1545 = 40%.

89. C

The number of patents filed by Germany was (32837+33936+33187) = 99960. The total number filed was (66084+66857+66972)= 199913. The percentage is, therefore, 100*99960/199913 = 50%.

90. E

To calculate the per capita patent filing we need to know the populations of the countries so there is no way of calculating this.

91. B

The overall growth is the increase between 2005 and 2006 divided by the starting point and then multiplied by 100 to make it a percentage. So, 100*(66857-66084)/66084=1.17%.

92. D

The amount spent is the spending per inhabitant multiplied by the population. The population of Ukraine dwarfs the other three countries combined and, therefore, so does its spending.

93. C

The amount spent is the spending per inhabitant multiplied by the population. Thus it is 1250*2240(thousand) = 2800 million or 2.8 billion.

94. A

The percentage increase is the amount of increase divided by the starting point and then multiplied by 100. This gives 100*(1022-911)/911 = 12%.

95. B

The local contribution is 9821 tonnes and their total contribution is (9821+19223+561) = 29605 and so the proportion of local aid is 9821/29605 = 0.33, which is a third.

96. C

The total aid donation is (6292+1019+871) = 8182 tonnes which, at an average cost of $1219 per tonne, is 8182*1219 = 9,973,858. Divide this by the population of Hungary (9,973,000) for an average cost of $1 per person.

97.   E

The total direct aid is (648+2901+871+561) = 4981 tonnes, of which, Austria's contribution was 648 tonnes. This gives a proportion of 648/4981 = 0.13. To make this a percentage we multiply by 100 to get 13%.

98.   D

The number of births is the rate multiplied by the population. This gives values of 62646, 63977, 60293 and 64093 respectively and so Slovakia had the most births.

99.   A

The number of births is the rate multiplied by the population. So, for Croatia this gives (4443*12.1) = 53760 and for Ireland it is (4187*12.8) = 53594. This is a difference of 166.

100.   D

The birth rate has fallen from 14.1 per thousand to 11.3 per thousand, a fall of 2.8 percentage points. The rate of decline is the difference (2.8) divided by the starting level (14.1) and multiplied by 100 to make it a percentage. 100*2.8/14.1 = 19.9%.

101.   A

The number of churchgoers is the percentage multiplied by the population. Greece has such a small population compared to the others it need not be calculated. The other three give values of 9.88m, 9.79m and 7.79m, hence France has the most churchgoers.

102.   B

The population increases from 11064 (thousand) by 351 (thousand) to 11,415,000, of which 21.9% go to church. 11415000*21.9 = 250 million which we need to divide by 100 to convert from a percentage which gives 2.5m.

103.   C

The percentage drop in attendance is the difference in attendance divided by the starting value and multiplied by 100 to make it a percentage. Thus: 100*(16.7-15.9)/16.7 = 4.8%.

104.   B

The percentage growth is the increase in sales divided by the starting level and then multiplied by 100. As this is a comparison rather than an absolute value that is sought, the *100 can be omitted. This gives expressions of 20/470, 11/210, 4/525 and 24/895 respectively and from among these options the result for 11/210, Morrisons' growth, is clearly the largest.

105.   A

The percentage contribution is Sainsbury's sales (525) divided by the total sales for that year (470+210+525+895) = 2100 and multiplied by 100 to make it a percentage. Thus: 100*525/2100 = 25%.

106.   E

A growth of 10% would have increased Asda's sales from 470 to 470*1.1 = 517. They actually sold 490, a difference of 27 in million litres.

107.   C

The average spending is the total amount spent divided by the population. This would be 2340(million)/58.645(million). The millions can be ignored so the answer is 39.90 euro per person.

108.   A

The increase in spending is (233-222) = 11 million euro and there are 11 million inhabitants and so the increase is 1 euro per person.

109.   E

The population increase of 163000 is just about 1%.

The increase in spending from 600 to 606 is also 1%. Therefore, the spending per person remains constant.

110.   A

The number of phone lines per head of population is the number of lines divided by the population of the country. However, from simple inspection it can be seen that only Andorra will produce a result below one half (0.5) and must, therefore, be the lowest.

111.   D

The percentage rate of growth is the increase divided by the starting value and then multiplied by 100 to make it a percentage. This gives 100*(230-200)/200 = 15%.

112.   B

The percentage of lines in Luxembourg is the number of lines there (247) divided by the total number of lines (36.5+247+210+21) = 514.5 and then multiplied by 100 to make it a percentage. So, 100*247/514.5 = 48%.

113.   E

The death rate fell from 24.1 to 21.7 per 100,000 over the period, a difference of 2.4.
   The number of deaths is the death rate (2.4) multiplied by the population (2,292,000) and divided by (100000) as the rate is per 100,000. This gives 2292*2.4/100 = 55.

114.   C

The decline in the death rate is the difference between the start and finish rates divided by the starting rate and then multiplied by 100 to make it a percentage. This gives 100*(27.1-24.1)/27.1 = 11%.

115.   A

The number of deaths is the death rate (17.2) multi-

plied by the population (35000) and divided by (100000) as the rate is per 100,000. This gives 35*17.2/100 = 6.

116.   E

The two journey times are 3:28 and 3:33. These give a combined time of 7hr 1min.

117.   C

The two journey times are 135 minutes and 159 minutes. To calculate how much shorter the first one is, divide the difference by the longer time and multiply by 100 to make it a percentage. Thus, 100*(159-135)/159 = 15%.

118.   A

The journey times are 2:25, 1:20 and 1:56 for the respective legs of the journey. These add up to 5 hours 41 minutes.

119.   D

The growth is the difference between the two values (5.8-5.0) divided by the starting value (5.0) and multiplied by 100 to make it a percentage. This gives 16%.

120.   B

The number of octogenarians is the percentage multiplied by the population. For Germany this is (82.1m*5.8%) = 4.76m and for France it is (62.6m*6.1%) = 3.82m, a difference of 0.94m or 940,000.

121.   A

The increase in the number of octogenarians is the increase in the rate (5.5%-5.3%) which is 0.2% multiplied by the population (9.3m). This gives 18600.

122.   E

Half of 1.2m is 0.6m or 600 thousand. There were 3603 thousand visitors to Denmark and so the proportion of foreign visitors is 600/3603 which is one sixth.

123.   C

A quick calculation shortcut can be made as follows. The growth is the difference between the 2001 and 2005 values divided by the 2001 value. Norway's growth is very small and Sweden's is less than 200 on a starting value of over 4000 which is less than 5%. So only the other two need be calculated. Finland is (2511-2297)/2297 = 0.09 and Denmark is (3743-3479)/3743 = 0.07 and so Finland has the highest growth.

124.   D

The per head visitor ratio is the number of visitors divided by the population. This gives (2633/4700) when both are in thousands. This is 0.56 visitors per head of population.

125.   D

The average density is the total population divided by the total area. Thus, 10440 (thousand) is divided by 30 (thousand) which gives 348 people per square kilometre.

126.   A

The growth in population is the difference in populations (45067-40970) = 4097 divided by the starting population (40970) and multiplied by 100 to make it a percentage. This gives 100*4097/40970 = 10%.

127.   E

The increase in population is the total population for 2008 (10667+63983+10618+ 45067) = 130335 (thousand) minus the total population for 2002 (10310+61426+10329+40970) = 123035 (thousand). 130335-123035 = 7300 (thousand) or 7.3 million.

128.   C

The percentage increase between any two years is the difference divided by the starting value and multiplied by 100. By inspection one can see that there are only two occasions in the table where an increase occurs: Italy 04-05 and Slovakia 05-06. The former gives a growth of 100*600/234600 = 0.26% and the latter gives 100*52/15628 = 0.33%.

129.   B

The number of marriages per thousand people is simply the number of marriages divided by the population (in thousands). So, for Ireland it is 20209/4187 = 4.83 and for Italy it is 235200/58645 = 4.01; the difference is about 0.8.

130.   A

The percentage drop in marriages is the difference in numbers between the two years divided by the starting value and multiplied by 100. Thus: 100*(18211-17919)/18211 = 1.6%.

131.   E

The percentage rise is the 2010 value (1239) minus the 1990 value (826) divided by the 1990 value and multiplied by 100. This gives 100*413/826 = 50%.

132.   D

The total spending is the number of weddings multiplied by the average spending per wedding. This gives 37250*5020 = 186995000 or 187m euro.

133.   B

The percentage change is the 2010 value (3730) minus the 2000 value (4520) divided by the 2000 value and multiplied by 100. This gives 100*-790/4520 = -17.5%, which is a fall of 17.5%.

134.   A

The number of men wearing larger than size 9

shoes is the sum of the percentages wearing size 10 (17.5), size 11 (9.6) and greater than size 11 (9.9) divided by 100 and multiplied by the total number of men (25 million). This gives (37/100)*25 million = 9.25m.

135.   C

The difference in the number of men wearing size 8 and size 9 shoes is the difference in percentages divided by 100 and multiplied by the number of men. This gives 25m*(23.7-19.8)/100 = 975000.

136.   E

The percentage of men wearing a particular shoe size is the number of men wearing it (2.4m) divided by the total number of men (25m) and multiplied by 100 to make it a percentage. This gives 100*(2.4)/25 = 9.6% which is the percentage of men wearing size 11s.

137.   B

The workforce is the number of unemployed divided by the percentage of the workforce that is unemployed and multiplied by 100. This has to be done for both men and women and then added together. So, (902/0.06) + (987/0.1) = 24900 (thousand) or 24.9m.

138.   C

The female workforce is the number of women unemployed divided by the percentage unemployed and multiplied by 100. The number employed is then the workforce minus the number unemployed. Thus, 100*(1050/12) = 8750. 8750-1050 =7700 (thousand) or 7.7m.

139.   E

The total number of women unemployed is (1266+987+1050+580) = 3883 and the total number of men unemployed is (1163+902+863+817) = 3745. This is a difference of 138 (thousand).

140.   D

The percentage growth is the increase divided by the starting point and multiplied by 100 to convert to a percentage. This give 100*(5274-2930)/2930 = 80%.

141.   E

Greece produced 1700kWh and the Netherlands 2737kWh. The difference is 1037kWh which is (1037/1700) = 0.61 times more. Multiply by 100 to convert to a percentage of 61%.

142.   B

The percentage of power generated by Denmark is their generation (6263) divided by the total generated by all four countries (2930+2067+1266+6263) = 12526 and multiplied by 100 to make it a percentage. 100*6263/12526 = 50%.

143.   B

The growth is the difference between the values for the two years divided by the starting level and multiplied by 100. However, we can see from inspection that Belgium has a growth of about 350/12000 which is very small, Norway is nearly 400/4800 which is less than 10% and Slovakia is about 350/6000 which is about 5%. In contrast, Estonia is about 170/800 which is about 20%, far more than the others.

144.   A

The per capita spending is the total amount spent divided by the population. This is 12394 (million)/10415 (thousand), which is 1190 euro per person.

145.   D

The overall growth between 2005 and 2006 is the total spent in 2006 (12723+996+5221+6581) = 25521 minus the total spent in 2005 (12394+911+5012+ 6318) = 24635 divided by the 2005 spending and multiplied by 100 to convert to a percentage. This gives 100*(25521-24635)/24635 = 3.6%.

146.   C

The per capita spending is the amount spent divided by the population. However, simple inspection reveals that while having the largest population Poland has spent the second least of all the countries; it has barely spent more than Ireland yet has nearly 10 times the population and must, therefore, have spent the least per head of population. Further, Poland is the only country where the population (in thousands) is higher than the amount spent in 2005.

147.   B

The growth is the difference in values divided by the starting value and multiplied by 100 to convert to a percentage. This gives 100*(25010-24281)/24281 = 3%.

148.   E

The total spending is the per capita spending multiplied by the population. This gives 2850*4187 (thousand) = €11933m. They actually spent 11893m so it would be a rise of €40m.

149.   B

The growth is the difference in numbers for the two years divided by the starting value. However, simple inspection shows that Germany's growth is so small that it appears flat on the graph and so is, therefore, the smallest increase. Along with their highest starting value this must make theirs the lowest growth.

150.   C

The total number of passengers travelling in 2005 was 1095 (million) which is (1095 million)/365 per day or 3 million.

6. Succeeding in Abstract Reasoning Tests

When first faced with an abstract reasoning test such as the one on this page, it can be a daunting experience. In each EPSO abstract reasoning test, you will see a text-based question (something similar to "Which of the following figures comes next in the series?"). Your eyes will scan the shapes in a haphazard fashion. You look at the first image, then the second. You quickly glance at the "answer figures" and get an idea. You then check all the shapes against that idea to find out whether it works. Then you realize that the figure you carefully selected would only fit the prospective pattern if just one figure in the question was a little bit different. Now it's time to start all over again.

Just as in the case of verbal reasoning tests, a systematic approach can produce results much more reliably and quickly. As part of such a systematic approach, we must mention that there are various abstract reasoning test types, depending on:

- the use or avoidance of colours
- the logical relationship between the various figures, whether they are part of a series, a grid, or if there is one figure which is the odd-one-out
- the number of dimensions in the test (two- or three-dimensional tests both exist)

Fortunately, it is now known that EPSO have chosen a type of abstract reasoning test that is very well defined:

- only black-and-white images are used (possibly with various shades of grey)
- only two-dimensional tests are given
- only series-type questions are used
- five items of the series are shown, and the candidate must select the next item in the series
- there are usually five answer options (though EPSO may vary this).

A typical abstract reasoning question: *Which figure is next in the series?*

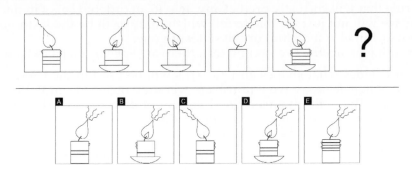

In abstract reasoning tests, it is extremely useful to identify the components. Let us look at these one-by-one:

- Building blocks: the building blocks of abstract reasoning tests are twofold:

  – Shapes and patterns are the actual visual objects that are used to construct the figures in the test: triangles, squares, circles, everyday objects (flowers, flasks, houses, and so on), as well as the physical properties of these objects (stripes, dotted or solid fill patterns, and so on)

  – Operations are various visual changes that these objects can undergo, such as colour inversion, multiplication, rotation, change of position, and countless others

- Rules: the rules of an abstract reasoning test are its essential component – they are the text-based description of what the relationship between the various shapes and patterns is, and between the various figures of an exercise

In this chapter, we will:

- Introduce how abstract reasoning tests are designed: insight into the thought process that is behind the creation of abstract reasoning tests will be very valuable when you are on the other side, that is, when taking such tests

- Introduce the various building blocks, typical shapes, patterns and operations that you will encounter in abstract reasoning tests

- Discuss how to approach abstract reasoning tests

- Provide tips on how to prepare for them

By quickly identifying the building blocks of the test and systematically looking for the above patterns and operations in each test question, you will be able to identify the rules that the question author invented to create the figures and the answer options. Consequently, you will be able to "generate" or "anticipate" the correct figure in your mind without even looking at the options. This method is highly reliable since you will not select one of the figures as the correct answer just because that particular shape seems the best or most suitable option: you will also have independent confirmation, that is, the rule and the figure you came up with yourself.

How Are Abstract Reasoning Tests Designed?

In this section, we will provide a look into the "workshop" of abstract reasoning test designers and, through a real test example, introduce how abstract reasoning exercises are designed.

As mentioned earlier, EPSO uses the series test type exclusively in its competitions. In this type of abstract reasoning test, the question is looking for the one figure that correctly completes a series of figures. A series is an abstract mathematical concept which describes a rule that will correctly predict any item in an ordered set of items. If we identify the rule, we will not just be able to tell which figure will be the sixth one (as in the example above), but also the ninth or the sixteenth one.

When designing an abstract reasoning test, there are specific steps to take:

1. The author decides what shapes and patterns will be used in the tests. Based on the sample test above, let's say we will use an everyday object (a candle) in our abstract reasoning test. This will give us a good variety of objects to work with: the candle itself, candlewick, flame, smoke, possibly a dish to hold the candle in, wax drops coming down the sides of the candle, and so on.

2. Next, the author has to keep in mind the difficulty of the test to be designed. It is

expected that in EPSO competitions for Assistants, the difficulty of the abstract reasoning test will fall into the "medium" difficulty category. The importance of difficulty during design lies in the fact that the number of different rules the author will come up with will determine the difficulty of the test.

3. Once the rules and the shapes/operations are identified and drawn, the author needs to come up with the one correct and several incorrect answer options. The incorrect options must not all be "completely wrong" – in a good (that is, tricky) abstract reasoning test, some of the incorrect answers are *almost* correct.

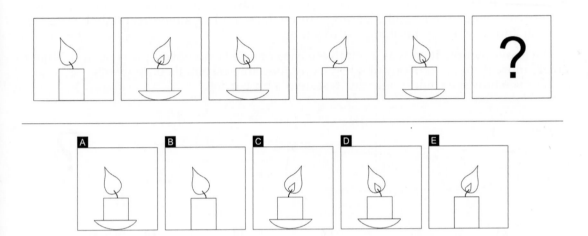

Consider the sample item above. We can identify the following building blocks:

- Candle with or without a dish
- Flame leaning left or right
- Candlewick with or without a "cone" around it

The first regularity you may notice is the direction of the flame. We might describe this as follows:

Rule #1: The candle flame alternates leaning left and right.

While this observation is certainly correct, it does not explain the presence or absence of the cone around the candlewick or the presence or absence of the dish under the candle. The appearance of these objects does not seem to follow any logical pattern.

We can, however, notice a rule in the relationship between these two objects which we might word as follows:

If the candle is on a dish, a cone is visible over the candlewick.

Our new rule, then, should be:

Rule #1: The candle flame alternates leaning left and right and if the candle is on a dish, a cone is visible over the candlewick.

We might at this point ask what will determine the appearance of the dish, but if we turn our attention to the answer options, we will realize that this will not be necessary.

- we are looking for a candle with a right-leaning flame: this immediately excludes A, B, and D

- we are looking for a figure where both the cone and the dish are either present or absent: this excludes E because it only features a cone but no dish

This will leave us with Answer C as the only possible correct answer. There are two very important observations to make here:

- Certain building blocks or patterns may not be relevant for the rule of the test – in our case, there is no logic governing which figures will feature the cone and the dish. Such irrelevant patterns are added to the test as *distractors* designed to make it more difficult to identify those components that are indeed relevant

- Some of the incorrect answer options are *less incorrect* than others: in our case, Answer E correctly included a right-leaning candle flame and was incorrect only because the dish and the cone did not appear together

The above sample item was a relatively easy one. It is, however, possible and usual to create more difficult versions of a test using the same essential components.

Let's see how we could make this test item a bit harder.

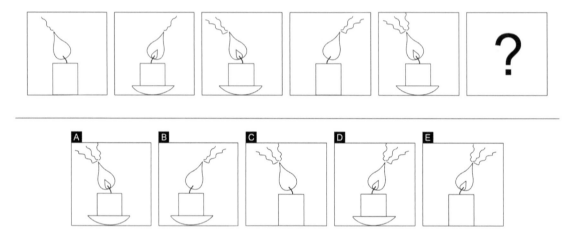

If you look at the above sample item, you will immediately realize that a new building block was included: smoke.

Before we identify the rule governing the smoke, notice that the rule we came up with above still holds:

Rule #1: The candle flame alternates leaning left and right and if the candle is on a dish, a cone is visible over the candlewick.

This rule, however, does not explain the number of wisps of smoke in the figures – consequently, any number of different images could be correct.

We need to identify the second rule:

Rule #2: The number of wisps of smoke increases by 1 every other turn.

Based on these two rules, we can correctly predict that the correct answer will have:

- Right-leaning flame

- Three wisps of smoke

- A dish and a cone or no dish and no cone

The only answer option that matches this description is Answer D.

We can make the test item even harder by introducing a few additional components:

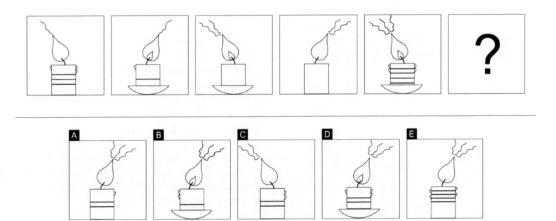

Notice that, again, a new rule must have been introduced because Rules #1 and #2 would be satisfied by Answer A, Answer B, Answer D and Answer E as well. In other words, we can only exclude Answer C based on the first two rules.

If we analyse the figures, we will notice that the number of stripes on the candles is always equal to the number of wax drips on the sides of the candle and, again, there seems to be no logic in how many wax drops appear in each image. We can describe this regularity as follows:

Rule #3: The number of stripes on the candle corresponds to the number of wax drips down the sides.

This rule will exclude Answer A (1 wax drip, two stripes), Answer B (2 wax drips, one stripe) and Answer D (3 wax drips, two stripes) as well, leaving Answer E as the only possible correct option.

As a summary, let us overview what techniques we can use to glimpse the thought process of the creator of the test item:

- Determining the building blocks (candle, dish, etc.) and the number of rules

- Watching out for distractors (e.g. the dish sometimes appears and sometimes does not)

- Eliminating answer options based on each rule we can identify

Patterns and Operations

Now that we have covered the basic components of abstract reasoning tests and the way they are designed, it is time to turn to the various patterns and operations that you must be aware of and able to recognize in order to quickly and efficiently take and success-fully pass abstract reasoning tests. It is of course impossible to take stock of all possible shapes and patterns, but we try to give a comprehensive overlook in the next section.

Rotation

The example top right on the next page shows a simple rotation by 90° clockwise. You can gain the necessary routine in identifying rotations by taking the time to sit down with a piece of paper and a pencil, draw various shapes and then redraw them after rotating them various degrees in either direction, clockwise or counter-clockwise.

The example below left shows a different kind of rotation. In strict geometrical terms, the relationship between the two figures is not rotation at all, yet for convenience's sake, we will discuss it in this section.

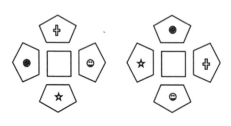

In the two figures, the small icons in the four pentagons around the rectangle in the middle swap places by each icon taking the place originally occupied by its neighbour in a clockwise direction. In some sense, we can say that the icons "rotate" along an imaginary circle running through the centres of the pentagons.

Axial Reflection

The two examples on the right show the geometrical operation called "axial reflection". The thin lines between the two figures in each of the two sets represent an imaginary mirror. In the first set A, the figure on the right is the reflection of the figure on the left in the "mirror" in the middle and vice versa. This is an example of a horizontal reflection.

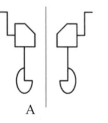
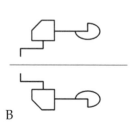

Set B represents a so-called vertical reflection. While for demonstration's sake the examples show the horizontal reflection side by side and the vertical reflection with one figure below the other, in real tests this may not always be the case.

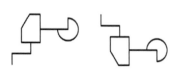

In the example on the left, the figure on the right is still the vertical "reflection" of the figure on the left, but the placement of the second figure does not correspond with where it would actually be in a strictly geometrical sense, that is, below the first image – this makes it harder to consider the relationship between the two figures as a reflection.

You can practice the recognition of this operation in the same cost-effective way as described above for rotations – all you need is paper, a pencil and loads of patience.

Patterns and Inversion

"Which of the following figures completes the series?"

In the example on the right, a new component is introduced – patterns. The example features three shapes:

- Stars

- Ellipses

- Rhombuses

We also notice three distinct patterns or *"fills"*:

?

- No fill (or solid white fill)

- Solid black fill

- Dots

Looking at the sample test, we notice that two "operations" take place:

- The shapes in each figure change places according to some rule

- The patterns (or fill) of the rhombuses and the ellipses also change according to some rule

- The pattern (or fill) of the star never changes

After further observation, we can establish the following rule regarding the patterns:

"If a rhombus has a dotted pattern, change it to solid black in the next step. If it has a solid black fill, change it to a dotted pattern in the next step. If an ellipse has a dotted pattern, change it to solid white in the next step. If it has a solid white fill, change it to a dotted pattern in the next step. Always leave the star's pattern unchanged."

There are of course many other combinations possible, involving more types of patterns and different relationships between them. Another typical case is the so-called inversion. In such tests, the solid colour fill (usually black or white) of each shape and object turns into its exact opposite, just like looking at pictures in a photo negative. Every shape with black fill becomes white, and vice versa.

The other component of our rule for the above example has to do with the positions of the shapes in relation to each other. We will discuss this in the next section.

Translation

In geometry, translation is an operation where each and every point of a shape is moved to a specified distance in a specified direction.

In the example on the right, each point of the triangle at the bottom is moved (or "translated") to the same distance and in the same direction, as indicated by the arrow or "vector" connecting the two shapes. The vector is only shown here for demonstration purposes and would not be visible in a real exercise. We must also keep in mind that the movement sometimes occurs along an actual shape that is part of the figure:

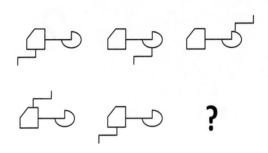

In the example on the left, the zigzagging line "migrates" around the other shapes in a counter-clockwise order. The movement is not a rotation or a reflection – the points of the zigzagging line are simply moved at a certain distance in a certain direction in each step of the series. Therefore the correct answer is a shape that is the same as the middle one in the top row.

Similarly to rotation, there is also a geometrically less accurate meaning of the term "translation". Looking at the sample question with the star, the ellipse and the rhombus, we may notice the following rule governing the placement of the three shapes in the figures of the series:

"Move each of the three shapes one position up. If the shape is already in the top position, it will now occupy the bottom position in the figure."

In the example, the six answer options were intentionally deleted. Based on the method described earlier in this chapter, we can mentally generate the correct figure based on the two rules we established for the series (copied below for convenience).

Rule #1:

"If a rhombus has a dotted pattern, change it to solid black. If it has a solid black fill, change it to a dotted pattern. If an ellipse has a dotted pattern, change it to solid white. If it has a solid white fill, change it to a dotted pattern. Always leave the star's pattern unchanged."

In the fifth item in the series (the figure that will take the place of the question mark), then, the ellipse will become dotted and the rhombus will become solid black. The star will remain white.

Rule #2:

"Move each of the three shapes one position up. If the shape is already in the top position, it will now occupy the bottom position in the figure."

In the figure we are looking for, the now black rhombus will take the bottom position, the now dotted ellipse will go to the middle, and the still white star will move to the top position.

Angles

In geometry, an angle is defined as a figure formed by two lines extending from the same point. In simple geometry, angles are usually given as being any number that is larger than zero and smaller than 360°.

When it comes to abstract reasoning tests, we need to be aware of angles for various reasons. In the case of identifying rotations, the rotation is usually done at a certain angle: 45°, 90° (also called a "right angle"), 180°, or 270°. Of course, rotation at any angle is possible, but due to the difficulty in identifying "custom" angles (say, 67°), such rotations are not likely to appear in EPSO's abstract reasoning tests.

When establishing the "rule" for a test question, we must always think about angles as well.

Consider the example below:

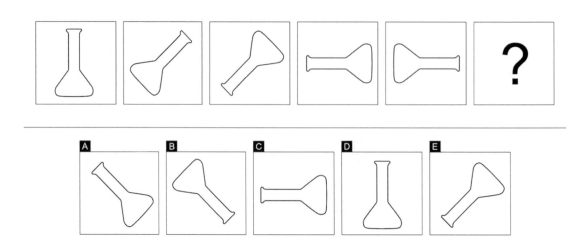

If we look at the images in the sample test above, we see a flask in various positions. After some further observation, we will notice that the flasks in the second, third and further figures are rotated at certain angles when compared to the flask in the first figure. We might describe this regularity based on angles as follows:

Rule #1: The flask is rotated around a fixed point 45 then 180 degrees, and then the cycle repeats.

Visual Arithmetic

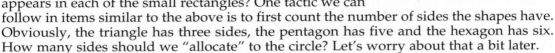

The last typical abstract reasoning component we discuss here is sometimes referred to as visual arithmetic.

If we look at the figure extracted from a real abstract reasoning test, we see a large outer rectangle with seven smaller rectangles along its sides. The top left rectangle is shaded, and there are various shapes in the other rectangles (the fact that not all rectangles contain shapes is not relevant for our purposes now).

What is the rule that could govern which kind of shape appears in each of the small rectangles? One tactic we can follow in items similar to the above is to first count the number of sides the shapes have. Obviously, the triangle has three sides, the pentagon has five and the hexagon has six. How many sides should we "allocate" to the circle? Let's worry about that a bit later.

The other question is what determines why a certain shape is placed in a certain position in the figure. Counting can again help us out. If we count the distance (defined as the number of rectangles) between the shapes and the shaded rectangle in a clockwise direction, we will notice that the position with the triangle, for example, is three steps away, the position with the rectangle is five shapes away, and so on.

We can now identify a rule:

The distance of a rectangle defined as the number of steps to be taken clockwise from the shaded rectangle is indicated by the number of sides the shape has inside that rectangle.

It is important to bear in mind that EPSO's abstract reasoning tests, similarly to all such well-designed tests, attempt to measure the candidate's intuition and intelligence both visually (identification of shapes, patterns, and so on) and logically (e.g. identifying relationships and numerical regularities).

Summary, Combinations and Approaches

In this chapter, we have overviewed various aspects of abstract reasoning tests:

- Test design, difficulty, rules and distractors
- Building blocks: operations, rules and patterns (rotation, reflection, angles, visual arithmetic, and so on)

Based on the difficulty of the test and the building blocks used, it is easy to see how many different combinations of tests can be created:

- A test with three rules based on rotation, pentagons, triangles and three different patterns (shaded, striped and dotted)
- A test with a single rule based on the number of circles inside a square
- A test with two rules involving windows on a house and the color of the chimney

The above list could of course be continued almost infinitely. The examples above were just meant to demonstrate the sheer number of building block and rule combinations that you as an EPSO test-taker can face. This is exactly why it is crucial to practice and familiarize yourself with an efficient method for identifying both the building blocks and the combination of rules that govern the given exercise – and of course to spot and then disregard distractor elements that do not play a role in establishing the rules of the test item.

Hints for Practicing

- If you feel that a geometrical operation (reflection, rotation, angles, etc.) is one of your weak points, do not shy away from sitting down with some paper and a pencil and draw various shapes and perform the operations on them until they become routine and you are able to recognize a 90°degree clockwise rotation of a complex shape in a couple of seconds

- Once you are familiar with all of the typical rules and operations as detailed above, start practicing on actual test questions, for example the ones in this book

- Since abstract reasoning tests are all about shapes, it is especially important to try to model the infrastructure of the exam while practicing – the EPSO test will be administered on a computer, which will make it harder (and stranger) to take than a paper-based test where you can scribble on the paper (even though you will be given scrap paper in the exam centre). If you have access to such services, try also to practice online.

It is also important to develop a systematic approach that you can take when solving each and every abstract reasoning test. One recommended approach is summarized below.

1. Quickly glance through the set of figures. Do not yet spend much time looking at the answer options at this stage.

2. Run through all the rules, operations and patterns you familiarised yourself with during practice and try to apply them to the set of figures. Start with the one that, based on glancing at the figures, intuitively seems the most promising "lead".

3. If you believe you have found the rule or rules governing the exercise, try to "generate" the correct answer figure in your mind or draw a sketch on a scrap paper.

4. Look at the answer options provided and match them against the one you came up with yourself. If a test item is based on multiple rules, you may still be able to exclude one or two of the answer options based on only the first rule. If you are able to do that, you can continue looking for the second rule with a smaller set of answer options to work with – thereby speeding up the process one rule at a time.

5. If you have found a match (and only one), you can mark that as the correct answer. If there are no matches, or multiple matches to your rule(s), they probably have a flaw. Apply your rule to all the figures in the test – this will most likely reveal the flaw, which you can then correct and "generate" a new, hopefully correct, answer figure in your mind.

6. While practicing, you may consider writing every idea and step down for each exercise to make sure you are aware of the logic and rules at play.

In the following chapter, you will find 100 abstract reasoning questions that you can use to start practicing right away.

7. Abstract Reasoning Test

100 Questions – Answers follow on from Question 100

1 Which figure is next in the series?

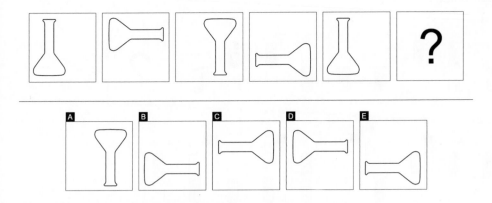

2 Which figure is next in the series?

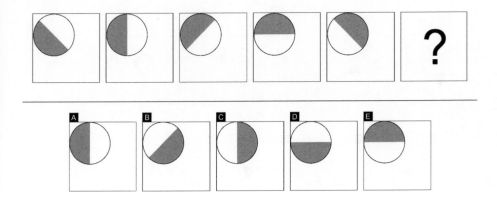

3 Which figure is next in the series?

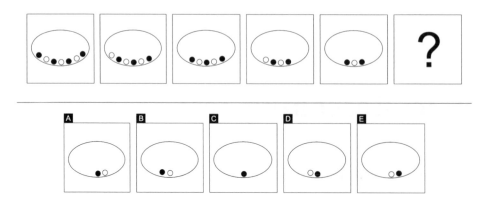

4 Which figure is next in the series?

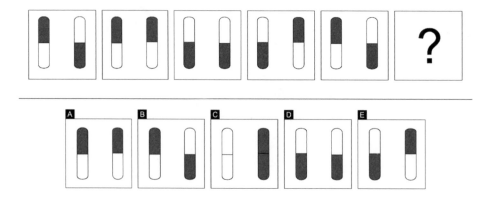

5 Which figure is next in the series?

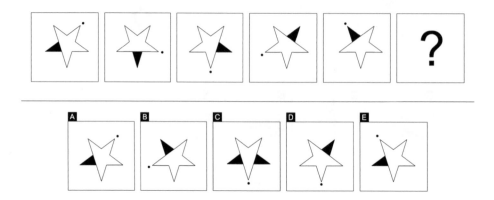

6 Which figure is next in the series?

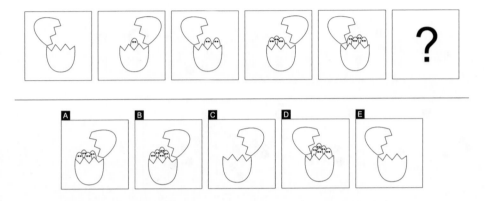

7 Which figure is next in the series?

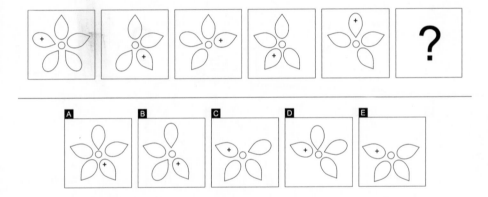

8 Which figure is next in the series?

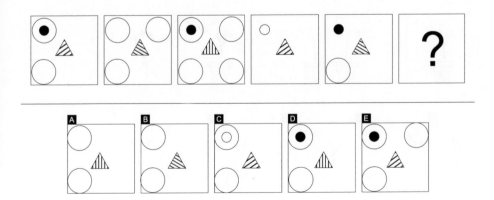

9   Which figure is next in the series?

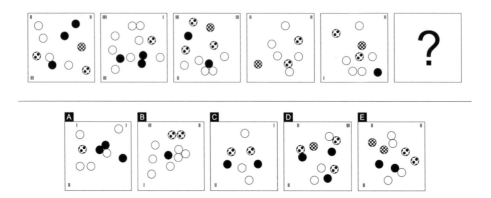

10   Which figure is next in the series?

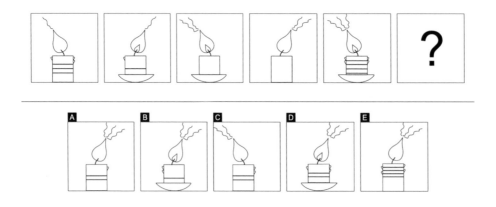

11   Which figure is next in the series?

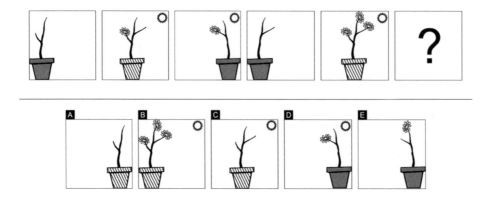

12 Which figure is next in the series?

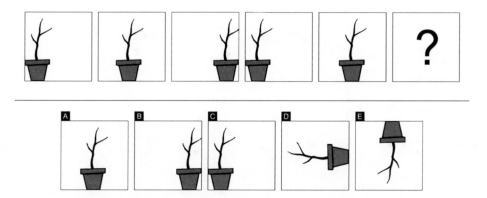

13 Which figure is next in the series?

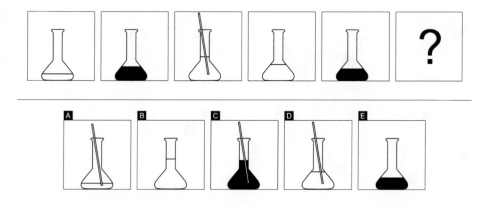

14 Which figure is next in the series?

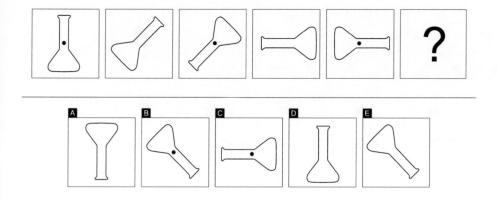

15   Which figure is next in the series?

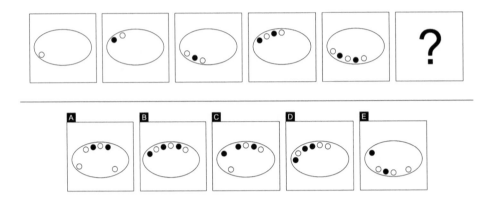

16   Which figure is next in the series?

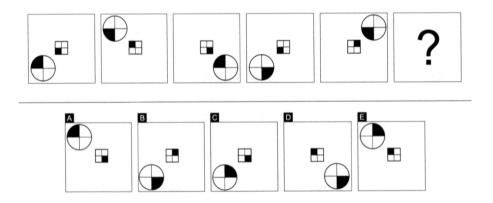

17   Which figure is next in the series?

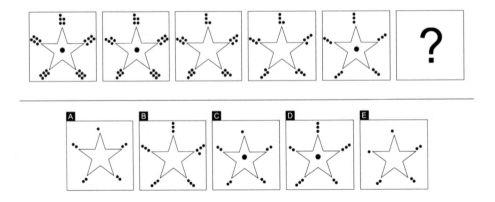

18 Which figure is next in the series?

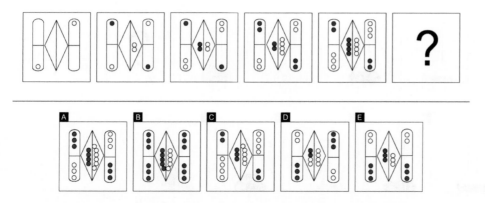

19 Which figure is next in the series?

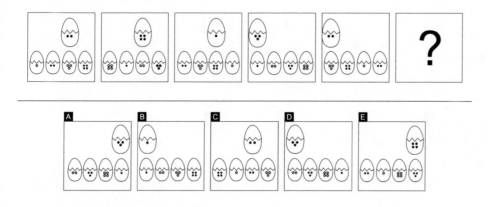

20 Which figure is next in the series?

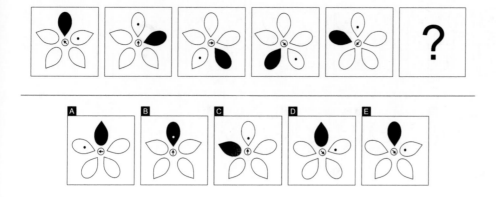

21   Which figure is next in the series?

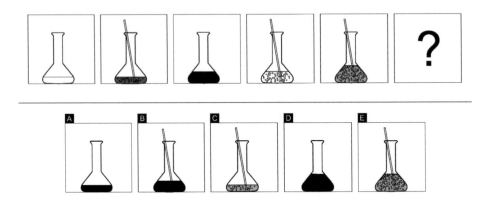

22   Which figure is next in the series?

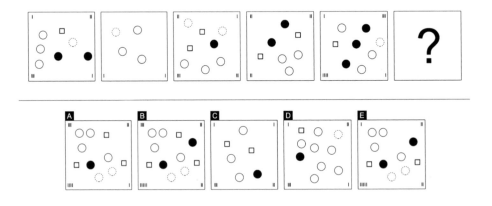

23   Which figure is next in the series?

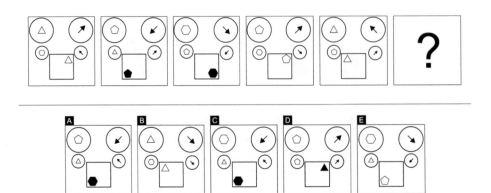

24 Which figure is next in the series?

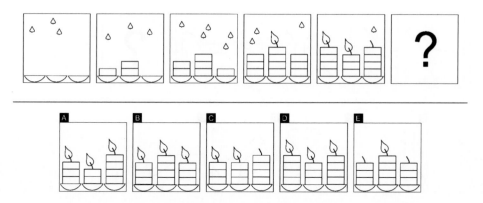

25 Which figure is next in the series?

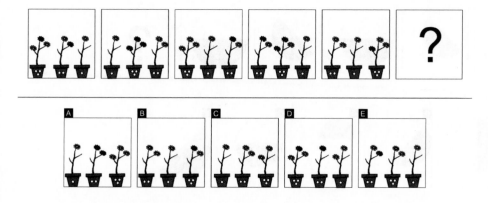

26 Which figure is next in the series?

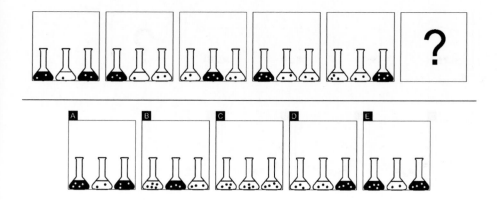

27   Which figure is next in the series?

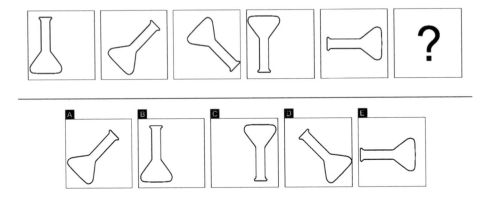

28   Which figure is next in the series?

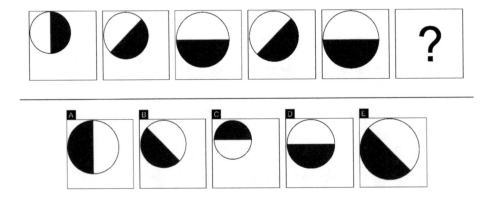

29   Which figure is next in the series?

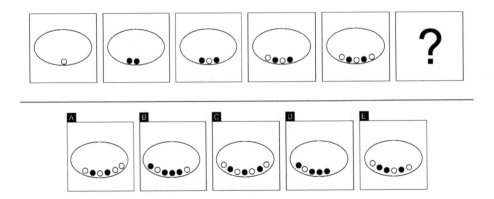

30 Which figure is next in the series?

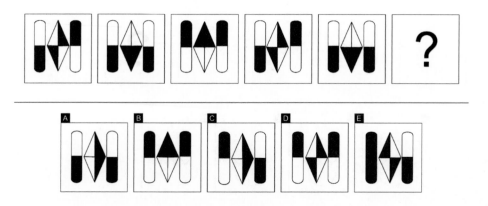

31 Which figure is next in the series?

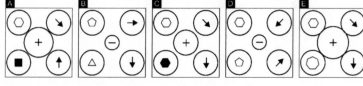

32 Which figure is next in the series?

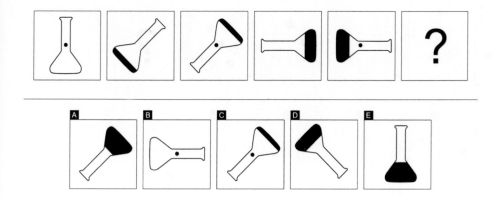

33   Which figure is next in the series?

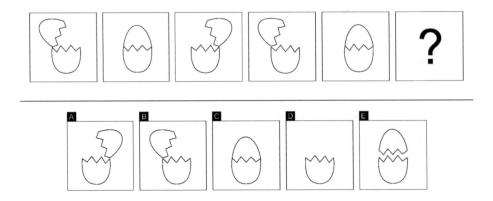

34   Which figure is next in the series?

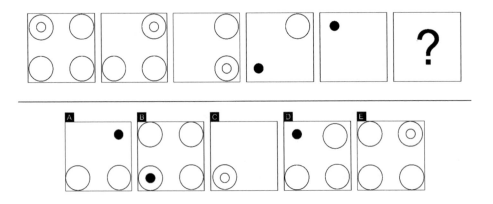

35   Which figure is next in the series?

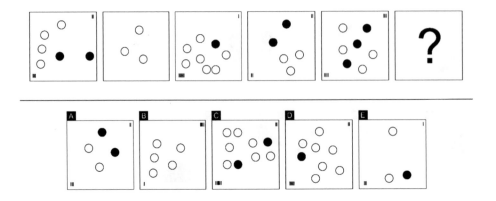

36 Which figure is next in the series?

37 Which figure is next in the series?

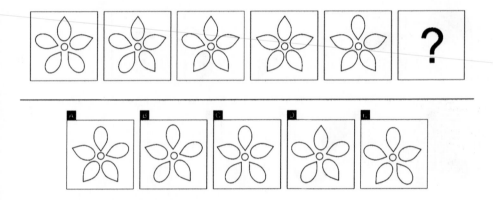

38 Which figure is next in the series?

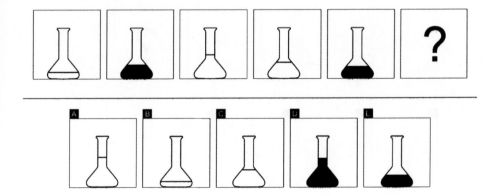

39 Which figure is next in the series?

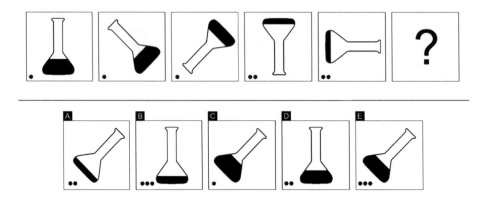

40 Which figure is next in the series?

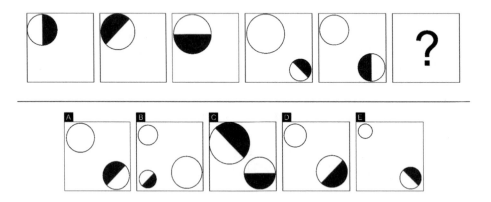

41 Which figure is next in the series?

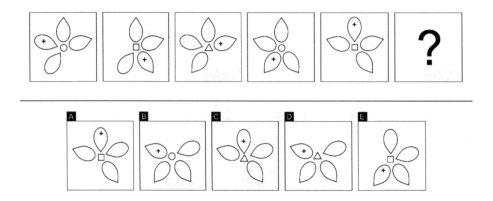

42 Which figure is next in the series?

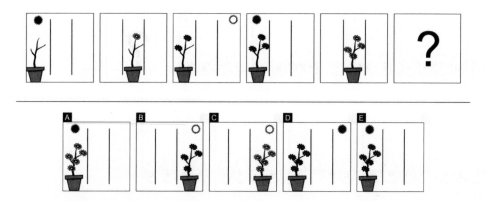

43 Which figure is next in the series?

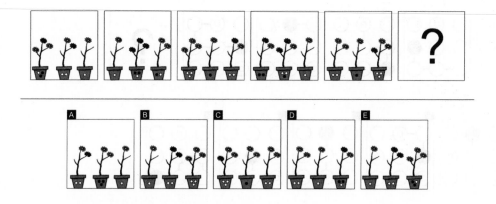

44 Which figure is next in the series?

- petals in rarh
on ery turn,
except shaded.
- shaded by defau
1.
- 2 shaded y " +
- none shaded y " -

45 Which figure is next in the series?

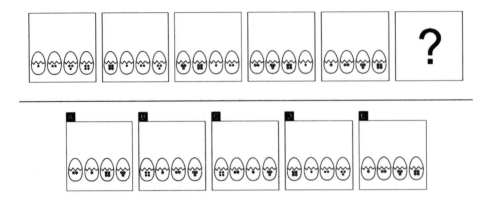

46 Which figure is next in the series?

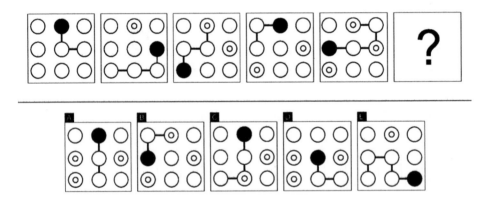

47 Which figure is next in the series?

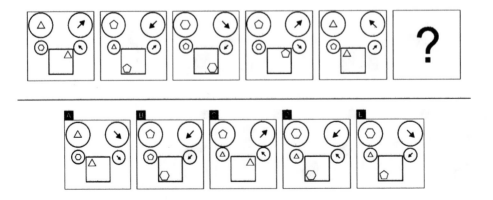

48 Which figure is next in the series?

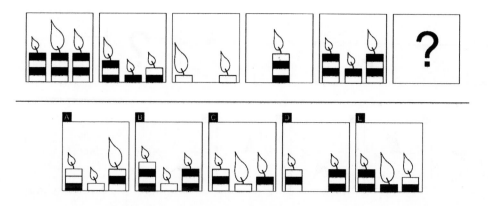

49 Which figure is next in the series?

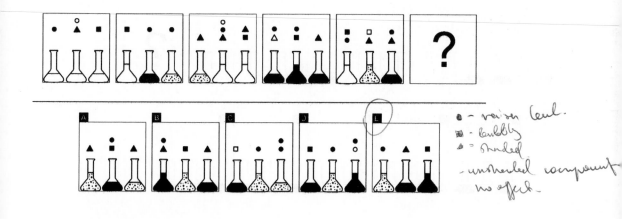

50 Which figure is next in the series?

51 Which figure is next in the series?

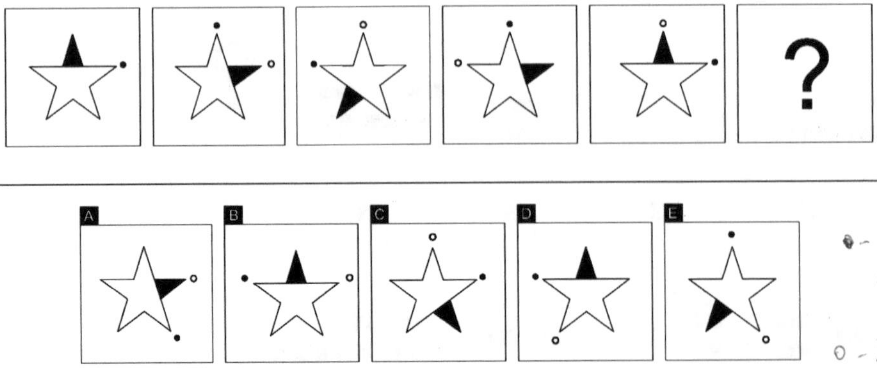

Shaded area moves increasing number of moves to clockwise. •- after/before shaded one alternately. o - follows where • has been.

52 Which figure is next in the series?

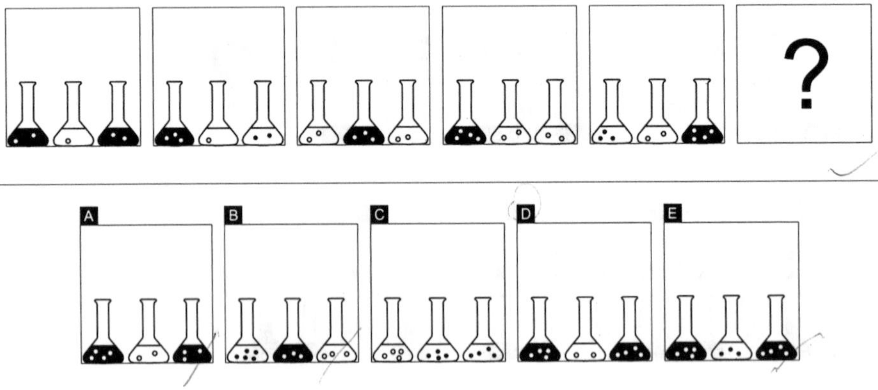

53 Which figure is next in the series?

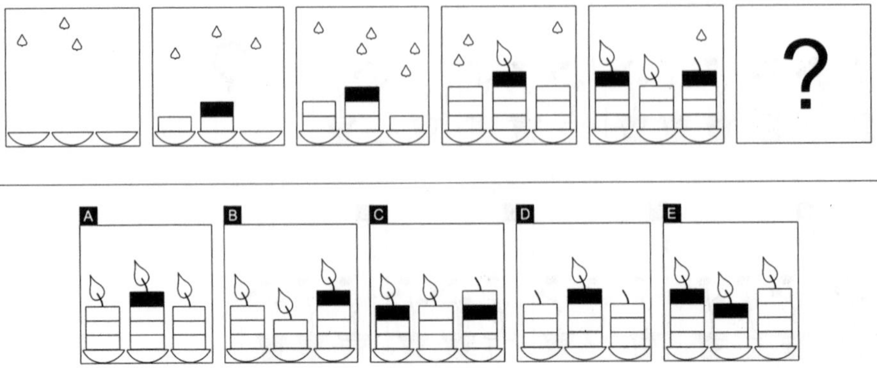

54 Which figure is next in the series?

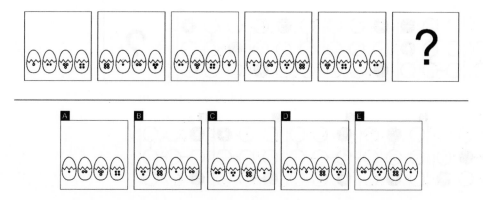

55 Which figure is next in the series?

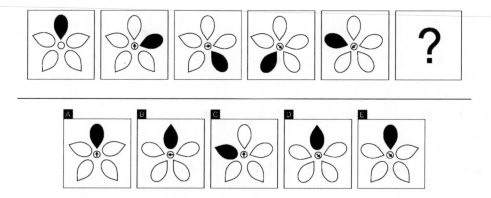

56 Which figure is next in the series?

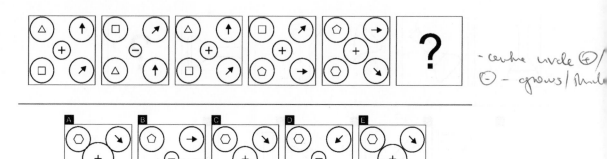

- centre circle ⊕/
  ⊖ – grows / shrinks

57 Which figure is next in the series?

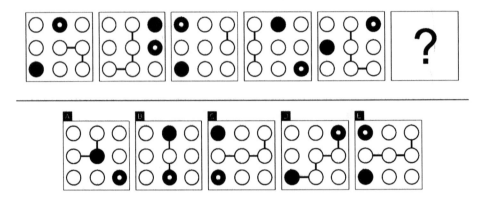

58 Which figure is next in the series?

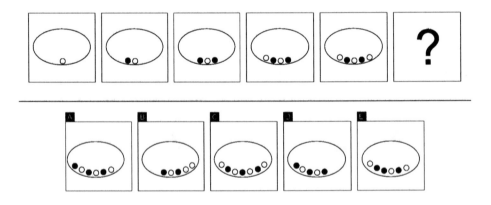

59 Which figure is next in the series?

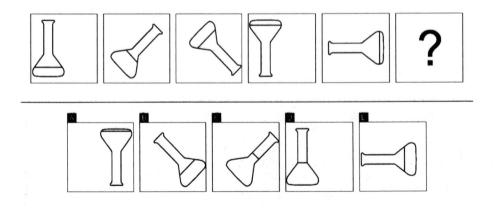

60 Which figure is next in the series?

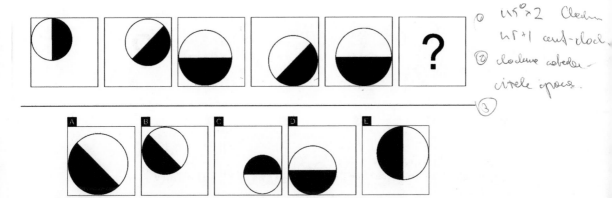

---

61 Which figure is next in the series?

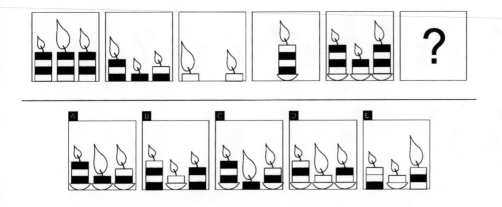

---

62 Which figure is next in the series?

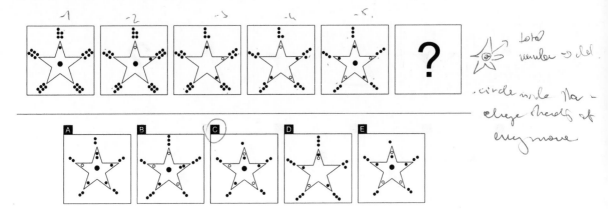

63 Which figure is next in the series?

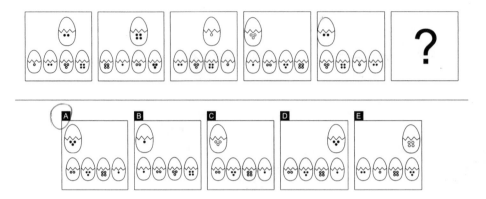

64 Which figure is next in the series?

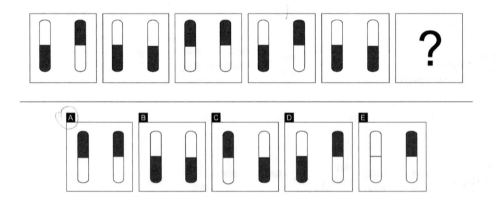

65 Which figure is next in the series?

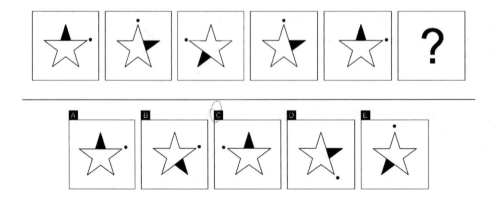

66   Which figure is next in the series?

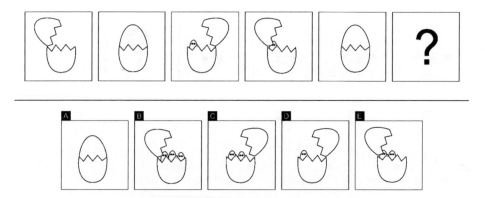

67   Which figure is next in the series?

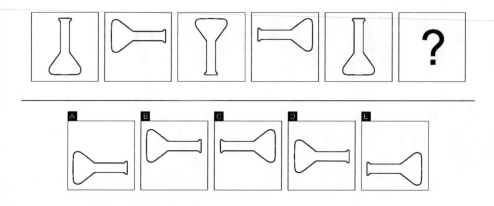

68   Which figure is next in the series?

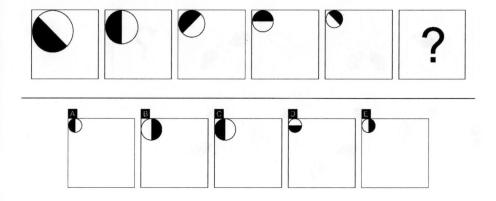

69 Which figure is next in the series?

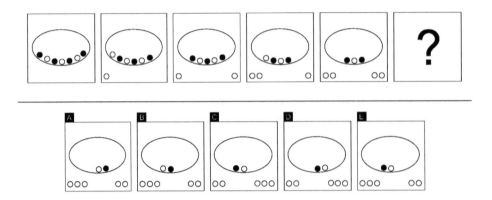

70 Which figure is next in the series?

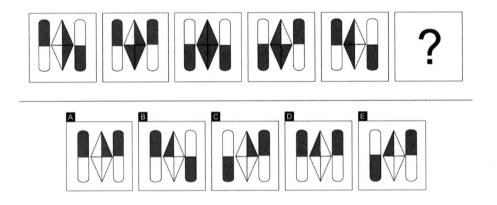

71 Which figure is next in the series?

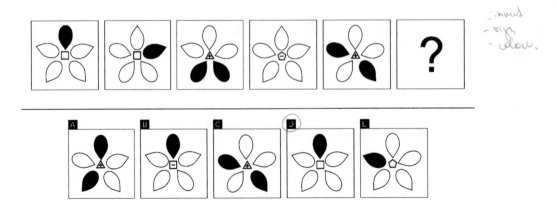

72 Which figure is next in the series?

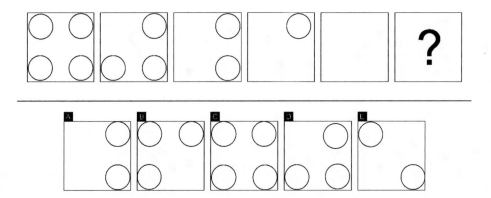

73 Which figure is next in the series?

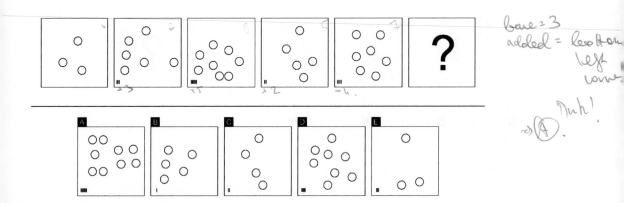

74 Which figure is next in the series?

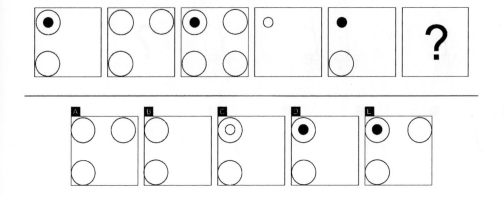

75 Which figure is next in the series?

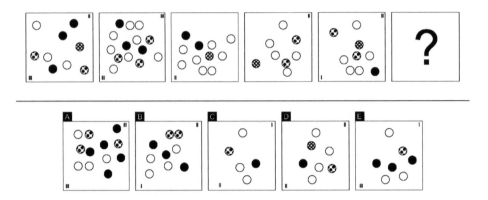

76 Which figure is next in the series?

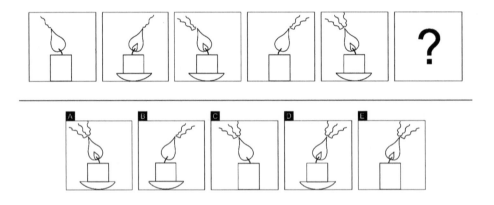

77 Which figure is next in the series?

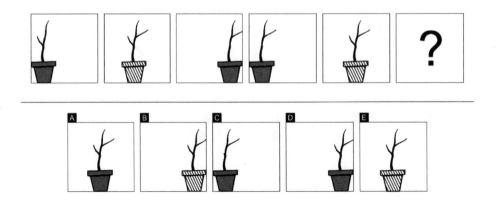

78 Which figure is next in the series?

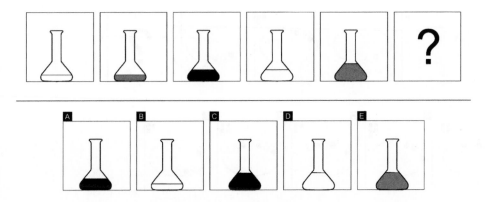

79 Which figure is next in the series?

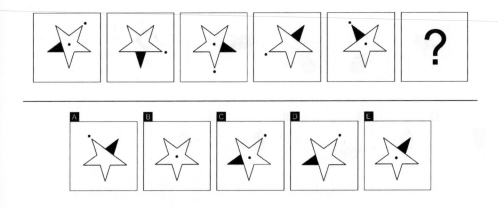

80 Which figure is next in the series?

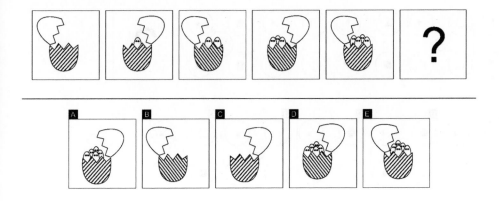

81　Which figure is next in the series?

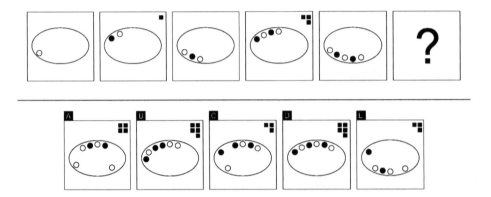

82　Which figure is next in the series?

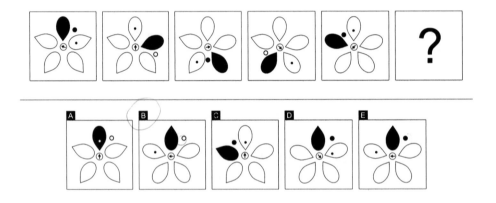

83　Which figure is next in the series?

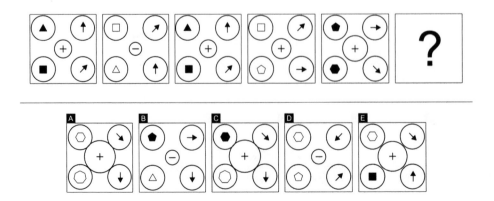

84 Which figure is next in the series?

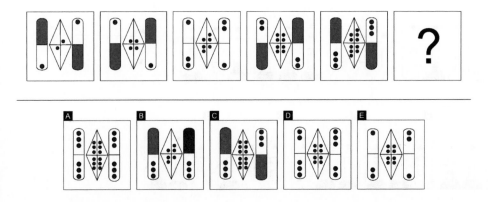

85 Which figure is next in the series?

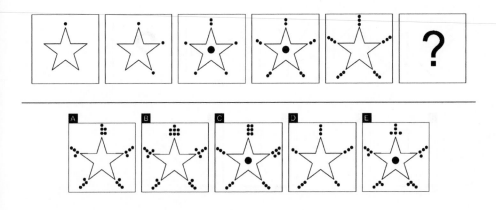

86 Which figure is next in the series?

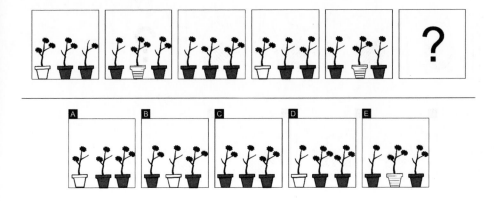

87   Which figure is next in the series?

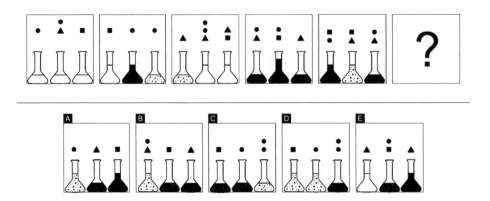

88   Which figure is next in the series?

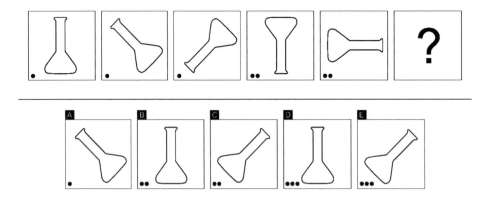

89   Which figure is next in the series?

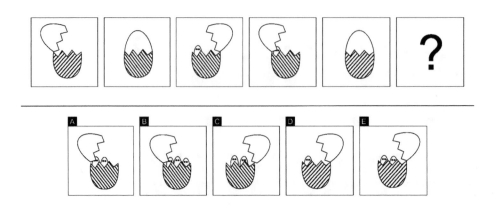

90 Which figure is next in the series?

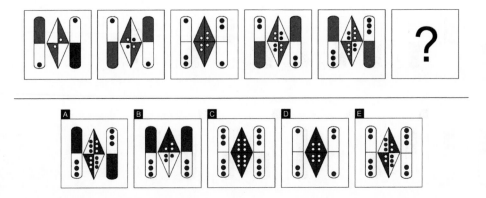

91 Which figure is next in the series?

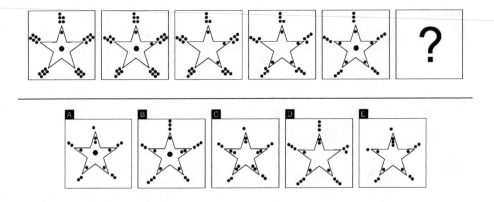

92 Which figure is next in the series?

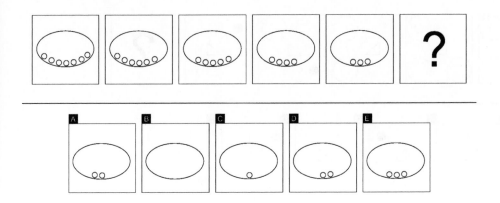

93 Which figure is next in the series?

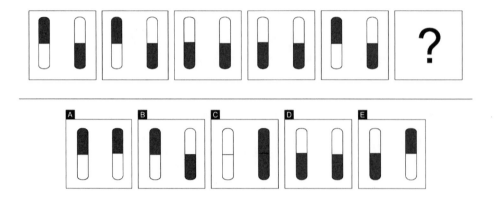

94 Which figure is next in the series?

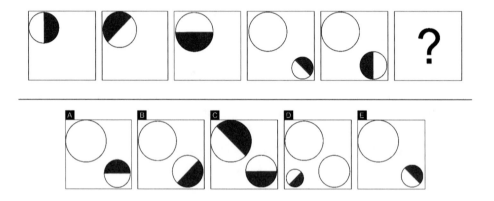

95 Which figure is next in the series?

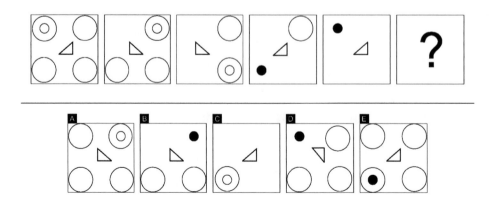

96 Which figure is next in the series?

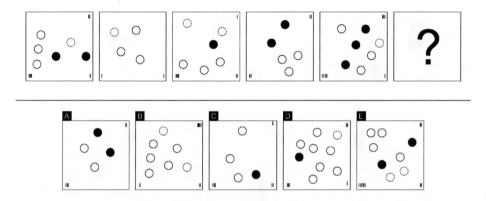

97 Which figure is next in the series?

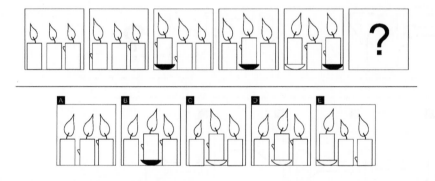

98 Which figure is next in the series?

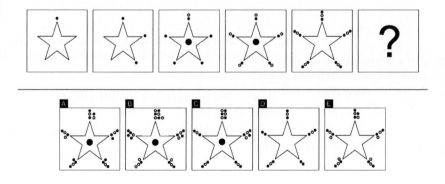

99 Which figure is next in the series?

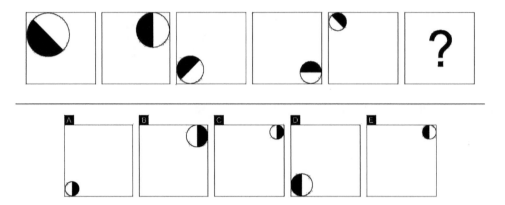

100 Which figure is next in the series?

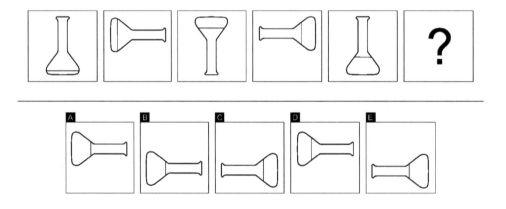

ANSWERS

1   D

Rule 1: The flask is rotating 90° clockwise every time. It remains in the same relative position every time when viewed as though it is the correct way up (i.e. bottom left corner).

2   C

Rule 1: The shaded area of the circle is rotating 45° clockwise every time.

3   D

Rule 1: One circle is removed each time from the left side of the line.

Rule 2: Each time a shaded circle is removed the circles composing the line move one place to the left.

4   A

Rule 1: The pill shape on the left is inverted every other time.

Rule 2: The pill shape on the right is inverted every time.

5   A

Rule 1: The shaded section of the star moves one point anti-clockwise each time.

Rule 2: At the same time, a spot rotates 1 point clockwise.

6   B

Rule 1: The top half of the egg alternates from left to right

Rule 2: The number of chicks in the egg increases by 1 each time

7   C

Rule 1: The petals invert in turn clockwise

Rule 2: The cross denotes the petal will disappear in the next frame for one complete cycle. The placing of the cross is random

8   A

Rule 1: A circle is added to each corner in turn, clockwise. When all 4 corners are full, the next turn is blank before starting again.

Rule 2: A smaller circle top L alternates black and white. When it is white, it is not visible against the larger circle (if applicable)

Rule 3: The direction of the central triangle's shading is at 90 degrees to one of the sides, rotating one side clockwise each turn.

9   B

Rule 1: The number of circles filled in black is shown in tallies in the bottom L corner.

Rule 2: The number of spotty circles is shown in tallies in the top R corner. The numbers of chequered and plain circles are irrelevant.

Rule 3: The number of circles that are touching is shown in tallies at the top L.

10   E

Rule 1: The candle flame alternates leaning left and right and if the candle is on a dish, a cone is visible over the candlewick

Rule 2: The number of wisps of smoke increases by 1 every other turn

Rule 3: The number of bands on the candle corresponds to the number of wax drips down the sides.

11   D

Rule 1: The plant pot alternates position, L, middle, R each turn.

Rule 2: If the pot is shaded, the plant has 1 twig. If the pot is striped the plant has 2 twigs.

Rule 3: When there is a sun, the plant has flowers (the number of flowers is irrelevant).

12   B

Rule 1: The plant pot alternates position, L, middle, R each turn.

13   A

Rule 1: the flask levels go up for three turns and then down for another three turns.

Rule 2: during the second stage of the rising fluid level and the second stage of falling fluid level, the fluid is shaded.

Rule 3: at the highest and lowest levels (the last level of rising and the last level of falling) there is a stirring stick in the pots (alternatively, we could say that the stirring stick appears after the fluid was shaded).

14   E

Rule 1: the flask alternates between rotating 45 and 180 degrees clockwise every turn around a fixed point.

Rule 2: The fixed point around which the flask rotates is shown on every other turn.

15   B

Rule 1: in every turn, a new circle is added to the bottom then in the next turn to the top of the oval shape. The already existing circles change their positions in every turn, either going to the top or the bottom of the oval shape according to their initial positions.

Rule 2: When a circle changes its position, it becomes shaded. At the next position change, it again becomes unshaded, and so on. Circles that freshly appear in the image always appear unshaded.

16   E

Rule 1: a circle divided into four segments wanders around the four corners of the square randomly and the corner in which the circle appeared in the previous turn marks the section which becomes shaded inside the circle in the next turn.

Rule 2: a square (also divided into four segments) appears in the middle of the image, and one of its segments becomes shaded – this is based on which corner of the main square the circle stands at in the given turn.

17   C

Rule 1: each point of the star has six circles above it, and in each turn an increasing number of these circles are taken away one by one going in a counter-clockwise direction.

Rule 2: a large black circle appears inside the star every time the total number of circles outside the star is an odd number.

18   A

Rule 1: in every turn, an unshaded circle is added to the top section of the right shape, and a shaded circle to the bottom section of the same shape in the following turn. The two sections of the left shape contain identical numbers of shaded and unshaded circles, but their places are flipped; the shaded circles appear in the upper section, while the unshaded ones appear in the lower section.

An alternative explanation: the top right and left bottom begin at count one with unshaded circles. In the next turn, shaded circles mirror in the top left and bottom right by catching up in count. Once caught up, the pattern repeats again with one more circle added, and so on.

Rule 2: the central shape is divided into two segments (left and right), and theses segments show how many circles the shapes on the sides had (the left side "collects" the shaded circles and the right side collects the unshaded circles) in the previous turn.

19   D

Rule 1: there are four eggs, each marked with 1, 2, 3 and 4 circles respectively. Each turn the egg on the far right side takes one then two steps to the left pushing the rest of the eggs to the right.

Rule 2: In every odd turn, the circles in those eggs are shaded where the number of circles is also odd. In every even turn, the circles in those eggs are shaded where the number of circles is also even.

Rule 3: a large central egg has a random number of circles inside it (between one and four), and the number of circles show which small egg it will appear above in the next turn.

20   A

Rule 1: every turn the shading goes around in a clockwise direction by one step at a time, and the petal which is shaded in a given turn is inverted. In the following turn the shading moves onward but the petal stays inverted.

Rule 2: an arrow in the middle shows which petal was shaded the previous turn.

Rule 3: in every odd turn, a black dot appears on the petal that will be shaded in the next turn. In every even turn, the black dot appears on the petal that was shaded in the previous turn.

21   D

Rule 1: The flask levels go up; two turns at low, two turns at medium, two at high.

Rule 2: The colour of liquid in the flask alternates from white to pale to dark to white, etc.

Rule 3: If a stirring stick is in the flask, you see bubbles in the liquid.

22   B

Rule 1: the tallies in the lower left corners show how many extra circles are present in each figure in addition to the standard three white circles.

Rule 2: the tallies in the upper right corners show how many of the extra circles are shaded.

Rule 3: the tallies in the lower right corners show how many circles with a dotted outline are added.

Rule 4: tallies in the upper left corners show the number of added unshaded squares to the image.

23   C

Rule 1: there are two circles in the upper half of the image and a square at the bottom. The left circle shows a shape and the right one a directional arrow. The square will have the shape which appeared in the upper left circle in one of its corners based on where the directional arrow pointed.

Rule 2: two small circles below the large ones show the shape and the directional arrow from the previous turn.

Rule 3: the shape in the square is shaded if it has more sides than the previous one had.

24   A

Rule 1: there are three dishes on the image and a random number of wax drops are dripping on them. Every drip turns into a candle segment the following turn. Once a candle reaches four segments a flame appears above it.

Rule 2: in every turn, after a candle has started burning, it will lose one segment per turn.

25   A

Rule 1: there are three potted flowers, each pot marked with one, two and three dots. In every turn, the pots randomly change places and the plants inside them have as many flowers as the number of dots on their pots.

Rule 2: in every turn, flowers are randomly shaded based on the number of dots the middle pot has.

26   E

Rule 1: there are three flasks in each figure and in each turn, the number of bubbles inside them in total grows by one. At the beginning, there are five bubbles altogether and their distribution is random.

Rule 2: in every turn, the flask with the highest number of bubbles becomes shaded (the bubbles become white). If there is more than one flask with the same high number of bubbles, all of them become shaded.

27   D

Rule 1: first the flask rotates 45 degrees clockwise, in the next item it rotates 90 degrees clockwise. Or we can say that every second flask rotates 45 degrees, while every alternate flask rotates 90 degrees.

Rule 2: the flask starts on the left side of the picture and takes one step to the right each turn. When it reaches the right edge of the picture, the cycle starts again from the left.

28   E

Rule 1: the shading rotates 45 degrees clockwise for two turns, then 45 degrees counter-clockwise for one turn.

Rule 2: while the shading rotates clockwise the circle is getting bigger, and while the shading rotates counter-clockwise the circle is getting smaller. The changes in the size of the circle are not uniform.

29   B

Rule 1: a single circle is added each turn, first to the left of the original one, then to the right.

Rule 2: the newly added circles alternate between being shaded and unshaded. The alternation for the circles added to the left and to the right side is counted separately. The first circle added to the left will be shaded, then the next circle added to the right will be shaded, but the second circle added to left will be unshaded, and so on. The central circle starts the series unshaded. Simply put: the newly added circles must carry a pattern that maintains every second circle as shaded.

Rule 3: The central circle switches from shaded to unshaded every time a shaded circle is added to the image.

30   B

Rule 1: first, the left shape is inverted (this results in the first image), then the right one, and this alternation repeats throughout the series.

Rule 2: in every third turn, both shapes are inverted.

Rule 3: the four quadrants of the central shape reflect the shading of the two shapes on its sides.

31   E

Rule 1: there are five circles in the image. The upper left circle has a shape, the upper right a directional arrow, while the circle in the middle has either a + or a - sign in it. The sign shows what happens with the shape (loses a side or gains a side) shown in the upper left circle and the result is shown in the lower left circle. The directional arrow in the upper right circle changes its facing whether there was a + sign in the central circle (the directional arrow rotates 45 degrees in a clockwise direction) or a - sign (the directional arrow rotates 45 degrees in an anticlockwise direction), and again, the result is shown in the lower right circle. The bottom two results will then form the upper shapes of the next image.

Rule 2: the central circle grows in size if there's a + sign in it, and shrinks if it is a - sign.

Rule 3: the lower left shape is shaded if it has an even number of sides.

32   D

Rule 1: the flask alternates between rotating 45 and 180 degrees clockwise every turn around a fixed center.

Rule 2: if the top of the flask passes either the 12'o clock or 6 o'clock positions in a given turn, the center around which the flask rotates is shown in that turn.

Rule 3: the flask starts as empty and every time the flask is not angled down the level of the liquid inside it increases.

33   A

Rule 1: the top half of the egg alternates between being on the left, in the middle "closing" the egg and on the right.

34   E

Rule 1: in every turn, a circle is removed going in an anticlockwise direction. Once every circle has been removed, there is a "blank" turn, where no circles appear, before the series starts again.

Rule 2: a smaller circle inside the large ones is going around in a clockwise direction, and if it lands on a space where the large circle is missing it becomes shaded.

35   C

Rule 1: the series starts with three circles, and the tallies in the lower left corners show how many extra circles are added to these three.

Rule 2: the tallies in the upper right corners show how many of the extra circles are shaded.

36   D

Rule 1: the three candles each start with a low flame, and in every turn, starting from the left, the flame of one of the candles increases. When all flames already increased, they start changing the direction in which they face one by one starting from the left.

Rule 2: In every second turn that a candle has a high flame, there is a dish under it.

37   A

Rule 1: The petals invert in turn clockwise

38   B

Rule 1: the flask levels go up for three turns and then down for another three turns.

Rule 2: during the second stage of the rising fluid level and the second stage of falling fluid level, the fluid is shaded.

39   A

Rule 1: the flask alternates between rotating 45 and 90 degrees counter-clockwise each turn around a fixed centre.

Rule 2: every time the top of the flask passes the 12 o'clock and 6 o'clock position, a black circle is added to the bottom of the picture.

Rule 3: every time the flask is upside down (that is, its top side of lower than its bottom side), the level of the liquid inside it decreases – in all other positions, the level of the liquid remains unchanged.

40   D

Rule 1: every turn the shading rotates 45 degrees in a clockwise direction, and after the rotation takes place the shaded and unshaded sections switch places.

Rule 2: the circle grows in size for three turns, after which it creates a smaller circle and its shading is transferred to the new circle. In the following turn, the shading rotation continues in the new (small) circle, while the old one remains empty.

Rule 3: the empty circles become smaller every turn.

41   D

Rule 1: The petals invert in turn clockwise

Rule 2: The cross denotes which petal to miss out next turn. The placing of the cross is random

Rule 3: The central shape alternates in turn: circle, square, triangle, circle, etc.

42   E

Rule 1: the potted plant has three stations where it can stand (left, middle and right). Starting on the left it takes an increasing number of steps to the right (when it reaches the right edge of the figure, the movement continues from the left again).

Rule 2: the plant has as many flowers as the number of steps it took in a given turn.

Rule 3: whenever the sun appears, the flowers are shaded.

Rule 4: the sun is shaded if it appears on the left side of the image.

43   E

Rule 1: there are three potted flowers, each pot marked with one, two and three dots. In every turn, the pots randomly change places and the plants inside them have as many flowers as the number of dots on their pots.

Rule 2: in every turn, flowers are randomly shaded based on the number of dots the middle pot has.

Rule 3: the dots on the pots are randomly shaded based on how many dots the pot in the middle has in a given turn.

44   B

Rule 1: in every turn, the shading of one or more petals may change depending on the sign in the middle of the flower and every petal with the exception of any shaded petals is inverted.

Rule 2: if there is a + sign in the middle of the image, two petals will be shaded instead of the standard 1, and if there is a - sign in the middle, no shading will take place in that turn. In the absence of a sign in the middle, 1 petal will become shaded. The special signs do not necessarily appear in every turn.

45   B

Rule 1: there are four eggs, each marked with 1, 2, 3 and 4 circles respectively. In every turn the egg on the far left side moves one step to the right, pushing the other eggs to the right.

Rule 2: In each egg that disappeared on the right side and reappeared on the left again, the circles invert colour.

46   A

Rule 1: there are 3x3 circles in the image and one of the circles is shaded. Links between the circles show the route the shaded circle will take the following turn. In the next turn, a new route is planned.

Rule 2: a dot appears in every previous station of the shaded circle.

47   D

Rule 1: there are two circles in the upper half of the image and a square at the bottom. The left circle shows a shape and the right one a directional arrow. The square will have the shape which appeared in the upper left circle in one of its corners based on where the directional arrow pointed.

Rule 2: two small circles below the large ones show the shape and the directional arrow from the previous turn.

48   E

Rule 1: there are three candles, each divided into four segments. The flame above them has three levels; small, medium and high. If a candle burns with a small flame it loses one segment the following turn, two segments with medium flame and three with high. If a candle completely burned down, it reappears the next turn with all four segments.

Rule 2: every odd turn the even segments of the candles are shaded, while every even turn the odd segments are (counting from the bottom).

49   E

Rule 1: there are three empty flasks on the picture and every turn different components are dropped into them, which have different effects on the flasks the following turn. If a triangle is dropped inside the flask becomes shaded, a square makes the flask bubbly, while the circle raises the level of the liquid inside the flask. Every turn the dropped components are selected randomly (between turn the flask "resets") and more than one can be dropped in a given flask.

Rule 2: every even turn an odd number of components are dropped into the flasks altogether, while every odd turn and even number of components are.

Rule 3: an unshaded component means that a given component had gone bad and it is no longer effective (that is, it will not have any effect on the liquid).

50   E

Rule 1: there are three pots of plants, and they can have either one, two or three flowers on them. The one with three flowers starts on the left side and every turn it moves one step to the right. The positions of the other two flowers are random and irrelevant.

Rule 2: if the plant with the three flowers appears on the far left side, its pot is unshaded, if it appears in the middle, the pot is stripped, and if it appears on the far right side, the pot is shaded. All other pots are always shaded.

Rule 3: whenever the pot of the plant with the three flowers is unshaded (that is, it is on the far left side) the flowers of the other two pots become unshaded too.

51   B

Rule 1: the shaded section moves an increasing number of points in a clockwise direction every turn.

Rule 2: the circle outside the star alternates between being 1 step after or before (going clockwise) the shaded section of the star.

Rule 3: an unshaded circle appears every turn showing where the shaded circle was in the previous turn.

52   D

Rule 1: there are three flasks on the picture and each turn the number of bubbles they have grow by one. At the beginning there are five bubbles altogether and their distribution is random.

Rule 2: every turn the flask with the highest number of bubbles becomes shaded (the bubbles become white). If there is more than one flask with the highest number of bubbles, all of them become shaded.

Rule 3: in the flask with the lowest number of bubbles, the bubbles are unshaded. If there is more than one flask with the same low number of bubbles, all of their bubbles are unshaded.

53   B

Rule 1: there are three dishes in the image and a random number of wax drops are dripping on them. Every drip turns into a candle segment the following turn. Once a candle reaches four segments a flame appears above it. Further wax drops above this candle will melt before reaching the candle, therefore will have no effect on it.

Rule 2: in every turn, after a candle has started burning, it will lose one segment per turn.

Rule 3: in every turn, the highest candle segment is shaded. If there are more segments of equal maximum height, all of them are shaded.

54   E

Rule 1: there are four eggs, each marked with 1, 2, 3 and 4 circles respectively. Each turn the egg on the far right side takes one then two steps to the left pushing the rest of the eggs to the right.

Rule 2: In every odd turn, the circles in those eggs are shaded where the number of circles is also odd. In every even turn, the circles in those eggs are shaded where the number of circles is also even.

55   B

Rule 1: every turn the shading goes around in a clockwise direction by one step at a time, and the petal which is shaded in a given turn is inverted. In the following turn the shading moves onward but the petal stays inverted.

Rule 2: an arrow in the middle shows which petal was shaded the previous turn.

56   A

Rule 1: there are five circles in the image. The upper left circle has a shape, the upper right a directional arrow, while the circle in the middle has either a + or a - sign in it. The sign shows what happens with the shape (loses a side or gains a side) shown in the upper left circle and the result is shown in the lower left circle. The directional arrow in the upper right circle changes its facing whether there was a + sign in the central circle (the directional arrow rotates 45 degrees in a clockwise direction) or a - sign (the directional arrow rotates 45 degrees in an anticlockwise direction), and again, the result is shown in the lower right circle. The bottom two results will then form the upper shapes of the next image.

Rule 2: the central circle grows in size if there's a + sign in it, and shrinks if it is a - sign.

57   C

Rule 1: in every turn, two circles are randomly shaded on the 3x3 table and links are drawn between the two shaded circles of the previous turn.

Rule 2: small white dots appear inside the shaded circles in every turn. In odd turns, they appear in the upper shaded circle, while in even turns, they appear inside lower shaded circle.

58   A

Rule 1: a single circle is added each turn, first to the left of the original one, then to the right.

Rule 2: the newly added circles alternate between being shaded and unshaded. The alternation for the circles added to the left and to the right side is counted separately. The first circle added to the left will be shaded, then the next circle added to the right will be shaded, but the second circle added to left will be unshaded, and so on. The central circle is always unshaded. Simply put: the newly added circles must carry a pattern that maintains every second circle as shaded.

59   B

Rule 1: first the flask rotates 45 degrees clockwise, in the next item it rotates 90 degrees clockwise. Or we can say that every second flask rotates 45 degrees, while every alternate flask rotates 90 degrees.

Rule 2: the flask starts on the left side of the picture and takes one step to the right each turn.

Rule 3: the level of the liquid gets higher in all stages where the flask is the right way up (that is, bottom at the bottom, top at the top), and gets lower in all stages when it is upside down. Nothing happens to the level when the flask is completely horizontal.

60   A

Rule 1: the shading rotates 45 degrees clockwise for two turns, then 45 degrees counter-clockwise for one turn.

Rule 2: while the shading rotates clockwise the circle is getting bigger, and while the shading rotates counter-clockwise the circle is getting smaller. The changes in the size of the circle are not uniform.

Rule 3: the circle goes around the corners of the square in a clockwise direction, increasing the steps it takes by 1 every turn.

61   A

Rule 1: there are three candles, each divided into four segments. The flame above them has three levels; small, medium and high. If a candle burns with a small flame it loses one segment the following turn, two segments with medium flame and three with high. If a candle completely burned down, it reappears the next turn with all four segments.

Rule 2: every odd turn the even segments of the candles are shaded, while every even turn the odd segments are (counting from the bottom).

Rule 3: Every second time a candle appears in a given position (left, centre or right), a dish will appear under the candle in that position.

62 C

Rule 1: Each point of the star originally had six circles attached to it. In each figure, an increasing number of circles are removed from the image going in a counter-clockwise direction. In the first figure, one circle is already removed from the 12'o clock position. In the second figure, a total of two circles are removed (one each from the next two points of the star going clockwise), then three, and so on.

Rule 2: a large black circle appears inside the star every time the total number of circles outside the star is an odd number.

Rule 3: in every turn, a circle is added to an inner point of the star going in a clockwise direction.

Rule 4: the circles added inside the star change their shading in every turn.

63 A

Rule 1: there are four eggs, each marked with 1, 2, 3 and 4 circles respectively. In each turn, the egg on the far left side takes one and then two steps to the right, pushing the rest of the eggs to the right as well, and then the cycle repeats.

Rule 2: First, the circles in those eggs are shaded where the number of circles is even. Then, in the next turn, the circles in those eggs are shaded where the number of circles is odd, and then the cycle repeats.

Rule 3: a large central egg has a random number of circles inside it (between one and four), and the number of circles shows above which small egg it will appear the following turn (above the one with the same number of circles).

Rule 4: the shading of the circles in the large egg is the opposite of that of the circles appearing in the small egg underneath.

64 A

Rule 1: first, the left shape is inverted (this results in the first image), then the right one, and this alternation repeats throughout the series.

Rule 2: in every third turn, both shapes are inverted.

65 C

Rule 1: the shaded section moves an increasing number of points in a clockwise direction every turn.

Rule 2: the circle outside the star alternates between being 1 step after or before (going clockwise) the shaded section of the star.

66 C

Rule 1: the top half of the egg alternates between being on the left, in the middle "closing" the egg and on the right.

Rule 2: every turn after the egg was closed a new chick appears inside the egg.

67 B

Rule 1: The flask is rotating 90° clockwise every time.

Rule 2: Looking at the picture with the flask the correct way up, it moves between three positions (left, centre and right). It moves as far as it can in one direction before changing direction. The sequence shown is from the centre to the left to the centre to the right to the centre. The next move would therefore be to the left.

68 E

Rule 1: The shaded area of the circle is rotating 45° clockwise every time.

Rule 2: The circle is getting smaller every time.

69 B

Rule 1: One circle is removed each time. This alternates between the circle furthest to the right and the one furthest to the left.

Rule 2: The circles alternate between being shaded and unshaded. The circle furthest to the right is always shaded.

Rule 3: When circles are removed, they appear at the bottom corner that is opposite to the side they have been removed from. None of these circles are shaded.

70 D

Rule 1: The pill shape on the left is inverted every other time.

Rule 2: The pill shape on the right is inverted every time.

Rule 3: Going clockwise, the next quadrant of the diamond is shaded until all are shaded. Continuing clockwise, the shading is then removed by one quadrant every time.

71 D

Rule 1: in every turn, the shading of one or more petals may change depending on the sign in the middle of the flower and every petal with the exception of any shaded petals is inverted.

Rule 2: if there is a + sign in the middle of the image, two petals will be shaded instead of the standard 1, and if there is a - sign in the middle, no shading will take place in that turn. In the absence of a sign in the middle, 1 petal will become shaded. The special signs do not necessarily appear in every turn.

Rule 3: the shape in the centre has as many sides as the number of the unshaded petals.

72   C

Rule 1: in every turn, a circle is removed going in an anticlockwise direction. Once every circle has been removed, there is a "blank" turn, where no circles appear, before the series starts again.

73   A

Rule 1: the series starts with three circles, and the tallies in the lower left corners show how many extra circles are added to these three.

74   B

Rule 1: A circle is added to each corner in turn, clockwise. When all 4 corners are full, the next turn is blank before starting again.

Rule 2: A smaller circle top L alternates black and white. When it is white, it is not visible against the larger circle (if applicable)

75   E

Rule 1: The number of circles filled in black is shown in tallies in the bottom L corner.

Rule 2: The number of spotty circles is shown in tallies in the top R corner. The numbers of chequered and plain circles are irrelevant.

76   D

Rule 1: The candle flame alternates in leaning left and right and if the candle is on a dish, a cone is visible over the candlewick

Rule 2: The number of wisps of smoke increases by 1 every other turn

77   B

Rule 1: The plant pot alternates position, L, middle, R each turn.

Rule 2: If the pot is shaded, the plant has 1 twig. If the pot is striped the plant has 2 twigs.

78   C

Rule 1: The flask levels go up; two turns at low, two turns at medium, two at high.

Rule 2: The colour of liquid in the flask alternates from white to pale to dark to white, etc.

79   D

Rule 1: The shaded section of the star moves one point anti-clockwise each time.

Rule 2: At the same time, a spot rotates 1 point clockwise.

Rule 3: A spot alternately appears and disappears in the centre of the star.

80   A

Rule 1: The top half of the egg alternates from left to right

Rule 2: The number of chicks in the egg increases by 1 each time

Rule 3: The stripes on the bottom half of the egg go top-right bottom-left for two turns, and then top-left bottom-right for two turns, and then the cycle repeats.

81   D

Rule 1: every turn a new circle gets added to the bottom then in the next turn to the top of the oval shape. The already existing circles change their position every turn, either going to the top or the bottom of the oval shape according to their initial positions.

Rule 2: When a circle changes its position, it becomes shaded. At the next position change, it again becomes unshaded, and so on. Circles that freshly appear in the image always appear unshaded.

Rule 3: In every even turn, small shaded squares appear outside the oval shape, in the top right corner. The number of squares is equal to the number of circles that were present inside the oval shape in the previous turn.

82   B

Rule 1: in every turn, the shading on the petals goes around in a clockwise direction by one step at a time, and the petal which is shaded in a given turn is inverted. In the following turn, the shading moves onward but the petal stays inverted.

Rule 2: an arrow in the middle shows which petal was shaded in the previous turn.

Rule 3: in every odd turn, a black dot appears on the petal that will be shaded in the next turn. In every even turn, the black dot appears on the petal that was shaded in the previous turn.

Rule 4: a single circle is going around between the petals of the flowers in a clockwise direction, and each time the black dot is in a neighbouring petal, it becomes shaded as well.

83   A

Rule 1: there are five circles in each figure. The upper left circle has a shape, the upper right a directional arrow, while the circle in the middle has either a plus (+) or a minus (-) sign in it. The sign shows what happens with the shape (loses a side or gains a side) shown in the upper left circle and the result is shown in the lower left circle. The directional arrow in the upper right circle changes its facing depending on whether there was a + sign in the central circle (the directional arrow rotates 45 degrees in a clockwise direction) or a - sign (the directional arrow rotates 45 degrees in an anticlockwise direction), and again, the result is shown in the lower right circle. The bottom two results will then form the upper shapes of the next image.

Rule 2: the central circle grows in size if there's a + sign in it, and shrinks if it is a - sign.

Rule 3: the lower left shape is shaded if it has an even number of sides.

Rule 4: the shape in the upper left circle is shaded if it has an odd number of sides.

84   A

Rule 1: the shadings invert every turn on both shapes and every third turn the shading is removed from them. Each turn a single circle is added to each unshaded section. These circles remain there even though they cannot be seen when the shading is over them.

Rule 2: the central shape's quadrants gain circles based on how many circles the two shapes on the sides have.

85   A

Rule 1: In every turn, an increasing number of circles are added one by one to the points of the star going in a clockwise direction. If there is already a circle at a given point of the star, the new one is added above or next to it.

Rule 2: a black circle appears inside the star if the total number of circles outside the star is even.

86   C

Rule 1: there are three pots of plants, and they can have either one, two or three flowers on them. The one with three flowers starts on the left side and every turn it moves one step to the right. The positions of the other two flowers are random and irrelevant.

Rule 2: if the plant with the three flowers appears on the far left side, its pot is unshaded, if it appears in the middle, the pot is striped, and if it appears on the far right side, the pot is shaded. All other pots are always shaded.

87   A

Rule 1: there are three flasks in each figure, and in every turn, different components are dropped into them, which have different effects on the flasks, as visible in the following turn. If a triangle is dropped inside the flask, the liquid becomes shaded; a square makes the flask bubbly, while the circle raises the level of the liquid inside the flask. In every turn, the dropped components are selected randomly, the liquid is reset to its default state between turns, and more than one component can be dropped in any given flask.

Rule 2: in every even turn, an odd number of components are dropped into the flasks altogether, while every odd turn an even number of components are dropped.

88   C

Rule 1: the flask alternates between rotating 45 and 90 degrees counter-clockwise each turn around a fixed centre.

Rule 2: every time the top of the flask passes the 12 o'clock and 6 o'clock position, a black circle is added to the bottom of the picture.

89   E

Rule 1: the top half of the egg alternates between being on the left, in the middle "closing" the egg and on the right.

Rule 2: every turn after the egg was closed a new chick appears inside the egg.

Rule 3: the stripes on the bottom half of the egg change direction every turn when the egg is closed.

90   C

Rule 1: the shadings invert every turn on both shapes and every third turn the shading is removed from them. Each turn a single circle is added to each non shaded section. These circles remain there even though they cannot be seen when the shading is over them.

Rule 2: the central shape's quadrants gain circles based on how many circles the two shapes on the sides have.

Rule 3: the central shape's shading is the opposite of the two shapes on the sides. The circles inside it can be seen even through the shading.

91   A

Rule 1: each point of the star has six circles above it, and in each turn an increasing number of these circles are taken away one by one going in a counter-clockwise direction.

Rule 2: a large black circle appears inside the star every time the total number of circles outside the star is an odd number.

Rule 3: in every turn, a circle is added to an inner point of the star going in a clockwise direction.

92   A

Rule 1: One circle is removed each time. This alternates between the circle furthest to the right and the one furthest to the left.

93   B

Rule 1: The pill shape on the left is inverted every other time.

94   B

Rule 1: in every turn, the shading rotates 45 degrees in a clockwise direction, and after the rotation takes place the shaded and unshaded sections switch places.

Rule 2: the circle grows in size for three turns, after which it creates a smaller circle and its shading is transferred to the new circle. In the following turn, the shading rotation continues in the new (small) circle, while the old one remains empty.

95   A

Rule 1: in every turn, a circle is removed going in an anticlockwise direction. Once every circle has been removed, there is a "blank" turn, where no circles appear, before the series starts again.

Rule 2: a smaller circle inside the large ones is going around in a clockwise direction, and if it lands on a space where the large circle is missing it becomes shaded.

Rule 3: the right angle of the triangle in the middle is facing the side of the figure opposite the one where the small circle is located.

96   E

Rule 1: the series starts with three circles, and the tallies in the lower left corners show how many extra circles are added to these three.

Rule 2: the tallies in the upper right corners show how many of the extra circles are shaded.

Rule 3: the tallies in the lower right corners show how many circles with a dotted outline are added.

97   B

Rule 1: the three candles each start with a low flame, and in every turn, starting from the left, the flame of one of the candles increases. When all flames have increased, they start changing the direction in which they face one by one starting from the left.

Rule 2: In every second turn that a candle has a high flame, there is a dish under it.

Rule 3: if there is wax dripping down the candle and also a dish under it, the dish becomes shaded. Wax drips appear randomly and are not relevant for the rules.

98   E

Rule 1 In every turn, an increasing number of circles are added one by one to the points of the star going in a clockwise direction. If there is already a circle at a given point of the star, the new one is added above or next to it.

Rule 2: a black circle appears inside the star if the total number of circles outside the star is even.

Rule 3: every even circle added to a given point of the star is unshaded.

99   C

Rule 1: The shaded area of the circle is rotating 45° clockwise every time.

Rule 2: The circle is getting smaller every time.

Rule 3: The circle moves from the top left to the top right to the bottom left to the bottom right then repeats the sequence.

100   A

Rule 1: The flask is rotating 90° clockwise every time.

Rule 2: Looking at the picture with the flask the correct way up, it moves between three positions (left, centre and right). It moves as far as it can in one direction before changing direction. The sequence shown is from the centre to the left to the centre to the right to the centre. The next move would therefore be to the left.

Rule 3: The liquid level in the flask is getting higher every time.

8.   Succeeding in Situational Judgement Tests

Situational judgement tests (or SJTs for short) present candidates with a series of hypothetical but realistic work-based scenarios in which they are required to make a decision. It is important to understand that even though called "tests", they are very different in nature from the verbal, numerical and abstract reasoning tests you will face during the recruitment process as they measure how you evaluate certain situations instead of testing your harder analytical skills and behaviours.

Situational judgement tests are employed because they can be used to consistently and fairly assess at an early stage behavioural attributes such as decision-making ability and interpersonal skills that are difficult to measure by other techniques.

SJTs are a fast-growing area in the selection and development field. The basic idea of presenting a relevant hypothetical situation has been in use in recruitment since the early 1900s, but SJTs in a format comparable to today's SJTs have been more prevalent since the 1940s, used in particular for predicting supervisory and managerial potential.

More recent research has found that SJTs are strong predictors of real-life job performance. This means that in the development or review of SJTs, those people doing well in the tests were also the people who performed well in role. Not only that, but SJTs seems to measure an additional aspect of performance that is not measured by other assessment tools such as ability tests or personality questionnaires. This suggests that the SJTs are tapping into a different skill, and one that is highly relevant to job performance.

According to EPSO, situational judgement tests will be used prior to the assessment phase, as part of the computer-based pre-selection process for Assistant profiles. However, it is important to note SJTs will not be eliminatory at the pre-selection stage. They are only taken into account if the candidate is accepted for the assessment phase; otherwise the conclusions that can be drawn from them are not communicated to the applicant. In practice, however, it is not inevitable that a situational judgement test will be found in an AST exam, particularly for AST1.

Theory behind Situational Judgement Tests

At the heart of social psychology is the idea that what makes us human is our ability to make sense of social situations. When we evaluate an important or new situation most of us try to understand the intentions of others in the situation, and possible causal explanations, to guide our response (e.g. "How would you react if you discovered that your colleague had leaked some confidential information to the press?").

Social psychology theory also holds that there is a similarity in how people evaluate situations, and that most people will have a shared expectation of what is an *appropriate* response. This theory forms the basis of why situational judgement tests can be used to provide an indicator of our likely behaviour in an EU job-context or elsewhere. By presenting the candidate with relevant hypothetical scenarios and a set of responses which have been previously scored for their level of effectiveness, it is possible to assess how appropriate the candidate's response selection is, and to use this information to predict their likely behavioural response if faced with similar situations in the role.

What They Measure

The name "situational judgement test" suggests that what is being measured is indeed "situational judgement" even though little research has been done to explore exactly what type of personal quality is being measured by SJTs. However, some evidence exists that what SJTs are actually tapping into is an aspect of "practical intelligence" or "general intelligence". It is likely that SJTs are indeed multi-dimensional; they measure a number of different constructs including social or behavioural judgement, practical or general intelligence and aspects of personality such as conscientiousness. In the EPSO assessment process the SJT has been specifically developed for the purpose of measuring the candidate's situational judgement in relation to selected EPSO competencies.

How They Are Developed

Robust situational judgement tests are developed in the same way as other psychometric tests. The particular job profiles EPSO is seeking to recruit for are analysed by experts to understand what type of workplace situations occur that are critical to achieving good performance outcomes. This is done by interviewing current EU officials, heads of unit, directors and subject matter experts to gain a number of perspectives on what is important and what would be effective behaviour.

At the same time, examples of how less effective behaviour could lead to less desirable outcomes are gathered. Once these situations are identified, they are written up as possible test scenarios: a paragraph or two that summarises the situation and a range of four or more response options (from *most desirable* to *least desirable*). The scenario and response options are crafted so that there is no "obvious" answer and even the "undesirable" options sound plausible. This is necessary to avoid "obvious" answers or the risk that candidates would be able to easily identify the "desired" answer.

Careful consideration is given to the design of the test introduction and instructions and the scenario wording, format and content. It is well known that in the case of public opinion surveys, how the question is formulated will significantly influence the answer. As this is certainly true for SJTs as well, even subtle details of presentation must be thought through carefully.

It is important that the SJT design fits within the organisational setting and the assessment process, and that it reflects realistic elements of the job role in question. However, EPSO has said that its situational judgement tests are designed so that they require no specialist knowledge to complete: they will be purely behaviourally-based assessments.

How They Work

The theory of planned behaviour states that an individual's behaviour in the past is a good predictor of their likely behaviour in the future. As with a standard competency based interview, this is the basis on which a situational judgement test is used to predict a candidate's job performance or suitability for the given job profile.

For each given situational judgement test, a *scoring key* is developed so that the candidate's response can be compared against this key. Initially, this can be developed by making rational judgements as to which are the most and least preferred responses to each scenario, based on the job analysis data collected in the design process and from additional evaluations made by subject matter experts.

The SJT can then be *validated* by demonstrating a clear relationship between good performance in the test and real-life good performance in the role. In order to validate the test design, and to select which scenarios will be in the final test, groups of existing job holders such as – for example – Assistants in the Committee of the Regions will be tested on the sample scenarios and their responses will be compared to their real-life competency-based job performance (as judged by their superior's appraisal ratings).

Those scenarios for which the high performers have consistently selected the most preferred response as their *own* most preferred response will be selected as good ones for the final test. If there are scenarios for which high performers consistently select different responses, these will be brought into question as to their appropriateness and dropped from the test. When used in the organisation's assessment process, the candidate's score in the SJT will be based on their performance across all scenarios within the test and a score will be given to each competency in question.

What They Look Like

When sitting the test, you will be presented with a number of seemingly equally-viable alternative courses of action and be asked to choose the most and least appropriate in your opinion; the questions will have limited or no direct relevance to the European Union but they will most likely relate to realistic workplace situations and working within hierarchies and with colleagues.

I would anticipate that each of the "situations" would measure one of the key competencies for the job (although you would not be informed which is being measured when answering each question) and also cross-check the consistency of your answers. Consequently, each competency will need to be measured more than once in order to reliably estimate your ability and therefore more than one scenario will relate to each competency. The test will have been designed especially for EPSO by expert occupational psychologists and I expect that it will contain from twenty-five to fifty questions.

Here is a sample SJT test scenario, designed to measure a generic "planning"-type competency (which is not itself a specific EPSO competency, but see below for a comprehensive sample test and explanations based on the EPSO competency framework). I have also included what I would judge to be the most and least effective courses of action (although this could vary according to exact competency definitions):

You have been approached by your superior and asked to deliver a project within a very tight deadline. You are pleased that your head of unit has approached you to work on the project but are concerned about delivering it within the timeframe given. What do you do?

A. Review and reprioritise the projects you are currently involved in so you can start work on the new project straight away.

B. Schedule a meeting with your head of unit to discuss options for delivering the project, suggesting colleagues that you would like to involve to ensure the project is delivered within the timeframe given. (**Most Effective**)

C. Develop a plan outlining how you intend approaching the project and use this to emphasise to your head of unit your concern about the deadline and ask if it can be extended.

D. Delegate the task to another person, stressing to them the importance of meeting the deadline. Retain an overview so that you can track progress and keep the ultimate credit for the work. (**Least Effective**)

The Candidate Experience

SJTs contribute to the assessment by being a two-way process for EPSO and the candidate.

EPSO can evaluate the candidate's responses to the scenarios against the structured scoring key and evaluate the extent to which the candidate's behaviour is likely to fit in with the competencies and way of working at the EU institutions.

The candidate is also able to take a view of what it would be like to work with the EU by reflecting after the test on the types of scenarios and response options presented. These may provide a general insight into what situations or behaviours might be expected in the role. Reviewing this chapter and trying out some of the practice questions later on is likely to prove beneficial for you: those candidates who are familiar with SJTs have been found to view the experience of completing SJTs as part of an assessment process more positively than those without that familiarity.

How to Prepare

It is difficult to prepare in advance of taking an SJT: a response to a situation that may be appropriate in one role may be inappropriate in another (e.g. the way you would react to a critique from your supervisor is very different from your reaction to an issue raised by an EU citizen affected by a policy you are covering). Therefore, your answers should draw from your intuitive, *honest* responses about how you would address such situations.

However, reviewing some practice questions (see sample test later in the chapter) can help to alleviate stress and allow you to focus on the *content* of the questions once you start the real test, rather than spending time becoming familiar with the *format*. Also, ensure that you are familiar with the EPSO competencies, as I anticipate that each scenario will be based around one of these. By doing this, you will be more aware of what is likely to be looked for across all the questions. Once again, however, it should be reiterated that you must be honest in your responses and not spend time trying to second-guess what is being looked for.

If you wished to, you could look up some reference material on current best practice thinking on areas related to the competencies being assessed. For example, as there is an EPSO competency entitled "Prioritising and Organising" (defined as "Prioritises the most important tasks, works flexibly and organises own workload efficiently"), you may benefit from doing some background reading on how to plan and organise a working day effectively, or how to cope with conflicting priorities as there is likely to be a question scenario based around this competency. Ideas for research topics on the other competencies are as follows.

- **Analysis and Problem Solving** – *Identifies the critical facts in complex issues and develops creative and practical solutions.* Research areas such as troubleshooting techniques, how to approach dealing with large amounts of information, techniques to stimulate creative problem solving, how to gather appropriate information.

- **Communicating** – *Communicates clearly and precisely both orally and in writing.* Research areas such as public speaking techniques, best practice in internal communications within organisations, how to engage an audience.

- **Delivering Quality and Results** – *Takes personal responsibility and initiative for delivering work to a high standard of quality within set procedures.* Research areas such as how to effectively balance quality and deadlines, how to judge when rules or procedures might be bent or broken.

- **Learning and Development** – *Develops and improves personal skills and knowledge of the organisation and its environment.* Research areas such as general self-improvement techniques, self-motivation, how to learn from mistakes, how to seek feedback from colleagues, how an organisation can use its learning capital.

- **Prioritising and Organising** – *Prioritises the most important tasks, works flexibly and organises own workload efficiently.* Research areas such as project management tools and techniques, how to prioritise effectively, how to distinguish the important from the urgent, how to respond to shifting deadlines and goalposts, when and how to delegate.

- **Resilience** – *Remains effective under a heavy workload, handles organisational frustrations positively and adapts to a changing work environment.* Research areas such as how to stay calm under pressure, how to keep an optimistic outlook, how to respond to criticism, how to balance work and home life, how to cope with ambiguity.

- **Working with Others** – *Works co-operatively with others in teams and across organisational boundaries and respects differences between people.* Research areas such as effective team working, working across organisational boundaries, how to support others.

However, it should be noted that this will be a lot of background work and it would be unrealistic to expect to become an expert in all of these areas prior to the assessment if you are not already. A better tactic might be to decide which one or two competency areas are your prime areas for development and focus upon these.

Tips for the Assessment itself

Several tips mentioned in the verbal reasoning chapter can be successfully applied for SJTs as well. Review and adapt those hints to match the specialties of SJTs.

- **Read Everything**: Read the scenario and each of the possible answers fully before responding. You may find that the answer that originally seemed to be the best does not turn out to be upon closer inspection. Remember that the options will be carefully worded and watch out for subtle differences in wording that could differentiate a truly exceptional response from an adequate one. If possible, try to judge which EPSO competency is being assessed so you have a good idea about what qualities they will be looking for you to emphasise.

- **Relative Answers**: Bear in mind that you are being asked to make *relative* judgements: you are not asked to say which courses of action are right or wrong. In other words, you may find that *all* of the possible responses are appropriate to some degree. In this case, just rank them in order of appropriateness to help you make the "most effective" and "least effective" decision.

- **Limited Context**: As with verbal reasoning exams, try not to bring in outside knowledge – base your responses solely on the information contained within the scenario itself. This is because your outside experience may colour your response in a way that means it is not relevant to the question being posed. To take a light-hearted example, you may know that in your team at work, they are all huge fans of pizza and therefore this would be a good way of motivating them. However, in the SJT test item, there may be no reference to this and the best way to motivate a team may well be to give a motivational talk. Therefore, your outside experience might negatively impact on your ability to perform well in the test.

- **Outcome Focus**: Take the time to consider what the possible *outcomes* would be, both positive and negative, of each of the courses of action you are considering. This will help you to narrow down the choices.

- **Communication is Key**: When a situation is described where you need to choose between handing responsibility for discussing an issue to your superior or discussing an issue with another party face-to-face, it is likely that the latter option will be preferred.

- **Internal Issues**: In a situation involving a conflict, try to look for options that favour keeping a certain issue in-house and involve only those affected by it; your loyalty to your unit or institution is highly valued.

- **Stay Positive**: When faced with a problem that may be resolved by making someone take the blame, avoid the temptation and try to act as fair as possible even if that means a disadvantage for you in the short term.

Though the primary focus of situational judgement tests is not your factual knowledge of EU procedures or administrative practice, it is advisable to read through the Code of Good Administrative Behaviour of EU officials. This includes fundamental principles such as lawfulness, proportionality, non-discrimination, consistency, objectivity and others which can *indirectly* help in your judgement of the questions. Another valuable source is EPSO's very own statement of the values based on which it aims to conduct its mission : integrity, ambition, professionalism, quality service, diversity and respect. If you bear these in mind when making your "situational judgement", it will surely yield the best result.

In the following pages, you can find a sample situational judgement test with detailed explanations, based on EPSO's competency framework.

SAMPLE SITUATIONAL JUDGEMENT TEST FOR ASSISTANTS

In this sample situational judgement test, you will be presented with **seven different situations**, along with a set of **four possible courses of action for each**. Instead of providing a comprehensive test that could evaluate your competency strengths and weaknesses (which is anyway close to impossible without a professional assessor's personal feedback or a dynamic evaluation tool), the goal is to give you a feel for what these tests are like so when facing the real exam, you can focus more on the content and not be surprised by the form.

Apart from the hints and techniques suggested above, we would also recommend that you *try to identify which EPSO competency is being assessed* before choosing one option that you think would be the most desirable and one option that would be the least desirable course of action in each situation. The above list of competencies should help you properly understand the detailed characteristics of each competency and thus assist in making your choice. The reason I recommend this approach is that this will help you to focus your response on the correct area instead of assuming a different context that might lead to misinterpretation. As a final note, I have written these scenarios so that they are likely to measure some of the qualities looked for under each of the EPSO competencies. However, these are not necessarily the exact format you will face as the number of answer options or other details might change. This nevertheless does not affect the core idea and methodology of SJTs, so the sample tests below should prove helpful whatever the final EPSO format is.

Situation One

You are scheduled to join a new unit next week, having requested a transfer from your current role as you had begun to feel as if your work was becoming rather predictable and dull. You are looking forward to your new role, but are aware that there are a range of new processes that you need to learn in order to perform effectively. There is no formal induction process into the new role. Which of the following are you most likely to do?

A. Wait until you begin in the new role as you have always learnt new processes best "on the job" in the past.

B. Speak to other people who work in the same area to find out which processes are the most important to know. Then plan your learning accordingly.

C. Meet with your new superior to discuss where the strengths and weaknesses in your knowledge lie and then plan your learning accordingly.

D. As you already have some idea of where you need to improve, begin learning some new processes straight away to avoid taking up other people's time.

Situation Two

You are in a meeting about time management, trying to give your views on how the current calendar system could be better used, when another person interrupts you saying that you are "talking nonsense" and then puts forward his views instead. The group all agree with the other person's idea even though you did not finish describing yours and you feel it still has merit. Moreover, the other person's idea has some obvious flaws. The group is about to move on to another topic of conversation. What are you most likely to do?

A. State that you, likewise, feel that the other person's idea is "nonsense" as well and that if he hadn't interrupted so rudely, he might have had a chance to hear your idea as well. Then proceed to give your views.

B. As the group is about to move on, don't hold up the meeting by disagreeing now, but send round an email that outlines your alternative idea afterwards, asking for feedback and whether you could call a subsequent meeting to discuss.

C. Let them proceed with the other person's idea, as it is the group consensus decision. However, do some preparation in advance to manage the fall-out when things go wrong.

D. Despite holding up the meeting, you state clearly and firmly that whilst you appreciate the other person's idea has merit, there are some drawbacks and you would like to suggest an alternative. Then proceed to give your views.

Situation Three

You are working as part of a team to discuss how to resolve a problem that has occurred with an IT payments system. The conversation seems to be going nowhere, with lots of people suggesting their own solutions but no-one listening. About halfway through you notice that the technical expert who was responsible for the problem has been quiet for most of the meeting, only contributing the occasional fact when asked by others. You know he is shy as you have worked with him for a while, but you definitely feel he could have something valuable to add. What do you do?

A. Suggest to the group that time is short and say that you think it is important that everyone's views are heard. Summarise what has been discussed and then ask for the technical expert's views directly.

B. Say nothing, as you do not wish to embarrass the technical expert by singling him out. Remain confident of the fact that there will come a point in the meeting at which he needs to be consulted in order for progress to be made.

C. Ask him for his views straight away, reminding the group that he is the technical expert and therefore he should have all the answers required. Because the meeting is already halfway through, you do not feel that there is enough time for discussions which might be irrelevant.

D. Suggest that the group pause for a moment and refocus on the purpose of the meeting. Then ask if anyone would like to comment on what we have covered so far whilst looking at the technical expert in the hope that they will take the opportunity to speak.

Situation Four

You are new to the role, it is the end of the day and you have just been approached by one of the junior Administrators who has an idea for how to handle the expense claims system differently. They have conducted some research about the most common expense types and have come up with a categorisation system that they say will make claiming expenses a far easier process. Apparently, they have the day free tomorrow to work on this and brief the rest of the team if you think it is a good idea. What do you do next?

A. Demonstrate your faith in your team member's judgement and give them the go-ahead to work on implementing the new system tomorrow.

B. Tell them they will not be able to work on the system tomorrow because you would like to look through the information and analyse it in more detail before arriving at a decision.

C. Tell them that they can work on the new system tomorrow as it sounds good in theory, but that they should not tell anyone else before you have had a chance to have a look through.

D. Start from scratch in analysing the expense claims system for yourself and see if you can suggest a new system that makes the process easier.

Situation Five

You have just been given responsibility for overseeing a project that involves the implementation of a new records system. These records seek to compile, in one place, hard copies of invoices and receipts relating to all projects completed over the past five years in your Directorate. Currently, no such system exists and records are kept by individuals in either hard or soft copies. As so much information is involved, you have been allocated 3 months to get the system up and running. How would you approach a task of this nature?

A. Work out who you will need to go to in order to get information and approach them individually with requests for hard or soft copies of invoices and receipts, hoping they will come back to you quickly enough to meet the deadline.

B. Identify the key milestones, risks and contingencies related to the project and pull together a project plan that you can refer to as the project progresses.

C. Because time is tight, begin working on the new system immediately, sending out requests for information held in soft copy to everyone in the Directorate and locating any hard copies of invoices or receipts on people's desks.

D. Arrange for individual meetings with everyone in the Directorate, beginning tomorrow, so that you can speak to them about the project and ask for any relevant information that they have.

Situation Six

You have been asked by a superior to help them in implementing a new security system. Basically, everyone now entering the building has to sign in at the register at the start of the day and sign out at the end of the day. They are also now required to wear a photo ID badge around their neck at all times. Your responsibility has been to inform people of the scheme and of the need to comply with this. So far, you have only managed to speak to five people but you have noticed that for the past three days since you spoke to them, they have not been following the new process. What do you do next?

A. Speed up your rate of telling people about the new scheme: the more people know about it, the more likely it is that people will follow it.

B. Speak to the people who have not complied, asking why and if also whether there are any tips they can give you for how to win other people over.

C. Try sending out an email to everyone that outlines the new process and encourages them to comply.

D. Pick people up as soon as they break with the rules and tell them to comply. Focus only upon the people you have told so far.

Situation Seven

You are responsible for compiling the results of an important opinion survey on how staff perceive the secretarial support function within your Directorate. It is running behind schedule: you are due to deliver the final report in two days' time. The work required is fairly basic data entry with some simple calculations required to get average scores. You already have a full diary and are feeling exhausted so would like to request that a secretary from another area is seconded to help. However, the people you need to speak to for permission are out of the office. You have been told that due to budget restrictions, temporary staff should not be hired at the present time. How do you approach the situation?

A. Decide to book an extra temporary member of staff anyway to help with the data entry and worry about the budget later: delivering the report on time is the most important issue.

B. Scale back the scope of the report and cover only what you have been able to complete in the available time. Afterwards, deliver a follow-up report that covers any additional data.

C. Work additional hours yourself in order to get the data entered, even if you already have a very busy schedule.

D. Decide to ask the other secretary to help anyway and worry about the permission later: delivering the report on time is the most important issue.

Answers with Explanations

Situation One

EPSO Competency: Learning and Development

Which did you think were the most and least desirable courses of action?

The most appropriate answer in this case is **Option C**. By understanding where the strengths and weaknesses in your knowledge lie and getting an expert opinion on this, you will have the ideal base upon which to plan your development. Your new superior is the ideal source, although you may also get some input from your current superior to help the discussion.

Option A may be a possibility, especially if you have a preference for active learning. However, this should follow from Option C, not replace it. It also reflects a rather ad hoc approach to personal development, rather than a planned, well considered one. Therefore, this is likely to be the least effective course of action.

Option B might be useful, but the advice is likely to be quite general, rather than applied to your role specifically. Also, the people in the job may not be performing all the tasks the head of unit wishes in the way in which the head of unit wishes them to be performed, so their advice may be flawed.

By choosing **Option D**, you will have missed out on the valuable chance to have your own opinion on what to develop validated or challenged by another. Ruling out this course of action because it may take up people's time before you have even checked with them is a missed opportunity.

Situation Two

EPSO Competency: Resilience

Which did you think were the most and least desirable courses of action?

The most appropriate answer in this case is **Option D**. It demonstrates great resilience to not only come back against a challenger that everyone else has agreed with, but also to do so in a calm and measured manner. It will be far more efficient to raise the point now, even if it means extending the meeting, as it ensures all subsequent discussions are relevant.

Option A is likely to simply cause antagonism by being equally rude in return.

Although your views will be heard by the group, they will also note your emotional reaction and may hesitate about engaging with you or giving you feedback in the future. Additionally, the person you were originally in conflict with may then feel obliged to argue back just because of the approach you adopted, in order to maintain his pride.

Option B may be acceptable, depending upon the timescales available, but it would show greater resilience to address the issue there and then, face to face. It also runs the risk of the rest of the meeting being unproductive because it will be based on the premise that the alternative idea will be adopted.

However, **Option C** is probably the least desirable as because you failed to speak out, now an entire plan's success is at risk: Option C almost feels like you are getting your own back on the other person through spite. It also shows a tendency to shy away from confrontation, which shows a lack of personal confidence.

Situation Three

EPSO Competency: Working With Others

Which did you think were the most and least desirable courses of action?

The most appropriate answer in this case is **Option A**. By pausing the meeting and summarising, this gives the chance to ensure everyone has the same understanding so far and also allows a pause for the technical expert to speak. Choosing Option A not only demonstrates empathy on your part, it also shows a certain drive to help the team achieve its goals.

Option B shows no real attempt to aid the team-working process and is therefore the least desirable option. It also abdicates responsibility for resolving the issue there and then yourself which would have aided the team-working process.

Option C shows a certain lack of appreciation for the technical expert's current mindset: this action may embarrass him and/or lead to him being unable to contribute by feeling too exposed. Introducing a pause in proceedings and then asking the technical expert to contribute in a non-threatening way shows far greater emotional intelligence.

Option D is unlikely to be successful as it seems from the scenario information that the technical expert is so shy or embarrassed that he may not pick up on your cue to speak. More direct action is needed to encourage his contribution.

Situation Four

EPSO Competency: Analysis and Problem Solving

Which did you think were the most and least desirable courses of action?

The most effective action in this case is **Option B**. It is likely to be unrealistic for you to make a sound judgement before you have reviewed the evidence and it sounds like there may well be some broader implications to consider before reaching a conclusion. There does not seem to be an urgent deadline for a decision, other than the fact of the team member having the free time tomorrow, and therefore a delay would probably be acceptable.

The least effective is **Option A**: this shows perhaps a tendency to shy away from detailed analysis and does not take into account the possible biases (or errors) of your team member in presenting their views to you. Although it may demonstrate loyalty to your teammate, it may result in a less than optimum outcome – especially considering you are new to the role and you presumably know little about your team member's reliability to date.

Option C would be a potentially good course of action at some point, as it will help you to review the person's system in more detail before "going public' with it. However, to approve this before having the chance for even a cursory review could result in wasted effort. Therefore it would be better to do Option B first.

Option D is a possibility if you had a lot of time, but it is an uneconomical way of problem solving if a lot of the research has already been conducted. It would be better to capitalise on the existing information, even if there are flaws in it, and once you have reviewed all the evidence you can then decide if a full analysis from scratch is required or not.

Situation Five

EPSO Competency: Prioritising and Organising

Which did you think were the most and least desirable courses of action?

The most appropriate answer in this case is **Option B**. In order to stand the best chance of successful delivery, an initial project plan with milestones, risks and contingencies is required. It sounds as if there will be multiple stakeholders to discuss with and multiple information sources to refer to; therefore by giving consideration to risks such as people being on holiday, or needing to request duplicates of lost invoices, contingency time can be allowed that will ensure the project is delivered on time.

Option A is a good idea, but doing this before a clear project plan is in place runs the risk of approaching people in the wrong order, or failing to consider other salient aspects of the project that may need to be resolved first (such as where to store the physical invoices and receipts). Taking some time to look at the bigger picture is more likely to lead to project success.

Option C reflects a very broad-brush approach. It may mean that some time is saved in planning, but it risks bothering people unnecessarily with requests for information. Also, by going ahead and removing hard copies from people's desks before seeking permission, you may be causing difficulties for the people involved if they need to locate the items at a later date. Option C is therefore probably the least effective course of action.

Option D is a good idea, but again perhaps reflects a rather broad-brush approach. Without either a project plan or a consideration of which people to involve, you run the risk of wasting your own and other people's time. It reflects a rather ad hoc approach, rather than a thoughtful and planned one to executing a project successfully.

Situation Six

EPSO Competency: Communicating

Which did you think were the most and least desirable courses of action?

The most appropriate answer in this case is **Option B**. Finding out which aspects of your communication worked and which did not work is going to be the best way of achieving success in future. It may well be that the non-compliance has nothing to do with your communication either: but at least by asking, you will have found out and can react accordingly.

Option A might work, but if there is something unclear about the way you are describing the new system, or the way in which you are phrasing your request is putting some people off from complying, then this is less likely to be effective. However, only speaking to five people in three days does not seem like many, so once you have done Option B then speeding up would be a good idea.

Option C represents taking a blanket approach to the issue. It ensures many people are told within a short time period. However, without knowing what has gone wrong with the first five people, you may repeat the same mistakes in how you are conveying the message. Coupled with Option B, this step may be a good precursor to face-to-face follow-ups.

Option D represents taking a more disciplinary stance. This is probably the least effective option as you have not only failed to seek out the reasons for non-compliance (and thus may repeat similar mistakes in the future), but by limiting yourself to only the first five people, you are delaying spreading the word to other people in the group.

Situation Seven

EPSO Competency: Delivering Quality and Results

Which did you think were the most and least desirable courses of action?

The most appropriate answer in this case is **Option D**. If extra resource is available from another team, this should help to ensure the deadline is met and with no additional cost implications. If the extra resource is not available, you are still free to pursue one of the other options, meaning that this gives you the most possible flexibility.

Despite demonstrating drive and determination, **Option C** runs the risks of errors being made due to fatigue. There is the additional risk that the other work you have running in parallel will also suffer as a result. Therefore, this answer falls down on the quality focus aspects.

Choosing **Option B** means that you fail to deliver the project objective. There is no indication that this course of action will be acceptable in the scenario and it is likely to be unsatisfactory to the stakeholders. Therefore it is probably the least appropriate answer.

Option A shows initiative, and should get the project delivered on time and with less chance of mistakes than working extra hours yourself (although a temp will still need to be fully briefed). However the extra budget goes beyond the remit of the project and this is therefore not an ideal solution as you will not have worked within the project objectives.

PART II
PRE-SELECTION – PROFESSIONAL SKILLS TESTS

About Part II

Testing of AST professional skills is carried out in both the pre-selection phase and in the Assessment Centre. However, there is a difference in emphasis between the two phases. In the pre-selection phase, the centre of attention is "prioritising and organising" tests which are needed for Assistants of every sub-profile, while in the Assessment Centre the tests cover specific knowledge in the chosen field of the exam. In Part II, we cover those tests used in the pre-selection phase.

These tests are designed to measure an individual's capacity to plan and organise. This could be in relation to their own or other people's time or resources. They can also measure the ability to prioritise issues. These are not psychometric tests that measure, for example, verbal or numerical reasoning skills; instead they measure what would more commonly be thought of as "behavioural competency" and they are frequently employed as part of a more complex Assessment Centre exercise that would be assessed by a trained individual. EPSO has decided to use these tests as part of the sifting process early on and therefore have automated a lot of the scoring that would normally be conducted by an assessor.

The forms of professional skills tests currently being used by EPSO include Organising and Prioritising tests, Computer Literacy tests and Accuracy tests. Exercises for each of these tests can be found in the following chapters.

In the **Organising and Prioritising Test** you are given a range of data in tabular format and asked to make a number of decisions based on the data. In some cases the answers involve basic calculations and there is, in an absolute sense, only one correct answer. In others you may be required to make judgements about the best use of resources, choosing a preferable option, even if another choice is not in itself wrong.

The **Computer Literacy Test** is relatively straight-forward as it covers main concepts and a practical knowledge of the most important Microsoft Office applications such as Word, Excel, PowerPoint and Outlook. It may also include generalist IT knowledge of basic security issues related to passwords, internet browsing, online searching, telephone management, mobile phone handling, USB keys and the fundamentals of wireless networks. This is of course not to say that candidates are expected to know as much as an IT expert; on the contrary, whatever would be needed for the work of an effective Assistant can be considered as relevant knowledge.

The **Accuracy Test** is what its name says: it involves spotting inconsistencies, typos, grammatical errors, misspellings or other discrepancies in complex charts and tables without actually dealing with the real content of these items. This means that no knowledge of the field or any in-depth analysis of a spreadsheet is required; the only competency tested here is your attention to detail and resilience under time pressure. This particular test is very similar to the task of a proof-reader who must ensure that a certain name is spelled in a uniform way throughout a document or a person's company ID number is consistently referred to everywhere it appears. It is strongly advised that you time yourself in order to simulate the exam environment as far as possible.

1. Organising and Prioritising Test

60 QUESTIONS – answers follow question 60

Glasgow – Edinburgh Bus Timetable: Journey Time 1hour 20mins (Q 1-3)			
Depart Glasgow		*Depart Edinburgh*	
Mon-Sat	Sun	Mon-Sat	Sun
0545	0800	0600	0745
0610	Every 2 hours until…	0620	Every 2 hours until…
0630	2000	0640	1945
Every 30 mins until…	2130	0700	2120
2230		Every 30 mins until…	
2330		2230	
		2330	

1. You live in Glasgow, 20 minutes' walk from the bus station. You are visiting a client in Edinburgh on Tuesday who is 5 minutes' walk from the bus terminus. Your meeting is scheduled for 10 o'clock. What is the latest time you can leave home?

A.   07:45

B.   08:00

C.   08:10

D.   08:30

E.   08:40

2. You need to be back home by 18:00. What is the longest possible meeting you can have?

A.   3h 20m

B.   2h 55m

C.   4h 40m

D.   5h 55m

E.   5h 10m

3. On Sunday you wish to visit a friend in Edinburgh who meets you at the bus station. You need to see each other for at least 3 hours. What is the earliest time you can arrive home?

A.   15:25

B.   12:35

C.   16:10

D.   14:30

E.   13:55

Project Cronos (Q 4-6)					
	Specification	*Implementation*	*Evaluation*	*Report*	*Day Unavailable*
Alan	X	X		X	2,9
Bella	X		X		3,7
Carol		X		X	1,4
Dmetri		X			2,8
Elaine			X	X	3,12

	Length of Phase (man-days)	*Maximum Simultaneous Workers*
Specification	4	2
Implementation	4	2
Evaluation	2	1
Report	1	1

4. In this project the implementation and evaluation phases are repeated until criteria are fulfilled and then the report is written. Assuming full availability of all team members, how long will the project take if three iterations are required?

A. 11 days   B. 16 days

C. 15 days   D. 12 days

E. 14 days

5. Given the unavailability shown, how long will a two-repetition project take?

A. 11 days   B. 13 days

C. 15 days   D. 12 days

E. 14 days

6. If Bella became completely unavailable due to illness, how long would a three repetition project take?

A. 13 days   B. 19 days

C. 20 days   D. 16 days

E. 17 days

7. You have to organise a conference call involving all five of the team members. The call is expected to last for 40 minutes. What is the latest time the call can be placed (CET)?

A. 10:20   B. 12:20

C. 15:20   D. 13:20

E. 14:20

8. What is the earliest time you can arrange a call for at least 4 members to participate?

A. 7:00   B. 7:30

C. 8:00   D. 8:30

E. 9:00

9. If the call needs to include Aaron and either Corre or Erin and either Bunte or Danielle, how long is the longest window of opportunity for the call?

A. 1h 45m   B. 1h 30m

C. 2h 15m   D. 1h 15m

E. 2h 00m

Conference Call (Q 7-9)					
Name	*Aaron*	*Bunte*	*Corre*	*Danielle*	*Erin*
Timezone	CET	CET+2	CET-1	CET+1	CET-1
Availability	0900 – 1200	1000 – 1200	1000 – 1200	0800 – 1130	0700 – 1000
	1300 – 1730	1345 – 1715	1230 – 1600	1400 – 1600	1300 - 1500

10. The meeting rooms shown can only be booked for whole hour slots. You need a room for a one-to-one performance review via video link with your remote manager at 11:00 for 1 hour. Which room would be most suitable?

A. Ulster   B. Munster

C. Leinster   D. Connacht

E. Eire

11. You need a room to show your team of 15 people the latest sales figures via a projector. The presentation will take less than one hour and the only time everyone is available is 12 o'clock. Which room should you book?

A. Ulster   B. Munster

C. Leinster   D. Connacht

E. Eire

Meeting Rooms (Q 10-12)					
	Ulster	*Munster*	*Leinster*	*Connacht*	*Eire*
Capacity	8	16	40	12	18
Projector	N	N	Y	N	Y
Video Phone	N	Y	N	Y	N
Monitor	N	Y	Y	Y	N
Wi-Fi	Y	Y	Y	N	N

12. You and your 4 senior managers need to make a video conference call with colleagues abroad. The call may take more than one hour and the only time everyone can make themselves available is 1 o'clock. Which room should you use?

A. Ulster   B. Munster

C. Leinster   D. Connacht

E. Eire

Room Bookings (Q10-12)									
	9-10	*10-11*	*11-12*	*12-1*	*1-2*	*2-3*	*3-4*	*4-5*	*5-6*
Ulster		X	X	X					
Munster	X	X	X				X		
Leinster	X			X					X
Connacht						X			
Eire					X			X	X

−   *X denotes room booked*

Manchester – Airport (Q 13-15)	
(Train Journey 25mins)	
Dep. Man	Dep. Airport
05:15	06:15
Every 15 minutes until…	Every 15 minutes until…
21:30	22:00
22:15	22:45

Manchester – Paris CDG (Q13-15)	
(Air Journey 1h 20mins)	
Dep. MAN (GMT)	Dep. Paris (CET)
07:05	07:00
07:35	07:30
08:15	08:15
11:20	12:00
14:15	15:15
17:20	17:20
18:00	17:40
18:40	18:10
21:00	20:50

Paris CDG – Paris (Q13-15)	
(Train Journey 20mins)	
Dep. Airport	Dep. Paris
0650	0610
0730	0700
Every 30 minutes until…	Every 30 minutes until…
21:30	21:00
22:15	21:45

13. You live in Manchester, 5 minutes walk from the station. You have a lunch appointment at 13:30 in Paris just outside the station. Assuming you must arrive at the airport 30 minutes before departure and it takes 15 minutes at each end to transfer between airport and railway station, what is the latest time you can leave home?

A.   6:20   B.   9:55

C.   6:55   D.   8:15

E.   7:30

14. The lunch lasts 1h 30mins. How much time can you spend sightseeing (including getting to the station) before you must catch the train to the airport to ensure you arrive home the same day?

A.   4h 30m   B.   2h 30m

C.   2h   D.   3h

E.   3h 30m

15. You catch the 17:00 train from Paris station. What time do you arrive home?

A.   20:15   B.   20:00

C.   19:00   D.   19:15

E.   20:30

16. You and another teacher are taking a group of 10 school children to France. You have a minibus and are prepared to drive for about an hour to take them to Disneyland and spend some time on the beach. Which accommodation is most suitable?

A.   Merlot   B.   Grenache

C.   Syrah   D.   Chardonnay

E.   Columbard

17. You, your partner and 3 other couples want to go on a golfing holiday and would like to be as close to a course as possible. You would like an easy walk to a restaurant and must have air conditioning. Which is the most suitable?

A.   Merlot   B.   Grenache

C.   Syrah   D.   Chardonnay

E.   Columbard

18. You and five friends have a budget of 200 euro each. You require a pool, air conditioning and close proximity to the shops. Which do you choose?

A.   Merlot   B.   Grenache

C.   Syrah   D.   Chardonnay

E.   Columbard

Holiday Homes in France (Q 16-18)					
	Merlot	*Grenache*	*Syrah*	*Chardonnay*	*Columbard*
Capacity	12	6	14	20	8
Pool	Private	Shared	Shared	Private	None
Air Conditioning	Y	Y	N	N	Y
Price (€)	1200	850	1200	1600	900

Distances to... (km) (Q 16-18)					
	Shops	*Beach*	*Restaurant*	*Disneyland*	*Golf Course*
Merlot	1	20	0.5	180	5
Grenache	4	10	0.1	220	20
Syrah	0.5	250	1	40	2
Chardonnay	10	1	6	50	5
Columbard	1	40	<1	60	1

19. You have to organise a training schedule. Only one course will be taught each day. What will be taught and where on Thursday?

A. Project management in Cassiopeia

B. Expense control in Cepheus

C. Report writing in Cepheus

D. Project management in Cepheus

E. Expense control in Cassiopeia

20. When and where will project management be taught?

A. Wednesday in Cepheus

B. Thursday in Cepheus

C. Thursday in Cassiopeia

D. Wednesday in Andromeda

E. Thursday in Andromeda

21. How many people will be taught on Monday and Tuesday combined?

A. 36   B. 34

C. 30   D. 28

E. 26

Training Schedule (Q 19-21)					
Course	*Time Management*	*Expense Control*	*Report Writing*	*Problem Solving*	*Project Management*
Enrolled	14	20	16	12	9
Tutor Available	Mon, Tue	Tue, Thu	Mon, Fri	Wed, Fri	Wed, Thu

Training Rooms (Q 19-21)			
Room	*Cepheus*	*Cassiopeia*	*Andromeda*
Capacity	25	15	12
Available	Mon, Thu	Tue, Thu	Tue, Wed, Fri

Training Course Hotels (Q 22-24)					
Hotel	*Traveller*	*Romano*	*Phoenix*	*Doric*	*El Greco*
Rating	3*	4*	3*	2*	4*
Gym	Y	Y	N	N	Y
Pool	N	Y	Y	N	Y
Wi-Fi	Y	Y	N	N	Y
Distance to Training Centre	0.5km	6km	5km	0.5km	1km
Cost (€)	80	110	75	60	140

22. You need to book a hotel for three of your staff for a training course. They will share a car and they need internet access for working during the evening. They have also requested use of a pool. Which hotel is the best option?

A. Traveller B. Romano

C. Phoenix D. Doric

E. El Greco

23. You are going on a training course for two days and require a hotel simply to sleep. You would like to be as close to the training centre as possible. Which should you choose?

A. Traveller B. Romano

C. Phoenix D. Doric

E. El Greco

24. You need to book a hotel for a senior manager who is attending a training course. He likes to use the gym in the morning and the pool in the evening. He also wants to walk to the training centre. Which is the best option?

A. Traveller B. Romano

C. Phoenix D. Doric

E. El Greco

25. You have a weekend retreat miles from anywhere which does not have broadband access. You need to access your e-mail via dial-up when visiting there. Which provider offers the most cost-effective solution?

A. Megalink B. Truspeed

C. Fastlink D. Netserve

E. Netlink

Internet Service Providers (Q 25-27)					
Provider	*Megalink*	*Truspeed*	*Fastlink*	*Netserve*	*Netlink*
Speed (Mb/s)	20	10	12	2	5
Download Limit (Gb)	100	40	40	10	10
Dial-up access	N	N	Y	Y	N
Help Desk	Y	Y	N	N	Y
Cost/month (€)	25	22.50	17.50	9.95	12.50

Stationery Stores (Q 28-30)				
	In Stock	*Ave. Weekly Usage*	*Order when Stock reaches…*	*Re-order Quantity*
Pads	40	12	25	50
Pens	120	50	100	250
Envelopes	220	80	160	500
Ring binders	30	4	20	20
Post-its	100	15	50	60

26. **You play a lot of interactive net games and download lots of videos and music totalling more than 30Gb/month. You are prepared to pay for fast speed. Who do you choose?**

A. Megalink   B. Truspeed

C. Fastlink   D. Netserve

E. Netlink

27. **You are setting up your home PC for the first time and need a lot of help. Your requirements are low as you only want access for a few e-mails and some internet shopping. Price is important to you. Which is your best option?**

A. Megalink   B. Truspeed

C. Fastlink   D. Netserve

E. Netlink

28. **You are in charge of the stationery stores which you check every Monday and order supplies if necessary which are delivered the same day. Today's stock level is shown for week 1. What will need ordering next week at week 2?**

A. Pads and Ring binders

B. Pads and Envelopes

C. Pens and Envelopes

D. Pens

E. Post-its

29. **Having placed the previous orders, during week 2 your department does a special mailshot which requires 200 additional envelopes. What needs ordering at week 3?**

A. Pads and Envelopes   B. Pads

C. Ring binders and Pens   D. Post-its

E. Post-its and Pads

30. **At week 4 you realise that you will not be at work the following week so you must order in advance (nobody else can do this for you). What needs to be ordered?**

A. Post-its and Pens

B. Envelopes and Pads

C. Ring binders and Pens

D. Ring binders

E. Ring binders and Post-its

Project Ouranos (Q 31-33)					
	Proposal	Draft	Review	Report	Day Unavailable
Callum	X			X	2,6
Edouard		X		X	2,12
Gabrielle	X		X		6,8
Jean	X			X	7,8
Liam		X	X		3,10

Length of Phase (man-days) (Q 31-33)	
Proposal	4
Draft	6
Review	8
Report	4

31. Each phase of the project must be completed in sequence and must have 2 people working on it at all times. If there are insufficient staff then the project stalls. Whose absence will cause the first delay in the project?

A. Callum   B. Edouard

C. Gabrielle   D. Jean

E. Liam

32. How many days will the project take with the given availability?

A. 12   B. 14

C. 16   D. 13

E. 15

33. If Liam re-arranges his commitments so that he is now available on day 3,

how many days will the project now take?

A. 11   B. 15

C. 14   D. 12

E. 13

34. You have to organise a video conference call involving all the team members. What is the longest possible call if all five people are to be involved?

A. 45m   B. 30m

C. 1h 30m   D. 1h 15m

E. 1h

35. Which single person would need to rearrange their availability to allow for a longer call?

A. Tina   B. Mia

C. Dee   D. Arnie

E. Ed

36. If Dee and Ed both extend their afternoon availability by 2 hours, by how much would this extend the maximum call length?

A. 2h   B. 1h

C. 0m   D. 15m

E. 45m

37. You need to book a car to take yourself and two colleagues, one of them disabled, to the airport for a 7a.m. flight. You need to be there at least 1hr before

Video Conference (Q 34-36)					
	Tina	Mia	Dee	Arnie	Ed
Timezone	CET-6	CET	CET+2	CET-1	CET+1
Availability (Local time)	0700 - 1100 1230 - 1545	0900 – 1200 1300 – 1700	0930 – 1115 1245 – 1545	1000 – 1300 1400 – 1530	0830 – 1130 1345 - 1500

Airport Transfers (Q 37-39)					
	Airways	*Avion*	*A1*	*Aircars*	*Ascendors*
Passengers	6	4	3	6	6
Hours of Operation	6 – 21	5 – 22	6 – 22	5 – 21	7 – 23
Wheelchair Access	Y	N	N	Y	N
Price (€)	35	40	30	40	45

departure because wheelchair access is difficult. Which car do you choose?

A. Airways   B. Avion

C. A1   D. Aircars

E. Ascendors

38. **You and a friend have to catch the midday flight to Paris. Which should you choose?**

A. Airways   B. Avion

C. A1   D. Aircars

E. Ascendors

39. **Five of you are going on a budget holiday and need to get to the airport. Every euro saved is an extra drink on the beach. Who do you choose?**

A. Airways   B. Avion

C. A1   D. Aircars

E. Ascendors

40. **You live in Amsterdam and have some important documents which need to be** signed by your client in Vienna and should only take about 5 minutes. Which is the best train to catch if you are to get back home the same day?

A. 5:15   B. 6:50

C. 7:20   D. 7:40

E. 8:40

41. **How much time do you spend waiting in stations on the journey in Q. 40 (including signing the documents)?**

A. 20m   B. 35m

C. 1h5m   D. 1h20m

E. 1h35m

42. **You are meeting a client in Frankfurt who can't leave Vienna until after mid-morning. You select your train to minimise your wait. How much time do you have in Frankfurt if you are both to catch your next available train?**

A. 20m   B. 45m

C. 30m   D. 55m

E. 1h10m

Train Timetable *Vienna – Amsterdam – Vienna; (Via Frankfurt)* (Q 40-42)							
Vienna	Frankfurt		Amsterdam		Frankfurt		Vienna
Dep.	*Arr.*	*Dep.*	*Arr.*	*Dep.*	*Arr.*	*Dep.*	*Arr.*
0430	0815	0620	0845	0515	0735	0650	1035
0720	1125	0840	1055	0740	1005	1020	1425
0915	1325	1025	1250	1025	1310	1205	1550
1230	1620	1440	1700	1350	1610	1420	1820
1440	1915	1705	1915	1710	1920	1705	2110
1730	2205	2020	2245	2100	2305	1945	2330

Mobile Phones (Q 43-45)					
Provider	*Skyway*	*Etherfone*	*ManyG*	*Scilink*	*Iridium*
Call Cost (€/min)	0.02	0.15	0.03	0.16	0.02
Text Cost (€)	0.02	0.06	0.02	0.05	0.03
Texts Included in Contract	300	0	500	0	200
Internet Access	Y	N	Y	N	N
Contract Cost (€/mth)	14.95	0	12.50	0	9.99

43. You need a phone for emergency use only, perhaps one call per month and never send text messages. Which is best for you?

A. Skyway   B. Etherfone

C. ManyG   D. Scilink

E. Iridium

44. You need a phone for your teenage child who sends over 20 text messages every day but makes very few calls. Which is best?

A. Skyway   B. Etherfone

C. ManyG   D. Scilink

E. Iridium

45. You need a phone with Internet access so that you can work on the move. You make a lot of calls totalling over an hour each day but send few text messages. Which is best for you?

A. Skyway   B. Etherfone

C. ManyG   D. Scilink

E. Iridium

46. You have a budget of €100 to get a printer to print the best possible quality in colour. Which do you choose?

A. Agfa   B. Daewoo

C. Epson   D. HP

E. Kodak

47. You need a departmental printer for printing colour brochures. Quality is paramount and there will generally be about 100 pages per day. Which do you choose?

A. Agfa   B. Daewoo

C. Epson   D. HP

E. Kodak

48. You need a printer to print large quantities of draft documents and e-mails, up to 8000 pages per day. Which do you choose?

A. Agfa   B. Daewoo

C. Epson   D. HP

E. Kodak

Office Printers (Q 46-48)					
Make	*Agfa*	*Daewoo*	*Epson*	*HP*	*Kodak*
Colour Print	Y	Y	N	N	Y
Type	Inkjet	Laser	Laser	Inkjet	Inkjet
Quality	4*	5*	5*	3*	3*
Speed (p/m)	12	3	5	20	14
Cost/page (€)	0.04	0.12	0.06	0.02	0.05
Price (€)	80	450	290	40	75

Strasbourg – Obernai (Q 49-51)					
(Bus Journey Time 80 mins)					
DEP. Strasbourg			*DEP. Obernai*		
Mon-Fri	*Sat*	*Sun*	*Mon-Fri*	*Sat*	*Sun*
0620	0800	0800	0600	0730	0830
0645	Every hour until…	Every 90 mins until…	0630	Every hour until…	Every 90 mins until…
0710	2200	2130	0740	2130	2200
Every hour until…			Every hour until…		
2110			2140		
2230			2250		

49. You live in Obernai, 5 minutes walk from the bus stop and need to attend a meeting in Strasbourg on Tuesday in an office 10 minutes walk from the bus terminus. The meeting is scheduled for 10:00 and lasts 1h 15m. You catch the first available bus home. What is the minimum time that you are away from home?

A. 4h
B. 4h 25m
C. 5h
D. 5h 35m
E. 6h

50. You live in Strasbourg and wish to visit friends in Obernai on Saturday for shopping and lunch. You spend 5h 20m with your friends. What is the earliest possible time you could get back to Strasbourg?

A. 15:10
B. 16:20
C. 18:00
D. 16:50
E. 17:10

51. You live in Obernai and wish to attend a memorial service in Strasbourg on Sunday. The service is at a church 10 minutes walk from the bus station and starts at 11:00 and lasts for 40 minutes. What is the minimum amount of time you can spend in Strasbourg?

A. 1h
B. 3h 20m
C. 2h 40m
D. 1h 40m
E. 2h 10m

52. You and your partner are going on holiday with two young children aged 4 and 6. You plan on spending a lot of time on the beach and your budget is tight. Where do you stay?

A. Seaview
B. Palace
C. Hydro
D. Marine
E. Grand

Holiday Hotels (Q 52-54)					
Hotel	*Seaview*	*Palace*	*Hydro*	*Marine*	*Grand*
Pool	N	Y	Y	Y	N
Restaurant	N	Y	N	N	Y
Air Conditioning	N	Y	Y	N	Y
Family Rooms	Y	N	Y	Y	N
Beach	20m	4km	200m	50m	6km
Cost/night (€)	70	95	90	90	80

53. **You and your partner are looking for a hotel that is convenient for the beach and it must have air-conditioned rooms. Which do you choose?**

A. Seaview   B. Palace

C. Hydro   D. Marine

E. Grand

54. **You and your partner like relaxing by the pool during the day and eating in the evening without having to drive out or get a taxi. Which is best suited for you?**

A. Seaview   B. Palace

C. Hydro   D. Marine

E. Grand

55. **You are tasked with organising training sessions, one each day for a week, keeping costs to a minimum. When and where will the Word training be held?**

A. Monday in Juno

B. Monday in Ceres

C. Thursday in Ceres

D. Wednesday in Ceres

E. Friday in Juno

56. **How much will Monday's training session cost?**

A. 45   B. 50

C. 60   D. 80

E. 100

57. **How many spare seats will there be in the classroom on Thursday?**

A. 4   B. 8

C. 5   D. 9

E. 2

58. **You have a large document in English which needs to be typed up in Mac Pages format as quickly as possible. Who do you use?**

A. Speedwell   B. Qwerty

C. Keyfast   D. Datablast

E. TypeRight

59. **You have a Spanish audio tape which needs transcribing. Your budget is very limited. Who do you use?**

A. Speedwell   B. Qwerty

C. Keyfast   D. Datablast

E. TypeRight

Training Courses (Q 55-57)					
Course	Word	Excel	Powerpoint	Databases	Windows
No. Enrolled	40	25	16	12	36
Tutor Available	Mon, Wed, Thu	Tue, Thu, Fri	Tue, Wed, Thu	Mon, Thu, Fri	Mon, Tue, Thu

Training Classrooms (Q 55-57)					
Room	Ceres	Juno	Pallas	Demeter	Hera
Capacity	40	40	20	30	20
Available	Tue, Wed, Fri	Tue, Fri	Tue, Wed, Thu	Mon, Thu, Fri	Mon, Tue, Wed
Cost (€)	100	89	50	60	45

Typing Services (Q 58-60)					
Name	*Speedwell*	*Qwerty*	*Keyfast*	*Datablast*	*TypeRight*
Words/min	80	85	70	90	75
Languages	Eng, Fr, Ger	Eng, Ger, Spa	Eng, It	Fr, Ger, Spa	Fr, Spa, It
Audio Transcription	Y	Y	N	N	Y
Mac Pages	N	Y	Y	N	Y
Cost/1000 wds (€)	6.50	6.50	7.00	7.50	6.00

60. **You have a 10000 word French transcript which needs typing up. You have a budget of €70 and need it doing as quickly as possible. Who do you use?**

A. Speedwell

B. Qwerty

C. Keyfast

D. Datablast

E. TypeRight

ANSWERS

1   C

Explanation: The buses arrive in Edinburgh at 20 and 50 minutes past each hour so you need to arrive by 09:50 which is the 08:30 bus from Glasgow. It is 20 minutes' walk to the bus stop so you need to leave by 08:10.

2   D

Explanation: To be home by 18:00 you need to be off the bus by 17:40 and so on the bus by 16:20. The last bus before this time is the 16:00 so you must leave the meeting by 15:55 which is 5h 55m after the meeting started.

3   A

Explanation: If you catch the 08:00 bus to Edinburgh you will arrive at 09:20. Three hours with your friend will bring it to 12:20. The next bus is then at 13:45 arriving back in Glasgow at 15:05 and it is 20 minutes' walk home.

4   C

Explanation: With two people working, the Specification will take 2 days. The implementation and evaluation takes 2+2=4 days but requires 3 iterations which is 12 days and the report requires 1 day for a total of 15 days.

5   D

Explanation: Alan is off on day 2 and Bella is off on day 3 which will add one day to the specification phase. There is enough cover for the two iterations of the implementation and evaluation cycle so it will take 8 days and the report takes one. This gives a total of 12 days.

6   B

Explanation: Alan is alone for the spec phase which now takes 5 days. Three repetitions of the implementation and evaluation would normally take 12 days but Elaine is off on day 12 when she is the only evaluator so it now takes 13 days. The report takes 1 day. This gives a total of 19 days.

7   E

Explanation: Bunte is unavailable from 10:00 and Corre is not available until 11:00 (CET) so there is no morning opportunity. In the afternoon, Erin is the last to become available at 14:00 and Danielle is the first to become unavailable at 15:00 so a 40 minute call must be placed by 14:20.

8   E

Explanation: Aaron is the fourth to become available at 09:00, which excludes Corre. The time window lasts until 10:00.

9   A

Explanation: There is a morning opportunity from 09:00 to 10:30 and an afternoon opportunity for Aaron, Bunte and Corre from 13:30–15:15, which is 1h 45m.

10   D

Explanation: Only Munster and Connacht have video phones and only Connacht is available at 11:00.

11   E

Explanation: Ulster and Connacht are too small, Munster doesn't have a projector and Leinster is unavailable at 12 o'clock.

12   B

Explanation: Munster and Connacht have the required video phone and both are available at 13:00 but as the call may take more than 1 hour Munster should be used.

13   C

Explanation: Because of the 1 hour time difference, the 11:20 flight arrives at 13:40 not 12:40 and is too late. To catch the 8:15 flight you need to arrive at the airport by 7:45 and at the airport station by 7:30. Hence you must catch the 7:00 train so you must leave home by 6:55.

14   A

Explanation: The last flight at 20:50 will arrive at Manchester at 21:10. You must arrive at the airport by 20:20. As it is 15 minutes walk from the station, you must get off the train by 20:05. This means you must catch the 19:30 train, giving you 4h 30m in Paris.

15   D

Explanation: The 17:00 train gets to the airport at 17:20 and the 15 minute walk gets you to check-in by 17:35, which is just in time for the 18:10 flight arriving at 18:30. You then get to the station for the 18:45 train arriving at 19:10 and it is 5 minutes walk home.

16   D

Explanation: Grenache and Columbard are too small, Merlot is too far from Disneyland and Syrah is too far from the beach.

17   E

Explanation: Grenache is too small, Syrah and Chardonnay do not have air conditioning. Both Merlot and Columbard are an easy walk to a restaurant but Columbard is much closer to the golf course.

18   A

Explanation: Only Merlot and Grenache have a pool and air conditioning. Both are within budget but Merlot is much closer to the shops.

19   B

Explanation: At first it appears there are two possibilities here. However, if project management is taught on Thursday then Expense control would have to be taught on Tuesday. There is no room big enough available on that day so Expense control must be taught on Thursday in Cepheus.

20   D

Explanation: Project management is available on Weds and Thurs but Expense control is scheduled for Thursday so it must be Wednesday. Andromeda is the only room available that day.

21   C

Explanation: If Expense control is on Thursday then the only two left for Monday and Tuesday are Time management and Report writing, giving a total of 30 people.

22   B

Explanation: Both the Romano and El Greco have a pool and wi-fi access so as the Romano is less expensive it would be the best option.

23   D

Explanation: The Traveller and the Doric are the closest to the centre and the Doric is the cheapest.

24   E

Explanation: Only the Romano and the El Greco have both a pool and a gym but the El Greco is within easy walking distance.

25   D

Explanation: Both Fastlink and Netserve offer dial-up access. The download speed and limit are meaningless for a dial-up link so Netserve is the more cost-effective solution.

26   A

Explanation: Netserve and Netlink are too restrictive on download limits and of the rest, Megalink provides the fastest service.

27   E

Explanation: Netlink provides the lowest price service that has a help desk.

28   C

Explanation: At week 2 the levels will be 28, 70, 140, 26 and 85. Pens and Envelopes need to be ordered bringing their levels to 320 and 640 respectively.

29   B

Explanation: The levels at week 3 will be 16, 270, 360, 22 and 70 which means only pads need to be ordered bringing their level to 66.

30   E

Explanation: By week five the stock levels will be 42, 170, 200, 14 and 40 which means that Ring binders and post-its will need to be ordered.

31   E

Explanation: Gabrielle and Jean can do the Proposal so that Callum's absence on day 2 has no effect. However, Liam's absence on day 3 leaves only Edouard available for the draft stage.

32   B

Explanation: The proposal takes 2 days. The draft should require 3 days, but an extra day is needed because of Liam's absence. The review starts on day 7. It should take 4 days but there is a delay because of Gabrielle on day 8 and Liam on day 10. The Report now starts on day 13 and takes 2 days, giving 14 days in total.

33   C

Explanation: The draft now finishes on day 5 and the review starts on day 6 but this now means that there is a double delay because of Gabrielle on days 6 and 8 and still a delay on day 10 because of Liam so the total remains the same.

34   A

Explanation: Tina is the main problem because she is so far west and doesn't become available until 1300 CET. At this point everyone is available until 1345 CET.

35   C

Explanation: Both Tina and Mia become available at 1300 CET so both would have to rearrange their time to extend the call earlier. However, Dee is the only person to become unavailable at 1345 CET.

36   D

Explanation: Arnie would have to finish at 1400 CET which would allow just an extra 15 minutes.

37   D

Explanation: Only Airways and Aircars have wheelchair access. You need to be at the airport by 6:00 at the latest so Aircars would be best.

38   C

Explanation: All the companies have cars that are big enough and operate at the right time. As A1 is the cheapest they would be the logical choice.

39   A

Explanation: Avion and A1 are too small. Of the others, Airways is the lowest price.

40   D

Explanation: The 14:40 from Vienna is the last return train that will get you home so you must arrive on the 14:25 in Vienna. Either the 05:15 or the 07:40 will allow this but the 07:40 involves far less waiting.

41   E

Explanation: You have 15 mins at Frankfurt (10:05 to 10:20), 15 mins at Vienna (14:25 to 14:40) and 1h 5m at Frankfurt (19:15 to 20:20).

42   B

Explanation: Your client will catch the 12:30 arriving in Frankfurt at 16:20. You should catch the 13:50 arriving at 16:10. You both have return trains at 17:05 which gives you 45 minutes together.

43   B

Explanation: For such a low call volume you do not need a contract phone. Both Etherfone and Scilink would be suitable but Etherfone would be slightly cheaper.

44   C

Explanation: 20 texts per day is about 600/month. With 500 free texts included in the contract this makes ManyG the best buy.

45   A

Explanation: Only Skyway and ManyG have Internet access and the lower call costs on Skyway will save you over €0.60 per day, more than offsetting the higher contract fee.

46   A

Explanation: Of the three that do colour the Daewoo is above budget and Agfa produces better quality than the Kodak.

47   B

Explanation: For top quality only the laser printers will do and as the Epson does not do colour then the Daewoo is it.

48   D

Explanation: There are not enough hours in the day for the laser printers to print so many pages. Quality is not an issue but speed is so the HP will be the most suitable.

49   E

Explanation: To get to the meeting for 10:00 you must leave home at 07:35 to catch the 07:40 bus which arrives at 9:00. After the 10 minutes walk you have 50 minutes to wait. You leave the meeting at 11:15 and 10 minutes back to the bus allows you to catch the 12:10 which will get you home at 13:35, 6 hours after you left.

50   D

Explanation: Catch the 08:00 bus in the morning to arrive in Obernai at 09:20. Spend 5h 20m with friends until 14:40 and catch the 15:30 bus back arriving at 16:50.

51   C

Explanation: Catch the 08:30 bus arriving at 09:50. Leave the church at 11:40 and walk back to the bus station to catch the 12:30 bus giving you 2h 40m in Strasbourg.

52   A

Explanation: The Palace and the Grand are a long way from the beach and don't have any family rooms. Of the others, the Seaview is the lowest priced and is also the closest to the beach.

53   C

Explanation: The Seaview and the Marine don't have air-conditioning and the Palace and the Grand are far from the beach.

54   B

Explanation: The Seaview and the Grand don't have a pool and the Hydro and the Marine don't have a restaurant.

55   D

Explanation: Word is available on Mon, Wed and Thu and the 2 rooms capable of hosting it, Ceres and Juno, are available on Tue, Wed and Fri. So, Word will be on Wednesday in Ceres.

56   A

Explanation: Word is on Wednesday and Windows, the next largest class must also be in Ceres or Juno. The only common day is Tuesday and Juno is the cheapest. Now, databases is the only course left for Monday. Both Demeter and Hera are available but Hera is the cheaper at €45.

57   E

Explanation: Having filled up Mon-Wed, this leaves Excel and Powerpoint. Powerpoint cannot be on a Friday, so must be on the Thursday. Pallas, with 2 free seats, is the most ecoomical option.

58   B

Explanation: Speedwell and Datablast do not do Mac Pages format and TypeRight doesn't do English. Qwerty is the faster of the remaining choices.

59   E

Explanation: Speedwell and Keyfast don't do Spanish and Datablast doesn't do audio tapes. TypeRight is the cheaper of the remaining two.

60   A

Explanation: Qwerty and Keyfast don't do French and Datablast would be too expensive. Although TypeRight is cheaper than Speedwell, Speedwell is the faster and it is within budget.

2. Computer Literacy Tests

50 Questions – Answers follow question 50

The answers to these questions may be found following question 50. Please note that all questions and answers refer to Windows and Microsoft Office products (Word, Excel, PowerPoint, and Outlook).

1   You have just received a new version of an old document but it still has the same name. How do save it with a different name?

     A   Open it, select all the contents of the current document and paste it into a new one and save with the required name.
     B   Use Windows Explorer to copy that file and rename it.
     C   Retype the contents in a new document.
     D   Use the Save As command.

2   What's the best way in Microsoft Word to create a table with custom rows and columns like the one shown below?

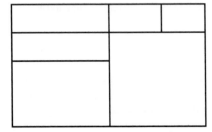

     A   Insert > Table, define rows and column accordingly
     B   Table > Draw Table
     C   Table > Insert > Table > Table Auto Format
     D   Can't say

3   Due to a hardware problem, your mouse is out of order. How do you select or highlight a paragraph in Word without using the mouse?

     A   Using the arrow keys
     B   Holding down Shift (+ Ctrl) and using the arrow keys
     C   Holding down Ctrl and using the arrow keys
     D   Edit > Select all

4 What does the blue wavy line mean in Word?

    A   It does not mean anything. It just decorates the text.

    B   It means the word may be incorrect in the context of its surrounding text or it shows formatting inconsistencies.

    C   It means that you misspelled the word.

    D   It appears after a correction is made.

5 Which of the following is not a social networking website?

    A   Xing

    B   LinkedIn

    C   Ebay

    D   Digg

6 If today's date is 23 September 2010, then which function is used to enter it in an Excel spreadsheet?

A1
A
1	9/23/2010
2
3

    A   =DATE()

    B   =DAY()

    C   =TODAY()

    D   =EDATE()

7 What is the use of this icon in Microsoft Excel?

    A   Decrease Indent

    B   Increase Indent

    C   Decrease number of Decimal places

    D   Increase number of Decimal places

8 In Microsoft Excel, which function can you use to calculate the number of rows in a given area of the sheet?

27	A	1
28	B	88
29	C	6
30	D	5
31	E	44
32	F	90
33	G	52
34	H	12
35	I	43

    A   VLOOKUP

    B   RTD

    C   ROW

    D   ROWS

9   Your boss asked you to check an Excel sheet that has a cell with the function NETWORKDAYS in it. What does it calculate?

    A   Returns the serial number of today's date
    B   Returns the serial number of a particular time of day
    C   Returns the number of whole workdays between two dates
    D   Returns the serial number of a particular date

10 You are asked to give a presentation about the allocation of tasks in your unit. You are in front of your audience and need to start it with one click. What is the shortcut to start the slideshow for a PowerPoint show?

    A   F7
    B   F5
    C   Ctrl + F1
    D   F6

11 What is the use of this icon in Microsoft PowerPoint?

    A   Draw a line
    B   Change the arrow style
    C   Change the line colour
    D   Change the dash style

12 Your boss has asked you to secure his PowerPoint presentation. How do you do it?

    A   Click File > Package for CD
    B   Click File > Permission > Restrict Permission As
    C   Click File > Permission > Do not distribute…
    D   There is no such option

13 What is the use of Shift + F6 in PowerPoint?

    A   Move clockwise among panes on the PowerPoint interface.
    B   Move counter-clockwise among panes on the PowerPoint interface.
    C   Switch between Slides and Outline tabs of the Outline and Slides pane of the Normal view.
    D   There is no such shortcut.

14 A part of a Word document is seen as shown below. What happened?

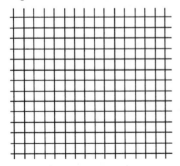

    A   A shape was drawn.
    B   A table with many rows and columns was created.
    C   Grids were enabled
    D   None of above

15 You want to present your text as shown in the figure - what is the best way to achieve that in Microsoft Word?

> The state of Alaska is in the northwest of the continent, with Canada to the east and Russia to the west across the Bering Strait. The state of Hawaii is an archipelago in the mid-Pacific. The country also possesses several territories in the Caribbean and Pacific.

    A   Select text +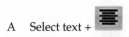

    B   Select text +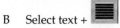

    C   Select text + 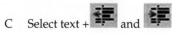 and

    D   Put the text in a table and adjust column

16 You have been asked by your colleague to edit an Excel chart. Which key moves the cursor from one cell to another in a table if the active cell is being edited?

    A   Tab
    B   Left arrow key
    C   Ctrl + Space
    D   Ctrl + Enter

17 You want to open more than two copies of the same document in Microsoft Word; what do you do?

    A   Reopen the same document.
    B   Copy contents to a new document.
    C   Select New Window option from the Window menu
    D   Copy the document from Windows Explorer then open both documents.

18 What is the role of this button in Microsoft Word?

    A   It saves the document as a webpage.
    B   It links web addresses and other items to the selected text or object in the document.
    C   It inserts an email address.
    D   It attaches files to the current document.

19 A document in Portrait orientation is printed in Microsoft Word:

    A   With smaller fonts to fit the same number of characters per line as in Landscape orientation.
    B   With fewer characters per line than if the same document is printed in Landscape orientation.
    C   With the same number of characters per line as if the same document is printed in Landscape orientation.
    D   None of the above

20 For a given paragraph, how can the formatting shown in the figure below be created in Microsoft Word?

The	or	is
United	America)	situated
States of	is a	mostly in
America	federal	central
(also The	constituti	North
United	onal	America,
States of	republic	where its
America	comprisi	forty-
(also	ng fifty	eight
referred	states	contiguo
to as the	and a	us states
United	federal	and
States,	district.	Washing
the U.S.,	The	ton, D.C
the USA,	country	

A   Format > Columns > Three Column preset.
B   Table > Insert three columns.
C   This format cannot be achieved in Word.
D   By placing the text in a three column frame.

21 What is the shortcut key to insert the current date in Microsoft Word?

A   Alt + Shift + D
B   Shift + D
C   Ctrl +Shift + D
D   Alt + I + T

22 Which icon will be used to convert the given shape into a 3D design in Microsoft PowerPoint?

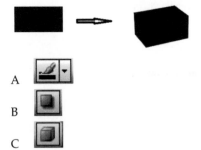

A

B

C

D   Draw the picture separately and then insert it.

23 You are preparing a PowerPoint presentation for your boss and you have added a chart to it. How can you change the format of that chart?

A   Delete the chart > Insert a new chart with a new format.
B   Double Click the chart > Edit the format.
C   Delete the slide > Create a new slide and insert the chart there.
D   None of the above.

24 Your boss has asked you to create a document and share it with others but not to let them edit it. How do you make a file available only for reading over a network, thereby prevent any modification or editing to it?

A Right click file >Properties > Hidden.
B Right click file >Properties > Read-only.
C Install special software and lock it.
D Right click file >Properties > Shared > Lock and Read.

25 Which shortcut allows you to quickly open the File Explorer (or Windows Explorer)?

A Ctrl + Shift + W
B Start button+ W
C Ctrl + Shift + E
D Start button + E

26 If the following checkbox is ticked and applied, a Windows feature is activated. Pick the correct description for that feature.

☐ Use StickyKeys   Settings

A When a mouse button is clicked on any window, it sticks to it to allow easy reorganization of your open windows.
B It allows keys pressed one after the other to perform actions which are commonly performed by holding down multiple keys.
C Activating this feature ignores brief or repeated strokes.
D It enables an on-screen keyboard to be controlled by the mouse.

27 What is the shortcut to create a new folder in Windows?

A Ctrl + Shift + N
B Ctrl + Alt + F
C Ctrl + Shift + F
D Start button + N

28 You are working on a spreadsheet and you want to select a particular bit of text and make repeated copies of it as shown in the figure. How can you achieve this result in Microsoft Excel?

abc		abcabcabc	

A RIGHT
B REPLACE
C REPT
D None of the above

29 You are working on a spreadsheet in Microsoft Excel and notice that some particular cells which have number values are displayed as negative numbers. How do you change them to currency values in the format - € 120.00?

A   Right click on cell > Format Cells > Number tab > Number category
B   Right click on cell > Format Cells > Number tab > Accounting category
C   Right click on cell > Format Cells > Number tab > Currency category
D   Right click on cell > Format Cells > Number tab > Custom category

30 Your colleague has to to prepare a chart for the unit's holidays but she needs to know which week of the year a certain days falls into. Which function is used in Microsoft Excel to convert the serial number of a day of the year (for example 322nd day) to a number representing which week that day falls in numerically within the year?

A   WEEKNUM
B   WEEKDAY
C   WORKDAY
D   NETWORKDAYS

31 You want to print your Excel spreadsheet, but there are several characters in your second row of the spreadsheet which are non-printable. How will you remove this error?

A   Use the function REMOVE
B   Use the function CLEAN
C   Use the function CODE
D   There is no function for this purpose

32 You are editing a list of your colleagues' names. From the following options, which function is used to sort values in descending order in Microsoft Excel?

A

B

C

D   None of these

33 Internet Explorer has a feature called Caret Browsing. Pick the best option that describes this feature.

A   This feature updates a particular part of a webpage instead of the whole page.
B   It translates a word or a line on a webpage.
C   It allows users to use navigation keys on the keyboard to select text and navigate within a webpage.
D   It highlights the domain name in the address bar and it makes the domain name or URL bold so that one can identify deceptive websites.

34 Suppose you have found a useful website for your daily work and want to add it to your favourites in Internet Explorer 7. Which button do you press to do that?

A

B

C

D

35 What is the shortcut to open a web link in a new tab on your browser?

A   Middle Mouse button
B   Right click > New tab
C   Ctrl + T
D   Double Right Click

36 What is the role of the '+' operator in a Google search for 'Hello +the'?

A   Forces Google to look for 'I' in 'Hello' during search.
B   It searches for results which contain either word.
C   It will search for results that include 'Hello' as well as the definite article 'the'.
D   It only returns results where the word 'Hello' is displayed in italics.

37 Your Head of Unit asked you to find a special PDF file online. How do you search exclusively for PDF documents in Google?

A   By adding file:pdf before or after the search term.
B   By adding filetype:pdf before or after the search term
C   By adding [pdf] before or after the search term.
D   By adding +pdf before or after the search term.

38 Which of the following characters ('operators') should be placed before the search term so that Google will search not only the search term itself but also its synonyms, translations and related items?

A   ~
B   ^
C   '
D   /

39 You are asked to pay for a hotel booking with a credit card. What is the best and primary way to know whether a website uses secure data transfer or not?

A   The website URL has the word 'secure' in it.
B   The website insists that its transactions are secure.
C   The URL of the webpage begins with 'https://'
D   It cannot be determined without special security software.

40 Your internet browser shows a lock sign shown in the figure at the bottom right corner while surfing the web. What does it mean?

- A   It means that some features of the active website are locked.
- B   It means that the website has locked its content to prevent copying.
- C   It means that certain features of the browser are locked and can only be used by purchasing the premium version.
- D   It means that the website uses secure data transfer.

41 You receive an email from an EU citizen at your official address and it has a strange attachment. Before opening an attachment, you should always check:

- A   The size of the attachment
- B   The file type or extension of the attachment
- C   The nature of the email that contains the attachment
- D   All of above

42 Where would you click to create a bulleted list in your email in Microsoft Outlook?

A

B

C

D

43 Which keyboard shortcut can you use to go to the Contacts page in Outlook?

- A   Ctrl + 3
- B   Ctrl + 4
- C   Ctrl + 5
- D   Ctrl + 8

44 For what purpose is this toolbar used?

- A   Editing Clip Art images
- B   Drawing and editing tables
- C   Inserting and editing a picture
- D   None of the above

45 You have started work in a unit that handles lots of personal and confidential data. How do you change the security level for handling incoming emails?

A   Tools menu > Options > Edit > Settings
B   Tools menu > Options > Security Tab > Select the security level
C   Tools menu > Options > Security Tab > Macro Security > Select the security level.
D   Tools menu > Options > Security Tab > Email options

46 Your boss has asked you to create a special email message. How will you add the following figure to your email in Outlook in an editable format?

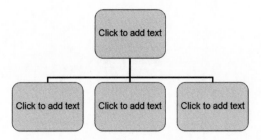

A   Attach an image file which has the required diagram
B   Draw the figure separately and insert it as a picture
C   Draw the figure through Auto Shapes
D   Click Insert > Diagram > Select the diagram type

47 Which is the default format used by Outlook to send an email that makes sure you can insert images, colours and various formatting options into your messages?

A   HTML
B   Rich Text
C   Plain Text
D   None of the above

48 You want to send an email to a friend about a charity organisation which should inform the receiver that the email is not very urgent to deal with. How will you do this?

A   Use the icon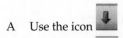

B   Use the icon

C   Use the icon

D   Use the icon

49   You work in a unit that deals with personnel matters. Given the sensitivity of your messages, you want to add a security label ('INTERNAL USE ONLY') to your email in Outlook which indicates in the message header the sensitivity of the message content. How will you accomplish this task?

   A   Add a Digital Signature and enter a privacy mark in it.
   B   Write the statement 'INTERNAL USE ONLY' in every message you compose.
   C   Change the macro security settings in your email
   D   None of the above

50   What is the use of the following shortcut: Ctrl + Shift + C

   A   Create a new note
   B   Create a new folder
   C   Create a new contact in the contact list
   D   Create a new calendar

ANSWERS

Q1   Correct Answer: D

Explanation: All the options above can be used to save a document with a different name, although using the Save As command from the File menu will save a lot of time.

Q2   Correct Answer: B

Explanation: Word offers creation of custom tables so instead of adjusting and formatting a table with fixed rows and columns, one can create a table from scratch using the Table > Draw Table option or edit an existing table using the same option.

Q3   Correct Answer: B

Explanation: Holding down the Shift key and then using the arrow keys selects the text. If the cursor is at the beginning of the paragraph, Pressing Shift + down arrow will select one line at a time. Pressing Shift + up arrow will deselect the selected text. Pressing Shift + right or left arrow will select or deselect one character at a time. If you also hold down Ctrl (in addition to Shift), you can use the right and left arrow keys to select words.

Q4   Correct Answer: B

Explanation: The blue wavy lines show inconsistencies in formatting and the highlighted word might be inconsistent with its surrounding text. It can be corrected by right clicking the faulty word and picking a correct option.

Q5   Correct Answer: C

Explanation: Ebay is an online marketplace for private and business vendors, whereas all other answer options have a 'social' element in them by connecting individual users who can jointly create content, contact each other and share information.

Q6   Correct Answer: C

Explanation: If you want to enter today's date in a particular cell then write =TODAY() and press enter. This function returns today's date.

Q7 Correct Answer: D

Explanation: This icon is used to increase the number of decimal places in a particular number selected. This icon can be used with fields which contain number values. It cannot be used with text values.

Q8 Correct Answer: D

Explanation: The function ROWS returns the number of rows in the selected reference or array.

Q9 Correct Answer: C

Explanation: If we want to calculate the number of working days between two given dates, then this function can be used.

Q10 Correct Answer: B

Explanation: F5 is used to start the slide show, whereas F7 is used to check spelling and F6 is used to go to the next pane clockwise on PowerPoint's interface.

Q11 Correct Answer: D

Explanation: There are multiple Dash styles provided by PowerPoint. This icon can be used to apply any of those for the drawn line.

Q12 Correct Answer: C

Explanation: If we want to make our PowerPoint file accessible only to a particular system, then the Do not Distribute option can be applied so that no other system can make amendments.

Q13 Correct Answer: B

Explanation: If we want to switch between active panes in a counter-clockwise direction, then this shortcut can be used.

Q14 Correct Answer: C

Explanation: Grids help organize the contents of a page and allow the user to see 'the big picture'. They can be enabled by first enabling the drawing toolbar > Draw > Grid.

Q15 Correct Answer: B

Explanation: The text shown in the figure is 'Justified', which can be accessed by selecting the text and clicking the Justify button in the Formatting toolbar.

Q16 Correct Answer: A

Explanation: Tab takes the cursor from one cell to other while the arrow key can only be used for this purpose if the selected cell is not being edited.

Q17 Correct Answer: C

Explanation: The New Window option from the Window menu opens the same document in a new window. This is very helpful when comparing different pages of the same document.

Q18 Correct Answer: B

Explanation: This button is the Insert Hyperlink button. Once some text or an image is selected and this button is pressed, it opens a browse window from which it allows one to link the word with the selected item. Once done, one can open the linked item by Ctrl + Clicking the hyperlinked text or image.

Q19 Correct Answer: B

Explanation: In Word, a Portrait print will have fewer characters per line as compared to a Landscape print which will have more characters per line.

Q20 Correct Answer: A

Explanation: The shown text is 'preset' in a three column format which can be found by clicking Format > Columns > Three.

Q21 Correct Answer: A

Explanation: By pressing Alt + Shift + D, Word inserts the current date. Similarly, by pressing Alt + Shift + T, Word inserts the current time.

Q22 Correct Answer: C

Explanation: A 2D picture can be changed to a 3D picture by applying the changes through a 3D design style.

Q23 Correct Answer: B

Explanation: Charts are added to PowerPoint slides by the Insert Chart icon. Its format can be easily changed by double-clicking on the chart and adjusting the format according to your requirements.

Q24 Correct Answer: B

Explanation: By making the file read-only, one can allow users over the network only to see and view the file but not to modify it.

Q25 Correct Answer: D

Explanation: Windows Explorer, which allows users to quickly navigate through folders and drives, can be opened quickly by using the Start button + E shortcut.

Q26 Correct Answer: B

Explanation: Sticky keys can be enabled if you do not want to hold several keys at once on the keyboard when using shortcuts. It allows you to press on one key at a time rather than multiple keys at once when you want to use, for example, Ctrl +Alt +Del. It can be activated in Control Panel > Accessibility Options.

Q27 Correct Answer: A

Explanation: To quickly create a folder, Ctrl + Shift + N can be used.

Q28 Correct Answer: C

Explanation: We can use the REPT function to set the text to be repeated and the number of times to repeat it.

Q29 Correct Answer: C

Explanation: Select the cell which needs conversion, then right click and select the Format Cells option. Now, select the Currency category in the Number tab. Choose the category and number of decimal places according to your requirements and click OK.

Q30 Correct Answer: A

Explanation: If we want to convert the serial number of a day of the year to its yearly position according which week of the year it falls into (e.g. 47th week), then this function can be used.

Q31 Correct Answer: B

Explanation: CODE returns a numerical code for the first character in a text string whereas CLEAN removes the non-printable characters in a text string. REMOVE is not a valid Excel function.

Q32 Correct Answer: B

Explanation: Select the column which is to be sorted in descending order and then click the Sort Descending icon in the toolbar.

Q33 Correct Answer: C

Explanation: Caret browsing allows use of the arrow keys to select text on a webpage and also navigate the page. It can be activated by pressing F7.

Q34 Correct Answer: C

Explanation: This button saves the page as favourite, Answer D allows you to view favourites, Answer A enables full screen mode while Answer B manages add-ons.

Q35 Correct Answer: A

Explanation: Tabs make movement between pages easier, as more than one Tab (new window) can be opened in the same Internet Explorer window.

Q36 Correct Answer: C

Explanation: Google ignores common words and characters such as how, where, the, digits and letters, so to force Google to include such words and digits, the '+' operator is used.

Q37 Correct Answer: B

Explanation: 'filetype: extension of file' forces Google to look only for files with the extension specified.

Q38 Correct Answer: A

Explanation: Tilde forces Google to search not only for the search term but also for its synonyms and translations. It is placed before the search term.

Q39 Correct Answer: C

Explanation: Secure website addresses mostly begin with 'https://' instead of 'http://'. One must make sure that before entering a credit card number or any similar confidential information on a website, the website URL should begin with 'https://'

Q40 Correct Answer: D

Explanation: The lock sign shows that the website is secure and can be trusted.

Q41 Correct Answer: D

Explanation: When an email is received with an attachment, you should always check the size of the attachment to see whether the file attached has a realistic size – a text file, for example, is usually quite small. You must also check whether the attachment has any suspicious file extensions (.exe, .vbs, and so on) and verify the nature of the email in which the attachment arrived.

Q42 Correct Answer: D

Explanation: A bulleted list is an unordered list with a special symbol beside each point indicated in the list. Icon A is used to increase indent, Icon B is used to decrease indent and Icon C is used to make an ordered list specified by numbers.

Q43 Correct Answer: A

Explanation: Ctrl + 4 is used to go to the Tasks page, Ctrl + 5 is used to go to Notes and Ctrl + 8 is used to go to the Journal.

Q44 Correct Answer: B

Explanation: You can insert a table in your email. The format of the table can also be changed using this toolbar.

Q45 Correct Answer: C

Explanation: There are different security levels provided in the Macro Security Level list. These levels are Very High, High, Medium and Low. Any of these can be chosen according to your requirements, although Low is usually not recommended.

Q46 Correct Answer: D

Explanation: There are different figures provided in the Insert > Diagram option. Here, we can add any of the required diagrams and also add text to it in the spaces allotted to make a meaningful diagram.

Q47 Correct Answer: A

Explanation: Outlook, by default, uses the HTML format to compose a mail and then send the message to the receiver.

Q48 Correct Answer: A

Explanation: Icon A is used to mark low importance emails, Icon B is used for high priority emails, Icon C is used to set permissions for different users to access email, and Icon D is used to create mail rules (for example: archive all emails with 'shampoo' in the subject).

Q49 Correct Answer: A

Explanation: Digital Signatures can be used to attach special security labels to the message which increases its security settings and makes it confidential. Click Options on the compose mail page > Security Settings > Tick the checkbox 'Add Digital Signature' > Enter the privacy mark in it.

Q50 Correct Answer: C

Explanation: We can add a new contact in our contact list by using the keyboard shortcut: Ctrl + Shift + C.

3.   Accuracy Test

These questions are intended to evaluate your attention to detail and accuracy under time pressure. In each of the following questions, you must decide which of the pieces of information in the final bar does not correspond with the data given in the table. Make sure to time yourself, allowing 9 seconds per question – so, for example, if you decide to try 20 questions in one go you should allow yourself 3 minutes. The answers can be found after Question 80.

Q 1

Tram ▦   Train ▤   Bicycle ⬴   Bus ⬛   Car ⬤

	Employee	Badge No.	Distance Travelled (Km)	Modes of Transport
1	Hans Gruber	TP 254	4.5	Tram, Train
2	Etienne Dupré	TP 635	6.8	Train, Bus
3	George Jones	TG 145	10.4	Car, Tram
4	Louis Cardin	TL 490	17.3	Car
5	Marie Theroux	RT 236	4.8	Bicycle, Bus, Tram

	Employee	Badge No.	Distance Travelled (Km)	Tram	Train	Bicycle	Bus	Car
1	Hans Gruber	TP 254	5.4	✓	✓			

A.   Employee

B.   Modes of Transport

C.   Badge No., Modes of Transport

D.   Distance Travelled

E.   Modes of Transport, Distance Travelled

Q 2

	Room	Booking Ref.	Booking Date	Room Facilities		
1	Windsor	WS/546	24/05/10			
2	Battenburg	BT/126	31/03/11			
3	Hanover	HV/480	09/10/11			
4	Bourbon	BB/1471	30/09/12			
5	Braganza	BZ/015	07/11/11			

	Room	Booking Ref.	Booking Date	Video	Phone	Fax	Wi-fi	Printer
5	Braganza	BZ/105	07/11/11		✓		✓	

A.	Booking Date, Room	B.	Room, Room Facilities
C.	Room Facilities	D.	Booking Date, Room Facilities
E.	Booking Reference		

Q 3

	Name of Farm	Subsidy	Value (€)	Type of Farming		
1	Richland Farms	GR 4593	1.36 M			
2	Boursin SE	GR 2460	15.8 M			
3	Weber GmbH	QR 2115	0.49 M			
4	M. Fermier	QR 2116	7.28 M			
5	Bacchus GmbH	GT 2561	2.78 M			

	Name of Farm	Subsidy	Value (€)	Fishery	Mixed	Fruit	Cereal	Dairy
4	M. Fermier	QR 2115	7.28 M	✓		✓		✓

A.	Value	B.	Dairy, Fruit
C.	Subsidy, Type of Farming	D.	Name of Farm, Value
E.	Subsidy		

Q 4

Box | Carpet | Chair | Table | Bookcase

	Building	Room	Delivery Date	Inventory
1	Berlaymont	B 270	19 Mar 2011	
2	Charlemagne	J 453	28 Feb 2010	
3	Breydel	G 773	14 Jul 2011	
4	Joyeuse Entrée	A 337	1 Dec 2010	
5	OIL	X 012	6 Jan 2012	

	Building	Room	Delivery Date	Box	Carpet	Chair	Table	Bookcase
2	Charlemagne	J 435	28 Feb 2010	✓			✓	

A. Room, Inventory

B. Delivery Date, Room

C. Room

D. Delivery Date, Inventory

E. Inventory

Q 5

Apple | Cherries | Carrot | Cake | Pretzel

	Employee	Department	Badge Number	Snacks
1	Hans Gruber	Justice	JUS/53X	
2	Yvette Weber	Catering	CAT/27L	
3	Jacques Durand	Maintenance	MAI/53C	
4	Brigitte Perrier	Parks	PAR/72S	
5	Michael Gartmann	Publicity	PUB/95Q	

	Employee	Department	Badge Number	Apple	Cherries	Carrot	Cake	Pretzel
2	Yvette Webber	Catering	CAT/27L	✓	✓		✓	

A. Employee, Snacks

B. Employee, Badge No.

C. Employee, Department

D. Department

E. Badge No., Department

Q 6

Solar · Gas · Oil · Nuclear · Wind

	Company	Location	Output (GWh)	Energy Supplied
1	Energy UK	Aberdeen	152.6	Gas, Oil, Wind
2	Finnish Energy	Helsinki	69.4	Wind, Oil
3	Energético Español	Madrid	324.1	Gas, Nuclear, Solar
4	Nederlandse Energiebedrijven	The Hague	89.5	Wind, Gas
5	Polskiej Energetyki	Warsaw	126.2	Oil, Nuclear

	Company	Location	Output (GWh)	Solar	Gas	Oil	Nuclear	Wind
3	Energético Español	Madrid	342.1	✓		✓	✓	

A. Company

B. Company, Output

C. Output, Energy Supplied

D. Company, Output, Energy Supplied

E. Company, Location

Q 7

Corn · Dairy · Barley · Eggs · Wheat

	Farm	Subsidy	Contract	Farm Produce
1	Nicholls Farm Group	£2.6m	3y 6m	Barley, Corn
2	Riley's Natural Produce	£1.8m	2y 4m	Eggs, Barley, Dairy
3	Bisch SA	€4.3m	1y 8m	Wheat, Barley
4	Nielson SEM	€2.3m	2y 6m	Corn, Wheat
5	Jørgensen Dairy	€0.8m	0y 6m	Eggs, Dairy

	Farm	Subsidy	Contract	Corn	Dairy	Barley	Eggs	Wheat
2	Riley's Natural Produce	£1.8m	2y 6m		✓		✓	✓

A. Farm, Contract, Subsidy

B. Farm, Contract

C. Subsidy, Contract

D. Contract, Farm Produce

E. Farm

Q 8

Trousers   T-Shirt   Fleece   Polo Shirt   Jacket

	Employee	Requisition Code	Order Date	Requisitions
1	Georgi Petrov	RQ-325A	10 Mar 2011	
2	Clara Schmid	RQ-625A	30 May 2011	
3	Riccardo Rossi	RQ-569B	14 Jun 2010	
4	Afonso Silva	RP-630A	28 Jan 2010	
5	Chris Jones	PQ-561C	13 Feb 2009	

	Employee	Requisition Code	Order Date	Trousers	T-Shirt	Fleece	Polo Shirt	Jacket
2	Clara Schmid	RQ-625A	30 Mar 2011		✓	✓		

A.   Order Date, Requisitions

B.   Requisition Code, Order Date

C.   Requisition Code, Order Date, Requisitions

D.   Requisition Code, Requisitions

E.   Employee, Order Date

Q 9

Email   Mail   Fax   Phone   Mobile

	Department	Budget	Annual Volume	Communications
1	Legal	€10.2m	356.2m	
2	Press	€20.7m	426.3m	
3	Revenue	€3.56m	2.36m	
4	Recruitment	€6.37m	6.45m	
5	Catering	€0.56m	2.45m	

	Department	Budget	Annual Volume	Email	Mail	Fax	Phone	Mobile
2	Press	€20.7m	426.3m	✓	✓		✓	

A.   Department, Budget

B.   Communications

C.   Department, Budget, Communications

D.   Budget, Communications

E.   Annual Volume, Communications

Q 10

	Function	Date	Number Attending	Menu
1	Inaugural Ball	24 Apr 2011	350	
2	Budget Committee	12 Sep 2012	75	
3	Royal Dinner	28 Jan 2011	680	
4	Prime Minister's Visit	5 Apr 2010	562	
5	Press Conference	31 Jan 2011	147	

	Function	Date	Number Attending	Meat	Seafood	Vegetarian	Cheese	Fruit
3	Royal Dinner	28 Jan 2010	860	✓	✓		✓	

A.   Date, Menu

B.   Date, Number Attending

C.   Function, Date

D.   Function

E.   Date, Number Attending, Menu

Q 11

	Delegate	Hotel and Room	Check In	Amenities
1	Olivier Blanchard	Excelsior 245	14/02/2011	
2	Marie Dubois	Le Grand 287	30/03/2010	
3	Henri Paladino	Hilton 1478	06/07/10	
4	Sylvain Vinet	Mayfair 165	02/01/2011	
5	Mattieu Poisson	Park Lane 654	16/06/2012	

	Delegate	Hotel and Room	Check In	Bar	3-D TV	Breakfast	Dinner	Pool
1	Oliver Blanchard	Excelsoir 245	14/02/2011		✓	✓	✓	

A.   Hotel and Room, Amenities

B.   Delegate, Hotel and Room

C.   Delegate, Amenities

D.   Delegate

E.   Delegate, Hotel and Room, Amenities

Q 12

| Plane | ✈ | Car | 🚐 | Truck | 🚚 | Ship | 🚢 | Train | 🚃 |

	Product	Code	Delivery Date	Transport Used		
1	Exhaust	EX265/1	24 May 2011	✈	🚚	
2	Spark Plugs	SP563/4	31 Jul 2011	🚐		
3	Transmission	TR490/2	13 Feb 2010	✈	🚃	🚚
4	Engine	EG697/6	15 Dec 2012	🚢	🚚	
5	Rear Axle	RA047/3	16 Aug 2011	🚚	🚃	

	Product	Code	Delivery Date	Plane	Car	Truck	Ship	Train
3	Transmission	TR490-2	13 Mar 2010	✓		✓		✓

A. Transport Used

B. Code, Transport Used

C. Delivery Date, Transport Used

D. Code, Delivery Date

E. Code, Delivery Date, Transport Use

Q 13

| Hydro Electric | | Oil | | Nuclear | | Wind | | Solar | |

	Country	Energy Output GWh	Revenue €m	Main Sources		
1	UK	589.3	985.2	Hydro	Nuclear	Oil
2	France	635.4	685.3	Nuclear	Solar	Hydro
3	Germany	486.4	632.1	Hydro	Wind	
4	Italy	268.4	268.1	Solar	Oil	
5	Spain	478.6	596.0	Solar	Wind	

	Country	Energy Output	Revenue	Hydro Electric	Oil	Nuclear	Wind	Solar
4	Italy	268.1	268.4		✓			✓

A. Energy Output, Revenue

B. Country, Revenue

C. Country, Energy Output

D. Energy Output, Main Sources

E. Country, Main Sources

Q 14

	Country	Subsidy Code	Length	Supported Industries		
1	Lithuania	QZ-574/2	1yr7m			
2	Greece	YT-6852/A	2yr 6m			
3	Ireland	TY-6852/A	4yr 5m			
4	Poland	JU-259/4	3yr 10m			
5	France	ER-574/2	0yr 9m			

	Country	Subsidy Code	Length	Forestry	Farming	Fishing	Poultry	Agriculture
2	Greece	TY-6852/A	2yr 6m		✓	✓		

A.   Subsidy Code, Supported Industries   B.   Country

C.   Length   D.   Subsidy Code, Length

E.   Supported Industries

Q 15

	Employee	Department	Order Date	Supplies Needed		
1	Alheid Schneider	Catering	12-12-2012			
2	Zoë Aucoin	Deliveries	14-07-2010			
3	Joseph Roylance	Logistics	30-05-2010			
4	Bruno Metzger	Crèche	28-01-2011			
5	Louis Garnier	Resources	31-01-2011			

	Employee	Department	Order Date	Pencils	Pens	Highlighters	Erasers	Cutters
1	Alheid Schnieder	Catering	12-2-2012		✓	✓	✓	

A.   Employee, Department   B.   Employee, Order Date

C.   Supplies Needed   D.   Order Date

E.   Department, Supplies Needed

Q 16

	Address	Order No.	Dispatched	Office Equipment		
1	12 Place de l'Europe, Paris	THL-568/K	14/02/2010	Bulb	Scissors	Basket
2	31 Georganstrass, Berlin	EKO-320/M	03/12/2012	CD	Basket	
3	245 Mayfair, London	KKL-554/R	30/06/2011	Scissors	Bulb	CD
4	16 Rue des Dentelles, Lyon	LPL-006/W	03/06/2010	Scissors	Basket	
5	341 Petersplatz, Frankfurt	WRF-568/Q	04/12/2011	Bulb	CD	Tape

	Address	Order No.	Dispatched	Bulb	Basket	Tape	CD	Scissors
4	16 Rue des Dentelles, Lyon	LPL-006/W	30/06/2011	✓			✓	✓

A. Dispatched, Office Equipment

B. Order Number, Office Equipment

C. Address

D. Address, Order Number

E. Office Equipment

Q 17

	Location	Owner	Grant	Requirements		
1	Petite Ferme, Nancy	M. Molyneux	€2.14m	Fence	Haystack	Seeds
2	Luft Bauernhof, Karben	H. Fuhrmann	€12.76m	Barn	Fence	
3	Pink Farm, Lostock	Mr. Lowry	£2.5m	Haystack	Tools	Seeds
4	Boundary Farms, Styall	Travis & Sons	£7.35m	Tools	Barn	
5	THP Farms, Stockton	THP Industries	£1.08m	Fence		

	Location	Owner	Grant	Barn	Fence	Haystack	Tools	Seeds
4	Boundary Farms, Styal	Travis & Sons	€7.35m	✓			✓	

A. Location

B. Location, Grant

C. Requirements

D. Owner, Requirements

E. Owner

Q 18

	Company	Frequency	Cost	Local Services
1	Peace and Quiet	Mon - Sun	£10 / hr	
2	Produce Locally	Mon - Fri	50p per item	
3	Porter & Sons	Mon - Sun	33p per item	
4	Jones Newsagents	Mon - Sun	45p per item	
5	Banners Help	Tue - Sat	£12.50 / hr	

	Company	Frequency	Cost	Newspaper	Milk	Fruit Vendor	Cleaning	Babysitting
4	Jones Newsagents	Mon - Sat	45p per item	✓	✓			

A.   Company, Frequency
B.   Company, Local Services
C.   Frequency, Local Services
D.   Cost, Local Services
E.   Company, Cost

Q 19

	Name of Ship	Port	Quota Tonnes/Yr	Catch
1	Gloria	Grimsby	1250	
2	Dawn Trader	Hull	2480	
3	Light of my Life	Rotterdam	26910	
4	Oceans Above	Marseilles	42690	
5	Mary Jane	Dover	27460	

	Name of Ship	Port	Quota Tonnes/Yr	Crab	Cod	Lobster	Oyster	Salmon
4	Oceans Above	Marseilles	42960		✓	✓	✓	

A.   Quota, Catch
B.   Port, Catch
C.   Name of Ship, Port
D.   Name of Ship, Quota
E.   Port, Quota

Q 20

Cathedral ✝ Battle Site ⚔ Architecture 🏛 Bridge 🌉 Church

	Location	Tourism Subsidy	Staff Required	Attractions
1	Banbury	£0.35m	125	Architecture, Bridge, Church
2	Hastings	£1.26m	634	Battle Site, Architecture
3	Culloden	£0.85m	459	Church, Battle Site
4	Mons	€2.89m	1362	Church, Cathedral, Battle Site
5	Cologne	€1.65m	1045	Cathedral, Architecture, Bridge

	Location	Tourism Subsidy	Staff Required	Cathedral	Battle Site	Architecture	Bridge	Church
5	Cologne	€1.65m	1045	✓	✓			✓

A. Location

B. Tourism Subsidy

C. Staff Required, Attractions

D. Attractions

E. Location, Tourism Subsidy

Q 21

Builder 🏠 Plumber 🚰 Electrician ⚠ Gasman 🔥 Decorator 🪣

	Urban Scheme	Location	Grant	Contractors
1	Obernai Millenium	Strasbourg	€23.54m	Builder, Plumber, Electrician
2	Salford Docks	Manchester	£124.6m	Plumber, Electrician, Gasman
3	Schwetzingen 2010	Heidelberg	€14.6m	Builder, Gasman, Decorator
4	Jyväskylä Renewal	Helsinki	€25.5m	Electrician, Plumber, Decorator
5	Zielonka Upgrade	Warsaw	PLN24580m	Builder, Electrician, Gasman

	Urban Scheme	Location	Grant	Builder	Plumber	Electrician	Gasman	Decorator
3	Shwetzingen 2010	Heidelberg	€16.4m	✓			✓	✓

A. Urban Scheme, Contractors

B. Urban Scheme, Grant

C. Contractors

D. Grant

E. Urban Scheme

Q 22

Chemical   Fire   Drought   Oil Slick   Nuclear Leak

	Location	Staff to Train	Budget	Disaster Drills		
1	London	3520	£0.23m			
2	Paris	4753	€1.36m			
3	Madrid	1254	€1.25m			
4	Innsbruck	4752	€2.31m			
5	Dublin	354	€0.014m			

	Location	Staff to Train	Budget	Chemical	Fire	Drought	Oil Slick	Nuclear Leak
5	Dublin	354	€0.14m		✓		✓	✓

A.   Location
C.   Budget
E.   Disaster Drills

B.   Location, Budget
D.   Budget, Disaster Drills

Q 23

Pelican   Eagle   Owl   Heron   Woodpecker

	Co-ordinator	Location	Donations	Endangered Species		
1	John Addams	Oswestry	£845,250			
2	Peter Sutcliffe	Burscough	£154,421			
3	Gusti Engel	Kitzbühel	€198,452			
4	Maria Rossi	Pescara	€452,474			
5	Edwina Curry	Peterborough	£145,420			

	Co-ordinator	Location	Donations	Pelican	Eagle	Owl	Heron	Woodpecker
4	Maria Rossi	Pecsara	€452,474		✓	✓		

A.   Co-ordinator, Endangered Species
C.   Location, Endangered Species
E.   Endangered Species

B.   Donations
D.   Location

Q 24

Disabled Driver		Road Train		Caravan		Camper Van		Motor-cycle	

	Country	Speed Limit km/h	Introduced	Vehicles Restricted
1	Finland	60	12-02-2010	Disabled Driver, Road Train, Caravan
2	UK	55	21-04-1999	Camper Van, Road Train, Disabled Driver
3	Italy	60	30-06-2001	Camper Van, Road Train
4	France	65	03-06-2010	Road Train, Disabled Driver
5	Germany	70	20-10-1984	Camper Van, Motorcycle, Disabled Driver

	Country	Speed Limit km/h	Introduced	Disabled Driver	Road Train	Caravan	Camper Van	Motor-cycle
1	Finland	80	12-02-2010	✓	✓		✓	

A. Speed Limit

B. Introduced and Vehicles Restricted

C. Introduced

D. Speed Limit and Introduced

E. Speed Limit and Vehicles Restricted

Q 25

Brown Bear		Caribou		Bactrian Camel		Wolf		Dromedary Camel	

	Country	Funding Body	Amount	Repopulation
1	Czech Republic	WWF	CZK21.23m	Brown Bear, Caribou, Wolf
2	Hungary	Wildlife Aid	HUF525.36m	Wolf, Caribou
3	France	Société protectrice des animaux	€7.21m	Brown Bear, Bactrian Camel, Wolf
4	Poland	The Wildlife Trust	PLN25.14m	Brown Bear, Wolf
5	Portugal	WWF	€14.3m	Bactrian Camel, Dromedary Camel

	Country	Funding Body	Amount	Brown Bear	Caribou	Bactrian Camel	Wolf	Dromedary Camel
1	Chech Republic	WWF	CZK21.23m	✓	✓			✓

A. Country and Amount

B. Amount and Repopulation

C. Repopulation

D. Country and Repopulation

E. Amount

Q 26

	Country	Man Hours Lost	Av. Days Closed / year	Road Closures		
1	Finland	1.26m	54.6	❄ 🌨		
2	Sweden	0.89m	35.6	☁ 🌨 ❄		
3	Denmark	0.45m	12.4	🌫 ☁		
4	Estonia	3.58m	84.2	❄ ⛈ 🌨		
5	UK	9.25m	35.2	🌫 🌨		

	Country	Man Hours Lost	Av. Days Closed/year	Ice	Flooding	Storm	Fog	Snow
5	UK	9.52m	35.2	✓	✓			

A. Country and Road Closures

B. Man Hours Lost

C. Road Closures

D. Man Hours Lost and Road Closures

E. Country and Man Hours Lost

Q 27

	Forest	Country	Area (km²)	Main Varieties		
1	Forêt de Mundolsheim	France	145.9	🌳 🌳 🌲		
2	Sherwood Forest	UK	632.4	🌳 🌳 🌳		
3	Oberpfälzer Wald	Germany	1452.6	🌲 🌳		
4	Schwarzsee	Austria	478.6	🌳 🌲		
5	Laruns	France	98.6	🌳 🌳 🌳		

	Forest	Country	Area (km²)	Elm	Oak	Ash	Birch	Pine
1	Forest de Mundolsheim	France	145.9		✓	✓		✓

A. Forest and Main Varieties

B. Forest

C. Area and Main Varieties

D. Area

E. Main Varieties

Q 28

	Ship	Captain	Income	Fishing Activities
1	Lady Jane	Jack Sparrow	£252600	
2	Maria Elena	Percy Sledge	£456148	
3	Wee Beauty	Cameron McCormick	£759200	
4	Le France	Jacques Gravois	€146320	
5	Wales and Whales	Ivor Lloyd	£362410	

	Ship	Captain	Income	Trawling	Line	Whale	Dolphin	Deep Sea
2	Marai Elena	Percy Sledge	£465148		✓			✓

A. Ship and Income

B. Ship and Fishing Activities

C. Ship

D. Captain and Fishing Activities

E. Fishing Activities

Q 29

	Company	Quota	Revenue	Logging Varieties
1	Exploitation Forestière du Dumbach	6.24m	€326.5m	
2	Ruhr Logging GmbH	45.2m	€452.1m	
3	Schwarzsee Lumber	12.6m	€66.2m	
4	Janakkala Logging	695.2m	€1263.5m	
5	Laruns SCS	145.3m	€896.2m	

	Company	Quota	Revenue	Conifer	Rowan	Beech	Alder	Chestnut
3	Schwarzee Lumber	12.6m	€66.2m	✓	✓	✓		

A. Company and Quota

B. Quota

C. Company and Logging Varieties

D. Logging Varieties

E. Quota and Logging Varieties

Q 30

	City	Bylaw	Free Parking Spaces	Vehicles		
1	Dublin	CV/125-5	1256	bicycle	taxi	disabled
2	London	459/6-VF	45876	electric car	taxi	motorcycle
3	Paris	148-68/GH	14523	disabled	bicycle	electric car
4	Berlin	457/52-TH	56214	taxi	electric car	
5	Lisbon	652/RT-63	1254	disabled	taxi	motorcycle

	City	Bylaw	Free Parking Spaces	Motor-cycle	Bicycle	Disabled	Electric Car	Taxi
3	Paris	148-68/GH	45876		✓	✓		✓

A. Bylaw

B. Bylaw and Vehicles

C. Vehicles

D. Bylaw and Free Parking Spaces

E. Free Parking Spaces and Vehicles

Q 31

	Zoo	Annual Revenue	No. Visitors	Most Popular Animals		
1	London Zoo	£16.2m	1.25m	lion	rhino	elephant
2	Zoo de Lyon	€8.95m	0.59m	rhino	bison	
3	Berlin Zoo	€12.6m	1.23m	bear	bison	elephant
4	Woburn Abbey	£7.23m	2.6m	elephant	lion	bear
5	Sofia Animal Sanctuary	€4.23m	0.78m	lion	rhino	

	Zoo	Annual Revenue	No. Visitors	Lion	Rhino	Elephant	Bison	Bear
4	Woburn Abbey	€7.23m	2.6m	✓		✓	✓	

A. Zoo and No. Visitors

B. No. Visitors

C. Annual Revenue and Most Popular Animals

D. No. Visitors and Most Popular Animals

E. Most Popular Animals

Q 32

	University	Date	Cost	Renovations		
1	Université Robert Schumann	14-05-2011	€1.23m	Lamp	Table	Bookcase
2	Glasgow University	21-02-2010	£2.36m	Table	Bed	Chair
3	Collège de Sorbonne	06-06-2008	€7.25m	Bookcase	Table	Chair
4	Heidelberg University	25-01-2001	€6.32m	Bed	Lamp	Chair
5	London College of Economics	07-12-2011	£0.36m	Lamp	Chair	Bookcase

	University	Date	Cost	Table	Bookcase	Bed	Chair	Lamp
3	Collége de Sorbonne	06-06-2008	€7.25m	✓		✓	✓	

A.	Renovations	B.	University and Renovations
C.	Date and Renovations	D.	Date
E.	University		

Q 33

	Company	Attendees	Date	Meeting Rooms		
1	Epcos Telekom	124	12 Mar 2011	Conference	Think Tank	Webinar
2	Nancy Télévision	245	14 Feb 2010	Conference	Think Tank	
3	Blodgers Inc.	682	15 Jun 2012	Conference	Development	Webinar
4	English-French Relations	742	26 Jul 2011	Think Tank	Development	Webinar
5	HTC UK	631	08 Dec 2011	Conference	Webinar	

	Company	Attendees	Date	Meeting	Conference	Think Tank	Develop-ment	Webinar
1	Epcos Telekom	142	12 Mar 2011		✓	✓		✓

A.	Attendees and Meeting Rooms	B.	Attendees
C.	Date and Meeting Rooms	D.	Meeting Rooms
E.	Date		

Q 34

	Employee	Badge No.	Distance Travelled (Km)	Modes of Transport
1	Paul Dubois	PT 765	14.6	
2	Ranulph Massey	PY 756	7.9	
3	Boris Mayer	PJ 149	4.6	
4	Luigi Vitone	KP 310	17.8	
5	Annette Pulver	PL 2250	8.4	

	Employee	Badge No.	Distance Travelled (Km)	Tram	Train	Bicycle	Bus	Car
3	Boris Mayer	PJ 149	4.6	✓			✓	

A.	Employee	B. Modes of Transport
C.	Badge No., Modes of Transport	D. Distance Travelled
E.	Modes of Transport, Distance Travelled	

A.   Employee

C.   Badge No., Modes of Transport

E.   Modes of Transport, Distance Travelled

B.   Modes of Transport

D.   Distance Travelled

Q 35

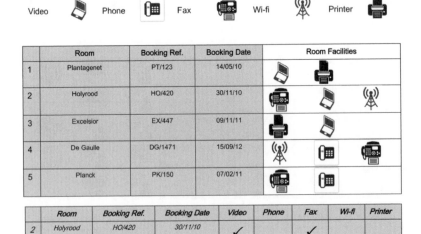

	Room	Booking Ref.	Booking Date	Room Facilities
1	Plantagenet	PT/123	14/05/10	
2	Holyrood	HO/420	30/11/10	
3	Excelsior	EX/447	09/11/11	
4	De Gaulle	DG/1471	15/09/12	
5	Planck	PK/150	07/02/11	

	Room	Booking Ref.	Booking Date	Video	Phone	Fax	Wi-fi	Printer
2	Holyrood	HO/420	30/11/10	✓		✓		

A.   Booking Date, Room

C.   Room Facilities

E.   Booking Reference

B.   Room, Room Facilities

D.   Booking Date, Room Facilities

Q 36

	Name of Farm	Subsidy	Value (€)	Type of Farming
1	Woodside Farm	GR 1049	2.91 M	
2	Takego	GR 1094	13.1 M	
3	Florian	GR 1078	1.02 M	
4	Wholefoods	GR 1111	7.50 M	
5	Gerbers	GR 1092	2.90 M	

	Name of Farm	Subsidy	Value (€)	Fishery	Mixed	Fruit	Cereal	Dairy
2	Takego	GR 1049	13.1 M		✓		✓	

A.	Value	B.	Dairy, Fruit
C.	Subsidy, Type of Farming	D.	Name of Farm, Value
E.	Subsidy		

Q 37

	Building	Room	Delivery Date	Inventory
1	Horlicks	2-23A	26 Jul 2009	
2	Excelsior	1-45B	17 Feb 2010	
3	John Bright	1-54B	13 May 2011	
4	Priestley	3-16A	13 Mar 2011	
5	Juan Carlos	4-30C	30 Oct 2012	

	Building	Room	Delivery Date	Box	Carpet	Chair	Table	Bookcase
3	John Bright	1-54B	13 Mar 2011	✓	✓		✓	

A.	Room, Inventory	B.	Delivery Date, Room
C.	Room	D.	Delivery Date, Inventory
E.	Inventory		

Q 38

Apple   Cherries   Carrot   Cake   Pretzel

	Employee	Department	Badge Number	Snacks
1	Cécile Lyes	Recruitment	CL-12/C	
2	Amanda Tamas	Press	AT-35/A	
3	Wale Fashina	Medical	WF-025/W	
4	Emily Grayson	Landscaping	EG-458/E	
5	Benjamin Bisch	Restoration	BB-162/B	

	Employee	Department	Badge Number	Apple	Cherries	Carrot	Cake	Pretzel
5	Benjamin Bisch	Landscaping	BB-162/B	✓				✓

A.   Employee, Snacks   B.   Employee, Badge No.

C.   Employee, Department   D.   Department

E.   Badge No., Department

Q 39

Solar   Gas   Oil   Nuclear   Wind

	Company	Location	Output (GWh)	Energy Supplied
1	Français de l'énergie	Paris	459.6	
2	Energy Efficient plc	Norwich	145.3	
3	Energy For All	Calais	36.2	
4	Power Are Us	Dublin	68.6	
5	Oil Consortium Ltd	Horwich	98.3	

	Company	Location	Output (GWh)	Solar	Gas	Oil	Nuclear	Wind
3	Energy Four All	Dublin	36.2	✓				✓

A.   Company   B.   Company, Output

C.   Output, Energy Supplied   D.   Company, Output, Energy Supplied

E.   Company, Location

Q 40

Corn 🌽 Dairy 🐂 Barley 🌾 Eggs 🥚 Wheat 🌾

	Farm	Subsidy	Contract	Farm Produce		
1	Olssen Farms	12.3mSEK	2y 3m	Corn	Dairy	
2	Ferguson's Farms	£4.5m	3y 4m	Dairy	Eggs	Corn
3	O'Leary's Produce	€6.4m	3y 0m	Eggs	Corn	
4	Tattersall's Dairies	£2.7m	2y 5m	Dairy	Eggs	
5	Blanc Farms	€7.2m	1y 4m	Barley	Wheat	Corn

	Farm	Subsidy	Contract	Corn	Dairy	Barley	Eggs	Wheat
1	Olsen Farms	12.3mSEK	3y 2m	✓	✓			

A. Farm, Contract, Subsidy

B. Farm, Contract

C. Subsidy, Contract

D. Contract, Farm Produce

E. Farm

Q 41

Trousers 👖 T-Shirt 👕 Fleece 🧥 Polo Shirt 👕 Jacket 🧥

	Employee	Requisition Code	Order Date	Requisitions		
1	Greta Braun	X357/23	14 Jun 2011	Jacket	Jacket	
2	Louis Blanc	X437/32	02 Jul 2011	Jacket	Trousers	Polo Shirt
3	Willem Bisch	X197/76	02 Jan 2011	T-Shirt	Jacket	
4	Boris Borg	X387/65	15 Dec 2010	Trousers		
5	Julio Carreras	X987/78	30 Nov 2011	T-Shirt	Jacket	Polo Shirt

	Employee	Requisition Code	Order Date	Trousers	T-Shirt	Fleece	Polo Shirt	Jacket
3	Willem Bisch	X197-76	02 Jul 2011				✓	✓

A. Order Date, Requisitions

B. Requisition Code, Order Date

C. Requisition Code, Order Date, Requisitions

D. Requisition Code, Requisitions

E. Employee, Order Date

Q 42

	Department	Budget	Annual Volume	Communications		
1	English	€0.56m	3.25m	@	✉	☎
2	French	€0.65m	3.56m	✉	@	
3	History	€1.2m	5.32m	☎	@	
4	Patents	€3.2m	4.56m	☎	✉	📱
5	Travel	€4.6m	6.54m	@	📠	☎

	Department	Budget	Annual Volume	Email	Mail	Fax	Phone	Mobile
1	English	€0.65m	3.25m	✓	✓			

A. Department, Budget

B. Communications

C. Department, Budget, Communications

D. Budget, Communications

E. Annual Volume, Communications

Q 43

	Function	Date	Number Attending	Menu		
1	Finance Committee	14 Oct 2011	52	Meat	Vegetarian	Cheese
2	New Department	16 Nov 2011	142	Seafood	Fruit	
3	Promotion	23 Feb 2012	67	Vegetarian	Meat	
4	Retirement	23 Jan 2011	154	Meat	Cheese	Fruit
5	Maternity Leave Party	28 Oct 2010	98	Seafood	Vegetarian	Fruit

	Function	Date	Number Attending	Meat	Seafood	Vegetarian	Cheese	Fruit
4	Promotion	23 Jan 2011	154	✓			✓	✓

A. Date, Menu

B. Date, Number Attending

C. Function, Date

D. Function

E. Date, Number Attending, Menu

Q 44

	Delegate	Hotel and Room	Check In	Amenities		
1	Sophia Mancuso	Rothsay 126	14 Feb 2011	Dinner	3-D TV	Bar
2	Loretta Baylfour	Tregarron 459	25 Apr 2011	Pool	Breakfast	
3	Harmony Everrett	St Asaph 147	16 Sep 2011	Dinner	Bar	Breakfast
4	Cornelia Swanson	Harlech 685	31 Oct 2010	Dinner	Breakfast	Pool
5	Cordelia Merriam	Windsor 685	28 Dec 2011	Breakfast	Bar	3-D TV

	Delegate	Hotel and Room	Check In	Bar	3-D TV	Breakfast	Dinner	Pool
5	Cornelia Merriam	Harlech 685	28 Dec 2011		✓	✓		✓

A. Hotel and Room, Amenities

B. Delegate, Hotel and Room

C. Delegate, Amenities

D. Delegate

E. Delegate, Hotel and Room, Amenities

Q 45

	Product	Code	Delivery Date	Transport Used		
1	Bananas	B659-148	14/02/2011	Ship	Truck	
2	Apples	A356-478	09/03/2011	Train	Truck	Car
3	Oranges	O145-689	25/10/2011	Ship	Train	
4	Peaches	P352-015	06/07/2011	Plane	Truck	
5	Kiwi Fruit	K698-478	30/03/2010	Ship	Train	Truck

	Product	Code	Delivery Date	Plane	Car	Truck	Ship	Train
3	Oranges	0145-689	25/10/2011			✓	✓	

A. Transport Used

B. Code, Transport Used

C. Delivery Date, Transport Used

D. Code, Delivery Date

E. Code, Delivery Date, Transport Used

Q 46

	Country	Energy Output GWh	Revenue €m	Main Sources
1	Portugal	458.1	682.1	
2	Sweden	369.2	468.0	
3	Finland	148.3	362.1	
4	Hungary	145.4	246.1	
5	Luxembourg	36.5	85.2	

	Country	Energy Output	Revenue	Hydro Electric	Oil	Nuclear	Wind	Solar
4	Hungry	154.4	246.1		✓	✓		

A. Energy Output, Revenue

B. Country, Revenue

C. Country, Energy Output

D. Energy Output, Main Sources

E. Country, Main Sources

Q 47

	Country	Subsidy Code	Length	Supported Industries
1	Belgium	SD-2456/L	1yr 6m	
2	Denmark	KU-564/4	3yr 8m	
3	Netherlands	RT-569/4	2yr 8m	
4	Latvia	OP-569/1	4yr 8m	
5	UK	WE-478/E	5yr 7m	

	Country	Subsidy Code	Length	Forestry	Farming	Fishing	Poultry	Agriculture
4	Latvia	OP-569/1	2yr 8m	✓	✓		✓	

A. Subsidy Code, Supported Industries

B. Country

C. Length

D. Subsidy Code, Length

E. Supported Industries

Q 48

	Company	Attendees	Date	Meeting Rooms		
1	Bolloré Société	635	14 May 2001			
2	Aleksandar Protich	745	07 Nov 2010			
3	Munchen-Benz	952	16 Oct 2011			
4	Silkeborg Stadion	630	03 Mar 2010			
5	Tivoli Sintra	145	07 Feb 2012			

	Company	Attendees	Date	Meeting	Conference	Think Tank	Develop-ment	Webinar
5	Tivoli Sinatra	145	03 Mar 2010	✓	✓		✓	

A. Company

B. Company and Date

C. Meeting Rooms

D. Company and Meeting Rooms

E. Date and Meeting Rooms

Q 49

	Employee	Department	Order Date	Supplies Needed		
1	Dagmar Eichelberger	Forensic Research	17 Mar 2011			
2	Alexis Rousseau	Biotech Lab	16 Feb 2010			
3	Harry Windsor	Environmental	30 Aug 2009			
4	Olivie Laurent	Quality Control	23 Apr 2011			
5	Otto Faber	Coroner	30 Nov 2011			

	Employee	Department	Order Date	Pencils	Pens	Highlighters	Erasers	Cutters
3	Harry Windsor	Enviromental	30 Aug 2009	✓	✓			✓

A. Employee, Department

B. Employee, Order Date

C. Supplies Needed

D. Order Date

E. Department, Supplies Needed

Q 50

Bulb   Basket   Tape   CD   Scissors

	Address	Order No.	Dispatched	Office Equipment	
1	390 Grand Rue, Nancy	249/KHT-5	24 Mar 2011	Tape	Basket
2	89 Marien Strass, Innsbruck	457/LUB-5	17 Jul 2011	Basket	Bulb
3	34 Bold Street, Lymm	473/NNB-5	14 Jun 2011	Scissors	Tape
4	65 High Street, Marple	630/MEL-9	05 Feb 2010	Basket	Bulb	Scissors
5	78 Sunset Drive, Rhyl	475/QZX-6	30 Jan 2009	Tape	Bulb

	Address	Order No.	Dispatched	Bulb	Basket	Tape	CD	Scissors
1	390 Grande Rue, Nancy	249/KHT-5	24 Mar 2011		✓	✓		

A.   Dispatched, Office Equipment   B.   Order Number, Office Equipment

C.   Address   D.   Address, Order Number

E.   Office Equipment

Q 51

Barn   Fence   Haystack   Tools   Seeds

	Location	Owner	Grant	Requirements		
1	Negro de Granja, Madrid	S. Ruiz	€4.25m	Seeds	Tools	Barn
2	Razzett Abjad, Valletta	M. Vella	€3.54m	Tools	Haystack	Barn
3	Kleiner Bauernhof, Gehspitz	H. Pfeffer	€1.08m	Fence	Barn	
4	Moorhouse Farms, Bury	Mr. Johnson	£0.45m	Haystack		
5	Pied Farm, Rochdale	Mrs. Leakie	£0.54m	Haystack	Fence	Tools

	Location	Owner	Grant	Barn	Fence	Haystack	Tools	Seeds
1	Negro de Granja, Madrid	S. Riuz	€4.25m	✓		✓	✓	

A.   Location   B.   Location, Grant

C.   Requirements   D.   Owner, Requirements

E.   Owner

Q 52

Newspaper   Milk   Fruit Vendor   Cleaning   Babysitting

	Company	Frequency	Cost	Local Services
1	Hands Are Us	Mon – Fri	£11.75 / hr	Cleaning, Babysitting
2	Help the Aged	Mon – Sun	75p per item	Milk, Fruit Vendor
3	Betty's Cleaners	Tue – Sat	£8.50 / hr	Cleaning
4	Jim's Care Scheme	Mon – Sun	£9.90 / hr	Babysitting, Cleaning, Fruit Vendor
5	Riley's News	Mon - Sun	25p per item	Newspaper, Milk

	Company	Frequency	Cost	Newspaper	Milk	Fruit Vendor	Cleaning	Babysitting
1	Hans Are Us	Mon - Fri	£11.25 / hr				✓	✓

A.	Company, Frequency	B.	Company, Local Services
C.	Frequency, Local Services	D.	Cost, Local Services
E.	Company, Cost		

Q 53

Crab   Cod   Lobster   Oyster   Salmon

	Name of Ship	Port	Quota Tonnes/Yr	Catch
1	Marie Hélène	Marseilles	36520	Lobster, Cod, Salmon
2	Jolly Fisher	Ramsgate	2450	Oyster, Crab
3	Red Snapper	Lisbon	7840	Cod, Lobster, Crab
4	United Fisheries III	London	6950	Cod, Salmon
5	Captain Haddock	Dublin	33660	Oyster, Salmon

	Name of Ship	Port	Quota Tonnes/Yr	Crab	Cod	Lobster	Oyster	Salmon
2	Jolly Fischer	Ramsgate	24450	✓			✓	

A.	Quota, Catch	B.	Port, Catch
C.	Name of Ship, Port	D.	Name of Ship, Quota
E.	Port, Quota		

Q 54

	Location	Tourism Subsidy	Staff Required	Attractions
1	Bannockburn	£1.61m	354	
2	Flanders	€4.26m	1675	
3	Edinburgh	£2.65m	1056	
4	Passchendaele	€1.72m	864	
5	Dresden	€0.98m	455	

	Location	Tourism Subsidy	Staff Required	Cathedral	Battle Site	Architecture	Bridge	Church
1	Bannockburn	€1.61m	354		✓	✓		✓

A.	Location	B.	Tourism Subsidy
C.	Staff Required, Attractions	D.	Attractions
E.	Location, Tourism Subsidy		

Q 55

	Urban Scheme	Location	Grant	Contractors
1	Toxteth Point	Liverpool	£12.6m	
2	Biederitz Renovations	Madgeburg	€3.65m	
3	Poggio di Roio	L'Aquila	€4.39m	
4	El Limonar	Cartagena	€7.68m	
5	Bairro Alto	Lisboa	€6.78m	

	Urban Scheme	Location	Grant	Builder	Plumber	Electrician	Gasman	Decorator
3	Poggio di Rolo	L'Aquila	€4.39m	✓			✓	✓

A.	Urban Scheme, Contractors	B.	Urban Scheme, Grant
C.	Contractors	D.	Grant
E.	Urban Scheme		

Q 56

Chemical   Fire   Drought   Oil Slick   Nuclear Leak

	Location	Staff to Train	Budget	Disaster Drills
1	Copenhagen	1425	DKK265.1m	
2	Valletta	854	€1.25m	
3	Amsterdam	4526	€1.26m	
4	Edinburgh	742	£0.45m	
5	Rotterdam	3692	€45.2m	

	Location	Staff to Train	Budget	Chemical	Fire	Drought	Oil Slick	Nuclear Leak
2	Valetta	854	€1.26m		✓	✓		

A.   Location

B.   Location, Budget

C.   Budget

D.   Budget, Disaster Drills

E.   Disaster Drills

Q 57

Pelican   Eagle   Owl   Heron   Woodpecker

	Co-ordinator	Location	Donations	Endangered Species
1	Paolo Gambini	Firenze	€150,125	
2	Jakub Zieliński	Kotka	€147,265	
3	Seamus O'Leary	Ballyboden	€256,265	
4	Bartosz Krawczyk	Zamość	PLN125,475	
5	Penrhyn Jones	Llandudno	£25,362	

	Co-ordinator	Location	Donations	Pelican	Eagle	Owl	Heron	Woodpecker
1	Paolo Gambini	Firenze	€150,215	✓	✓		✓	

A.   Co-ordinator, Endangered Species

B.   Donations

C.   Location, Endangered Species

D.   Location

E.   Endangered Species

Q 58

Disabled Driver	Road Train	Caravan	Camper Van	Motor-cycle

	Country	Speed Limit km/h	Introduced	Vehicles Restricted
1	Ireland	50	07-12-1985	
2	Malta	60	30-09-1988	
3	Spain	50	24-04-1985	
4	Poland	70	31-01-2004	
5	Austria	60	28-01-1984	

	Country	Speed Limit km/h	Introduced	Disabled Driver	Road Train	Caravan	Camper Van	Motor-cycle
3	Spain	50	24-04-1988		✓	✓		✓

A. Speed Limit

B. Introduced and Vehicles Restricted

C. Introduced

D. Speed Limit and Introduced

E. Speed Limit and Vehicles Restricted

Q 59

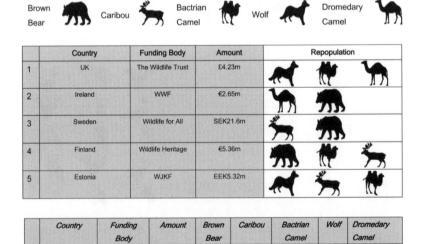

Brown Bear	Caribou	Bactrian Camel	Wolf	Dromedary Camel

	Country	Funding Body	Amount	Repopulation
1	UK	The Wildlife Trust	£4.23m	
2	Ireland	WWF	€2.65m	
3	Sweden	Wildlife for All	SEK21.6m	
4	Finland	Wildlife Heritage	€5.36m	
5	Estonia	WJKF	EEK5.32m	

	Country	Funding Body	Amount	Brown Bear	Caribou	Bactrian Camel	Wolf	Dromedary Camel
2	Ireland	WWF	£2.65m	✓		✓		

A. Country and Amount

B. Amount and Repopulation

C. Repopulation

D. Country and Repopulation

E. Amount

Q 60

	Country	Man Hours Lost	Av. Days Closed / year	Road Closures
1	Germany	2.36m	42.3	
2	France	26.1m	32.6	
3	Belgium	4.63m	12.3	
4	Poland	96.2m	57.2	
5	Czech Republic	96.3m	56.2	

	Country	Man Hours Lost	Av. Days Closed/year	Ice	Flooding	Storm	Fog	Snow
1	Gemany	2.36m	42.3			✓		✓

A.   Country and Road Closures

B.   Man Hours Lost

C.   Road Closures

D.   Man Hours Lost and Road Closures

E.   Country and Man Hours Lost

Q 61

	Forest	Country	Area (km²)	Main Varieties
1	Białowieża Forest	Poland	152.2	
2	New Forest	UK	241.3	
3	Kolmården Forest	Sweden	2310.5	
4	Forêt noire	France	145.3	
5	Dartrey Forest	Ireland	53.2	

	Forest	Country	Area (km²)	Elm	Oak	Ash	Birch	Pine
3	Kolmården Forest	Sweden	2130.5			✓		✓

A.   Forest and Main Varieties

B.   Forest

C.   Area and Main Varieties

D.   Area

E.   Main Varieties

Q 62

Trawling   Line   Whale   Dolphin   Deep Sea

	Ship	Captain	Income	Fishing Activities
1	Rose Marie	Paul Anchor	£146230	
2	Le Charles de Gaulle	Didier Laurent	€453210	
3	Black Adder	Mick O'Day	£745210	
4	Gisela	Macon Bosch	€895210	
5	Porta Doone II	Howard Wilde	£456327	

	Ship	Captain	Income	Trawling	Line	Whale	Dolphin	Deep Sea
5	Porta Doone II	Howard Wild	£456327			✓	✓	

A.   Ship and Income

B.   Ship and Fishing Activities

C.   Ship

D.   Captain and Fishing Activities

E.   Fishing Activities

Q 63

Conifer   Rowan   Beech   Alder   Chestnut

	Company	Quota	Revenue	Logging Varieties
1	Sustainable Logging plc	14.6m	£56.3m	
2	Popular Sawmills	63.2m	£152.3m	
3	Scierie de Molsheim	452.0m	€785.2m	
4	News International	478.2m	£126.3m	
5	Dupont Lumber	12.3m	€65.2m	

	Company	Quota	Revenue	Conifer	Rowan	Beech	Alder	Chestnut
1	Sustainable Logging plc	16.4m	£56.3m	✓			✓	✓

A.   Company and Quota

B.   Quota

C.   Company and Logging Varieties

D.   Logging Varieties

E.   Quota and Logging Varieties

Q 64

	City	Bylaw	Free Parking Spaces	Vehicles		
1	Innsbruck	BN-98/625	3652			
2	Vienna	ER-859/14	1458			
3	Madrid	478-LK/74	7456			
4	Bucharest	459-WQ/256	456			
5	Helsinki	43-LP/145	1486			

	City	Bylaw	Free Parking Spaces	Motor-cycle	Bicycle	Disabled	Electric Car	Taxi
1	Innsbruck	BN-89/625	3652	✓			✓	✓

A. Bylaw

B. Bylaw and Vehicles

C. Vehicles

D. Bylaw and Free Parking Spaces

E. Free Parking Spaces and Vehicles

Q 65

	Zoo	Annual Revenue	No. Visitors	Most Popular Animals		
1	Rome Zoo	€24.3m	3.65m			
2	Parc animalier de l'Orangerie	€14.5m	4.36m			
3	Madrid Zoo	€25.6m	8.6m			
4	Knowsley Safari Park	£36.2m	12.6m			
5	Amsterdam Park	€14.6m	3.24m			

	Zoo	Annual Revenue	No. Visitors	Lion	Rhino	Elephant	Bison	Bear
5	Amsterdam Park	€14.6m	3.42m		✓	✓		

A. Zoo and No. Visitors

B. No. Visitors

C. Annual Revenue and Most Popular Animals

D. No. Visitors and Most Popular Animals

E. Most Popular Animals

Q 66

	University	Date	Cost	Renovations		
1	Edinburgh University	17-02-2010	£6.32m			
2	Université Louis Pasteur	09-09-2009	€14.23m			
3	University of Chester	08-12-2010	£0.25m			
4	Università di Bologna	02-03-2011	€3.65m			
5	Faculté de pharmacologie d'Alsace	23-04-2009	€12.5m			

	University	Date	Cost	Table	Bookcase	Bed	Chair	Lamp
1	Edinburgh University	09-09-2009	£6.32m	✓	✓			✓

A.	Renovations	B. University and Renovations
C.	Date and Renovations	D. Date
E.	University	

Q 67

	Company	Attendees	Date	Meeting Rooms		
1	Monopoly Ltd.	1365	30 Jun 2011			
2	Weber & Co.	254	31 Jan 2009			
3	Lloyds TSB	962	28 Feb 2010			
4	Koenig and Hummel GmbH	753	27 Apr 2009			
5	Les Bouloungeries de Pierre	225	05 May 2008			

	Company	Attendees	Date	Meeting	Conference	Think Tank	Development	Webinar
3	Lloyds TSB	962	8 Feb 2010	✓			✓	

A.	Attendees and Meeting Rooms	B. Attendees
C.	Date and Meeting Rooms	D. Meeting Rooms
E.	Date	

Q 68

Tram 🚋 Train 🚈 Bicycle 🚲 Bus 🚌 Car 🚐

	Employee	Badge No.	Distance Travelled (Km)	Modes of Transport		
1	Manuel Del Piero	WF 985	24.6	Tram	Train	
2	Franka Iverson	MR 430	14.8	Train	Bus	
3	Stanislaw Rakowski	RG 478	5.1	Car	Tram	
4	Adriana Calvo	TL 490	6.4	Car		
5	Robert Sheargold	QZ 340	4.6	Bicycle	Bus	Tram

	Employee	Badge No.	Distance Travelled (Km)	Tram	Train	Bicycle	Bus	Car
4	Adriana Calvo	TL 940	6.4				✓	✓

A. Employee

B. Modes of Transport

C. Badge No., Modes of Transport

D. Distance Travelled

E. Modes of Transport, Distance Travelled

Q 69

Video 💻 Phone 📞 Fax 📠 Wi-fi 📡 Printer 🖨

	Room	Booking Ref.	Booking Date	Room Facilities		
1	Getty	GY/546	12/04/10	Video	Fax	Phone
2	Oporto	OP/126	16/06/09	Fax	Phone	
3	Madrid	MD/4451	09/09/10	Printer	Wi-fi	
4	Victoria	VT/1447	30/09/12	Printer	Phone	Fax
5	Hope	HP/632	03/12/11	Wi-fi	Video	

	Room	Booking Ref.	Booking Date	Video	Phone	Fax	Wi-fi	Printer
5	Hope	HP/632	03/11/12	✓			✓	✓

A. Booking Date, Room

B. Room, Room Facilities

C. Room Facilities

D. Booking Date, Room Facilities

E. Booking Reference

Q 70

	Name of Farm	Subsidy	Value (€)	Type of Farming
1	Coverdale	AT 230	0.5 M	🚜 🐟
2	Provencale	AN 109	0.8 M	🍒 🥛 🌾
3	Gillatti	AF 229	0.9 M	🌾 🚜 🍒
4	Rabenaut	AG 111	0.4 M	🚜 🐟
5	Bloemenfarm	AH 107	0.75 M	🍒 🥛

	Name of Farm	Subsidy	Value (€)	Fishery	Mixed	Fruit	Cereal	Dairy
1	Coverlade	AT 230	0.8 M	✓	✓			

A. Value

B. Dairy, Fruit

C. Subsidy, Type of Farming

D. Name of Farm, Value

E. Subsidy

Q 71

	Building	Room	Delivery Date	Inventory
1	Jean Monnet	JM 154	16 Jun 2011	🪑 📦 📚
2	Euroforum	EF 362	30 Dec 2010	🪑 📚
3	HITECH	HT 015	08 Apr 2010	🪑 🧍
4	BECH	BE 262	25 Jun 2011	📦 🪑 🪑
5	Maison de L'Europe	ME 626	08 Sept 2010	🧍 📚 📦

	Building	Room	Delivery Date	Box	Carpet	Chair	Table	Bookcase
4	BECH	BE 626	25 Jun 2011	✓		✓		✓

A. Room, Inventory

B. Delivery Date, Room

C. Room

D. Delivery Date, Inventory

E. Inventory

Q 72

Apple   Cherries   Carrot   Cake   Pretzel

	Employee	Department	Badge Number	Snacks		
1	Boris Gruber	Roads	RD 569A	Cake	Cherries	Pretzel
2	Jacqueline Kennedy	Transport	TP 365C	Carrot		
3	Pierre Blanc	Legal	LG 069B	Cherries	Apple	Cake
4	Jean-Luc Marceau	Catering	CT 145L	Apple	Pretzel	
5	Lukas Schmid	Research	RH 365V	Cake	Cherries	Pretzel

	Employee	Department	Badge Number	Apple	Cherries	Carrot	Cake	Pretzel
3	Piere Blanc	Legal	LG 609B	✓	✓		✓	

A. Employee, Snacks   B. Employee, Badge No.

C. Employee, Department   D. Department

E. Badge No., Department

Q 73

Solar   Gas   Oil   Nuclear   Wind

	Company	Location	Output (GWh)	Energy Supplied		
1	Energy for Life	Basingstoke	245.2	Nuclear	Solar	
2	Autrian Énergie	Innsbruck	756.3	Gas	Oil	Nuclear
3	People Power	Stockholm	64.2	Oil	Wind	
4	Blowing in the Wind	Reading	12.3	Wind		
5	Natural Power	Copenhagen	62.0	Wind	Solar	

	Company	Location	Output (GWh)	Solar	Gas	Oil	Nuclear	Wind
2	Austrian Énergie	Innsbruck	765.3		✓	✓	✓	

A. Company   B. Company, Output

C. Output, Energy Supplied   D. Company, Output, Energy Supplied

E. Company, Location

Q 74

	Farm	Subsidy	Contract	Farm Produce			
1	Bengtsson Farms	€7.23m	4y 6m				
2	Richland Dairies	£14.6m	5y 9m				
3	Van Dyke Produce	€32.6m	6y 8m				
4	Robinson's Beef Farm	£35.2m	6y 6m				
5	Marino & Son	€0.8m	1y 3m				

	Farm	Subsidy	Contract	Corn	Dairy	Barley	Eggs	Wheat
5	Marino & Son	£35.2m	6y 6m	✓		✓	✓	

A. Farm, Contract, Subsidy

B. Farm, Contract

C. Subsidy, Contract

D. Contract, Farm Produce

E. Farm

Q 75

	Employee	Requisition Code	Order Date	Requisitions		
1	Hans Solo	3987-G	14-06-2010			
2	Irene Rhodes	3085-M	15-03-2012			
3	Paul Schofield	2947-B	06-06-2009			
4	Peter Andre	3495-V	05-04-2011			
5	Sara Gimp	1976-R	31-01-2011			

	Employee	Requisition Code	Order Date	Trousers	T-Shirt	Fleece	Polo Shirt	Jacket
5	Sarah Gimp	1976-R	31-10-2011	✓	✓	✓		

A. Order Date, Requisitions

B. Requisition Code, Order Date

C. Requisition Code, Order Date, Requisitions

D. Requisition Code, Requisitions

E. Employee, Order Date

Q 76

Email		Mail		Fax		Phone		Mobile	

	Department	Budget	Annual Volume	Communications		
1	Energy	€3.25m	63.1m	Phone	Email	
2	Morgue	€2.14m	25.3m	Mail	Fax	
3	Coroner	€0.65m	1.54m	Mail	Phone	
4	Investigation	€7.8m	3.98m	Fax	Mobile	Email
5	Environmental	€0.115m	1.26m	Email	Phone	Mobile

	Department	Budget	Annual Volume	Email	Mail	Fax	Phone	Mobile
4	Coroner	£7.8m	3.98m	✓		✓		✓

A. Department, Budget
B. Communications
C. Department, Budget, Communications
D. Budget, Communications
E. Annual Volume, Communications

Q 77

Meat		Seafood		Vegetarian		Cheese		Fruit	

	Function	Date	Number Attending	Menu		
1	Swedish Ambassador	30 Mar 2011	1450	Vegetarian	Seafood	Cheese
2	UNICEF	31 Oct 2011	2147	Seafood	Meat	Fruit
3	Opening of Parliament	13 Oct 2011	3652	Vegetarian	Meat	Cheese
4	State Visit	04 Aug 2011	2652	Seafood	Cheese	Fruit
5	Presidential Dinner	27 Jul 2012	1496	Meat	Vegetarian	Fruit

	Function	Date	Number Attending	Meat	Seafood	Vegetarian	Cheese	Fruit
3	Opening of Parliament	31 Oct 2011	3652	✓	✓			✓

A. Date, Menu
B. Date, Number Attending
C. Function, Date
D. Function
E. Date, Number Attending, Menu

Q 78

	Delegate	Hotel and Room	Check In	Amenities
1	Ralph Malph	The Royal 129	14 Mar 2011	
2	Paul Roberts	The Ambassador 496	30 Jul 2011	
3	Henry Stephenson	The Grand 147	17 Mar 2012	
4	Gillian Murdoch	The Empire 654	23 Feb 2012	
5	Francine Towers	The Annan 652	27 Oct 2010	

	Delegate	Hotel and Room	Check In	Bar	3-D TV	Breakfast	Dinner	Pool
3	Henri Stephenson	The Grand 147	17 Mar 2012	✓		✓		

A.   Hotel and Room, Amenities

B.   Delegate, Hotel and Room

C.   Delegate, Amenities

D.   Delegate

E.   Delegate, Hotel and Room, Amenities

Q 79

	Product	Code	Delivery Date	Transport Used
1	Prosthetics	P368/125	14/02/2010	
2	Mechanical Heart	MH452/425	21/03/2012	
3	Blood	B369/421	17/03/2011	
4	Dialysis Machine	DM785/147	03/02/2011	
5	MRI Scanner	MS639/560	08/08/2010	

	Product	Code	Delivery Date	Plane	Car	Truck	Ship	Train
2	Mechanical Heart	MH425/452	21/03/2011		✓	✓	✓	

A.   Transport Used

B.   Code, Transport Used

C.   Delivery Date, Transport Used

D.   Code, Delivery Date

E.   Code, Delivery Date, Transport Used

Q 80

Hydro Electric   Oil   Nuclear   Wind   Solar

	Country	Energy Output GWh	Revenue €m	Main Sources		
1	Slovakia	475.3	892.1			
2	Slovenia	250.6	352.0			
3	Romania	450.3	986.3			
4	Estonia	682.0	1263.2			
5	Malta	36.5	74.2			

	Country	Energy Output	Revenue	Hydro Electric	Oil	Nuclear	Wind	Solar
2	Slovakia	250.6	352.0	✓	✓		✓	

A.   Energy Output, Revenue

B.   Country, Revenue

C.   Country, Energy Output

D.   Energy Output, Main Sources

E.   Country, Main Sources

ACCURACY TEST – ANSWERS

1. D

The distance travelled should be 4.5km.

2. E

Booking Reference should be BZ/015.

3. C

Subsidy should be 2116 and Type of Farming should not include Fruit.

4. C

Room should be J453.

5. A

Name should be Yvette Weber and Snacks should be Apple, Cherries and Carrot.

6. C

Output should be 324.1 and Energy Supplied should be Gas, Nuclear and Solar.

7. D

Contract should be 2y 4m and Farm Produce should be Eggs, Barley and Dairy.

8. A

Order Date should be 30 May 2011 and Requisitions should be Fleece and Polo Shirt.

9. B

Communications should be Email, Mail and Mobile.

10. B

Date should be 28 Jan 2011 and Number Attending should be 680.

11. B

Delegate should be Olivier Blanchard and Hotel and Room should be Excelsior 245.

12. D

Code should be TR490/2 and Delivery Date should be 13 Feb 2010.

13. A

Energy Output should be 268.4 and Revenue should be 268.1.

14. A

Subsidy Code should be YT-6852/A and Supported Industries should have Poultry and Fishing.

15. B

Employee should be Alheid Schneider and Order Date should be 12-12-2012.

16. A

Dispatched should be 03/06/2010 and Office Equipment should be Scissors and Basket.

17. B

Location should be Styall and Grant should be '£'.

18. C

Frequency should be Mon-Sun and Local Services should not include Milk.

19. A

Quota should be 42690 and Catch should include Crab, Cod and Oyster.

20. D

Attractions should be Cathedral, Architecture and Bridge.

21. B

Urban Scheme should be Schwetzingen and Grant should be €14.6m.

22. D

Budget should be 0.014 and Disaster Drills should include Oil Slick, Nuclear Leak and Chemical.

23. C

Location should be Pescara and Endangered Species should include Eagle and Pelican.

24. E

Speed Limit should be 60 and Vehicles Restricted should have Disabled Driver, Roadtrain and Caravan.

25. D

Country should be Czech Republic and Repopulation should include Brown Bear, Caribou and Wolf.

26. D

Man Hours Lost should be 9.25m and Road Closures should include Snow and Flooding.

27. B

Forest should be Forêt de Mundolsheim.

28. A

Ship should be Maria Elena and Income should be £456148.

29. C

Company should be Schwarzsee Lumber and Logging Varieties should include Rowan, Conifer and Alder.

30. E

Free parking spaces should be 14523 and Vehicles should include Disabled, Bicycle and Electric Car.

31. C

Annual Revenue should be £ and Most Popular Animals should include Elephant, Lion and Bear.

32. B

University should be Collège de Sorbonne and Renovations should include Bookcase, Table and.Chair.

33. A

Attendees should be 124 and Meeting Rooms should include Meeting, Conference and Webinar.

34. B

Mode of Transport should be Bicycle and Tram.

35. C

Room facilities should also include Wi-fi.

36. E

Subsidy should be 1094.

37. D

Delivery Date should be 13 May 2011 and Inventory should be Table and Carpet.

38. D

Department should be Restoration.

39. E

Company should be Energy For All and Location should be Calais.

40. B

Farm should be Olssen Farms and Contract should be 2y 3m.

41. C

Requisition Code should be X197/76, Order Date should be 02 Jan 2011 and Requisitions should be Polo Shirt and Fleece.

42. D

Budget should be €0.56m and Communications should be Email, Mail and Phone.

43. D

Function should be Retirement.

44. E

Delegate should be Cordelia Merriam, Hotel and Room should be Windsor 685 and Amenities should be Breakfast, Bar and 3-D TV.

45. B

Code should be O145-689 and Transport used should be Ship and Train.

46. C

Country should be Hungary and Energy Output should be 145.4.

47. D

Subsidy Code should begin with O not 0 and Length should be 4yr 8m.

48. B

Company should be Tivoli Sintra and Date should be 07 Feb 2012.

49. E

Department should be Environmental and Supplies Needed should have Pens, Pencils and Highlighter.

50. C

Address should be Grand Rue.

51. D

Owner should be Ruiz and Requirements should have Seeds, Tools and Barn.

52. E

Company should be Hands Are Us and Cost should be £11.75.

53. E

Name of Ship should be Fisher and Quota should be 2450.

54. E

Location should be Bannockburn and Tourism Subsidy should be £.

55. A

Urban Scheme should be Poggio di Roio and Contractor should include Plumber, Builder and Decorator.

56. B

Location should be Valletta and Budget should be 1.25m.

57. B

Donations should be €150,125.

58. B

Introduced should be 1985 and Vehicles Restricted should have Camper Van Caravan and Motorcycle.

59. B

Amount should be € and Repopulation should include Dromedary and Brown Bear.

60. A

Country should be Germany and Road Closures should include Snow and Flooding.

61. C

Area should be 2310.5 and Main varieties should include Pine and Birch.

62. D

Captain should be Howard Wilde and Fishing Activities should include Whale and Deep Sea.

63. E

Quota should be 14.6m and Logging varieties should include Chestnut, Conifer and Beech.

64. A

Bylaw should be BN-98/625.

65. D

No. Visitors should be 3.24m and Most Popular Animals should include Bear, Rhino and Elephant.

66. C

Date should be 17-02-2010 and Renovations should include Chair, Table and Bookcase.

67. C

Date should be 28-Feb-2010 and Meeting Rooms should include Conference and Meeting.

68. C

Badge No. should be TL 490 and Modes of Transport should be Car only.

69. D

Booking date should be 03/12/11 and Room Facilities should not include a Printer.

70. D

Name of Farm should be Coverdale and Value should be 0.5 M.

71. A

Room should be BE 262 and Inventory should be Box, Table and Chair.

72. B

Employee should be Pierre Blanc and Badge No. should be LG 069B.

73. B

Company should be Autrian Énergie and Output should be 756.3.

74. C

Subsidy should be €0.8m and Contract should be 1y 3m.

75. E

Employee should be Sara Gimp and Order Date should be 31-01-2011.

76. A

Department should be Investigation and Budget should be €7.8m.

77. A

Date should be 13 Oct 2011 and Menu should be Vegetarian, Meat and Cheese.

78. C

Delegate should be Henry Stephenson and Amenities should be Bar and Dinner.

79. E

Code should be MH452/425, Delivery Date should be 21/03/2012 and Transport Used should be Ship, Train and Truck.

80. E

Country should be Slovenia and Main Sources should be Nuclear, Wind and Oil.

PART III

THE ASSESSMENT CENTRE FOR ASSISTANTS

1.   About Assessment Centres and Exercises

What is an Assessment Centre?

An "Assessment Centre" (or AC for short) is a way of assessing potential performance in a role; applied to a group of participants by trained assessors using various diagnostic tools. Assessment Centres were first used in the 1950s and are now regularly used by organisations to assess staff, whether for recruitment, personal development or internal promotion. In essence, an Assessment Centre consists of asking candidates to complete a varied set of exercises which are designed to simulate different aspects of a role and work environment.

Candidates are observed by a team of assessors who make judgements on the candidates' performance by completing a set of standardised competency rating forms which describe what "good" and "poor" performance looks like. As a candidate you will be observed by a number of assessors throughout the event, to minimise the likelihood of any bias on the part of assessors. According to the Chartered Institute of Personnel and Development's "Recruitment, Retention and Turnover Survey", 34% of employers now use Assessment Centres when recruiting managers, professionals or graduates. This figure will inevitably grow as organisations seek to make more accurate selection and promotion decisions.

Assessment Centres are one of the most fair, objective and effective ways of identifying high-potential candidates who will fit in with a role and an organisation's culture. Research shows them to be far more predictive of future job performance than individual tasks, such as an interview. This is because a number of different assessors get to see you perform over a long period of time and have the chance to see what you can *actually* do in a variety of situations (rather than what you might *say* you do in an interview).

An additional advantage that I have found when running ACs is that they offer potential employees a realistic preview of the types of tasks they will be required to perform in the role. On a number of occasions when feeding-back to candidates they have told me that, regardless of how they actually performed at the Assessment Centre, they have decided that the role is not for them as they did not enjoy the tasks they were required to perform. This is obviously only going to benefit you in the long-run: it is far better for you to decide now tha t you are less well suited to a particular EU role than once you have accepted an offer and are in the post.

For those of you that are interested in the research angle, I have included a table below that summarises research conducted at the University of Manchester by Dr. Mike Smith and Prof. Ivan Robertson. It compares the predictive power of a range of assessment methods. To help you interpret it, a score of zero suggests that the prediction is no better than random chance. A score of one would mean that the selection technique offered a perfect prediction of future performance. You can see from this table that no technique is perfect but that Assessment Centres offer the best chance to predict future performance effectively.

The EPSO Assessment Centres typically last between half a day and one day, depending upon the role. In my experience, a single Assessment Centre usually contains up to twelve people, although EPSO may decide to run multiple streams on the same day given the large number of candidates. The Centres will be conducted by EPSO personnel who have been trained by an external body in best Assessment Centre practice, and they might be assisted

Predictive Power of Various Assessment Methods

(Mike Smith/Ivan Robertson, University of Manchester)

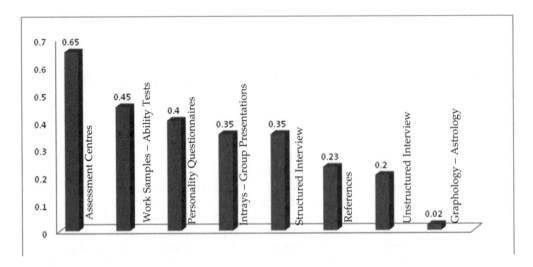

by accredited external consultants. Assessment Centres are time consuming and expensive affairs: for this reason, they are the last stage in the EPSO selection process so that there are smaller numbers of preselected candidates to deal with.

I hope that these opening comments have given you some confidence in the validity of the process. In the chapters that follow, I will be revealing a large number of hints and tips to help you perform well at an Assessment Centre. Some of these are based upon knowledge of actual EPSO processes gained from publicly available sources; other hints are drawn from my experience of designing and running Assessment Centres and what types of behaviours have earned candidates a positive result in similar past situations.

You should bear in mind two important points when reading these chapters. Firstly, it is hard to "fake" a good performance at an Assessment Centre. Trying to act in a manner completely contrary to your natural style over an eight hour period and across multiple assessments can be mentally taxing and may actually cause your performance to suffer. If the behaviours you are trying to convey do not come at all naturally, you will be found out. Secondly, it is contrary to both your and EPSO's interests to find yourself in a role for which you are neither behaviourally nor motivationally suited. As well as underperforming, you are likely to experience greater levels of stress and job dissatisfaction if you are placed in a role that you are not well suited to.

That said, it is possible to prepare yourself for what is coming in the Centre by reading the advice in the following chapters and thinking about your approach in advance. I tend to actually encourage this for all prospective Assessment Centre candidates, as it places everyone on a "level playing field" and minimises the likelihood that the Assessment Centre process causes a poor performance, rather than it being a true reflection of someone's ability. By going into the event with your eyes open and having planned how you can show off your strengths to their maximum advantage, you will give yourself the best possible chance for success, not to mention that the assessment tasks will not take you by surprise if you are fully aware of what to expect.

The Role of Competencies

EU staff selection procedures are now competency driven, and no longer purely based on knowledge. This is certainly because research has found that the ability to learn and retain knowledge is only one small aspect of the personal qualities that go towards making a successful employee. The way I tend to define competencies is "groupings of related behaviours, traits and motivations that each predict successful performance in a particular aspect of a role". The EPSO selection process is built around a set of competencies that are relevant to all roles within the organisation to some extent. Some competencies are more or less important for certain roles and will therefore carry more or less weight in the final decision making process. According to EPSO's latest practice, the list of competencies and the matching exercises are published in the Notice of Competition.

The EPSO competencies and definitions for Assistants' (AST) roles are as follows (with titles and definitions taken from the EPSO website). I have also provided an example of where each competency might be well measured:

Analysis and Problem Solving – Identifies the critical facts in complex issues and develops creative and practical solutions. This competency is measured in an e-tray exercise and in the structured interview and also possibly in the organisation and prioritisation test. For example, positive behaviours in the e-tray exercise would include making correct assumptions and analysis of e-mails and data presented in charts (such as instructions from superiors, service offers and quotes for a task that needs to be completed) and poorer behaviour would include taking only a surface look at issues and missing subtleties such as politically contentious aspects, long-term ramifications of short-term decisions or missing the inherent relations between different groups of information. (For example: a request made by a colleague needs to be cross-checked with company policy, instructions from your superiors and budgetary constraints must also be considered, therefore you will be expected not to accept assumptions before drawing any conclusion). Similar issues are measured in the structured interview, e.g. how you managed to overcome a challenge in the work place or identified the core issue in question. *See the feedback and scoring guide in the In-tray and Structured Interview chapters below.*

Communicating – Communicates clearly and precisely both orally and in writing. The most natural place for this competency to be measured is the structured interview. I would expect better responses not only to be grammatically correct but also to convey something of the candidate's passion, conviction and understanding of the "big picture", especially if requested to adopt a role that involved assisting a senior EU official. For example, a sentence such as "We were gonna recommend more money be spent" is grammatically poor and emotionally sparse. A better way of expressing the same concept would be "I believe it is essential that we allocate more funds to the international trade development project to guarantee its success". The fundamental principles of communication apply: your message must be clear, sufficiently concrete, and underpinned by strong relevant arguments and data; it must be well structured both visually and logically, and its presentation should be done in a compelling manner. *See further tips on effective oral and written communication in the chapters below.*

Delivering Quality and Results – Takes personal responsibility and initiative for delivering work to a high standard of quality within set procedures. This competency is measured in the e-tray exercise or the professional skills tests in Part II of this book: for example, positive actions could include making sure you meet the time limit for the task by introducing time- and project-management methods into the exercise (adding milestones, allocating time for the exercise and other ideas, even in a relatively short one hour exercise setting). Poorer actions could be trying to make ineffective short-cuts by using superficial assumptions before the possible options had all been explored and evaluated fully, or arbitrarily interpreting the rules set by the assessors – for example if your task is to "identify the three speakers for a conference", you should not identify two or rather four by saying "that number was only a suggestion".

Learning and Development – *Develops and improves personal skills and knowledge of the organisation and its environment.* This is assessed by self-report in the structured interview, as it is hard to measure these behaviours in another way in a day-long Assessment Centre. Better candidate responses would include examples of when they have proactively decided to undergo additional learning or training to enhance their employability or skills, such as enrolling in a seminar on the EU financial regulation or on a computer literacy course; this may be shown by presenting the self-development books you have recently read or mentioning the wine tasting course you signed up for. A poorer candidate response would show little evidence of attempting to proactively improve their knowledge or skills, outside what has been mandated by their studies or employment, or talking negatively of the "burdens" posed by the trainings your current or previous employer "imposed" on you. *A large number of tips and hints can be found in the chapter on the structured interview.*

Prioritising and Organising – *Prioritises the most important tasks, works flexibly and organises own workload efficiently.* This type of competency is measured by an organising and prioritising exercise and the accuracy test (for AST3), along with the structured interview and the e-tray exercise (also for AST1). From the large amount of data you are presented with in such exercises, it will be important to identify key priorities – in other words, those requiring immediate action (e.g. short deadline items). A less strong performance on this competency would likely be indicated by a haphazard approach to tasks, or tackling them in the exact order they are presented to you rather than by their importance. *More ideas and hints will be offered in the in-tray chapter.*

Resilience – *Remains effective under a heavy workload, handles organisational frustrations positively and adapts to a changing work environment.* As it would be unethical to place candidates under excessive stress during an assessment (though the e-tray exercise and other skills tests will have lots of time pressure built in), this is also measured through the structured interview, where candidates are asked about previous stressful experiences they have encountered. Therefore it is crucial that you try to recall such experiences when preparing for the Assessment Centre so that you will not be left without any ideas when the question is put to you. A better response might be if a candidate were to describe a time when they remained calm and focused when faced with a tight deadline and multiple competing demands (e.g. your boss assigned you two projects where the deadlines seemed unrealistic). A poorer response would be to dwell on the difficulties you had with a colleague when under pressure without providing an explanation of how the situation was effectively resolved. In addition to the interview, I sometimes try to simulate a relatively low-level of stress by asking candidates a series of challenging questions after their interview: I will even express contrary opinions on purpose to see how they respond. *More tips will be offered in the chapter on the structured interview below.*

Working with Others (in a Team) – *Works co-operatively with others in teams and across organisational boundaries and respects differences between people.* This competency is measured by the structured interview and the e-tray exercise. Effective behaviours could then include candidates making a more abstract consideration of which stakeholders to consult as part of their plans. (In an EU context, this means you will not only be expected to show a co-operative approach with your fellow candidates, but also to understand the decision-making procedures and stakeholder consultation mechanisms of the European Commission and other institutions; this should then be integrated into your approach.) Poorer responses would include interrupting or belittling others' point of view in a non-professional way (e.g. by saying "this idea doesn't make any sense") or failing to consider various interests in a situation. *You will find further ideas about how to make the most of this competency in the chapters about the structured interview and the in-tray exercise.*

One last issue worth mentioning is the "ability to apply specialist knowledge in the field", which is measured by the computer literacy test or other profile (or domain) specific interview or computer-based test that you may be required to sit, depending on whether you are taking an AST1 or AST3 exam.

In terms of how the competencies are actually used, as part of the Assessment Centre design, they are "mapped" to each of the Assessment Centre exercises, depending upon where they would be best observed. EPSO specifies that each of the EPSO competencies is observed twice over the course of the event. This is a good idea, as it prevents someone's rating being overly affected by a particularly bad or good performance in just one exercise.

The table below shows a competency matrix illustrating which exercises EPSO may use to measure different competencies. An X denotes which competency could be measured. This is a *generic* AST-type matrix for illustration purposes and the exact matrix might vary between competitions. You should check the Notice of Competition or the invitation letter to the Assessment Centre for any information it provides on this topic.

Competence	In-Tray	Structured Interview	Accuracy Test	Organising and Prioritising Test	Computer Literacy Test
Analysis and Problem solving	X	X		X	
Communication		X			
Delivering results	X			X	X
Learning and development		X			
Prioritising and organising	X	X	X	X	
Resilience		X	X		
Working in a team	X	X			

As a general rule, in order to help assessors score the candidate's performance on each exercise, each competency will then be further defined by a range of positive and negative indicators on a bipolar scale. For example, here are three possible indicators for a generic "Planning"-type competency (non EPSO-specific):

Sample Competency Name: Planning	
Sample Competency Description: Adopts a methodical and structured approach to work.	
Negative Indicators	**Positive Indicators**
– Only sets an end goal, no checkpoints along the way	– Sets clear checkpoints to track progress
– Plans contain no contingency time	– Builds contingency into plans
– Treats all tasks as equally important – fails to prioritise	– Assigns appropriate priorities to issues
... etc	... etc

Once the Assessment Centre is underway, assessors will make copious notes on everything you say and do during each exercise. Afterwards, they will rate you on each competency that has been linked to each particular exercise on the matrix, using a prescribed performance scale. EPSO uses a scale of 1-5 for Linguists and 1-10 for all other profiles.

Following an Assessment Centre a group of assessors will meet to discuss the results for each candidate and reach a group consensus about each candidate's ratings for each competency.

How to Maximise Your Chance of Success

In order to give your best possible performance, I recommend the first step to be researching the details of the Assessment Centre EPSO has prepared for your role or profile – length, activities, etc. This will be either provided in your invitation letter or on the EPSO website and you can expect to find relevant information in the Notice of Competition as well. As with any selection process, thorough preparation is the key to maximising the outcome of your assessment. As a next step, read and consider the general guidance about how to approach Assessment Centres given below, before proceeding to the exercise-specific guidance we provide later.

How to Prepare

- **Invitation Letter**: Read the invitation letter/e-mail carefully as this will tell you what exactly to expect at the centre though in a less detailed form.

- **Research**: Make sure you carry out some research on the EU and EPSO websites and on the EU Test Book and Online EU Training facebook pages, and on the internet in general (e.g. relevant news articles, job discussion boards; see further information in other chapters of this book and recommended websites below).

- **EU Knowledge**: Apart from techniques, I strongly suggest that you try to learn and remember the basics of the EU's history, institutions, decision-making system, structure and policies. This will help you speak the right "language" of an international public administration and you can also relate to the case study much better if you are familiar with the big picture.

- **Questions**: It is also worth thinking of a few questions you can ask if given an opportunity. You might, for example, find yourself seated at lunch beside an assessor: if you have prepared a selection of questions and topics for discussion relating to the role or the EU, you will make a strong impression (even though this will not form part of the formal assessment). If you have a contact in the EU, phone them up and talk to them about the role and what it is like to work there, or you can also find blogs and Facebook pages with such content.

- **EPSO Competencies**: Think about what skills and attributes EPSO is looking for. Review the competency framework, job description or other material sent to you, with the objective of identifying the main skills and attributes required to be successful in the post. Write out a bullet-point checklist of these core capabilities to help fix them clearly in your mind, because the exercises in the Assessment Centre will be designed to measure your abilities in these areas.

- **Local Preparation Resources**: Check with a Brussels-based or your local careers service or training firms, as some run workshops and presentations on how to successfully prepare for Assessment Centres. See if you can practice similar exercises and gain feedback before attending. There are also online training services you can access wherever you are including live and recorded webinars at www.eutraining.eu.

- **CV**: Look over your application and CV to refresh your memory about their contents – a surprising number of candidates fail to refresh their CV or leave unprofessional typos and inconsistencies within. As this is something you can certainly avoid, better do so.

- **Practicalities**: Think about the practical things such as travel arrangements, timings and what you are going to wear. Deciding upon these in advance will reduce stress closer to the time. (As the Assessment Centres are located in Brussels, you should always find out whether public transport companies are planning a strike for the day of your assessment or whether certain sections of the metro or bus lines are expected to be temporarily unavailable; by no means should you risk arriving late in the early morning traffic jam. EPSO itself publishes information on issues affecting access on the exam day, provided they have prior notice.)

- **Introduction**: At the beginning of an Assessment Centre, all delegates are normally asked to introduce themselves and then they may be asked to briefly tell the others about themselves. So it is good practice to prepare a 30-60 second introductory pitch about yourself and your background beforehand. Say something memorable, preferably about an achievement related to the job profile you are aiming at. But do bear in mind that you will only have about 60 seconds maximum, so practise beforehand and keep it short and sharp.

- **Special Needs**: Make it clear well before the session if you have any special needs so that there is a chance to make appropriate amendments to the process. For example, large text versions of the materials should be available for anyone who is visually impaired or extra time may be available for people with dyslexia. Access considerations will be important for wheelchair users. EPSO will be used to making such adaptations and it will only benefit your performance on the day, so do let them know. If you require reading glasses or a hearing aid, please be sure to take these with you.

- **Relax**: Make sure you have a good night's sleep before the Assessment Centre; being tired will impact on your performance. This also means that you should try not to take an early morning flight or train but arrive in town the day before.

- **Know Yourself**: Take some time for self-awareness raising and reflection. Being aware of your own development areas is the first step to being able to address them. How much of an awareness and understanding do you actually have about your behaviour in certain situations? Are you already aware of any development needs? For example, if you're part of a project team charged with completing a task, how do you behave? Do you have a tendency to be nervous and lost for words? Nervous and talk too much? Bossy? Passive? Find it hard to get your point heard? Is your picture of yourself accurate? It may be worth consulting with other people who know you well, to help identify any development points you could work on. Consider what you need to work on in advance of the Assessment Centre and find opportunities to practise and gain feedback on your progress.

- **Positive Thinking**: Maintain a positive frame of mind. Whilst you need to visualise yourself being successful in completing an Assessment Centre to guard against lack of confidence, over confidence can have a detrimental effect on candidates where they fail to pay sufficient attention to the tasks. Perhaps try some thought experiments in advance where you work through various scenarios that could arise at the Assessment Centre and picture how you would deal with those successfully. For example, how would you respond if the person you are having a structured interview with says that they disagree with your viewpoint? This will not only help reduce tension but also assist in dealing with these situations should they arise in reality.

- **Simulation**: Another good method could be simulating certain exercises with a friend or other exam candidates; the help of someone knowledgeable in recruitment could certainly help but even without such person you can test or "challenge" each other in a simulated environment.

- **Communication Skills**: Good communication skills are always helpful, no matter what the exercise. Many applicants attending Assessment Centres can find it quite daunting, especially when they feel that they are in direct competition with so many others, so they tend to keep a low profile at first. But this is an opportunity to get noticed, and it will be looked upon very favourably if you are seen to be mingling with the group when the opportunity arises. Have a think about this when preparing for the day. Prepare some questions that you feel comfortable to ask the other individuals in the group. Aim to talk to as many of the other candidates as you can – including a range of nationalities, ages and genders – before the end of the day because this will be noted, not to mention the valuable pieces of information you can gather as well, including your impressions of the others' skills, background and experience vis-à-vis your own. (An excellent collection of articles and books on the "fine art of small talk" can be found under http://www. debrafine.com/articles.html)

- **Open Questions**: Also, showing that you are confident, friendly and proactive will come across well with the other candidates which may bode well for any activity. Remember that any questions you ask should be open and straightforward to encourage a dialogue. Open questions that start with "what", "why", "how", "where" and "when" should be a good start.

- **Honesty**: Make sure you remember how to use any technology applications and speak all languages that you have mentioned in your CV even if there is little chance these will be tested (if you listed basic knowledge of Croatian to make a better impression, don't risk being caught by an assessor who just started his beginner's course and may wish to test his knowledge with you!).

Tips for the Assessment Itself

- **Dress Code**: Unless otherwise instructed, wear business dress.

- **Contingency Plan**: Build plenty of time into your journey for unexpected delays. Make sure you set off with the full address of your destination and a contact telephone number. If you are delayed and are going to be late, ring to advise the Assessment Centre as soon as you can – though this is definitely not going to compensate for setting out late or unprepared.

- **Checklist**: Ensure you take with you anything that you have been asked to bring, such as photographic ID, supporting documents and your invitation to the Assessment Centre.

- **Instructions**: At the beginning of the assessment, you should receive an initial briefing about the timetable of exercises, location of rooms etc. Prior to each exercise, you will be given instructions describing the task, your role, timeframes, equipment etc. Take time to think and absorb this information. Follow any instructions carefully and ask questions if there is something you do not understand or wish to understand further.

- **Remember Names**: It may be useful to make a note of the names of the EPSO representatives you meet, and when in conversation with assessors or candidates drop those names into conversation.

- **Socialise**: Talk to the other candidates. Remember that you are not necessarily in competition with the other candidates so treat them as allies rather than rivals. *If you all perform well, you might all be successful.* Your performances will all be judged against the competency indicators, not against each other; therefore this is a crucial issue to bear in mind.

- **Approach Each Exercise Afresh**: Do not be dismayed if you struggle in some of the exercises. The Assessment Centre is designed to thoroughly explore all of the attributes for the job, so you might find that you do not perform as well as you hope to in every single exercise. If you feel that you have let yourself down on some of the exercises, do not dwell on your mistakes and agonise over them, because that will create a negative attitude that might bring down your overall performance. Just accept it, and concentrate fully on the next task, seeing this as a new opportunity to demonstrate your potential. Remember that many candidates will have a slow start, and very few, if any, will perform well on all of the tasks. You can still score highly over the whole event, even if you have performed badly in one exercise.

- **Be Yourself**: It's much easier and fairer to be yourself, rather than putting on an act. It's very easy to fall into the trap of making assumptions about what the assessor is looking for in a new recruit and trying to second-guess what they want to hear or see. The best approach is to be yourself at all times. It has been proven that when you behave normally, rather than trying to create a false image of yourself, you will come across as being a lot more relaxed and confident, and will therefore present a better picture of yourself. If "the real you" is not what EPSO is looking for in that particular competition, the profile is obviously not meant for you, so perhaps you should reconsider which other EPSO profile or position your skills, style, background and aspirations make you best suited to.

- **Stay Calm**: Remember it is normal to feel nervous before the day. A shaky voice or clammy hands are not unusual symptoms and therefore it is recommended that you arrive ten to fifteen minutes early to give yourself time to relax. Be polite to everyone you meet. Stay calm, focused and positive throughout the Assessment Centre.

- **Lunch Break**: You are not being formally observed during breaks and lunch, but you should remain professional at all times. Do not over-indulge, become flippant or over-confident. Take the opportunity to ask questions, talk to other candidates or assessors and show a strong interest in the position.

- **Mobile Phone**: Turn off your mobile phone (and make silent any other electronic device that beeps) before the start of the assessment session.

- **Time Limit**: The exercises will have strict time limits. Make sure to bring a watch with you and check the clock carefully during timed exercises – over-running is not allowed. Try to work through the tasks quickly but accurately. Use all of the time allocated to you and make sure to plan your time prudently before starting an exercise (e.g. if you have 40 minutes available, split it into 10-25-5 minute segments to allow enough time for an outline, drafting and revision). Even if you have finished the task, take the final few minutes to review your response (or preparation work in the case of preparing to give a presentation).

- **Decision Timescale**: EPSO should let you know when they expect to have made a decision (usually within 2 months of the last day of the exam) and how you will be notified of the end result but do not be scared to ask if this has not been made clear.

- **Positive Ending**: Remember to thank the assessors for their time before you leave.

After the Assessment

- **Enquiries**: If you do not hear from EPSO by the deadline stated (or two to three weeks later at the latest), write or telephone to enquire whether a decision has been made.

- **Reserve List**: If you are placed on the reserve list, your name will appear on the EPSO website and be published in the Official Journal of the EU. Once this happens, you are eligible to be recruited by any EU institution (see more details in the relevant chapter on the recruitment procedure and flagging system).

- **Job Offer**: Once you receive an offer, make sure it is the right role and job profile for you before accepting. Take into consideration the following; they may all impact on what makes the offer you accept the right decision for you.

- **Job Content** (while this is largely determined by the exam you are sitting, it may nevertheless differ greatly depending on what the actual job is, so it's worth asking for more details and trying to search online for this profile; it is also worth checking the Directorate General's or institution's organigram online to see the type of positions that exist there).

- **Location** (are you willing to relocate to Luxembourg? Or to a Commission delegation in e.g. Sri Lanka, Japan or elsewhere?)

- **Working Hours** (while the Staff Regulations of EU officials have strict rules on working hours, the intensity can vary according to the job profile; if your unit deals with for example financial affairs or external trade, it may require more intensive day-to-day work than some other administrative job profiles)

- **Salary Level** (this is almost exclusively determined by the competition's grade that you were sitting for, though smaller adjustments called "steps" within a given grade are possible, based on your work experience)

- **Mobility Requirement** (if the work is in the European Parliament or in another institution but dealing with Parliamentary affairs, you may have to spend four days a month in Strasbourg (though for Assistants this is a less common requirement); or if you work for e.g. the Commission's Directorate General for Trade, you may be required to travel extensively)

- Impression of the **organisational culture** of the institution or directorate

- **Keep Rejection in Perspective**: If you are unsuccessful – do not take it personally! You are simply not the most suitable applicant for that specific position at the current time; you can of course apply again for an EU exam any time in the future.

- **Feedback**: EPSO provides feedback to all AC candidates and this is an essential part of the Assessment Centre process. Even if you do not get the job, remember that attending the Assessment Centre is a significant learning experience for you, and feedback can provide invaluable insights for the future. There is also no harm in using the day as a networking opportunity, with both the panel and the other delegates. Your career is a long path and you never know when or where these people may turn up in the future.

- **Self-development**: Learn from your mistakes. Once the dust has settled after the Assessment Centre, take stock of the situation. Summon up the courage to be brutally honest with yourself: make a list of areas with room for improvement, and then take appropriate action. Knowing yourself is one of the keys to success, because if you can identify the gaps in your knowledge (e.g. you realise that you need to know more about Microsoft Excel or the basics of online security), pinpoint the skills you need to gain or develop (e.g. improve your time management skills or work better in a team under pressure), and then rectify these deficiencies by attending training or enrolling in various courses, you will greatly improve your attractiveness and value to the EU and other organisations in your chosen field. Once you have addressed these areas, you will enter the next Assessment Centre with much greater confidence, and greater chance of success.

Lastly, assessors do understand that Assessment Centres can be daunting and will do all that they can to put you at ease. It may help to bear in mind that it is only those people who have passed through the preliminary selection stages and those that EPSO thinks are more likely to successfully carry out the job that are asked to attend – so be confident and positive. Indeed, the Assessment Centre as a whole should be viewed as a two-way process. Use it as an opportunity to find out what you want to know about the role and the organisation. Judge the extent to which you enjoy the tasks you are required to perform and the extent to which you gel with the EPSO or EU representatives you meet.

2. The Structured Interview

Description and Purpose

The interview must surely be the most widely-used selection tool. Its use is based on the idea that past behaviour is a good indicator of future performance. Most organisations now include at least one interview at the Assessment Centre, even when there has been a previous interview stage.

Interviews come in a variety of formats and can be one-to-one or panel, formal or informal, general or technical, competence-based or biographically-based, structured or more open and flexible. The interview is generally classed by assessors as a "secondary" source of evidence. This means that it carries less weight in the overall decision as performance is based upon the candidate's own self-report (rather than directly observed behaviours). This also means that it is the easiest exercise to perform well in, so this really is your best opportunity to shine.

The interview format used by EPSO is described as a "competency-based structured interview". It contains questions related to three or four of the competencies that are relevant to the role being recruited for. EPSO states that a structured interview will be used as part of the recruitment process for all EU institution roles.

The fact that the interview is "structured" means that it will follow a consistent format across all candidates. This is in contrast to a more fluid, unstructured exploration of a candidate's CV that other organisations use. Research suggests that taking a structured approach offers the best chance to predict future behaviour. In practice, this means that everyone will receive the same instructions; the interviews will be the same length and will usually focus on the same competency areas (and thus cover the same questions).

The interviewer will ask you to talk about example situations where you have demonstrated the relevant competencies. For example, a question for a generic "Teamwork" competency may be as follows:

- *"Tell me about a time when you had to deal with conflict within a team you were part of"*

The interviewer is then likely to ask follow-up probing questions in order to explore your responses more fully. The exact probes asked will vary depending upon your answer to the starter question. For example:

- *"What caused the conflict?"*

- *"What did you do?"*

- *"What was the outcome?"*

- *"With hindsight, what would you do differently?"*

How to Prepare

Consider the types of questions you may be asked based upon the previously outlined

EPSO competencies and have a think about relevant situations you can draw upon from education, work and leisure activities. A helpful way to do this may be to ensure that you have a good, detailed example to fill each of the four quadrants below. This is a completed example, but you are strongly advised to create your own.

		EXPERIENCE FOCUS	
		PEOPLE	**TASK**
EXPERIENCE TYPE	*POSITIVE*	E.g. • *Working successfully with team on final year project* • *(EPSO competencies – Working With Others, Analysis and Problem Solving, Prioritising and Organising)*	E.g. • *Project managing end of year university ball* • *(EPSO competencies – Prioritising and Organising, Delivering Quality and Results, Resilience)*
	NEGATIVE	E.g. • *Relationship troubles with other charity workers.* • *(EPSO competencies – Communicating, Working With Others)*	E.g. • *Data analysis for end of year project – not knowing the correct statistical techniques.* • *(EPSO competencies – Learning and Development, Resilience)*

Consider Your Experiences: First, consider and write down your key achievements and general life experiences in a structured manner. Which of those were task focused and which were people focused? By task focused, I mean those experiences that were primarily related to resolving a problem or issue or delivering a result (such as launching a marketing campaign or compiling a risk analysis) that involved minimal contact with others. By people focused, I mean those experiences that had a large component of interactions with others such as a joint drafting exercise, a team meeting that you coordinated etc.

Find Positive and Negative Examples: Then, try to consider experiences of both a positive and a less positive nature or outcome (and how you learned and grew from the negative experience). This is valuable in case you are asked to describe a time when things did not go so well (e.g. "please tell me about a mistake you made at your current workplace and describe how you reacted to it"), and avoids you becoming flustered or put off by the question. For these types of questions, you need to ensure that you can talk about how you either overcame the negative experience on that occasion, or have done so in subsequent similar situations.

Link with Competencies: Next, make a note against each example, indicating which of the EPSO competencies they are relevant to. Using this method, you should have a comprehensive list of examples for the interview. If you have had previous interviews for other posts at other employers, consider how you could have improved your approach and how you could have answered certain questions more effectively.

Prepare for Follow-up Questions: Be aware that sometimes an interviewer will simply ask you for a second example once you have already described one situation. This is designed to find out if a candidate only has one "star answer" for a competency. Make sure that you are not caught out by this and have multiple examples in mind. Prepare answers to classic "difficult" questions such as "what are your biggest weaknesses"?

Further sample questions can include:

- *What is your main motivation for working in the EU?*

- *What makes you suitable for an EU post?*

- *What role or position do you see yourself in, in 5-10 years?*

- *Can you describe situations where you acted in a pro-active manner?*

- *What would you do if you discovered that your colleagues were breaking some administrative rules?*

- *Describe a stressful situation in your current job. How did you react to it?*

- *What does success mean to you?*

Your Questions: Although in most cases this opportunity will not arise, you should nonetheless consider what questions you may wish to ask the interviewer about the EU institution and the role if you get the chance. Be mindful of the impression your questions give. Making your first question one that enquires about holidays or the next pay rise may give the interviewer the impression that you are not intrinsically interested in either the EU institution or the role.

Likewise, try not to ask questions to which answers could easily be obtained by a bit of basic research (e.g. what a certain institution deals with). Asking about the organisation's future strategies (such as a unit's future tasks after the changes of the Lisbon Treaty) in a particular area may be a more suitable question. It is a good idea to have some questions prepared (even if you already have the answers): it will show you are keen to learn about the organisation from the interviewer and will allow them to feel good about themselves when providing you with the information you seek.

Such questions could refer to the interviewer's experience about how the EU's continuous enlargement has changed the institutions' organisational culture; you may ask about the changes in policy focus triggered by the global financial crisis; or you may choose to ask about life in Brussels (Luxembourg or elsewhere) for young families etc.

You could also try a few more testing questions such as how they differentiate the opportunities they offer from those available at other organisations or what they think the most challenging part of the job profile of an Administrator or Assistant is. However, only use questions where you have a genuine interest in the answer – avoid questions that are merely designed to impress, as you may not be able to follow up with further thoughtful questions or responses if the interviewer gives a fuller response than you expected them to.

Tips for the Assessment itself

- **Introduction**: The interviewer is going to inform you which competencies are to be covered during the interview. If you have become familiar with the EPSO competencies in advance, then you can ensure that your responses are tailored around the competency under discussion and that you provide relevant answers that help both your assessment and the assessor's job as well. For example, if you are asked a question under the Prioritising and Organising competency, do not spend a long time describing your teamwork: focus your answers on the planning, prioritising, monitoring and organising-type behaviours that you displayed at the time. At the start of the interview, the assessor will give you two minutes to introduce yourself. Some candidates choose to do this from a CV focused angle ("this is what I've done so far"), while others apply a motivational perspective ("I'm very keen to work for the EU").

- **Active Listening**: You should listen carefully to what you are being asked; it is perfectly acceptable for you to take a moment to think before responding (you can always say to the interviewer: "If I understand your question correctly, you are asking if […]. Let me think about that for a moment…" which wins you time to think the issue over).

- **Clarification**: If you are unsure what information a question is aimed at getting from you, ask for clarification: "could you please clarify what you'd like to learn about me here?"

- **Respond to the Question**: Keep your answers focused (e.g. when asked about your most recent work experience regarding workplace conflicts, do not start by introducing your CV and professional background or how you got your most recent job; keep your focus on the question with only a few words on the overall context). Begin with a broad outline of the situation, and then proceed to give details about what behaviours and personal qualities you displayed rather than spending a lot of time describing technical details (for example "I arranged… I instructed… I persuaded…" are all good, but avoid going into details such as "I used my knowledge of EU Employment policies, specifically regarding the working time directive that deals with the following list of issues…[long explanation follows]").

- **Personal Achievements**: The interviewer is interested in what you did personally, so make sure this is clear and avoid using collective terms such as "we (made a project plan)" or "the group (came up with the solution)" or "company X launched (an initiative)". Instead, make statements such as "I (suggested we begin with a project plan)". This can be hard if the situation you are describing was genuinely a group process, but you should always be clear about the role you played in helping a group arrive at its decision. At the same time, avoid giving the impression of being an overly confident or egocentric candidate.

- **Respond Concisely**: In order to allow the interviewer time to probe your response if required, focus your answers. For example, if you were responsible for a particular piece of legal translation work, outline the situation in around five sentences ("I was given the task of ensuring the timely and precise translation of a tender procedure"), what you did in another five ("I created a project plan and milestones, identified the team members, outlined the work methodology…") and the outcome in another five ("we managed to deliver the translation within deadline"). The interviewer is then free to probe you around the specific details they are interested in. If you are not sure whether you have given enough information, you can always ask. If your answers are too verbose, you may damage your chances because if what you are saying is irrelevant to the competency (e.g. you explained in detail the IT applications used for the translation while the question essentially focused on project management skills), the interviewer will have less time to ask questions about the areas they really need to understand. In short, keep your focus strictly on the management and interpersonal side of the events.

- **Confidentiality**: Do not disclose the name of the company or organisation you mention in your responses; it is enough to say "when I worked for a firm" or "when I was a project manager" unless the interviewer wishes to know more. Similarly, never disclose the full name of a person with whom you had a conflict or use him or her as an example to describe a situation.

- **Stick to the Point**: Resist the temptation to describe a situation in unnecessary detail (e.g. "I had a Spanish colleague who had just moved to Latvia where he was travelling in neighbouring countries almost every weekend") unless certain facts are relevant because they affected or explained a certain behaviour you wish to emphasize.

- **Methodology and Motivation**: When asked "how did you respond to this situation", aim to provide an answer that concentrates on the methodology or motivation side ("I understood there is a tension between us so I tried to discuss the situation face to face") instead of describing unrelated facts ("I proposed we have lunch in the company canteen as it had just opened on the sixth floor"); when asked "how did you facilitate the teamwork" avoid fact-driven but less relevant answers such as "I heard from the IT department that Microsoft had come out with a great program that runs on Windows XP, so given that we had this operating system, it sounded like a good idea". Instead, focus on your behaviours, solutions, methods, motivation, feelings and ideas.

- **Taking Notes**: It is important to allow the interviewer to write down as much information as possible in order to assess your answers afterwards. Watch the interviewer's note taking. If they seem to be having trouble keeping up with your answers, you should slow down, pause and allow them to catch up. Conversely, if they have stopped taking notes, or put their pen down, this indicates they are likely to have all the information they need on for this competency *or* you are currently giving them detail that is irrelevant. Pause, and perhaps ask if what you are telling them is useful and relevant.

- **Be Honest**: Interviewers are trained to probe your responses; if you are embellishing the truth then they may well find out as you begin to falter under increasingly detailed questioning.

- **Trick Questions**: You will seldom, if ever, be asked "trick" questions in a professionally run interview.

- **EU Jargon**: Explain any jargon or acronyms you use. Avoid using slang expressions. For example, if you are sitting a competition for general administrators and you use the term "absorption capacity", make sure you show that you understand it by explaining its meaning in plain terms; similarly, if you are sitting a specialist competition for e.g. data protection officials, your interviewer may not be an expert in that field even if he or she is an EU official, therefore try to read the interviewer's non-verbal cues regarding their knowledge of the field and adjust your vocabulary accordingly. Similarly, if you talk about previous work and use industry jargon such as "the PHP programmer had a conflict with the Java scripter", make sure you do not overload the interviewer with expressions they may not be familiar with.

- **Stay Calm**: Aggressive interviewers are probably just acting and looking for your response; staying calm and professional is the best way to respond to this.

- **Loyalty**: Never belittle or give away secrets of any past or present employers – the interviewer will see this as unprofessional and be concerned about you doing the same if you were to leave the role you are applying for. For example, avoid saying something like "I left my last company because it was run by people who were incompetent".

- **If Stuck:** If you find you are completely stuck for an answer and do not have an example to offer, then it is worthwhile trying to make one of your other experiences "fit" the question if at all possible. You may begin by saying "I have never experienced precisely that situation, but let me tell you about a similar situation when..." Even if your response does not help you on this particular competency, it should count as further evidence towards other competencies covered by the interview, not to mention your resourcefulness.

- **Body Language**: Consider your body language during the interview: this is one of the key aspects interviewers will observe and weigh in almost as much as your words. Keep your arms unfolded and adopt a generally "open" posture. Lean slightly forward in the chair and maintain good eye contact with the interviewer (even if they themselves break eye contact to make notes). Smile, nod and repeat back their questions to show you are listening. Be careful of your body language "leaking signals" that you are uncomfortable with a question or subject area: for example, avoid pained expressions when asked a difficult question – look interested, motivated and positive instead. A good exercise can be a simulation with a friend who, while asking you questions, takes notes on your body language and you analyse it together afterwards. You may also wish to have yourself recorded and then try to improve your overall performance; a professional coach can also be of great help.

- **Flash Cards**: Some interviewers may allow you to refer to "prompt cards" (or "flash cards") during the interview. It is worthwhile preparing some of these in advance: you can always check with the interviewer if these are acceptable at the beginning of the session. Keep them short and focused: one or two words bullet-pointed against each of the competencies to help remind you of relevant examples. Do not fall into the trap of writing out examples verbatim and then simply reading your notes out loud during the interview: this will not impress the interviewer and will make you less agile and able to respond to follow-up probing questions.

SAMPLE STRUCTURED INTERVIEW

In the following section, we have provided a sample structured interview of the type that you will be facing as part of the EPSO recruitment process. We have begun with an outline of the typical topics to be covered in the introduction to the interview. We have then gone on to provide examples of the type of questions you may be faced with, followed by all competency areas we identified that are reflective of the types of areas looked for as part of the EPSO recruitment process. It should be stressed that these are of course not the exact questions you will be facing as part of your structured interview; however, they should be very useful in understanding the likely question format. They will also help you consider how you may be able to best phrase your skills and experience to fit with the way these types of interview are structured. After the questions, we have provided example candidate answers to two of the questions so that you can actually have a go at assessing a response against typical assessor guidelines and see how your rating compares to that of an actual assessor.

Interview Introduction

When the interview starts, you will be given a short introduction by the interviewer. This is designed to give you information about how the interview will run, put you at ease and allow you to ask any questions you have about the interview process. It is unlikely that there will be time to discuss the role in depth at the structured interview stage: check with the interviewer whether such questions are appropriate if you wish, but they may best be saved for another time.

The interviewer will cover the following topics in the introduction:

- **Time Available**: Given the large number of EPSO candidates, it will likely be around 40 minutes. The interviewer may tell you that they will move you on if they feel they have enough information on a particular competency. Some interviewers are better at this than others, so make it easy for them by keeping your answers concise and then asking them if they would like any more information.

- **Definition of a structured interview**: This will introduce the format of the session and explain what a competency is. They may describe the EPSO competencies at this point.

- **Notes**: The interviewer is likely to inform you that they will be taking notes throughout and to ask you to excuse them if they break eye contact.

- **"Warm up" Questions**: Before the formal competency-based questions begin, you will be asked some more general questions designed to "warm you up" before the interview proper begins. These may or may not be assessed. Questions like "Tell me about your studies" or "What was the subject of your dissertation" are less likely to be assessed than a question like "Tell me what motivated you to apply for this role".

Questioning

This sample interview is split into seven competency areas. Each competency has two "starter questions": these would be asked of all candidates. They are then followed by a selection of probing follow-up questions. These are designed to not only gain more detail about an example, but also to really test those candidates who have fabricated their answers: it is likely they will falter under this level of detailed questioning.

Competency Area One: Learning and Development

This competency area is concerned with how well a candidate utilises the power of learning. This includes learning and developing personally, as well as managing the learning of the organisation.

Question One: Tell me about a time that you proactively decided to expand your knowledge of a certain subject.
[Possible situations to think of: you were assigned a task by your boss and you did extra in-depth research online, interviewed industry experts and wrote studies on the topic out of your own personal curiosity; you signed up to a course outside work as you were so motivated to learn about a subject; you volunteered to give lectures on a topic and prepared a presentation about it.]

Follow-up Probes:

- Why was it important to do so?
- What approach did you take? Why?
- What difficulties did you encounter?
- How successful were you?
- What would you have done differently, with hindsight?
- How have you applied this since?

Question Two: Tell me about a time you received valid negative feedback about the work you completed.
[Possible situations to think of: you were not precise enough in your written report and your superior called your attention to the problem; you failed to fully respect or negligently overlooked a certain rule which caused some loss to your company; you did not act or talk properly in a professional meeting and your superior discussed ways of improvement with you; you did not organise your work efficiently and you missed a deadline or forgot about a task which caused delays or tensions in the team.]

Follow-up Probes:

- How did you find out how the other person felt about your work?
- How did you feel when you received the feedback?
- How did you respond?
- With the benefit of hindsight, how might you have handled the situation differently?
- What further feedback have you received on this area since that time?

Competency Area Two: Planning and Organising

This competency area is concerned with how well a candidate manages time and resources in order to achieve their objectives. It includes both initiating projects and keeping them running to schedule once they are underway.

Question One: Tell me about a time when an unexpected problem arose during a project that you were responsible for resolving.
[Possible issues to think of: a certain note or background briefing you were asked to prepare and a crit-

ical input was not provided to you in time; you were requested to organise an event and unforeseen extra expenses arose; a computer or server collapsed in a critical period of executing a certain task; a person whose contribution was crucial to the project refused to participate or declined to take part; personal conflicts within a team prevented the project from timely and accurate delivery.]

Follow-up Probes:

- How did you become aware of the problem?
- What was its potential impact on the project?
- How did you respond?
- What was the outcome?
- What feedback did you receive on the project?
- With the benefit of hindsight, how could you have improved your handling of the situation?
- How have you applied this learning since?

Question Two: Tell me about a particular project or task you were involved with in which taking a planned approach was essential.
[Possible issues to think of: you were asked to organise a consultation or conference and this required practical planning efforts; you were asked to create a strategic financial or marketing forecast for your organisation; the completion of a compliance or a special qualification course while working full time required in-depth time management and planning; a certain project such as redecorating a house or a work-related issue in which the sequence of steps and creation of milestones was of crucial importance and it required proper step-by-step planning.]

Follow-up Probes:

- What factors did you need to take into account in your planning?
- How did you do this?
- How did you track progress?
- What was the outcome?
- What feedback did you receive?
- With the benefit of hindsight, what would you have done differently?
- How have you applied this learning since?

Competency Area Three: Resilience (Coping Under Pressure)

This competency area is concerned with how a candidate responds to pressure at work. It includes the extent to which they display their feelings and their general levels of optimism. It also measures how well they respond to changing circumstances.

Question One: Tell me about a time you were working under intense time pressure to complete a project or task.
[Possible issues to think of: an event that had to be ready by a certain non-negotiable deadline (anniversary, Christmas party, national holiday, exam); a business project or legal obligation

where any delay would have caused significant loss of revenue or reputation or downgrading in rating (tax report deadline, application for a tender, legal obligations)]

Follow-up Probes:

- How had this situation arisen?

- How did it make you feel?

- How did this situation affect your behaviour?

- What was the outcome?

- With the benefit of hindsight, how could you have approached the situation differently?

- How have you applied this learning in subsequent similar situations?

Question Two: Tell me about a time that you felt particularly disappointed or let down in a work situation.
[Possible issues to think of: a promise regarding your possible promotion was not kept; a work input you really counted on did not arrive at all or came too late; you expected a certain project to be completed in time but it was not; you had an assumption (that you would get a better office room or you would be asked to take part in a new project team or you would be sent on your company's annual bonus trip) and expected it to happen in a certain way but it did not, thus you felt exposed (and possibly a little naïve).]

Follow-up Probes:

- How did your emotions manifest themselves?

- How did this affect your behaviour?

- How did others react to your behaviour?

- How did you "move on" from this situation?

- With the benefit of hindsight, how might you have handled this situation differently?

- How have you applied this learning in subsequent similar situations?

Competency Area Four: Working in a Team

This competency area is concerned with how effectively a candidate works with other people – be they colleagues, officials from other EU institutions or other stakeholders. It measures co-operative tendencies as well as general interpersonal sensitivity. It also covers how effectively a candidate may utilise the diverse skills and backgrounds of others.

Question One: Tell me about a time when you experienced a difficulty in a working relationship with someone
[Possible issues to think of: you had a conflict with someone above or below you in the hierarchy (manager or secretary) due to a misconception of your position or role in the organisation; a colleague seemed jealous of your job profile or your benefits or the way you were treated by your superiors and thus harboured negative feelings about you; due to miscommunication, conflicts arose in a project team working under tense circumstances and heavy time pressure.]

Follow-up Probes:

- Had the relationship always been difficult? If not, what prompted the change?

- What made it difficult?
- How did you respond to the situation?
- How did the other party respond?
- What was the ultimate outcome?
- What feedback did you receive from others on how you handled the situation?
- With the benefit of hindsight, how would you have approached the situation differently?
- How have you applied this learning in subsequent similar situations?

Question Two: Tell me about a time when you needed to work as part of a team to accomplish an objective.
[Possible issues to think of: the organisation of an event or delivery of a development project was assigned to you and two other colleagues to work in a team; you were part of the team or you were asked to lead it; conflicts and management techniques required handling team members who were more senior than you and did not accept your authority; you had different concepts or ideas than the coordinator or leader of the team; some team members failed to deliver their share in the proper quality or in time and the way you handled this; rivalry between the team members.]

Follow-up Probes:

- What role did you play in the team?
- To what extent did you tailor your approach towards different group members?
- How did you decide on decisions facing the group?
- What differences of opinion arose? How did you deal with these?
- What did you do to facilitate the teamwork process?
- What was the outcome?
- With the benefit of hindsight, what would you have done differently?
- How have you applied this learning to subsequent similar situations?

Competency Area Five: Communicating with Clarity

This competency area is concerned with how effectively a candidate communicates facts and opinions to others. It includes both oral and written communication. Effective communication is measured not just by clarity and accuracy, but also by successfully gaining the interest and attention of the audience and by adapting to suit their needs.

Question One: Tell me about a time that it was important that your communication captured the attention and interest of another party.
[Possible issues to think of: you had to make an important presentation to secure buy-in or funding from others; you needed to convey important health and safety information; your communication was going to resolve an important training needs gap; you were facing a particularly cynical or stubborn audience who had proven to be resistant to the idea you were presenting in the past.]

Follow-up Probes:

- How did you know what would appeal to the other party?
- What tactics did you employ?

- What reaction did you get? How do you know?
- What was the outcome?
- With the benefit of hindsight, what would you have done differently?
- How have you applied this learning to subsequent similar situations?

Question Two: Tell me about a time when you had to communicate a complex concept in layman's terms.
[Possible issues to think of: you were explaining technical aspects of your role to a non-expert audience during a job interview, during a networking event or at a conference; your manager wished to know the impact of a technical issue without hearing the detail behind it; a new starter in your department required training in a new system or process; you were seeking buy-in from stakeholders to the value of what you were proposing, but they would not respond well to lots of technical details.]

Follow-up Probes:

- How did you know the other party would find the content complex?
- How did you approach the task?
- Why did you decide on the approach you took?
- To what extent do you feel you were successful? How do you know?
- With the benefit of hindsight, what would you have done differently?
- How have you applied this learning to subsequent similar situations?

Competency Area Six: Analysing and Problem Solving

This competency area is concerned with how a candidate approaches the resolution of complex issues. A systematic approach to gathering relevant informaion and then formulating solutions that are both innovative and pragmatic is important. It also includes the creation of multiple alternative courses of action where possible.

Question One: Tell me about a time that you had a large amount of information to analyse.
[Possible issues to think of: you were new to a role and needed to assimilate lots of information relating to your daily tasks, organisational structure, systems and stakeholders quickly; you were preparing a report for your superior or a stakeholder about a particular issue where it was important to consult a wide range of sources and media; you were responsible for financially reporting on the performance of a venture; you personally conducted a research project that entailed large amounts of data (e.g. survey results, observations).]

Follow-up Probes:

- What type of information was it?
- How did you approach the task?
- How did you distinguish essential from non-essential information?
- To what extent did you trust the information you were presented with? How did this affect your approach?
- How did you feel while conducting the task?
- What was the outcome?

- With the benefit of hindsight, what would you have done differently?
- How have you applied this learning to subsequent similar situations?

Question Two: Tell me about a time when you successfully resolved a key problem or issue that you were facing at work.
[Possible issues to think of: a persistent problem with an inefficient process was overcome by an innovative solution you suggested; a project encountered an obstacle that could have threatened to stop the project in its tracks but you found a way round it no-one else had thought of; you were tasked with finding ways of making a task more commercially efficient; a team you managed were facing persistent absence issues which you successfully investigated and then resolved.]

Follow-up Probes:

- What made this problem an important one to resolve?
- What did you suggest? How did you arrive at this suggestion?
- How innovative would you rate your idea as being?
- How well did it work in practice?
- What feedback did you receive?
- With the benefit of hindsight, what would you have done differently?
- How have you applied this learning to subsequent similar situations?

Competency Area Seven: Delivery and Results

This competency area is concerned with how effectively a candidate meets their work objectives to a high standard of quality. It covers the extent to which they are proactive and thrive in challenging situations. It also includes the extent to which candidates follow relevant rules and regulations where appropriate.

Question One: Describe to me your most challenging work project to date.
[Possible issues to think of: a challenging situation in which you took the initiative and acted proactively to achieve a good project outcome; a project you managed where you made sure procedures were followed and/or quality standards were met in the face of pressure to do otherwise; a recent example of when you took responsibility for meeting stretching project milestones and objectives.]

Follow-up Probes:

- What made it challenging?
- How did this make you feel and act?
- How did your behaviour and attitude compare to others in the same situation?
- What were the delivery expectations? To what extent were these met?
- What feedback did you receive?
- With the benefit of hindsight, what would you have done differently?
- How have you applied this learning to subsequent similar situations?

Question Two: Tell me about a time when you had to make a judgement call between meeting a deadline and quality of the end product.
[Possible issues to think of: a time when you took on responsibility for an existing project that was running behind schedule, and had to evaluate what was essential and what could be done to a lesser

degree in order to meet the deadline; a time when the client's requirements changed but the deadline remained, and you had to balance quality of the additional output requirements with meeting the strict deadline.]

Follow-up Probes:

- Why was such a judgement call necessary?
- What did you decide?
- What was the impact of your decision?
- What steps did you take to mitigate the impact of this?
- What feedback did you receive?
- With the benefit of hindsight, what would you have done differently?
- How have you applied this learning to subsequent similar situations?

Summaries, Ending the Interview

After each competency is completed, the interviewer is likely to summarise your examples back to you, to check that they have understood correctly. This is your chance to correct any misunderstanding or add in additional important information that has been left out – so listen carefully. They may also ask if you have anything else to add around this competency. Only give them extra information if you have a really good example that you simply could not give through the questions they asked – otherwise, this could cut into the time you have available on other competencies.

Once all the questions have been asked, the interviewer may again offer you the chance to contribute final examples (although this is less common): again, only do so if you have a relevant, fantastic example that you were not able to give in answer to the questions posed. Keep it short and simple – the interviewer will ask for more information if they need it. Assuming there are no opportunities for questioning the interviewer about the role at this stage, you should thank them for their time and move onto the next exercise in your schedule.

Sample Candidate Responses

In this section, we have included sample summary transcripts for a candidate's answers around two of the competencies. Read their responses and then using the scoring criteria we provide afterwards, try to decide how well you think the candidate has performed. Then, read the Assessment of Performance section to see how your views compare to those of a professional assessor. In each of the examples that follow we have focused on the candidate's response to the question and follow up probes and, for ease of reading, have omitted the probes themselves from the text.

Competency Area Four: Working in a Team

> **Question:** Tell me about a time when you experienced a difficulty in a working relationship with someone
>
> Sample Candidate Response: Let me have a think…. Yes, when I was working as a project manager for company X, there was a colleague in particular who I struggled to build a really good relationship with.
>
> *continued on the next page…*

He was the same level in the hierarchy as me but I was relatively new to the firm. Despite my behaving in what I felt was a professional and competent manner, this person used to frequently make little sarcastic comments to me and did not seek to include me when interesting new pieces of work came up. I got on well with other members of staff, so I don't know why there was a problem with him in particular. I did make attempts to try and help the relationship, for example I would include him on emails when I suggested a social evening out to a nice Japanese restaurant. However, it all came to be an open conflict when a project report we had been assigned to work on together was not delivered by the deadline. This person had not informed me of some critical information, which meant I had much shorter timescales than I realised; I was really frustrated especially because I was supposed to go on holiday after handing in the report. When this happened, I made sure that my manager was aware of the background to the situation and I told my colleague I was disappointed he had not kept me informed as communication is key to the type of work we are involved in.

Things did change a little after this incident. Even though I was really upset, I decided to change tactic and stopped inviting him to social events, but instead set up review meetings and milestones in our diaries whenever we were working on a project together to make sure no important points got missed. Overall, I think it was just one of those things – you can't expect to get on with everyone, can you? We were very different people and I think we now have a professional relationship: but we will never be best of friends or anything.

Scoring Criteria

For this competency, the following would be indicators of a **positive response**:

- Includes relevant others in decision making

- Praises the contributions of others

- Works co-operatively across organisational areas

- Actively listens to others

- Effectively utilises the diverse range of backgrounds, skills and motivations of their team

- Shows a concern for the emotional state of others

The following would be indicators of a **poor response**:

- Makes decisions in isolation without consulting others

- Ignores or belittles the contributions of others

- Adopts a silo mentality, does not co-operate with other organisational areas

- Ignores others

- Works with others without regard to individual differences in background, skills or motivations

- Shows no concern for the emotional state of others

Assessment of performance: So, how well did you feel the example candidate did? Overall, assessors would be likely to grade this as a poorer response against the scoring criteria. On the positive side, the candidate did make an attempt (however small) to build the relationship through the social event invitations and the candidate also put measures in place to improve future communication. However, there was far more scope for the candidate to have openly explored the other party's feelings and motives for behaving in the way that he did. The candidate allowed the interpersonal relationship issue to get in the way of collaborative decision making, which ultimately had a detrimental effect on delivery.

Competency Area Two: Planning and Organising

Question: Tell me about a particular project or task you were involved with, in which taking a planned approach was essential

Sample Candidate Response: In my last role, I was given responsibility for organising the translation of a range of promotional literature for a forthcoming international conference on global migration. I needed to consider a lot of factors such as when I was going to speak to the original copywriters, completing the actual translations, how to identify and approach peer-reviewers, setting up the back-translation process and allowing time for amendments. I decided that the best thing to do would be to set up a project plan in Microsoft Project. I identified each of the required tasks and I highlighted where the potential pitfalls were. I set deadlines and checkpoints but also built in additional time to allow for unforeseen events that could arise. I made sure to assign responsibilities and stakeholders to each of the tasks.

I did find that certain events arose that threw the plan off a little. For example, the back-translation took longer than expected which reduced the time I had available for amendments. I have to admit, this got me rather worried as I feel the final stage is the most critical for identifying those final errors that can detract from the quality of a professional finished product. As a result, I asked the back-translators to send me through their work in sections immediately as it was completed, rather than waiting until it was all ready; so that I could also begin the review and amendment process immediately. In hindsight, this was not such a good idea, because as the back translation progressed I found that they would frequently revisit their earlier work in the light of the more recent translations and terminology and send me over multiple updated versions which became difficult to track. If I were faced with a similar situation in the future, I would simply work extended hours once the back translation was complete, or perhaps see if I could bring on extra human or IT resource.

In the end, the promotional leaflets were ready by the deadline and met with great feedback from my manager and conference delegates.

Scoring Criteria

For this competency, the following would be indicators of a **positive response**:

- Prioritises tasks appropriately
- Sets realistic deadlines and milestones
- Monitors progress
- Adapts to changes in plans effectively
- Manages own workload effectively
- Conducts preparation in advance

The following would be indicators of a **poor response**:

- Makes incorrect prioritisation judgements
- Fails to set realistic deadlines and milestones
- Allows projects to continue without monitoring
- Becomes flustered and ineffective when plans need to change
- Works inefficiently or becomes overwhelmed with workload
- Fails to prepare in advance

Assessment of performance: Overall, assessors would be likely to grade this as a good response against the scoring criteria. On the positive side, the candidate adopted a highly planned approach to the task by identifying the key stages, setting up monitoring procedures and allowing contingency time. The project was also delivered by the deadline and met with positive feedback. There was, however, some indication that the candidate panicked when faced with changing circumstances and worked in a less efficient manner, even though they did recognise this and said they would follow a different approach in the future.

3.   The In-Tray Exercise

As discussed earlier, Assistants have to pass practical skills tests that include various tasks relating to attention to detail, IT skills and computer literacy. Given its complexity and highly challenging nature, we focus here on the so-called in-tray (or its computer-based version, the e-tray) exercise that aims to gauge candidates' organising, planning and multi-tasking skills in a simulated work environment.

Description and Purpose

In-tray (also called "in-basket") exercises ask you to assume a particular role in a ficti-tious company or an EU institution and work through an in-tray of items such as letters, memos, reports, requests, organigrams, calendars, e-mails and problems. They are typi-cally used to measure harder, analytical-type competencies as well as planning-type competencies. The usual length is between one and two hours.

EPSO has chosen to use what is referred to as an "e-tray exercise", which is the same as an in-tray exercise but is computer-based and uses an e-mail inbox. Like the paper equiva-lent, this will be a mix of requests, memos, phone messages and general information. Your task is to decide on priorities and appropriate actions to take. They usually consist of a range of issues of varying degrees of importance and urgency, some of which may well be related.

The e-tray usually has one key difference to a traditional in-tray in that it may be dynamic: in other words, e-mails continue to arrive throughout the exercise that add to your knowl-edge about a situation and may even cause you to dynamically change your mind com-pletely about the best way to deal with a scenario. Some e-tray exercises provide a multiple choice format (e.g. a number of actions to choose from), whereas others allow a free-text response (e.g. a space to write a narrative answer). Many include both alternatives. According to EPSO, an e-tray is part of the recruitment process for Assistant roles only.

How to Prepare

The best way to prepare for an e-tray exercise is to try the sample in-tray exercise in this book and then go online to practice – see the links at the end of this chapter. You might also be able to visit a career service to see if it runs mock in-tray exercise sessions. More broadly, it may help to search online to find current business e-mail etiquette and gen-eral time management tips (see recommended links below).

Consider your general approach when faced with a large amount of information to digest and then work with. Do you tend to be slow and methodical, or quicker and less concerned with the detail? Ask for feedback from those who know you well. I find that there are two primary ways that people do poorly in e-trays: rushing through to complete all tasks with too little thought for the detail; or spending far too much time analysing the detail and fail-ing to complete all the tasks. An effective balance must be struck.

Another aspect to consider is how you tend to prioritise your workload. E-trays typi-cally require you to distinguish the *urgent* from the *important* issues. Urgent issues are those that have a relatively short deadline for a response or resolution, regardless of how critical they are. Important issues are those which will ultimately contribute significantly towards fulfilling the overall objectives of your job, but may not need to be completed straight away. For example, finding a nice photo of your unit's away-day for inclusion in the "Commission En Direct" internal newsletter that is being published tomorrow may be urgent, but it is unlikely to be important. Similarly, researching new, more efficient software programmes for managing your unit's budget next year in a more systematic way may be important, but it is probably not urgent. Make sure that you understand the difference between the two, as this will help you to prioritise more effectively. A good way to keep your focus is continuously asking yourself the question "what is the next action I must take"?

Tips for the Assessment itself

Full Coverage: Read through all the correspondence swiftly before doing anything and only then assess the tasks required and come back to the items that you consider more worthy of your time.

Notes: Make notes on rough paper or the erasable slate given at the Assessment or Exam Centre of key pieces of information (names, dates, events, relationships between these etc; the exercise may have hard-to-remember names or similar names to make your task more challenging) as you read through. This will help you work quicker and more accurately.

Clarity: Make sure you clearly state what you would do in response to each issue (e.g. a request for a meeting for your director; a problem raised by a colleague in your unit regarding his annual holiday entitlement etc.), according to the instructions.

Dates and Deadlines: Make sure to identify the sending date of the e-mail or the date shown on a fax message as these may be relevant information to understand the situation. In some cases a relative deadline ("within 30 days") may depend on your understanding of these pieces of information.

Types of Action: this can essentially mean the following: those issues needing immediate or urgent action; those you can delegate; those you can defer (delay); and those you may be able to drop (ignore). If you can successfully identify which action (or inaction) to choose for each, you are halfway done with the exercise!

Priorities: If something is urgent but insignificant (see the example above), deal with it quickly and decisively, or decide if anything actually needs to be done at all.

Sender: Always identify who the message is from as the sender's importance to the organisation may be a crucial factor. Make sure you act accordingly depending on whether the sender is internal (staff) or external (a citizen, stakeholder, a Member State diplomat, trade union activist or journalist).

Deferring: For tasks that you decide to defer, note how you will act on them when you have time. Make sure to keep a thorough track record of all such items and ensure you do not forget about them under the time pressure of the exercise. Identify any deadlines or further information you may need to request. See if you can negotiate for an extended deadline, if this seems appropriate or if it is technically possible in the exercise.

Delegating: For tasks you delegate, the background information will normally have references indicating to whom you can do this (e.g. you may see someone is your team's Administrative Assistant from their job title in an e-mail or from an organisation or department structure chart): include this detail in your response to show your understanding of the context.

- **Multiple Solutions**: Remember, there are many possible ways to resolve the issues in an e-tray: there is seldom just one "right answer". You will need to indicate the most and least suitable choice and there might even be two levels within each. Consider all possibilities (and present these in your answer if you are asked to do so): however, present one as your definite chosen opinion, mentioning why you decided against the other possibilities ("I turned down the meeting request from the NGO because they were not registered in the Commission's stakeholder registry" or "I accepted the more expensive plane ticket offer from the travel agency despite our unit's limited budget because the schedule was much better", etc.).

- **Calculations**: Be careful with questions that require you to make exact calculations. Typically, some of the multiple choice answers listed will be common calculation errors for that problem and can be misleading.

- **Time Management**: Manage your time so that you deal with everything in your e-tray, but do not rush and miss out key information or act in a way that conflicts with a decision you need to take on another e-tray item. If at all possible, leave five minutes at the end to proof read what you have written before the time is up (but do not rush the task in order to guarantee this).

- **Dates**: As well as keeping track of real time, take note of the dates on which e-mails were sent to help in your prioritisation decisions and better understanding the context.

- **Dynamic Version**: E-mails in an e-tray exercise will often arrive slowly at first and then get faster as time progresses. It is important that you do not begin to select random answers at the end as they will be testing to see how you perform under pressure.

- **Relevance**: Usually, more information than is necessary will be provided in order to distract you and test your prioritisation skills. Remember that assessors want you to identify essential, key points rather than over-analyse information and get overwhelmed by detail. At times you will have to make a judgement call based on what information is available, even though it may not seem fully complete.

- **Open-ended Responses**: If you have the option of a "free text" response (rather than multiple choice), assessors may well be judging your written communication skills (clarity, sophistication of vocabulary, spelling, hyphenation) as well as your analytical and reasoning skills (quality of your arguments, issues raised, understanding of the context). Work out an outline of what you want to say and the points you need to make and in a logically constructed order. Keep it concise and use bullet points where appropriate as this can save time, help you focus your attention better and only write down the key concepts or arguments. Beautifully crafted prose isn't expected – just good, clear, plain language. Typically, no spell-checker is provided, so you must be certain to use words that you can spell confidently. If you are asked to respond to an e-mail, make sure you respond in a style appropriate to the e-mail you have been sent.

SAMPLE IN-TRAY EXERCISE FOR ASSISTANTS

This exercise is designed to assess how you:

- *Analyse information and create solutions*
- *Communicate clearly in writing*
- *Focus on delivery*
- *Plan and organise*

The exercise has three parts below. First, there is a **"Candidate Booklet"**, which explains what the test involves and how you are to tackle it. Second is the **"In-Tray file"** which provides all the copies of emails, memos and other documents you need to tackle the exercise. Finally, there is a **"Scoring Guide"** which allows you to look in detail at how you performed in the test.

CANDIDATE BOOKLET

In this exercise you are to assume the role of an Assistant to the Director in the European Economic Agency (EEA)*. You have only just taken over this role, which reports to your director and to the assistant of the Director General. Your predecessor left suddenly due to illness, preventing you from having any handover time together.

Your job is a highly demanding one as your director is in charge of nine EU Member States' economies. The director has launched an initiative to organise a high-level conference on the competitiveness of the EU economy, and your predecessor had just left the position before they could undertake to make the preparations for this event. You are therefore the linchpin to make the conference happen, ensuring smooth logistics, a challenging programme, a budget under control, conference and travel arrangements for speakers and other related issues.

You have three tasks:

1.	*Organising*	*40 minutes (recommended)*
2.	*Analysing and decision making*	*25 minutes (recommended)*
3.	*Written communication*	*15 minutes (recommended)*

Instructions for the three tasks are given in this candidate booklet.

You have **80 minutes** in total to complete this exercise. It is up to you to divide up your time between the tasks but suggested times are indicated above.

You may use a calculator.

For the purposes of this exercise, today's date is **Monday 2nd August.**•

> *When you have ensured that you can work on this simulation undisturbed for 80 minutes, start your timer and turn over.*

* *Disclaimer: please note all persons, email addresses and other information are fictitious and were created solely for the purposes of this simulation exercise. Where actual institutions and other entities are mentioned in the exercise this is only to offer a more realistic simulation but all documents are entirely fictitious. The European Economic Agency does not exist.*

TASK 1 – Organising

Your task is to sort through and action the items in your in-tray. A table is provided on the following page for your answers (please add extra pages as needed).

• You may deal with items individually or in groups of related issues. List the issue in the first column.

• Each in-tray item is numbered. In the second column, note which item or items relate to that issue.

• In the third column, indicate what priority you allocate to the issue: H (high), M (Medium) or L (Low), explaining briefly why you think it deserves that priority. Priority should reflect both importance and urgency.

• Under the Proposed Action column, list how you would deal with the issue. You will need to give enough detail for the assessor to understand your response. Ensure that you state what is to be done, when and who will be involved.

• Whilst in real life you might have access to other people or information to help you decide your actions, for this exercise you will need to proceed on the basis of the information provided.

• You have rough paper to assist your working or if you need more space for your answer. Please ensure that your name is at the top of any pages you wish the assessor to see.

• You should spend **40 minutes** of your total 80 minutes on this task.

TASK 2 – Analysing & deciding

Referring to the in-tray:

• Outline the costs and budget for the conference

• Explain what steps you will take to control costs, explaining your reasoning.

You should spend **25 minutes** completing this activity.

Write your answer on a clean sheet of paper.

TASK 3 – Written Communication

Write a letter to your choice of a keynote speaker to fill one of the vacancies in the conference schedule. Your letter should include the following points as a minimum:

• An invitation to attend the conference, explaining what it is about

• A request to speak at the conference and why you would like them to

• An outline of when you want them to speak and for how long

• A suggested topic or request for their ideas on a suitable topic

• Details about travel, accommodation and the financial arrangements.

Y ou should spend **15 minutes** completing this activity

`*TASK 1 ANSWER TABLE*   *Please add extra sheets as necessary*

Issue	Item(s)	Priority: H, M, L	Proposed action
Example *European Parliament Event on Financial Regulation*	0,24	M *The event is not until next year and the letter does not give any deadline for response, but it would be good to build a relationship with them*	– *Get Peter Van Meer's views on how involved we should be* – *Check if we have enough spaces to offer their team places at our conference* – *Write back to M. De la Tour with thanks, offer our involvement, and encourage them to attend our event*

You

From:	Michelle Gaplin <michelle.gaplin@eea.eu >
To:	YOU <you@eea.eu>
Sent:	Monday, 2 August 13:18

Subject: Welcome

Dear <YOU>,

Welcome to the European Economic Agency and the directorate of Member States' Economies. As you are aware, we are dealing with extremely interesting topics that are even more relevant these days. Our colleagues have a lot of expertise but we also like to think of ourselves as a team that helps and supports each other all the time.

We cover 9 Member States, namely Slovenia, Italy, Cyprus, Spain, Denmark, Finland, Greece and Estonia: quite a number of languages and cultures are represented here, not to mention the highly diverse nature of these countries' economies. We monitor, analyse and proactively report on the economic developments here while contributing to the overall strategic thinking of our Agency on how to enhance economic governance and make Europe more competitive globally.

Your position as assistant to the Director is a crucial element in the daily operation of our directorate. I'm sorry that María, your predecessor, had left so abruptly and no handover file could be made; I nevertheless hope your demonstrated organisational skills will help you catch up quickly.

As briefly mentioned at the job interview, your first and foremost task will be to help organise the upcoming conference "European Competitiveness in a Global Context". Its purpose is to provide a lively debate and forum of exchange for policy experts and researchers on how Europe can best reposition itself to become more competitive globally. As the European Economic Agency is the lead organiser, we wish to give the conference an economic approach rather than focusing on competition policy, IT infrastructure or other areas. The conference is scheduled for 11-12 October (Monday-Tuesday); its language is English and we still need to confirm 12 speakers and one keynote speaker for the dinner, some of whom will be on a discussion panel, while others will give 20-minute speeches followed by questions.

The idea of the conference came from our Director and was supported by other colleagues, therefore he is very keen on its success and you can count on his input in case you need any.

An important aspect is the budget: we have had to cut back on various expenses and the expenses must be very carefully managed. We can therefore only cover economy class tickets and a 4* hotel for speakers, and it would be very much appreciated if the keynote speakers could be diplomatically suggested to cover their related costs. We do have, nevertheless, a budget for a reception after the event for all speakers and participants. In any case, the final total budget cannot exceed 36,000 EUR (net), which is a strict request from our ADMIN unit. This can be challenging as the conference will be free for all the 200-300 delegates (exact number to be decided later, based on cost projections), though we do not pay speakers any fees given the international exposure such event could offer to an invitee.

Lastly, I do wish to thank you for agreeing not to take a summer vacation until the conference – I know it shows your commitment to the success of the event.

Please read thoroughly the assembled information and paperwork to get a good idea of what needs to be done. I unfortunately will not be able to assist you with any questions as I am leaving today for an official mission to Austria. Though the rest of the directorate is either on holiday or on various missions, I'm sure you'll be able to cope with all the tasks by yourself!

Best regards,

Michelle Gaplin
Assistant to the Director General
European Economic Agency (EEA)

ITEM 2

Organisational structure of the European Economic Agency (extract)

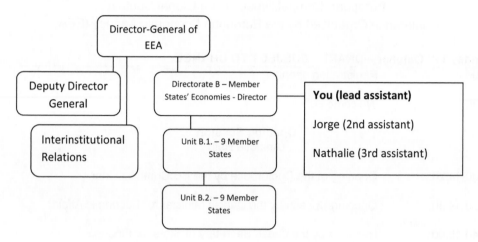

ITEM 3

EUROPEAN ECONOMIC AGENCY EVERYONE

From:	Agency HR BUDGET <dg-hr-budget@eea.eu >
To:	Everyone <everyone@eea.eu>
Sent:	Monday, 2 August 14:32
Subject:	[BUDGET NOTICE] Hotel costs and booking procedure reminder

The Agency's HR & Budget Directorate would like to remind all staff of the revised hotel booking regulations concerning events and conferences. According to the note HR 477/552, all hotel bookings in the framework of official missions and events organised by the Agency involving guests staying overnight and official visits to the Commission by third parties requiring hotel reservations are to be made via our contract partner, EUbooker Ltd.

All staff involved in organising such missions and visits are reminded that other booking providers or direct booking at a hotel cannot be accounted as official expense or it requires the signature of the Deputy Director General for exceptional approval.

The only exception to this rule is an urgent reservation that must be done within 48 hours and for no more than 2 person nights or less. In such cases any hotel within the maximum daily allowed rate is permissible but this must be followed by consequent approval of the hierarchy within 3 working days.

IMPORTANT: bulk bookings, i.e. booking for at least 40 person nights (for example, 4 nights for 10 persons or 8 nights for 5 persons) must be done via another provider, Discount Bookers SA. Our framework agreement with this company and EUbooker Ltd. are valid until 31 Dec 2014, therefore all staff is advised to make sure that any advance booking does not go beyond this date.

For further information and contact details of the bookers see the Intranet's "Mission & Hotels" section.

Disclaimer: All contents of this message are aimed at the person the message was originally sent to. The institution cannot take any responsibility for modified and forwarded messages sent to any other recipient.

ITEM 4

European Competitiveness in a Global Context
Conference Organised by the European Economic Agency (EEA)

Monday 11th October – DRAFT – SUBJECT TO CHANGE

13.00	Registration opening
13.30	Welcome coffee

Opening Session
(Aristotle Hall)

14.00-14.20	Opening of the Conference by the EU Commissioner
14.20-14.40	Opening Speech by the Danish Minister for Economic Affairs
14.40-15.00	Remarks by the Greek Secretary of State for Finance
15.00-15.40	Coffee break

Parallel Session I: The rulebook for European economic discipline: time for reform?
Chair: Financial Times Brussels Correspondent
Conference Hall (Victor Hugo Room)

15.40-15.45	Introduction by the Chair
15.45-16.15	The Single Market and Financial Supervision in the EU (*TBC*)
16.15-16.45	The Stability and Growth Pact: Obstacle or Miracle? (*TBC*)
16.45-17.25	Discussion and questions with the floor – Moderator (*TBC*)
17.25-17.30	Conclusions by the Chair
17.30	Cocktail for participants (Grand Reception Hall)

Parallel Session II: How do European economies compare to China and the USA?
Chair: **TBC**, European Echo's financial journalist
Conference Hall (Schuman Salon)

15.40-15.45	Introduction by the Chair
15.45-16.15	Macroeconomic benchmarks in the EU, USA and China: who performs better in what? (*TBC*)
16.15-16.45	Employment, inflation and interest rate – a novel approach (*TBC*)
16.45-17.25	Discussion and questions with the floor – Moderator (*TBC*)
17.25-17.30	Conclusions by the Chair

ITEM 4 – cont.

17.30	Cocktail for participants (Grand Reception Hall)

Evening Programme: with invitation only

20.30	Dinner for Speakers and Senior Guests Keynote Speaker on the main challenges facing the EU (*TBC*)

Tuesday 12th October – DRAFT – SUBJECT TO CHANGE

8.00	Registration
8.30	Welcome coffee
9.00-9.10	Opening of the second day by the Director General of the European Economic Agency

Morning session: Structural reforms and competitiveness

9.10-9.30	The political factor of reforming the economy: why it doesn't work and what can be done about it (*TBC*)
9.30-9.50	"Are we there yet?" – Definitions of competitiveness inside and outside the EU (*TBC*)
9.50-10.10	Pensions, debt, savings and other threats to sustainable economies (*TBC*)
10.20-10.50	Coffee break
10.50- 11.25	Sociology and economics: how geographical, cultural and linguistic roots affect economic performance (*TBC*)
11.25-12.25	Discussion and questions with the floor – Moderator: (*TBC*)
12.25-12.30	Conclusions by the Chair
12.30-12.40	Conclusions by the President of the EEA Governing Board
12.45-14.00	Buffet lunch for participants
14.30	Close

ITEM 5

María Swentla (Your predecessor)

From:	Michelle Gaplin <michelle.gaplin@eea.eu>
To:	María Swentla <maria.swentla@eea.eu>
Sent:	Thursday, 22 July 15:02
Subject:	Conference speakers

María,

I was just told that you will be leaving the unit very soon. We will certainly miss you and let me wish you good luck in your next endeavour.

Since there are still a few days left before your departure, please find below a few ideas to keep in mind when starting to prepare the upcoming competitiveness conference, especially regarding the speakers who should be given an early warning as soon as possible to secure their availability.

When discussing with your colleagues who could make for a suitable speaker, please ensure that each person we invite:

- Speaks fluent English
- Has a high level of visibility and presents regularly at various conferences
- Has a significant volume of relevant publications in respected journals
- Has been active in the past months/years in terms of publications
- Is pro-European or (s)he has a respected standing in the eyes of our audience
- Is likely to be available to travel to Brussels for the planned days of the conference

Do not hesitate to ask me if you need further information.

Michelle

ITEM 7

European Economic Agency – DIRECTORATE B

From:	European Economic Agency ADMIN <eea-admin@eea.eu>
To:	Member States' Economies Unit <ms-eco@eea.eu>
Sent:	Wednesday, 4 August 17:02
Subject:	[IMPORTANT] Budget limitations

The European Economic Agency's ADMIN unit would like to call your attention to the following notice.

Due to an unexpectedly high travel budget in the first semester, the Directorate's conference and mission budget has been overspent on a pro rata basis. As a result, the Director has issued a warning to all staff to only approve expenses that are absolutely necessary to carry out the core tasks of the units.

Until the next budgetary year starting on 1 January, all expenses above 475 EUR must be approved by the Director. Priority will be given to expenses related to economic analysis while certain requests may be postponed or rejected unless their necessity is clearly justified.

Staff is also requested to have items pre-approved by their head of unit before turning to the Director's assistant to streamline the workflow. Head of units are well aware of these measures and their pre-screening will be necessary to maintain efficiency.

ITEM 6

YOU

From:	Printer Magic <sales@printermagic.com>
To:	YOU <you@eea.eu>
Sent:	Wednesday, 4 August 15:02
Subject:	Re: Quote request for conference printing

Dear Sir/Madam,

Thank you for your interest in Printer Magic's services and for contacting us for a quote. My name is Pieter Stevens, corporate account manager and sales expert who shall be your point of contact if you need any further information on our products or services.

Please find below a small summary chart of the items you had requested a quote for and our proposed rates based on volume discounts. We can also offer a large variety of services and gifts, as detailed below.

Product/service	Net unit price (EUR)	Discount (>50 units)	Discount (>200 units)	Discount (>500 units)
Printing of 16-page conference brochures in colour, glossy paper, single sided	12.32	4%	7%	12%
Printing of 16-page conference brochures in mix (4 in colour, 12 in B&W), glossy paper	5.65	4%	7%	12%
Conference fliers in semi-colour (4 colours)	2.56	4%	7%	12%
Printed copy of all speakers' slides with binder (max. 150 pages in B&W), basic paper	18.00	4%	7%	12%
USB memory stick for each participant with the conference materials, with EU or conference logo	15.02	4%	7%	12%
Professional desktop publishing and editing service	1840.00	4%	7%	12%
Delivery of all materials and items (in Brussels)	172.00	FREE	FREE	FREE
Service fee and flat rate processing fee (compulsory)	350.00	-	-	-

You will see in the above chart that we can offer a large selection of options depending on your needs. We can also undertake the professional editing of all your documents for a single flat-rate fee if you wish. Another highly popular feature we offer is the USB keys that can be branded for your organisation or event, and we upload the conference materials so that guests will not have to carry around large folders or binders with the programme. Being environmentally conscious, this is also a highly eco-friendly solution to avoid unnecessary printing.

Our satisfied clients include the European institutions' Brussels offices, Shell, Citibank and various other companies in Belgium and the Netherlands.

Discount: further to the above discounts, we can offer a special 3% discount on all items if you file your order with us before the 12th August.

Please do not hesitate to contact me for further assistance.

Yours sincerely,
Pieter Stevens
Account manager and sales expert
Printer Magic

Eve Ponnier
Member of the European Parliament

Director General of the European Economic Agency
Brussels

Dear Director General,

The European Parliament very much welcomes your initiative to organise the conference on European competitiveness this year. This newly established "tradition" is a great way to involve academia, private sector and policy makers in the public discussions on how to make Europe compete in a global world.

As an MEP and as vice-chairwoman of the Competitiveness Committee of the EP, I would like to express our strong interest in this year's event. We are positive that either our committee chair or a member could provide valuable input to the discussions, given our expertise in the field of public finances and sustainable growth. If you are planning a similar structure as last year, a panel discussion or a keynote address seems a perfectly suitable forum to express the EU's only directly elected institution's position on these very timely issues.

As your Agency is keen on supervising and steering Member States' stability and convergence, the Parliament can provide valuable expertise on these topics. Dovetailing EEA initiatives on improving economic performance and budgetary discipline is a common interest to all institutions.

Our Committee Chair, Mr. Jeremy Sabo is at your disposal to discuss a topic you consider appropriate for him or another member to address. For technical or logistical arrangements, our committee's secretariat is available at <u>cc-secretariat@parliament.eu</u>

I look forward to your thoughts at your earliest convenience.

Yours sincerely,

(signed)

ITEM 9

EUROPEAN ECONOMIC AGENCY EVERYONE

From: Agency SECURITY <<u>eea-security@eea.eu</u> >
To: Everyone <<u>everyone@eea.eu</u>>
Sent: Thursday, 5 August 09:32
Subject: [SECURITY ALERT] New badges introduced in 5 units from 1 September

Due to increased security measures, the Agency's Security department will issue a new type of security badge that will be compulsory for all staff wishing to enter Agency units and all other European institutions located in Brussels as of 1 September.

All staff, especially those working in the Agency or paying frequent visits there are requested to pass by the Agency's security office any weekday between 9.00 – 12.00 to have their badges replaced.

The current badges of those working in the Agency will be deactivated as of 1 September 06:00 and it will no longer be possible to pass through the electronic gates without registering at the reception desks first with the current badges. Therefore all staff is reminded not to wait until the last day and you are requested to have your badge replaced as soon as possible.

Before obtaining the new badge, an official photo will be taken in Agency's security office, which will then be uploaded into the local online directory accessible from all European institutions but not to the general public. You may nevertheless request that this photo not be used in the intranet directory either, due to data protection reasons.

A valid passport, ID card or other certified document issued by a local or national authority is needed before the new badge can be handed over. Please ensure that you have such document with you as otherwise the Agency's security department will not be in the position to issue your new badge.

ITEM 10

Ms. María Swentla　　　　　　　　　　　**The Manager**
European Economic Agency　　　　　　**Royal Hotel Brussels**
Member States Unit　　　　　　　　　**Rue Archimedes 89**
Brussels　　　　　　　　　　　　　　manager@royalhotel.be

Brussels, 4 August

Dear Madam,

Pursuant to your request of last week to pre-book our conference rooms, I am happy to confirm their availability as follows. Please note that all prices are exclusive of VAT. Further, I have pre-registered your booking for all of the following services, which needs to be confirmed before the 20th August to ensure their availability.

- **The Aristotle Hall**: a maximum capacity of 250 seats and three video cameras to stream the event for possible viewing in other halls or online. Fee: 2450 EUR/day

- **The Schuman Room**: a maximum capacity of 150 seats and further 50 standing. Fee: 1820 EUR/day

- **The Victor Hugo Room**: a maximum capacity of 180 seats and further 30 standing. Fee: 2070 EUR/day

- **The Grand Reception Hall**: a maximum capacity of 500 standing guests if round high tables are placed at every 25 m2 area. Fee: 650 EUR/hour

- **A VIP room**: next to the above facilities, we can provide for the organisers and VIP guests a discreet welcome room where refreshments can also be served with a maximum capacity of 6 persons. Fee: FREE in case any two of the above halls are reserved, otherwise 400 EUR/day

Apart from the above conference and reception rooms, we can also provide the following facilities:

- **Conference screen** in all rooms for projector screening with laptop, 290 EUR/day/room

- **Microphone with professional audio assistance** and possibility of recording, 120 EUR/day/room

- **Video streaming** for those located in other halls or to the general public online, 420 EUR/day/room

- Coffee, refreshment drinks, bio finger food, cocktails and champagne (see below)

- Full catering in our 2 Michelin-star restaurant "The Rainforest" (see below)

Royal Hotel – Brussels　　　　　　　　　　　　　　　Tel: (32) 2 55 55 55 55
"Where Quality Reigns"　　　　　　　　　　　　　　　reception@royalhotel.be

ITEM 10- cont.

- Regarding our rates per delegate, please find these below:

- **Visitor delegate** (only refreshment and finger food): 32 EUR/day/person

- **Lunch delegate** (refreshment, finger food and buffet lunch): 46 EUR/day/person

- **Dinner delegate** (refreshment, finger food and buffet lunch, dinner with 4 courses, wine and refreshments): 82 EUR/person

- **Hotel fees based on individual rooms**: 148 EUR/person/night including buffet breakfast

Please note that above 50 delegates per day, 5 organisers can be catered for free of charge. We also offer a great volume discount of 12% on any of the above fees, including hotel rooms for 50 or more delegates or guests .

I wish to mention here that on your planned event date (9-10 October) we currently have all the above rooms available, except for the Schuman Room which is tentatively reserved for the 10th October, but the guest will need to confirm this within two weeks. Additionally, there is a large wedding on the 8th October (Sunday) before your conference; therefore we unfortunately cannot offer any hotel rooms for speakers or guests arriving on Sunday.

We sincerely hope the above services and fees will meet with your approval. Should you have any questions or need further information, myself or my colleagues will be happy to assist you.

Yours sincerely,

The Manager

Royal Hotel – Brussels
"Where Quality Reigns"

Tel: (32) 2 55 55 55 55
reception@royalhotel.be

ITEM 11

YOU

From:	Manuel Del Río <manuel.del-rio@eea.eu >
To:	Maria Swentla <maria.swentla@eea.eu>
Sent:	Friday, 30 July 16:32
Subject:	Re: Competitiveness conference – potential speakers

Hi María,

Hope all is well with you! It's been a while since we last met; I remember your son is about to start school in September, right?

Regarding your message, I was very glad when you wrote about researching potential speakers, it sounded like a task exactly for me!

I looked around the Agency's library and asked some colleagues as well for ideas. Here is a list of 11 names, though I'm not sure all of them will meet your criteria. In any case, have a look at it and let me know if I should keep looking for more ☺

So here goes the list:

Name	Number of publications in academic magazines/journals, books (counted at a 5x rate), last publication	Quotation ranking	Academic level, Affiliation	English knowledge	Availability	Comments
Wilfried Schwarz	34, 10 months ago	Top 80	PhD, Leipzig University	Medium	Probably yes	
Elaine Rosen	29, 2 months ago	Top 600	PhD, Wisconsin University, USA	Fluent	Probably yes	Controversial views on the convergence criteria, may be critical
Yaroslav Igortsky	31, 4 months ago	Top 140	Managing Partner, PriceWaterhouseCoopers Moscow	Fluent	Unknown	
Leo Komorski	12, 8 months ago	n/a	MA in International Economics, The Brussels Economic Think-Tank	Fluent	Probably yes	Somewhat junior researcher, but he has published very interesting studies
Erica Appelbon	147, 2 months ago	Top 300	PhD, University of Utrecht	Fluent	Probably yes	Highly regarded academic
Garos Srinac	23, 7 months ago	Top 800	Economic correspondent, Serbian Times	Medium	Unknown	Despite being a journalist, he has authored quite many academic studies
Juan-Miguel García	65, 5 months ago	Top 500	PhD, New Mexican University, USA	Fluent	Unknown	

ITEM 11 – cont.

David Ma	34, 1 year ago	Top 700	PhD, State University of Beijing, China	Good	Probably yes	Highly regarded Chinese academic who could give a special perspective to the event
Angelika Wolfgang	194, 3 months ago	Top 250	PhD, Economic Research Institute of Vienna	Fluent	Probably no	
Aneta Georgescu	84, 9 months ago	Top 450	MA, Senior Advisor to the Romanian Government	Fluent	Unknown	

Just let me know if you need anything else, see you soon,

Manuel

p.s.: pass my greetings to your family!

ITEM 12

YOU

From:	Brochure King <king@borchureking.be>
To:	YOU <you@eea.eu>
Sent:	Friday, 6 August 19:12
Subject:	Re: Quote request for conference printing

A good day from Brochure King!

We at Brochure King were thrilled to have your price quote request in our inbox. While others simply print flyers and folders, we do magic in print: you will always be amazed at the quality of our work or we provide a full money back guarantee. What more could you ask for?

Regarding your specific questions, we can offer you our very best rates especially created for the European Economic Agency's Conference.

A sales representative will call you in two days to discuss any questions you may have.

Rest assured – you are in good hands when Brochure King takes care of your order!

Best regards,
Your Royal Team

Product/service	Net unit price (EUR)	Discount (>150 units)	Discount (>300 units)	Discount (>500 units)
16-page conference brochures in B&W, glossy paper, single sided	6.12	7%	11%	18%
16-page conference brochures in colour, glossy paper, single sided	15.23	7%	11%	18%
16-page conference brochures in mix (4 in colour, 12 in B&W), glossy paper, single sided	5.02	7%	11%	18%
16-page conference brochures in mix (4 in colour, 12 in B&W), glossy paper, double sided	4.72	7%	11%	18%
Conference fliers in full colour	4.12	7%	11%	18%
Printed copy of all speakers' slides with binder (max. 250 pages in 4 colours), quality paper	17.12	7%	11%	18%
Editing service for all materials (per day)	542.12	7%	11%	18%
Delivery of all materials and items (in Brussels)	FREE	FREE	FREE	FREE
Service fee (obligatory)	520.00	-	-	FREE

ITEM 13

Conference costs spreadsheet in progress

	How many	Price per unit (EUR, net)	Discount (%)	TOTAL (EUR, net)	Comment
Visitor delegates (50-100)		32	12	0	
Lunch delegates (2x as many as visitors)		46	12	0	
Dinner delegates (including organisers)	8	82	12	577	
Speakers (no hotel, considered as dinner delegate)	7	82	12	505	
Speakers (hotel fee plus lunch delegate fee)	11	194	12	1,878	
Venue costs (Aristotle Hall)	1	2,450	12	2,156	needed only for 1 day
Venue costs (Schuman Room)	2	1,820	12	3,203	needed for 2 days
Venue costs (Victor Hugo)	2	2,070	12	3,643	needed for 2 days
Venue costs (Grand Reception Hall, per hour)	4	650	12	2,288	for the reception at the end of day 1
Venue costs (equipment, approximately)			12	4,717	3 video streaming, 5 microphone units for 2 days, 5 conference screens with laptop for 2 days
Venue costs (various)	1	500	12	440	various items that may come up
Printing costs (brochures, 16 page single sided glossy, 4/12 colour)					
Printing costs (slide handouts, 200 pages, with binder)					
Printing costs (USB, branded)					
Travel costs for speakers (average)	18	650		11,700	average cost per speaker regardless of means of transport
GRAND TOTAL					
With 20% Extra Contingency Cost					
Sponsorship income	10	2,000			(if any, e.g. logos in conference brochure or info booths in the foyer)
Total COST with sponsorship					

ITEM 14

YOU

From: Alicia Tomas <alicia.tomas@eea.eu>
To: YOU <you@eea.eu>
Sent: Monday, 9 August 11:42
Subject: Re: Speakers for the conference

Dear <YOU>,

As you may have heard, María had asked me to contact a few potential speakers for the October conference before she left, and I already got some replies. I'd be grateful if you could take over the file from me as you are now fully in charge of this event.

Here is the list of speakers whom I had contacted and the answers they gave:

- Mr. Louis Van Oprec from the World Bank cannot attend as he will in Japan in the period.

- Ms. Angelika Perez, Banco Santander's chief macroeconomics analyst cannot come either but she has shown lots of interest in the event and asked to be kept in touch about the final programme and speakers.

- Mr. Piotr Lewarewski, Governor of the Bank of Poland, can attend the whole conference.

- Mr. George Morisson from the International Monetary Fund (IMF) Washington Headquarters can come to the whole event.

- Ms. Catherine Fillory from the London School of Economics could attend the 2nd day but asked to have a confirmation ASAP as her diary is under pressure.

- Ms. Indhira Gupta from the Indian Research Council on Europe can come for one day but not the whole conference, and when she learned that Ms. Fillory might be attending, she expressed her wish to meet up with her if possible.

- Mr. Stefan Engelström from the University of Malmö can and would very much like to attend but he must leave by 2pm on the second day. As he lives in Northern Sweden, it's rather complicated for him to travel and could arrive on Sunday 10th (due to lack of connecting flights), so he would need an extra day of accommodation.

- Mr. Ted Rothkorn from the US Council of Economic Advisers can arrive at 3pm on day one and must leave right after dinner the same day.

- Ms. Vanessa Erbrock from the Transatlantic Institute of Brussels can attend the second day from 10.30 until 15.30 due to childcare issues.

This in total means 7 speakers can make it, though I understand it might be a challenge to shuffle them in the right order. As far as I understand, there are altogether 12 slots and a keynote speaker to fill, so you probably need to seek more speakers to fill in these slots.

Hope this helps in your preparations – please let me know if you can manage from this point on.

Thank you,

Alicia

ITEM 15

WORKING FOR THE EEA? WISH TO SOCIALIZE MORE?

Here is a chance to meet colleagues in a fun way and also contribute to charity!

The Staff Union for Healthy Officials is organising a

PUB QUIZ

on 27 August at 19.30 in the Kitty O'Shea's Irish Pub

Fee: 20 EUR, of which 15 EUR goes to the charity

"Prevent Cancer for a Better Tomorrow"

In loving memory of colleagues and relatives who died from cancer

More information and sign up:

Social-events-staff-union@eea.eu

Join us in a fun evening for a good cause!

ITEM 16

European Economic Agency ADMIN

From:	European Economic Agency ADMIN <eea-admin@eea.eu>
To:	Everyone <everyone@eea.eu>
Sent:	Wednesday, 11 August 16:42
Subject:	[ADMIN NOTICE] Frequent Flyer Points

The European Economic Agency ADMIN would like to remind all staff that based on the note ADMIN/4458/12 and due to the limited budgetary resources available until the end of the year, those who have completed a large number of official missions in the past months and have consequently accumulated frequent flyer points or air miles are requested to use these points for any upcoming official trip instead of requesting a ticket from our contract travel agency or using the points for purchasing personal flights.

Thank you for your cooperation in this matter. Should you have any technical questions for combined trips or overseas missions, please contact the Agency's ADMIN secretariat at the above e-mail address.

ITEM 17

http://eea.eu/eu2050/index_en.htm

European Economic Agency: EUROPE 2050

Europe 2050: A strategy for competitive and social growth

Over the last two decades, we have witnessed the decline of Europe's economies and the timely responses given by the continent's leaders. This crisis has reversed much of the progress achieved in Europe in the past ten years. We are now facing high levels of unemployment, slow structural growth and excessive levels of debt. The economic situation is improving, but the recovery is still fragile. At the same time, the world is moving fast and long-term challenges – globalisation, pressure on resources, climate change, ageing – are intensifying.

Europe can only succeed if it acts as a Union. The Europe 2050 strategy sets out a vision of Europe's social market economy for the first half of the 21st century. It shows how the we can come out stronger from the crisis and how it can be turned into a sustainable and inclusive economy delivering high levels of employment, productivity and social cohesion. To deliver rapid and lasting results, stronger economic governance will be required.

Useful links

Strategy for growth and jobs

Public consultation on the future EU 2050 strategy

Committees call on European regions and cities to join in the debate

ITEM 18

euroview.com

HEADLINE NEWS

Surprise loss of European competitiveness

JEREMY TODDER

16 August @ 09:27 CET

EUROVIEW / BRUSSELS - New figures released by the EUSTATIX office have shown a surprise contraction in the continent's growth during the second quarter of this year, a further difficulty for the EU which is already struggling to cut a large public deficit and revive an ailing banking sector.

- Print

- Comment article

Despite a surge in exports, data from the EU's statistical office indicated that the EU's gross domestic product (GDP) fell by 1.2 percent in the three months up to the end of June when compared to the previous quarter.

This contrasts with Eurozone figures which show growth at a whole 1 percent.

As Elaine Rosen from the University of Wisconsin pointed out, "European governments must learn what budgetary discipline means or else they face austerity measures". The highly respected American professor has been one of the main supporters of fiscal cutbacks to preserve competitiveness.

The new figures showed a decline in GNP of 1.3 percent in the second quarter, compared with a fall of 0.2 percent in the first, leading Erica Appelbon from the University of Utrecht to describe the economy as "getting worse by the day". Ms Appelbon, an internationally renowned expert on the EU budget, has recently issued a study on EU public finances in the framework of a research programme initiated by the European Economic Agency.

But economists suggest the EEA may be forced to review its annual growth forecast, with European bonds and stocks coming under renewed pressure after the news on Thursday.

Government hints that holders of subordinated bonds in the nationalised banks may not receive their full returns also weighed on markets. According to David Ma of Beijing University, a leading commentator on G20 issues since he predicted with unmatched accuracy the collapse of capital markets several years ago, this can prove to be a huge risk in European solvency.

The European Bank has recently suggested that Eurozone governments may struggle to reduce their massive budget deficit this year in line with targets set by the EEA.

ITEM 19

EN

ECONOMIC COMMITTEE OF
THE EUROPEAN UNION

PRESS

press.office@econ-com.eu   http://www.econ-com.eu/Newsroom

Brussels, 28 July   14021/85

The Committee today reached agreement on a general approach, pending the opinion of the European Parliament, on a draft directive aimed at strengthening mutual assistance between member states in the balance of payment assistance.

The directive will be adopted at a forthcoming Council meeting, once the Parliament's opinion is available.

The draft directive is aimed at better fulfilling the member states' needs with regard to the recovery of taxes in the framework of public finances, providing an overhaul of directive 22/398/EEC on the basis of which the member states have engaged in mutual assistance since 1986.

National provisions on recovery are limited in scope to national territories, and hedge funds have taken advantage of this to organise insolvencies in member states where they have debts. Member states therefore increasingly request the assistance of other member states to recover taxes, but existing provisions have only allowed a small proportion of debts to be recovered.

The Presidency of the Council has welcomed the agreement as it will significantly help Europe improve its long-term competitiveness by recovering lost public revenues. Further discussions on the implementation would be needed, and an impact assessment along with a public consultation on further measures is envisaged. The key remaining issue is how to tackle the relationship between IMF and EU efforts on balance-of-payment cooperation.

ITEM 20

YOU

From:	Juanita Sánchez <juanita.sanchez@imf.org>
To:	YOU <you@eea.eu>
Sent:	Tuesday, 17 August 07:48
Subject:	Change of flight schedule for Mr. Morrison

Dear <YOU>,

I am contacting you in reference to the European Economic Agency's invitation to the European Competitiveness conference in October this year on behalf of the International Monetary Fund (IMF) Deputy Managing Director, Mr. George Morisson.

Mr. Morisson was due to arrive on Monday 11 October at 11.00 am in Brussels, but due to an unforeseen urgency he will need to attend a meeting in Peru the previous days. As it is rather complex to organise the route from Lima to Brussels, it seems he will arrive at 10.28 on Tuesday 12 October. Unfortunately, this change also means that the flight cost will amount to 2342 EUR (on business class).

I apologise if this has caused any inconvenience in your planning and I trust you will be in the position to make the necessary arrangements in the conference schedule.

I would like to kindly request that you confirm that Mr. Morisson's new schedule and the travel arrangements are agreed.

I look forward to hearing from you at your earliest convenience.

Yours sincerely,

Juanita Sánchez
Personal Assistant to the Deputy Managing Director
International Monetary Fund - Washington Bureau

ITEM 21

The Minister for Economics
Kingdom of Denmark

Director General of the European Economic Agency
Brussels

12 August

Dear Director General,

Due to personal and health issues, the Minister has decided to step down from his post two weeks ago on 1st August. According to the decision of the Prime Minister, he will be replaced as Minister for Economics by Mr. Lars Nedergaard, former Minister of Agriculture.

On behalf of the Minister, I would like to inquire whether this change would affect your kind invitation that you have passed for the upcoming conference on European Competitiveness in a Global Context. Mr. Nedergaard is highly competent, with a PhD in chemistry from the Humboldt University of Berlin. If possible, he would prefer to give the opening remarks in German or Italian instead of English.

Please kindly contact the cabinet secretariat to discuss administrative issues further via e-mail at minister-secretariat@oem.dk

Yours sincerely,

(signed)

For reference, please find below a short biography of the Minister:
Born in 1971, Mr. Nedergaard studied agricultural economics at the Coppenhagen Technical University, followed by studies of pharmacology at Aalborg University. After obtaining a PhD in chemistry at the Humboldt University of Berlin, he became an advisor to the Minister of Health in the Danish Government. For the last two years, Mr. Nedergaard has held various positions in the government such as state secretary for rural affairs, chair of the German-Danish Cooperation Council and most recently Minister for Agriculture.

ITEM 22

YOU

From:	Peter Komarno <peter.komarno@eea.eu>
To:	YOU <you@eea.eu>
Sent:	Wednesday, 11 August 15:34
Subject:	Re: Keynote speaker ideas – can you help?

Hi <YOU>,

I am coming back to you regarding your question about possible keynote speakers.

It was quite hard to gather the three suggestions that you asked for, but I did my best:

1. The Bulgarian EU Affairs Minister: highly competent guy who knows what he's talking about; has been giving lots of public speeches and lectures on the financial crisis, structural reforms, sustainable development and other related topics. Speaks perfect English but there have been rumours he might become his country's nominee for the new European Council President. As he travels quite extensively, he will probably be in Canada for the G8 summit the days before the conference, which may add to the travel costs (though he might choose to cover that himself).

2. The French State Secretary for Competitiveness: though not ministerial level, she is quite known for her strong support for the convergence criteria and strict budgetary policies (which makes her less popular in the government, but that's a different story). I heard her speak once, it was OK though not outstanding, and as a French politician she will surely be reluctant if not unwilling to give a speech in English. Otherwise she will almost certainly be in Brussels at the time of the conference since there will be a Council meeting that day so it would be probably easy to get her to participate.

3. The Czech Permanent Representative, who is an economist, although he is not really involved in any competitiveness issue. A few weeks ago he was invited by a think tank to present his governments' ideas on economic governance, and he impressed the audience with a very lively presentation. The problem is that he may be sent to become his country's OECD ambassador in October, though this is not yet confirmed. Even so, Paris is not far away so that should not prevent him from giving a keynote. By the way, he is more Francophone than English-speaking, but his English is not bad either.

I hope this helps in your selection – feel free to let me know if I can be of further help.

Best regards,
Peter

IN-TRAY SCORING GUIDE

Having completed the in-tray exercise for yourself, you can now look at how an assessor might evaluate your response. This section outlines 4 competency areas of the sort commonly used to score in-trays. Each competency is marked on a scale from 1 – 5:

1	2	3	4	5
Poor	Weak	Adequate	Good	Excellent
The response was wrong or absent and would have made the situation worse	The actions were limited and basic. There would be little impact either way on the situation.	The response was reasonably effective. The situation was partly resolved.	A range of effective actions were applied, largely resolving the situation.	The response was wide-ranging, resolving the immediate issues and addressing longer-term and wider factors too.

Competency 1: Planning & Organising

For this competency, the following indicators would be seen as part of a **good response**:

Task 1

- Prioritised tasks appropriately – refer to the table below for an example of an effective way to prioritise the in-tray items.

- Set realistic timescales for actions listed

- Took account of speakers' availability for compiling the schedule

- Described how they would prepare for a decision, e.g. who they would speak to, how they would identify the financial and human resources required

- Adapted effectively to changes in plans, e.g. took account of the Minister's replacement and identified that it would be better to replace him

Task 2

- Took steps to monitor progress on budget and spending, e.g. built in milestones

General

- Managed workload effectively: completed all 3 tasks in the time allowed

The following would be seen as part of a **poor or weak response**:

Task 1

- Prioritised ineffectively (see table below), e.g. listed all items as High priority, or misjudged relative priorities

- Dealt with items individually rather than tackling groups of related issues

- Did not give any timescales for actions, or was unrealistic (e.g. proposed to complete everything within a very short timescale)

- Gave little detail around how they would go about proposed actions, e.g. made snap decisions without having considered resources or availability

- Did not adapt to necessary changes (e.g. took no account of the Minister's replacement, did not recognise a speaker's changed availability and increased travel costs)

Task 2

- Did not mention ongoing monitoring of budget and spending
- Didn't allow any contingency fund

General

- Managed time badly in the exercise: did not finish all 3 tasks in the time allowed

Issue	Items	Priority	Reasons
Arranging speakers	4, 5, 8, 11, 14, 18, 20, 21	H	Time is getting short. Good speakers are essential to a successful conference. Some speakers need confirmation ASAP. Travel costs will go up the later it is left.
Key note speakers	8, 11, 14, 18, 19, 20, 21	H	It is critical to the conference to firm up a good list of speakers and some are getting booked up.
Other speakers	4, 5, 11, 14, 18	H	
Danish speaker	20, 21	M/H	A decision is needed promptly because if the substitute is not accepted, an alternative will be needed. This just affects one speaker, however.
EP involvement	8, 19	M/H	A significant stakeholder wants prompt acknowledgement and might fill a needed gap as a speaker/discussion panel member. However, this is just one stakeholder.
Budget	3, 6, 7, 10, 12, 13, 16, 20	H	Getting the budget right is a key deliverable for the conference and could lead to embarrassment if exceeded. It needs tackling promptly as costs could rise if not addressed now, e.g. speakers with cheaper travel costs might not be available.
Hotel bookings/venue	3, 7, 10	H	Confirming the venue is urgent or the conference might not be able to run.
Speaker travel	7, 20, 22	M	The speaker's flight needs confirming promptly, and has a bearing on budget control, but this only affects one person.
Printing	6, 7, 12	M	No deadline specified. This is important to get right for the conference, but there appears to be time in hand to achieve it.
Security passes	9	L	This is important, but is quick to do, doesn't affect anyone else and not immediately urgent
Quiz night	15	L	The sender is not necessarily expecting a response from the candidate. It is an optional activity.

Competency 2: Analysing and Creating Solutions

For this competency, the following indicators would be seen as part of a **good response**:

Task 1

- Coped well with complexity; grouped the items into logical themes and recognised interrelationships (e.g. hotel orders, speaker arrangements, printer orders)

Task 2

- Challenged data, e.g. considered requesting further discount from hotel, looked into travel costs
- Considered multiple options for resolving issues, produced several suggestions for controlling costs
- Suggested creative ideas, e.g. that speakers use their air miles to pay for their flights, that keynote speakers are only offered 24 hours free at the conference, seeking further sponsors, etc.
- Gathered information to inform decision making; compiled an accurate and complete list of all the costs
- Acted on special offers in a timely manner (e.g. Printer Magic's extra discount)

Below is a sample budget spreadsheet (note that this is not *the* correct answer, just one of many possible answers)

	How many	Price per unit (EUR, net)	Discount (%)	TOTAL (EUR, net)
Visitor delegates	80	32	12	2,253
Lunch delegates	160	46	12	6,477
Dinner delegates (including organisers)	8	82	12	577
Speakers (no hotel, considered as dinner delegate)	7	82	12	505
Speakers (hotel fee plus lunch delegate fee)	11	194	12	1,878
Venue costs (Aristotle Hall)	1	2,450	12	2,156
Venue costs (Schuman Room)	2	1,820	12	3,203
Venue costs (Victor Hugo)	2	2,070	12	3,643
Venue costs (Grand Reception Hall, per hour)	4	650	12	2,288
Venue costs (equipment, approximately)			12	4,717
Venue costs (various)	1	500	12	440

Printing costs (brochures, 16 page glossy, 4/12 colour)	300	5	17	1,250
Printing costs (slide handouts, 200 pages, with binder)	300	17	4	4,931
Printing costs (USB, branded)	300	15	8	4,146
Travel costs for speakers (average)	18	450		8,100
GRAND TOTAL				**46,563**
WITH 20% EXTRA CONTINGENCY COST				**55,876**
Sponsorship income (if any)	10	2,000		20,000
Total cost with sponsorship				**35,876**
TOTAL DELEGATES	*248*			
TOTAL SPEAKERS	*18*			

Task 3

- Made practical, workable suggestions to the speaker for a topic linked to other items such as the Communication on EU2050 or specific ideas about competitiveness based on the draft programme, current events, news or other facts. (e.g. on the role of China's currency policy affecting European economies or the relations between the G8, G20, US and the EU, the role of the IMF in the international financial system)

- Gave a logical and considered justification for inviting the speaker

The following would be seen as part of a **poor or weak response**:

Task 1

- Struggled with the complexity of the exercise; tackled items 1 by 1 rather than by theme. Did not recognise where an item was superseded or added to by subsequent information (e.g. the change of speakers' availability, or not mixing the two printers' offers for various items such as USB keys and slide printouts etc.)

Task 2

- Accepted the given figures at face value without trying to negotiate further discount or find other ways to cut costs (e.g. did not try to use additional discounts, accepted speakers' special travel requests without trying to find alternative arrangements)

- Produced very few ideas for controlling costs

- Demonstrated little or no creativity, e.g. didn't use the hint provided of using frequent flyer points to offset costs

- Produced an incomplete and/or inaccurate summary of the costs

Task 3

- Made an impractical suggestion to the speaker for a topic or gave no ideas (e.g. suggested to speak on competition law instead of competitiveness)
- Gave an illogical justification for inviting the speaker, or none at all

Competency 3: Communicating with Clarity

For this competency, the following indicators would be seen as part of a **good response**:

Task 1

- Used an appropriate level of detail / conciseness, e.g. wrote in note form but giving enough information to understand what was proposed and how

Task 2

- Presented the summary of costs clearly
- Wrote a clear, precise and fluent explanation of their proposals for controlling costs

Task 3

- Wrote a clear and fluent letter to the potential keynote speaker, with appropriate structure in paragraphs including introductory and valedictory greetings.
- Avoided jargon or explained it in the letter
- Caught the attention and interest of the audience, e.g. by pointing out the benefits of attending the conference, through a warm tone, etc
- Conveyed the key points, explaining effectively why the speaker might want to speak at the conference, and reiterated the main point at the end
- Used a suitably professional tone for a respected audience

The following would be seen as part of a **poor or weak response**:

Task 1

- Was over-concise so that their proposals were not clear, or wrote in too much detail for the time allowed (e.g. actually drafted full responses)

Task 2

- The summary of costs was presented unclearly, without sufficient structure
- Proposals for controlling costs were not clear, hard to follow or contradictory

Task 3

- Wrote unclearly, imprecisely or in a disjointed manner to the potential keynote speaker. The letter was unpolished, hard to follow or contradictory, or lacked sufficient information or structure to fully understand
- Used jargon or made excessive assumptions about understanding
- Wrote in a flat, dull or uninteresting tone, e.g. a list of bullet points, or used an inappropriately informal style
- Failed to convey the key points; confusing, missing or obscuring important messages.

Competency 4: Focusing on Delivery

For this competency, the following indicators would be seen as part of a **good response**:

Task 1

- Took responsibility for meeting objectives. Actions listed would achieve the goal to successfully organise the conference within budget

- Followed established guidelines and procedures (e.g. booked night's accommodation before the conference for a given speaker in line with item 3 guidance)

- Took the initiative and acted without being told, e.g. in noting need to book flights for speakers once confirmed

Task 2

- Noted need to follow guidelines and procedures in, e.g. booking flights, staying within budget, using private air mile points if possible etc.

- Used their initiative to suggest ways to control costs

General

- Produced a good volume of work across the exercise to a good standard of quality

- Followed the instructions given and fulfilled the tasks set as requested (e.g. included all the requested points in the letter in task 3)

The following would be seen as part of a **poor or weak response**:

Task 1

- Did not take responsibility for meeting the objective to successfully organise the conference within budget. Actions were not sufficient to achieve the objective, and/or they deferred actions and decisions to a higher authority

- Did not follow established guidelines and procedures (e.g. the hotel reservation policy as requested by the circular e-mail to all EEA employees)

- Took no initiative, only acting under specific instructions rather than identifying where something needed to be done, e.g. in noting need to book flights for speakers once confirmed

Task 2

- Did not mention need to follow guidelines and procedures in, e.g. booking flights

- Did not use their initiative to suggest ways to control costs

General

- Produced a poor volume of work across the exercise and /or to a low standard of quality

- Did not follow the instructions given, failing to fulfil the 3 tasks requested (e.g. did not cover all the requested points in the letter in task 3)

Summary of scores

Competency	Score (1-5)
Planning and organising	
Analysing and creating solutions	
Communicating with clarity	
Focusing on delivery	

7. Sample Assessment Centre Reports for Assistants

In this chapter, I provide two sample reports in which fictitious candidates' performances at an EPSO Assessment Centre are evaluated against the EPSO competency headings. This type of report will be used internally to compare candidates' performances so as to help make the decision and also will be used to give feedback to the candidates themselves. You will be offered a written feedback report following the Centre. If you are unsuccessful, this report can help to illuminate your strengths and weaknesses and you can use it to improve your performance at Assessment Centres in the future. If you are successful, then it will often form the basis of your first personal development discussion with your new head of unit or be part of your personal profile for future career development.

As stated, the two candidates are fictitious, and the exercises quoted may not be exactly the ones that EPSO will use to measure each competency. However, these are reasonable mappings and this will give you an indication of what such summary reports look like. I have included two reports – one representing a good performance overall, the other representing a poorer performance (although of course there is variation within each).

EXAMPLE REPORT ONE – MR. X

Summary

Overall, Mr. X performed well at the Assessment Centre and he is recommended as a potential candidate for an Assistant role.

His key **strengths** emerged as follows:

– Strong quality and cost efficiency focus

– Strong at keeping his professional knowledge up to date

– Remains calm and focused on delivery when under pressure

– Strong analytical skills and formulates creative solutions

– Good team working and networking ability in order to gain co-operation

– Communicates clearly both orally and in writing

His key **development needs** emerged as follows:

– Needs to focus more on personal development of softer skills

– Becomes flustered in speech when under pressure

– His creative ideas need to be more practical to implement

– Should remember to always include contingencies and monitoring procedures in plans

More detailed ratings by competency follow.

Delivering Quality and Results

In the e-tray/in-tray, Mr. X clearly outlined how he would address each issue and included quality control procedures at various points such as review meetings and peer review of documentation. He mentioned various administrative policies and procedures of the Directorate (given in the background brief) that he would adhere to in the implementation. He sought to add additional value by mentioning a number of ways to save money in implementing the new processes and also how the team could operate in a more efficient manner.

Overall Rating: 5

Learning and Development

In the structured interview, Mr. X described a number of ways he kept his skills up to date, including going to training courses to update his skills in the latest versions of the MS Office suite, as well as attending training courses in advanced techniques. He gave evidence of how he subsequently applied this learning. He also took evening classes in financial management to help his understanding of accounting practices. Mr. X was less strong on developing his softer skills. He tends to receive feedback on an ad hoc basis and has never sought to collect this proactively in a structured way. He has sought to develop some of his interpersonal skills, such as team working, but this tended to consist of just attending a relevant training course with little evidence of putting what he has learnt into practice subsequently.

Overall Rating: 3

Resilience

In the interview, Mr. X described an occasion where he needed to work for a prolonged period of extended hours due to a last minute change to the specifications on a series of reports he was producing. Despite feeling that it was going to be difficult to complete, he rearranged his calendar and worked evenings and weekends to ensure the report was finished on time and to specification. This did make Mr. X feel quite tired for a while afterwards, but he feels the extra effort was rewarded with a report that was very well received. During the interview, Mr. X was sometimes flustered by questions when he could not think of an answer straight away, but otherwise spoke confidently.

Overall Rating: 4

Analysis and Problem Solving

In the in tray/e-tray exercise, Mr. X had obviously understood the background information well, as he uncovered a number of important themes and trends. His suggested ways of dealing with the problems showed some novel thinking as well as the ability to think of the longer-term implications of current courses of action. He presented a number of possible alternatives, evaluated their pros and cons and then came to a reasoned judgement about which to recommend. Some of his ideas sounded good in theory, but were unlikely to be practical to implement. His budgetary calculations were all 100% accurate.

Overall Rating: 4

Working with Others

In the interview, Mr. X described how it was important for him in his last role to build relationships quickly when he arrived, as he needed to gain co-operation from people in different parts of the business in order to ensure his new manger's project was completed on time. He did this effectively and proactively through a series of emails and meetings. He described some potentially contentious situations, such as dealing with a Director who refused to respond to emails, which he handled with maturity and tact and resulted in a positive outcome. He sees networking as a crucial part of achieving results when you have no direct authority over others and gave examples of how he has got to know different people's unique motivations in order to get their co-operation.

Overall Rating: 5

Communicating

In the interview, Mr. X's responses were generally concise and to the point. He varied his tone when he became excited by a particular topic, which helped to retain the interest of the interviewer. He sometimes hesitated and stuttered when he could not think of an answer straight away, which lost some impact. Also, on two occasions the examples he gave were not in direct response to the question and included some superfluous detail.

In the in-tray/e-tray exercise, Mr. X structured his written email response in an easy to follow manner. He began with an overview of the situation and then proceeded to run through the issues clearly. He ended with a short conclusion and summary which tied up the email clearly.

Overall Rating: 4

Prioritising and Organising

In the in-tray/e-tray exercise, Mr. X set clear priorities for which issues he would address first and which could wait until later. He set some tentative dates and milestones for implementation, although he did not build any contingency time into his plans. However, the time allocated for the tasks seemed realistic. Mr. X identified where different responsibilities would lie with other people although he did not describe how he would monitor whether these were being met.

Overall Rating: 3

Professional Skills Test

In the data entry professional skills test, he scored better than 70% of the population, which is an above average score. His accuracy was moderate: he got 20 questions correct out of 30 questions attempted (there were 30 questions overall): this suggests he might benefit from slowing down and considering the responses more carefully in future. These results suggest that he will be comfortable in entering data quickly and accurately into spreadsheets, which forms a key part of the role.

Overall Rating: 4

EXAMPLE REPORT TWO – MR. Y

Summary

Overall, Mr. Y performed fairly poorly at the Assessment Centre and he is not recommended as a potential candidate for the Assistant role.

His key **strengths** emerged as follows:

- Ability to identify possible sources of risk
- Has undergone training in order to develop
- Does not allow work pressure to limit his work output
- Confident responding to questions
- Can draw out key points from a body of information
- Makes accurate financial calculations
- Proposes practical, workable solutions
- Identifies risk
- Recognises the importance of good project management practice

His **key development** needs emerged as follows:

- Needs to develop greater drive to reach objectives
- Would benefit from a more focused approach to developing own knowledge and skills
- Needs to work on controlling his defensiveness when challenged
- Would benefit from going into greater analytical depth when reviewing information
- May shy away from working in a team when this option is available
- Avoids networking and needs to broaden strategies for gaining buy-in from stakeholders
- Both written and verbal communication lack structure and clarity
- Whilst he recognises the importance of good project management practice, there is little evidence that he actually puts this in place.

More detailed ratings by competency follow.

Delivering Quality and Results

In the in-tray/e-tray exercise, although Mr. Y did not seem to contravene any of the Directorate policies or guidelines in his recommendations, he did not explicitly refer to the need to follow them either. He mentioned a number of possible risks to the work being delivered on time, but he gave a vague response on how to mitigate these risks ("review things as they develop"). He also suggested that it was not that important to deliver the project 100% to the original specification, as long as SOMETHING was delivered by the deadline. He produced a very brief length of email response in the time available.

Overall Rating: 2

Learning and Development

In the interview, Mr. Y seemed to adopt a rather casual approach to self development. When he has undergone self development (e.g. training courses), this has not been proactively sought out. In terms of his personal development, Mr. Y adopts a similar approach. He got rather defensive in the interview when asked about his development areas, stating "I don't have any". When pushed, he admitted to having feedback from his supervisor that he can be a little aggressive towards others, so he has tried to be more welcoming since. He has not sought any feedback on how he has progressed on this issue.

Overall Rating: 1

Resilience

In the interview, Mr. Y stated that he never becomes stressed under pressure and gave a number of examples of when he was working to very tight deadlines and kept calm and succeeded in getting a resolution. His tactic in these situations tends to be to work harder and not to think about even trying for a work-life balance, which stops him from feeling frustrated. When answering questions, he appeared fairly confident but did become defensive (as shown by flushing red and issuing short, terse, answers) when asked about times that things did not go well in the past.

Overall Rating: 3

Analysis and Problem Solving

In the in-tray/e-tray exercise, Mr. Y uncovered most of the main points from the background information, although he seemed to miss some of the subtler information in the dataset, such as the fact that the materials would not make it to the venue in time for the first session. His solutions all sounded practical and workable, although they were not particularly innovative. Mr. Y's suggestions were all presented at a fairly superficial, top-line level: there was more scope for him to give detail on how they would be implemented in practice. He tended to shy away from detailed calculations of financials, but those that he did include were accurate.

Overall Rating: 2

Working with Others

In the interview, Mr. Y described how he generally enjoys working as part of a team, but in all of his examples he made the decision to work alone and then speak to people later if they asked to, rather than working as a team from the outset. He stated that he generally dislikes networking as he sees it as "fake". When asked how he gets co-operation from others he replied that "it's down to them if they co-operate or not: if they don't, they'll be the ones facing the consequences". He says that he generally feels the best approach when there is conflict is to move on and not dwell on it, which shows a certain reluctance to deal with these issues openly.

Overall Rating: 1

Communicating

In the interview, Mr. Y's responses were quiet and mumbled. He spoke very quickly which made it hard to follow what he was saying. He gestured with his hands while talking which helped to emphasise key points. His answers became short and aggressive in tone when asked for negative evidence, which betrayed sensitivity.

In the in-tray/e-tray exercise, Mr. Y's email did not follow a clear structure, instead just launching straight into his recommendations and the detailed analysis behind them. He used some jargon without explanation and he did not include a summary at the end, instead just ending abruptly after discussing the finances.

Overall Rating: 1

Prioritising and Organising

In the in-tray/e-tray exercise, Mr. Y was clear about the need for a planned implementation, but did not go into details of what such a plan would look like. He mentioned some key stakeholders and what actions he would assign to them. He gave a considered view of the risks facing the plan's implementation and made some suggestions for how to overcome these. He mentioned the importance of contingency time, but did not go into specifics. Likewise, he mentioned that we need to "monitor progress" without elaborating on how this should be done.

Overall Rating: 2

Professional Skills Test

In the proofreading professional skills test, he scored better than 30% of the population, which is a below average score. His accuracy was strong: he got 10 questions correct out of 10 questions attempted (there were 30 questions overall): this suggests he may benefit from speeding up in his responses in order to get a better total score. These results suggest that he may find it a challenge to proof read quickly enough in order to be proficient in the role.

Overall Rating: 2

Further Reference

A wide range of internet sources of further information on Assessment Centres can be accessed via *www.eu-testbook.com*

The European Parliament

By Richard Corbett, Francis Jacobs and Michael Shackleton

This book is a must-read for anyone hoping to work at the European Parliament, explaining every aspect of how the Parliament is elected, organised and does it work.

"An invaluable guide to the institution's history, power and politics"
Jerzy Buzek, President of the European Parliament

"Recognised in academia and among practitioners as the authoritative guide to the European Parliament"
Herman Van Rompuy, President of the European Council

8th edition Published June 2011
ISBN 978-0-9564508-5-2

Further details and latest news at

www.europesparliament.com

How the EU Institutions Work and...
How to Work with the EU Institutions

Edited by Alan Hardacre

This is a practical step-by-step guide for anyone who wants to understand the way EU institutions and decision-making work. It fully explains the role of the key players – Commission, Council and Parliament – as well as bodies like the EESC and CoR and how these interact with business lobbies, local governments, NGOs and other interest groups. It provides an excellent foundation stone for anyone planning a career in the EU institutions

"A very insightful tool for citizens, political and private actors",
Maroš Šefčovič, Vice-President of the European Commission

"A first ... a real nuts and bolts approach to how the EU legislative process functions",
Diana Wallis MEP, Vice-President of the European Parliament

June 2011

ISBN 978-0-9564508-6-9

Further details and latest news at

www.europesparliament.com